Legitimate by Nature?

Legitimate by Nature?

Examining the Legitimisation Activities Implemented by the International Criminal Tribunal for Rwanda

Claire Boost

eleven

Published, sold and distributed by Eleven
P.O. Box 85576
2508 CG The Hague
The Netherlands
Tel.: +31 70 33 070 33
Fax: +31 70 33 070 30
email: sales@elevenpub.nl
www.elevenpub.com

Sold and distributed in USA and Canada
Independent Publishers Group
814 N. Franklin Street
Chicago, IL 60610, USA
Order Placement: +1 800 888 4741
Fax: +1 312 337 5985
orders@ipgbook.com
www.ipgbook.com

Eleven is an imprint of Boom uitgevers Den Haag.

ISBN 978-94-6236-259-8
ISBN 978-90-5189-202-4 (e-book)

On dit qu'avant d'entrer dans la mer,
une rivière tremble de peur.
Elle regarde en arrière le chemin qu'elle a parcouru,
depuis les sommets, les montagnes,
la longue route sinueuse
qui traverse des forêts et des villages,
et voit devant elle un océan si vaste
qu'y pénétrer ne parait rien d'autre
que devoir disparaître à jamais.
Mais il n'y a pas d'autre moyen.
La rivière ne peut pas revenir en arrière.
Personne ne peut revenir en arrière.
Revenir en arrière est impossible dans l'existence.
La rivière a besoin de prendre le risque
et d'entrer dans l'océan.
Ce n'est qu'en entrant dans l'océan
que la peur disparaîtra,
parce que c'est alors seulement
que la rivière saura qu'il ne s'agit pas
de disparaître dans l'océan,
mais de devenir océan.

Khalil Gibran ~ La Peur

Preface

The chameleon on the front cover represents the multifaceted nature of legitimacy. Chameleons are known for their ability to change colour in response to their environment, thanks to the pigments and photonic crystals (amino acids) found in their skin.[1] Like a chameleon, the concept of legitimacy changes with its environment.

Specifically, organisational legitimacy enables organisations to adapt to – and interact with –their environment and stakeholders. This chameleonic nature of legitimacy highlights the delicate balance organisations face when seeking to meet the wants and needs of all stakeholders, while simultaneously adapting to the complexities of their environment. As a result, the legitimacy challenges faced by organisations present themselves in different forms – from both the internal and external organisational environment – and are perceived at different times and in different ways. Similarly, legitimisation, the process by which something is made legitimate (or acceptable) to a society, is as complex and multifaceted as the concept of legitimacy itself.

The light blue colour on the cover of this book matches the blue found on the Rwandan flag, which *"symbolises happiness and peace"*;[2] and the blue of the United Nations flag,[3] which *"represents peace in opposition to red, for war."*[4] Established by the United Nations Security Council, the International Criminal Tribunal for Rwanda (ICTR) also made use of this colour for its own flag.

With thanks to Mireille Kastermans and Edouard Boost for their contributions to the cover.

1 Jérémie Teyssier, Suzanne V. Saenko, Dirk van der Marel and Michel C. Milinkovitch, *Photonic crystals cause active colour change in chameleons*, Nature communications, 2015, 6(1), pp. 1-7.

2 Rwanda: *Law N° 34/2008 of 08/08/2008 on characteristics, description, ceremonial and respect of the national flag [Rwanda]*, 8 August 2008, Article 5(3).

3 United Nations General Assembly, *Resolution 167 (II)*, A/RES/167(II), 20 October 1947.

4 United Nations website, 'UN emblem and flag': https://www.un.org/en/about-us/un-emblem-and-flag.

Table of Contents

Administrative Map of Rwanda (1993)

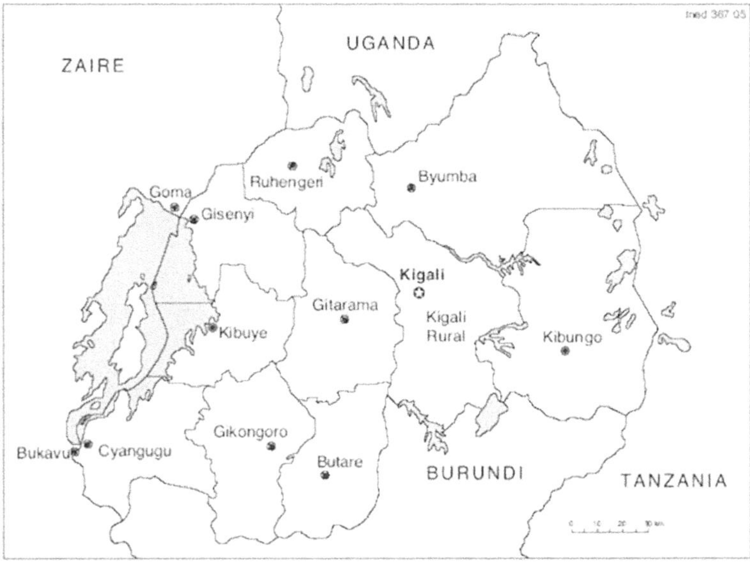

Administrative Map of Rwanda's Five Provinces (2021)

Map of Great Lakes Region (2021)

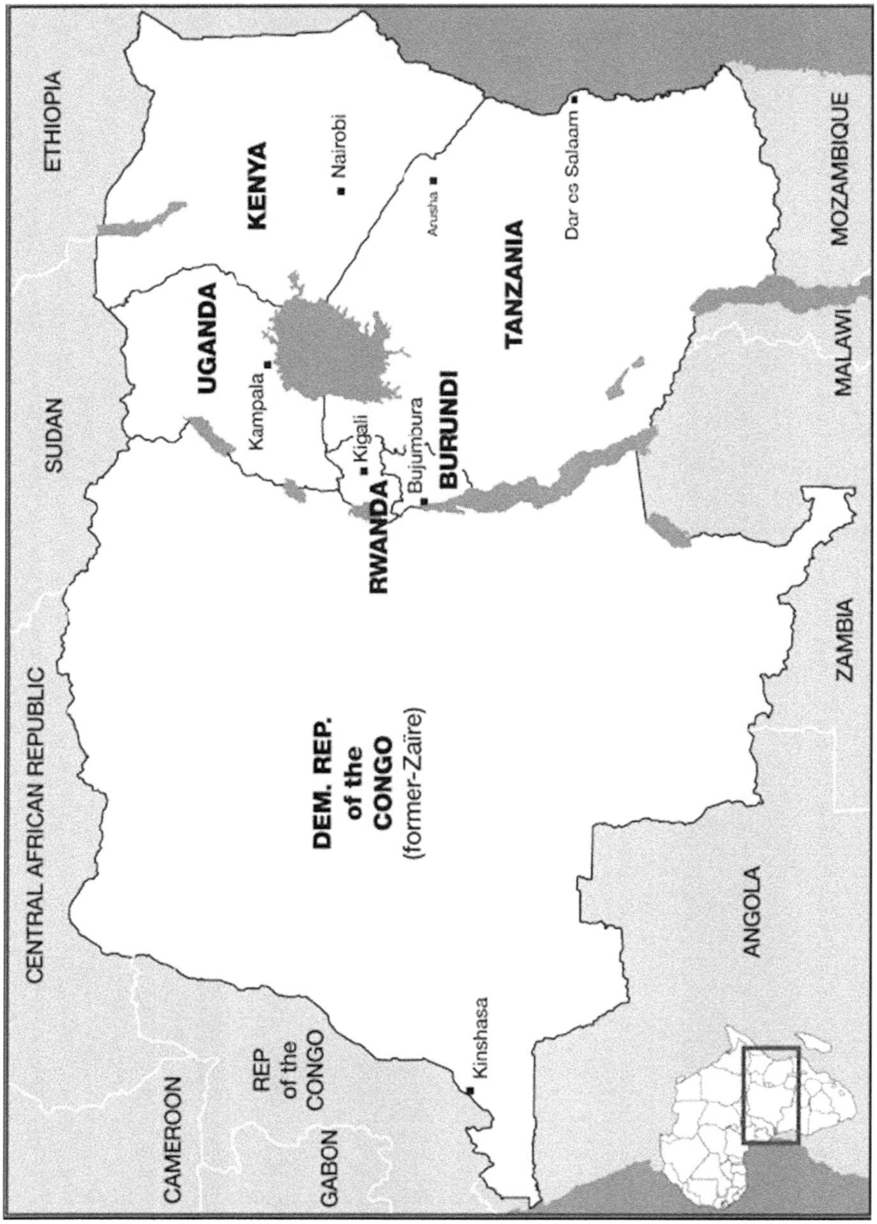

List of Abbreviations

ACABQ	Advisory Committee on Administrative and Budgetary Questions
AICC	Arusha International Conference Centre
ASF	Avocats Sans Frontières
AVEGA	Association des Veuves du Génocide Agahozo
CDR	Coalition pour la Défense de la République
CNLG	National Commission for the Fight Against Genocide *French: Commission Nationale de Lutte contre le Génocide*
COPORWA	Communauté des Potiers du Rwanda
DRC	Democratic Republic of Congo
EAC	East African Community
EIDHR	European Instrument for Democracy and Human Rights
ERSPS	External Relations and Strategic Planning Section
GFTU	Genocide Fugitive Tracking Unit
GLIHD	Great Lakes Initiative for Human Rights Development
ICC	International Criminal Court
ICTR	International Criminal Tribunal for Rwanda
ICTY	International Criminal Tribunal for the former Yugoslavia
IMT	International Military Tribunal (Nuremberg)
IMTFE	International Military Tribunal for the Far East (Tokyo)
IR-MCT	International Residual Mechanism for Criminal Tribunals *Formerly the Mechanism for International Criminal Tribunals (MICT)*
IWGA	International Work Group for Indigenous Affairs
LAF	Legal Aid Forum
MRND	National Revolutionary Movement for Development *French: Mouvement Révolutionnaire National pour le Développement*
NATO	North Atlantic Treaty Organization
NCST	National Council for Science and Technology
NGO	Non-Governmental Organisation
NURC	National Unity and Reconciliation Commission
OTP	Office of The Prosecutor
RCN	Réseau Citoyens-Citizens Network
RPE	Rules of Procedure and Evidence
RPF	Rwandan Patriotic Front
RTML	Radio Télévision Libre des Mille Collines
SCSL	Special Court for Sierra Leone

STL	Special Tribunal for Lebanon
UN	United Nations
UNAMIR	United Nations Assistance Mission for Rwanda
UR	University of Rwanda
UK	United Kingdom
USA	United States of America

Glossary of Key Terms

Legitimacy (empirical)	The perception or belief that an individual, a group, an organisation or a system is legitimate.
Legitimacy (normative)	A set of standards by which an individual, a group, an organisation or a system is judged to be legitimate.
Legitimacy (input)	Assesses the legitimacy of an organisation based on the systems or structures through which it was established or selected.
Legitimacy (output)	Assesses legitimacy based the output or performance of an organisation.
Legitimacy (throughput)	Assesses legitimacy based on the processes that shape how decisions are made.
Legitimacy challenge	An event or situation that threatened the legitimacy of the ICTR.
Legitimacy type	A categorisation introduced by Suchman (1995) that distinguishes between pragmatic, moral and cognitive legitimacy.
Legitimacy type (cognitive)	Cognitive legitimacy relates to the collective societal goals and interests an organisation's stakeholders.
Legitimacy type (moral)	Moral legitimacy reflects the ethics and values of the organisation's stakeholder(s).
Legitimacy type (pragmatic)	Pragmatic legitimacy addresses the immediate needs and interests of the organisation's stakeholder(s).
Legitimisation	The process of gaining, maintaining and/or repairing legitimacy.
Legitimisation activity	An activity that is implemented in order to gain, maintain and/or repair legitimacy.
Legitimisation strategy	A plan that aims to gain, maintain and/or repair legitimacy.
Organisational environment	The stakeholders that affect the operations, resources and performance of an organisation.
Organisational legitimacy	The study of legitimacy in relation to organisations and organisational behaviour.
Stakeholder	An individual, a group, an organisation and/or a system that had an interest in the work of the ICTR, and could either affect and/or were affected by the ICTR's activities.

"Peace in the long term, cannot be achieved unless the population is confident that redress for grievances can be obtained through legitimate structures for the peaceful settlement of disputes and the fair administration of justice."[*]

* United Nations Security Council, *Rule of law and transitional justice in conflict and post-conflict societies.* Report of the Secretary-General, S/2004/616, 23 August 2004, para. 2. Retrieved from: https://www.securitycouncilreport.org/atf/cf/%7B65BFCF9B-6D27-4E9C-8CD3-CF6E4FF96FF9%7D/PCS%20S%202004%20616.pdf.

1 Introduction

On 1 May 1998, the former prime minister of Rwanda, Jean Kambanda, pleaded guilty to the crime of genocide at the International Criminal Tribunal for Rwanda (ICTR)[1] located in Arusha, Tanzania.[2] Four months later, on 2 September 1998, the first conviction for the crime of genocide was pronounced by Trial Chamber I in the case of Jean-Paul Akayesu,[3] a Rwandan mayor involved in mass killings that targeted the Tutsi population living in the Gitarama Province.[4] These events were ground-breaking, marking the first time that individuals had been prosecuted and convicted for committing crimes of genocide;[5] signalling the recognition of the heinous crimes committed in Rwanda in 1994 and an end to impunity for those in positions of power,[6] whilst also making a significant contribution to the development of international criminal law.[7]

The Tribunal also set a legal precedent when acts of sexual violence were recognised as crimes of genocide during the trial of Akayesu,[8] and when broadcasts by Radio Télévision Libre des Mille Collines (RTML) and articles published in Kangura were acknowledged as tools used for the *"direct and public incitement to commit genocide"* during the joint

---

1 Formal name: *International Criminal Tribunal for the Prosecution of Persons Responsible for Genocide and Other Serious Violations of International Humanitarian Law Committed in the Territory of Rwanda and Rwandan Citizens Responsible for Genocide and Other Such Violations Committed in the Territory of Neighbouring States between 1 January and 31 December 1994.*

2 ICTR, *Prosecutor v. Jean Kambanda*, Judgment and Sentence, ICTR-97-23-S, 4 September 1998, para. 3; ICTR Press release, *Ex-Rwandan Prime Minister Jean Kambanda pleads guilty to genocide*, 1 May 1998. Retrieved from: https://unictr.irmct.org/en/news/ex-rwandan-prime-minister-jean-kambanda-pleads-guilty-genocide.

3 ICTR, *Prosecutor v. Jean-Paul Akayesu*, Judgment, ICTR-96-4-T, 2 September 1998, p. 179.

4 In 2005, Rwanda's original 12 provinces were abolished and replaced with four provinces and the City of Kigali. A key reason given for this change was to remove reminders of the 1994 genocide (interviewees G1, CS5 & CS6). As a result, the Gitarama Province now forms part of the Southern Province. Retrieved from: https://www.gov.rw/government/administrative-structure#c4493.

5 The Nuremberg and Tokyo Military Tribunals addressed crimes against peace, war crimes and crimes against humanity (London Agreement, Charter of the International Military Tribunal, 8 August 1945, Article 6; Charter of the International Military Tribunal for the Far East, 19 January 1946, Article 5). In 1961 Adolf Eichman was charged with crimes against the Jewish People, crimes against humanity, war crimes and membership of hostile organisations (District Court of Jerusalem, *Prosecutor v. Adolf Eichman*, Judgement, Case No. 40/61, 11 December 1961, para. 16).

6 Catherine Cisse, *The End of a Culture of Impunity in Rwanda? Prosecution of Genocide and War Crimes before Rwandan Courts and the International Criminal Tribunal for Rwanda*, Yearbook of International Humanitarian Law, 1998, 1, pp. 161-188.

7 Robert Cryer, Darryl Robinson and Serge Vasiliev, *An Introduction to International Criminal Law and Procedure*, Cambridge University Press, 2019, pp. 207-208.

8 ICTR, *Prosecutor v. Jean-Paul Akayesu*, Judgment, ICTR-96-4-T, 2 September 1998, para. 731.

trial of Ferdinand Nahimana, Jean-Bosco Barayagwiza and Hassan Ngeze.[9] As explained by the judges: "*Without a firearm, machete or any physical weapon, he [Nahimana] caused the death of thousands of innocent civilians.*"[10] Furthermore, in 2006 the Appeal Chamber took judicial notice that "*there was a genocide in Rwanda against the Tutsi ethnic group*" between April and July 1994,[11] recognising that crimes of genocide had been committed against the Tutsi population in Rwanda and provided a public record of this judicial fact.[12]

There are, however, individuals (including academics, former ICTR staff members and representatives from civil society organisations) who bring the fore another side of the ICTR, for example, the series of highly controversial acquittals and sentence reductions for senior military and political leaders involved in the genocide.[13] In fact, the ICTR's reputation was questioned even before its inception in November 1994, when the Rwandan delegation to the United Nations (UN) contested the adoption of UN Resolution 955 from which the Tribunal would be established.[14]

As one of the mechanisms established to contribute to the rebuilding of Rwanda following such a brutal conflict, it was vital for the ICTR – established to prosecute those most responsible for the 1994 genocide that took place in Rwanda – to be perceived as a legitimate organisation. Furthermore, in addressing the international crimes committed on Rwandan soil through an international criminal tribunal, the ICTR needed to establish itself as an independent and impartial court, while working alongside the new Rwandan government.[15]

---

9 ICTR, *Prosecutor v. Ferdinand Nahimana, Jean-Bosco Barayagwiza and Hassan Ngeze (Media Case)*, Judgment and Sentence, ICTR-99-52-T, 3 December 2003, para. 979-1039.

10 *idem.*, para. J99, p. 359.

11 ICTR, *Prosecutor v. Édouard Karemera, Matthieu Ngirumpatse and Joseph Nzirorera*, Decision on Prosecutor's Interlocutory Appeal of Decision on Judicial Notice, ICTR-98-44-AR73(C), 16 June 2006, para. 33-35; ICTR Press Release, *ICTR Appeals Chamber takes Judicial Notice of Genocide in Rwanda*, 20 June 2006. Retrieved from: https://unictr.irmct.org/en/news/ictr-appeals-chamber-takes-judicial-notice-genocide-rwanda.

12 Interviewees A10, CS6, CS7, CS22, G4, M2, T5, T9, T20 & T22; Tim Gallimore, *The Legacy of the International Criminal Tribunal for Rwanda (ICTR) and its Contributions to Reconciliation in Rwanda*, New England Journal of International and Comparative Law, 2007, 14, p. 240.

13 Interviewees A10, M2, J3, J4, CS10, CS17, G2, T1, T2, T5 & T22; Yolande A. Bouka, *In the Shadow of Prison: Power, Identity, and Transitional Justice in Post-Genocide Rwanda*, American University, 2013a; Kingsley Moghalu, *Rwanda's Genocide: The Politics of Global Justice*, Palgrave Macmillan, 2005; Valerie Oosterveld and John McManus, *The Cooperation of States with the International Criminal Court*, Fordham International Law Journal, 2002, 25(3); Victor Peskin, *International Justice in Rwanda and the Balkans: Virtual Trials and the Struggle for State Cooperation*, Cambridge University Press, 2008.

14 United Nations Security Council, *The Situation Concerning Rwanda.* Provisional Report of the 3453rd Meeting, S/PV.3453, 8 November 1994, pp. 14-16. Retrieved from: https://digitallibrary.un.org/record/167764/files/S_PV.3453-EN.pdf.

15 Mark A. Drumbl, *Atrocity, Punishment, and International Law*, Cambridge University Press, 2007, pp. 110-111; Barbara Oomen, *Justice Mechanisms and the Question of Legitimacy. The Example of Rwanda's Multi-layered Justice Mechanisms*, in: Kai Ambos, Judith Large, and Marieke Wierda (eds.), *Building a Future on Peace and Justice*, Springer Berlin Heidelberg 2009, pp. 188-189.

The ICTR held an ambitious mandate aimed not only at prosecuting those responsible for gross human rights violations in Rwanda, but also at contributing *"to the process of national reconciliation and to the restoration and maintenance of peace"*[16] and sending *"a strong message to Africa's leaders and warlords"*[17] that impunity would no longer be tolerated. In doing so, the ICTR promoted itself as a key player in striving towards *"international peace and justice"*.[18]

Given the challenging environment in which the ICTR was operating and the high expectations placed on the success of this international criminal tribunal, the research aims to understand how the Tribunal sought to establish itself as a credible court of law in a post-conflict environment by exploring the legitimisation activities implemented by the ICTR in order to gain, maintain and repair its legitimacy, especially when faced with legitimacy challenges. The main objective of this research is therefore to *examine how the ICTR implemented legitimisation activities to gain, maintain and/or repair its legitimacy.*

In doing so, the study aims to inform the work of existing and future international criminal courts, particularly in relation to their work in (post-)conflict environments. It is particularly important to emphasise the value of legitimacy as a critical resource for international criminal courts, and to remove the notion that courts are legitimate by nature, due to their legal status and role in upholding the rule of law.

By examining the concept of legitimacy and its importance for international criminal courts, this research seeks to understand the dynamics of organisational legitimacy for international criminal courts and tribunals by focusing on the legitimisation activities implemented by the ICTR. In order to answer the main research question, this study explores the following sub-questions:

- Why was legitimacy important for the ICTR?
- What challenges did the ICTR face that threatened its legitimacy?
- How did the ICTR respond to the threats to its legitimacy?

By focusing solely on the legitimisation activities of the ICTR, this study uses a single case study approach,[19] examining the actions implemented from the creation of the Tribunal through UN Resolution 955 in November 1994 to its closure on 31 December 2015. For the purpose of this research, the Tribunal will be referred to as one single entity; however, Chapters 4, 5 and 6 demonstrate that the task of legitimisation was taken on by specific departments within the ICTR – namely the External Relations and Strategic Planning

16 United Nations Security Council, *Resolution 955*, S/RES/955, 8 November 1994, p. 1.

17 Original ICTR website, 'Homepage', Relevance for Peace and Justice. Retrieved from: https://web.archive.org/web/20070729015547/http://www.unictr.org/default.htm.

18 *ibid.*

19 Robert K. Yin, Case Study Research: Design and Methods, Sage: London, 2009.

Section (ERSPS) – and/or by individuals – for example the president, the registrar and ICTR spokespersons.

In order to provide context for the research approach, and the main research question and sub-questions, the following sections in this chapter offer background information related to the topics addressed in this research. The first section describes the aftermath of the 1994 genocide in Rwanda, resulting in the establishment of the ICTR. This is followed by a section on legitimacy, which introduces the concept of organisational legitimacy, in particular the perceptions of legitimacy in the context of a post-conflict setting. The third section in this chapter links the two previous sections to the main focus of this research: first describing the importance of legitimacy for international courts working in post-conflict environments, followed by introducing some of legitimacy challenges faced by the ICTR over the course of its lifespan, and finally highlighting the three main objectives of this study. The fourth section of this chapter provides an outline of the chapters of this book.

1.1 The Events and Aftermath of the 1994 Genocide

Reports of extreme violence within Rwanda hit media outlets in early April 1994, following the downing of the presidential plane on 6 April, which killed Rwandan President Habyarimana and Burundian President Ntaryamira, who were returning from peace talks in Arusha along with eight others. In response to the news of the plane crash, the Rwandan Presidential Guard immediately erected roadblocks in and around the capital city of Kigali, and soon after reports of killings started to emerge.[20] During the subsequent days, weeks and months, violence surged throughout the country and a steady stream of refugees started fleeing to the neighbouring countries of Burundi, the Democratic Republic of Congo (DRC), Uganda and Tanzania.[21] Urged on by radio broadcasts, aided by soldiers and militia groups (namely the "*interahamwe*"),[22] and facilitated by roadblocks and security

20 BBC, *Rwanda presidents' plane 'shot down'*, 6 April 1994. Retrieved from: http://news.bbc.co.uk/onthisday/hi/dates/stories/april/6/newsid_2472000/2472195.stm; The Guardian, *Thousands massacred in Rwanda*, 9 April 1994. Retrieved from: https://www.theguardian.com/world/1994/apr/09/rwanda; New York Times, *Anarchy Rules Rwanda's Capital And Drunken Soldiers Roam City*, 14 April 1994. Retrieved from: https://www.nytimes.com/1994/04/14/world/anarchy-rules-rwanda-s-capital-and-drunken-soldiers-roam-city.html; Penal Reform International, *Eight years on... A record of Gacaca monitoring in Rwanda*, 2006, Glossary. Retrieved from: https://cdn.penalreform.org/wp-content/uploads/2013/05/WEB-english-gacaca-rwanda-5.pdf.

21 The Guardian, 9 April 1994; New York Times, 14 April 1994.

22 The Kinyarwanda word *interahamwe* "*derives from two words put together to make a noun, intera and hamwe: Intera comes from the verb gutera' which can mean both to attack and to work. It was documented that in 1994, besides meaning to work or to attack, the word gutera could also mean to kill. Hamwe means together. Therefore Interahamwe could mean to attack or to work together, and, depending on the context,*

checkpoints set up throughout the country, ordinary Rwandans used clubs and machetes to hunt down, mutilate, rape and kill members of their community.[23]

Over the course of the next 100 days, ordinary men and women of all ages killed approximately 800,000 of their fellow Rwandan citizens.[24] The majority of the victims were men, women and children from the Tutsi ethnic group, and those considered '*moderate*' Hutu.[25] The targeted killings concluded a four-year-long civil war fought between the Hutu government and the Rwandan Patriotic Front (RPF).[26]

The number of deaths recorded between April and July 1994 amounts to approximately 10% of the Rwandan population (estimated at approximately 7 million at the time), with roughly 8,000 men, women and children killed every day.[27] This figure represents roughly 84% of the Tutsi population living in Rwanda in 1994.[28] Aside from the sheer volume of deaths, reports estimated the number of killers at 750,000, which accounted for approximately one in four Rwandan adults at the time.[29] By the end of the conflict, Rwanda was left in ruins: schools, hospitals, banks, government buildings and other public and

---

to kill together." It was the name used by the youth wing established in 1992 by the Hutu government, the National Revolutionary Movement for Development (MRND), which played a key role in the 1994 genocide (ICTR, *Prosecutor v. Jean-Paul Akayesu*, Judgment, ICTR-96-4-T, 2 September 1998, para. 151).

23 Alison L. Des Forges, *Leave None to Tell the Story: Genocide in Rwanda*, Human Rights Watch, 1999, pp. 10-12. Retrieved from: https://www.hrw.org/reports/1999/rwanda/.

24 The UN estimates that 800,000 people lost their lives during the 1994 genocide (United Nations Security Council, *Report of the Independent Inquiry into the actions of the United Nations during the 1994 genocide in Rwanda*, S/199/1257, 15 December 1999); the Government of Rwanda refers to over one million Tutsi and moderate Hutu victims of genocidal violence (Retrieved from: https://www.gov.rw/about); while Human Rights Watch places the number closer to 500,000 victims (Des Forges, 1999, pp. 15-16).

25 '*Moderate*' Hutu makes reference to Rwandan citizens from the Hutu ethnic group who tried to save the lives of their Tutsi compatriots. The term also encompasses those that supported the power-sharing agreement negotiated during the Arusha Accords, which would have enabled the Tutsi-led RPF to gain power and to work alongside the Hutu government. (Des Forges, 1999, p. 39; Penal Reform International, 2006, p. 13; Marijke Verpoorten, *The Death Toll of the Rwandan Genocide: A Detailed Analysis for Gikongoro Province*, Population, 2005, 60(4), p. 333).
Members of the Twa ethnic group were also involved in the conflict, both as perpetrators and victims; yet, they are rarely mentioned in relation to the 1994 genocide in Rwanda (Interviewees G2 & CS10). The ethnic divisions that were intrinsic to Rwandan society prior to and during the 1994 genocide no longer exist in Rwanda. Since 2001, identifying individuals with the ethnic labels – Hutu, Tutsi or Twa – is considered as "*divisionist*" in Rwanda (Rwanda, *Law No. 47/2001 of 2001 on Prevention, Suppression and Punishment of the Crime of Discrimination and Sectarianism* [Rwanda], 18 December 2001).

26 With a growing number of Tutsi refugees living in Uganda, the Rwandan Patriotic Front (RPF) was established in Kampala in 1988. The aim of this political and military movement was to return to Rwanda and to overthrow the Rwandan government. The RPF launched their first major attack against the Hutu government in Rwanda on 1 October 1990, marking the start of the Rwandan Civil War (Des Forges, 1999, pp. 15-16; Drumbl, 2007, p. 81; Kingsley Moghalu, *Rwanda's Genocide: The Politics of Global Justice*, Palgrave Macmillan, 2005, pp. 13-14).

27 Des Forges, 1999, pp. 15-16; United Nations Security Council (1999). *Report of the Independent Inquiry into the actions of the United Nations during the 1994 genocide in Rwanda*, S/199/1257, 15 December 1999.

28 Verpoorten, 2005, pp. 332-333.

29 Penal Reform International, *Eight years on ... A record of Gacaca monitoring in Rwanda*, 2006.

private property had been destroyed or ransacked; there was a lack of food and clean water, and the streets of Kigali were empty of people. Outside the capital entire communities had been torn apart; fields and farms had been destroyed and were left deserted. Furthermore, the country was scattered with bodies left in fields and on roads where roadblocks had been abandoned.[30]

In an attempt to rebuild the country, the new *National Unity* government, led by members of the victorious RPF,[31] and including both Hutu and Tutsi government officials, emphasised a policy of "*national unity and reconciliation.*"[32] In an effort to end the ethnic violence that had afflicted the country since 1959, laws were adopted to ensure that all citizens identified as Rwandans, essentially removing any distinction based on Tutsi, Hutu or Twa ethnic groups.[33] Furthermore, national re-education programmes were launched in the form of solidarity camps (*ingando*) and civic education trainings (*itorero*) as a means to reconcile past conflicts and instil new civic values.[34]

Following the extreme violence that had taken place on Rwandan soil, the new government was also determined to see justice served. Despite the lack of human resources and judicial infrastructure, the Rwandan government instituted national prosecutions against those implicated in the genocide using both the conventional national court system (from 1996) and later on – in response to the bottleneck of cases waiting for trial at national courts – community-based gacaca courts (from 2002 to 2012).[35] The Rwandan government also requested the assistance of the international community to prosecute those most

---

30 Augustine Brannigan and Nicholas Jones, *Genocide and the Legal Process in Rwanda: From Genocide Amnesty to the New Rule of Law,* International Criminal Justice Review, 2009, 19(2), p. 197; Carla Ferstman, *Domestic Trials for Genocide and Crimes Against Humanity: The Example of Rwanda*, African Journal of International and Comparative Law, 1997, 9, p. 859; Moghalu, 2005, p. 37.

31 The new government was headed by a Hutu president, Pasteur Bizimungu, and a Tutsi vice-president, Paul Kagame, who also acted as minister of defence (Scott Straus and Lars Waldorf (eds.), *Remaking Rwanda: State Building and Human Rights After Mass Violence*, University of Wisconsin Press, 2011, p. 32).

32 *idem.*, pp. 8 & 31-32.
Several efforts were made as a way to promote reconciliation and unity among Rwandans, including the establishment of the National Unity and Reconciliation Commission: https://www.nurc.gov.rw/.

33 Straus & Waldorf, 2011, pp. 10-12; Rwanda, *Law No. 47/2001 of 2001 on Prevention, Suppression and Punishment of the Crime of Discrimination and Sectarianism*, 18 December 2001; Rwanda, *Law No. 33n bis/2003 of 2003 Repressing the Crime of Genocide, Crimes Against Humanity and War Crimes*, 6 September 2003; Rwanda, *Organic Law N° 30/2008 of 25/07/2008 relating to Rwandan Nationality*, 25 July 2008.

34 Interviewees J1, CS3, CS5, CS10, CS12, CS21, G1 & G4; Janine Natalya Clark, *National unity and reconciliation in Rwanda: A flawed approach?* Journal of Contemporary African Studies, 2010, 28(2), pp. 138-140; Penal Reform International, 2006, Glossary; Straus & Waldorf, 2011, pp. 8-9.

35 Clark, 2010, p. 137; Penal Reform International, 2006; William A. Schabas, *Genocide Trials and Gacaca Courts*, Journal of International Criminal Justice, 2005, 3(4), 879-895; Sylo Taraku and Gunnar M. Karlsen, *Prosecuting Genocide in Rwanda: The Gacaca System and the International Criminal Tribunal for Rwanda,* Oslo: Norwegian Helsinki Committee, 2002, pp. 14-19.

responsible for the international crimes committed in Rwanda, in particular the members of the previous regime that had fled to foreign countries.[36]

1.1.1 *The International Criminal Tribunal for Rwanda (ICTR)*

> "Nothing emboldens a criminal so much as the knowledge he can get away with the crime. That was the message the failure to prosecute for the Armenian massacre gave to the Nazis."[37]

In line with Articles 29 and 41 of the UN Charter,[38] the UN Security Council created new functions for itself in the early 1990s, namely the establishment of two international criminal tribunals: the International Criminal Tribunal for the former Yugoslavia (ICTY) and the ICTR. These two international criminal tribunals were created to prosecute individuals for international crimes, determine judicial facts and decide on the sentencing of former political and military leaders.[39]

With Rwanda's basic infrastructure in ruins, a severe lack of qualified personnel, overcrowded prisons, and new laws being drafted by Rwandan legislators, the new Rwandan government requested the assistance of the international community to establish an international tribunal that would focus on prosecuting those most responsible for planning, inciting and committing gross human rights violations that had ravaged the country from 1990 to 1994.[40]

Up to that point, the UN had been known for its peacekeeping efforts during the Rwandan conflict, which had started with the arrival of the United Nations Assistance Mission for Rwanda (UNAMIR) in 1993.[41] However, from July 1994 onwards, the UN

---

36 United Nations Security Council, *Letter dated 94/09/28 from the Permanent Representative of Rwanda to the United Nations addressed to the President of the Security Council*, S/1994/1115, 29 September 1994. Retrieved from: https://digitallibrary.un.org/record/197773?ln=en.

37 David Matas, *Prosecuting Crimes Against Humanity: The Lessons of World War I*, Fordham International Law Journal, 1989, 13, p. 104.

38 United Nations, *Charter of the United Nations*, 24 October 1945, Article 29: "*The Security Council may establish such subsidiary organs as it deems necessary for the performance of its functions*";
UN Charter, 1945, Article 41: "*The Security Council may decide what measures not involving the use of armed force are to be employed to give effect to its decisions, and it may call upon the Members of the United Nations to apply such measures*".

39 Axel Marschik, *The Security Council as World Legislator?: Theory, Practice and Consequences of an Expanding World Power*, New York University School of Law, International Law and Justice Working Papers, 2005, 18, pp. 4-6.

40 United Nations Security Council, *Letter dated 94/09/28 from the Permanent Representative of Rwanda to the United Nations addressed to the President of the Security Council*, S/1994/1115, 29 September 1994. Retrieved from: https://digitallibrary.un.org/record/197773?ln=en.

41 The United Nations Assistance Mission for Rwanda (UNAMIR) was established by United Nations Security Council Resolution 872 (S/RES/872) on 5 October 1993. It was composed of troops from Belgium,

took on a different role by becoming actively involved in transitional justice efforts throughout the country,[42] and on 8 November 1994, the UN Security Council adopted Resolution 955,[43] establishing the first international criminal tribunal on the African continent.[44]

> "The Security Council [...] decides hereby, having received the request of the Government of Rwanda (S/1994/1115), to establish an international tribunal for the sole purpose of prosecuting persons responsible for genocide and other serious violations of International Humanitarian Law committed in the territory of Rwanda and Rwandan citizens responsible for genocide and other such violations committed in the territory of neighbouring States, between 1 January 1994 and 31 December 1994."[45]

Through the adoption of UN Resolution 955, all UN member states agreed to cooperate with the ICTR and to take measures, through their domestic legal systems, to enable the execution of the Resolution, namely by tracking and arresting fugitives that had fled to other countries.[46] The ICTR had jurisdiction over individuals rather than states or organisations (as had been the case with the International Military Tribunals in Nuremburg and Tokyo following World War II),[47] and claimed primacy over national investigations and prosecutions: the Tribunal could therefore take over proceedings held at a national level at any stage. However, the UN Security Council assured the Rwandan government that they would be notified prior to any decision taken by the ICTR regarding the commutation or enforcement of sentences, as stipulated under Articles 26 and 27 of the ICTR Statute.[48]

Bangladesh, Ghana, and Tunisia, and was operational until March 1996 (United Nations Security Council, *Resolution 1029*, S/RES/1029, 12 December 1995, para. 1).

42 United Nations Rwanda. See website: http://www.rw.one.un.org/who-we-are/united-nations-rwanda.

43 United Nations Security Council, *Resolution 955*, S/RES/955, 8 November 1994.

44 Cryer et al., 2019, p. 137; Peskin, 2008, p. 167.

45 UN, Resolution 955, S/RES/955, 8 November 1994.

46 United Nations Security Council, *Statute of the International Criminal Tribunal for Rwanda (as amended on 31 December 2010)*, 8 November 1994. Retrieved from: https://unictr.irmct.org/sites/unictr.org/files/legal-library/100131_Statute_en_fr_0.pdf.

47 Cryer et al., 2019, p. 118.
The International Military Tribunal in Nuremberg or the Nuremberg Trial (1946-1946); and The International Military Tribunal for the Far East (IMTFE), also known as the Tokyo War Crimes Tribunal or the Tokyo Trial (1946-1948).

48 ICTR Statute, 2010, Articles 26 & 27; Cryer et al., 2019, p. 138; Alette Smeulers and Fred Grünfeld, *International Crimes and Other Gross Human Rights Violations: A Multi- and Interdisciplinary Textbook*, Brill, 2011, p. 44.

1.1.2 *Operating Structure of the Tribunal*

On 31 August 1995, an agreement was reached with the government of Tanzania to locate the Tribunal in Arusha.[49] Housed predominantly in the Arusha International Conference Centre (AICC) in the north of Tanzania, the ICTR consisted of three main organs: the Chambers, (including the Appeals Chamber located in The Hague) led by the ICTR president and consisting of 16 ICTR judges and their staff; the Office of the Prosecutor (OTP), headed by the chief prosecutor and responsible for all investigations and prosecutions of individuals involved in crimes that fell under the ICTR's jurisdiction; and the Registry led by the registrar and responsible for administrative tasks related to the functioning of the Tribunal.[50]

Although independent from each other, the ICTY and the ICTR shared the chief prosecutor and appellate judges to ensure a coherence in their judicial operations, and to increase the effectiveness of the resources allocated to them.[51] This changed in 2003 when the tribunals were assigned one chief prosecutor each.[52]

1.1.2.1 The Chambers

The Chambers formed the judicial organ of the ICTR, and consisted of 16 judges from 16 different UN member states and their staff.[53] The ICTR originally had two trial chambers based in Arusha, and an appeals chamber based in The Hague that was shared with the ICTY. In 1998, an additional trial chamber was built in Arusha to speed up trials.[54]

The ICTR judges were elected by the UN General Assembly in accordance with the UN staff recruitment protocol, which took into account the need for "*equitable geographic distribution*", and consisted of representatives from both the common law and civil law legal systems.[55] The judges were each elected for a four-year term and could be re-elected

49 ICTR, *1st Annual Report*, A/51/399-S/1996/778, 24 September 1996. Retrieved from: https://unictr.irmct.org/sites/unictr.org/files/legal-library/960924-annual-report-en.pdf.

50 ICTR website, 'About the ICTR': https://unictr.irmct.org/en/tribunal.

51 Cryer et al., 2019, p. 138; United Nations Security Council, *ICTR Rules of Procedure and Evidence* (as amended on 13 May 2015), 29 June 1995, rule 13(4).

52 ICTR, *Completion Strategy Report*, S/2003/946, 6 October 2003; United Nations Security Council, *Resolution 1503*, S/RES/1503, 28 August 2003.

53 The original number was 11 judges for the two Trial Chambers and the Appeals Chamber, this increased to 14 in 1998, when a third Trial Chamber was built. On 30 November the UN Security Council voted to increase the number to 16 judges (Yves Beigbeder, *International Criminal Tribunals: Justice and Politics*, Springer, 2011, p. 89; UN, ICTR RPE, 29 June 1995, rule 11 (1); ICTR website, 'Chambers': https://unictr.irmct.org/en/tribunal/chambers).

54 United Nations Security Council, *Resolution 1165*, S/RES/1165, 30 April 1998; ICTR, *4th Annual Report*, A/54/315-S/1999/943, 7 September 1999, para. 5.

55 William A. Schabas, *The UN International Criminal Tribunals: The Former Yugoslavia, Rwanda and Sierra Leone*,Cambridge University Press, 2006, p. 595; United Nations Secretariat, Application of the principle

for additional terms.[56] Candidates were nominated by UN member states and a selection was made by the UN Security Council from a list of 22 to 33 names.[57] The 16 judges then elected the president of the Tribunal.[58] From 1995 until its closure in 2015, the ICTR had a total of six presidents:

- Judge Laïty Kama	(Senegal)	1995 to 1999
- Judge Navanethem Pillay	(South Africa)	1999 to 2003
- Judge Erik Møse	(Norway)	2003 to 2007
- Judge Charles M. D. Byron	(St. Kitts & Nevis)	2007 to 2011
- Judge Khalida Rachid Khan	(Pakistan)	2011 to 2012
- Judge Vagn Joensen	(Denmark)	2012 to 2015

The president's role was to represent the ICTR at the UN General Assembly meetings and to assign judges to the different chambers (including to the Appeals Chamber in The Hague).[59] Once established, each chamber elected its own president.[60]

1.1.2.2 The Office of the Prosecutor (OTP)

The OTP was the organ responsible for investigating and prosecuting the crimes that fell under the jurisdiction of the ICTR. The chief prosecutor was nominated by the UN Secretary-General and appointed by the Security Council for a four-year term, renewable once. The senior staff of the OTP were appointed by the UN Secretary-General on the recommendation of the chief prosecutor, who was assisted by a deputy prosecutor.[61] Over the course of its 20-year existence, the ICTR had a total of four chief prosecutors:

- Richard Goldstone	(South Africa)	1995 to 1996 *[ICTR & ICTY]*
- Louise Arbour	(Canada)	1996 to 1999 *[ICTR & ICTY]*
- Carla Del Ponte	(Switzerland)	1999 to 2003 *[ICTR & ICTY]*
- Hassan Bubacar Jallow	(Gambia)	2003 to 2015 *[ICTR]*

In addition to the ICTR's location in Tanzania – where the detention facilities and courtrooms were located, and the judges and the registrar had their offices – the Tribunal

of equitable geographical distribution of the staff of the United Nations Secretariat, JIU/REP/81/10, Geneva, July 1981; UN, ICTR RPE, rule 11 (1).

56 UN, ICTR RPE, 29 June 1995, rule 12 *bis*(3).

57 *idem.*, rule 12 *bis* (1)(c).

58 *idem.*, rule 13(1).

59 *idem.*, rule 12 *ter* (2).

60 *idem.*, rule 13 (7).

61 Schabas, 2006, p. 600; UN, ICTR RPE, Article 15; ICTR website, 'Office of the Prosecutor': https://unictr.irmct.org/en/tribunal/office-prosecutor.

also had an office in Kigali, from which OTP staff conducted their investigations and initiated criminal proceedings; the Kigali office was led by the deputy prosecutor.[62] The geographical spread of the Tribunal's activities was further emphasised by the fact that from 1994 to 2003 the chief prosecutor was stationed at the ICTY's OTP offices in The Hague, the Netherlands.[63]

The chief prosecutor was responsible for investigating and prosecuting of cases for both the ICTY and the ICTR until 28 August 2003, when the UN Security Council amended Article 15 of the ICTR Statute by adopting UN Resolution 1503, splitting the work of the chief prosecutor into two separate functions: one at the ICTY and the other at the ICTR.[64] In September 2003, Hassan Bubacar Jallow, from Gambia, was appointed as the new chief prosecutor for the ICTR, while Carla Del Ponte remained in her former position of chief prosecutor for the ICTY.[65]

1.1.2.3 The Registry

The administrative organ of the ICTR was called the Registry and was led by the registrar, who oversaw the management of the Tribunal's internal and external operations. Given the unique character of international criminal courts and tribunals, and the ICTR's location in Arusha with operations in The Hague and Kigali, the ICTR Registry was given a complex set of responsibilities, and was considered the most diverse organ of the Tribunal in terms of its tasks and responsibilities.[66]

In addition to managing the ICTR's administration, the Registry provided legal and judicial support for the work of the two other organs, the Chambers and the OTP. It also oversaw the contracts and expenses of defence teams, and managed the detention of the accused and the Witness and Victim Support Section.[67] The registrar served a four-year term, which was extended by the UN Secretary-General in consultation with the president of the Tribunal. The staff working at the OTP were also approved in consultation with the UN Secretary-General.[68] Between 1995 and 2015, a total of four registrars were employed by the ICTR:

---

62 Peskin, 2008, p. 172.
63 Moghalu, 2005, pp. 127-130; Schabas, 2006, p. 594.
64 ICTR, *Completion Strategy Report*, S/2003/946, 6 October 2003; UN, Resolution 1503, S/RES/1503, 28 August 2003.
65 ICTR Press Release, *The Security Council Appoints Separate Prosecutors for the two ad hoc UN Tribunals*, 4 September 2003. Retrieved from: https://unictr.irmct.org/en/news/security-council-appoints-separate-prosecutors-two-ad-hoc-un-tribunals; UN Press Release, *Security Council splits prosecutorial duties for Rwanda, Yugoslavia Tribunals, unanimously adopting Resolution 1503 (2003)*, 28 August 2003. Retrieved from: https://www.un.org/press/en/2003/sc7858.doc.htm.
66 Schabas, 2006, pp. 607-608; UN, ICTR RPE, 28 August 2003, rule 16; ICTR website, 'Registry': https://unictr.irmct.org/en/tribunal/registry.
67 *ibid.*; ICTR website, 'Defence and Detention': https://unictr.irmct.org/en/tribunal/defence.
68 UN, ICTR RPE, 29 June 1995, rule 16 (3).

- Andronico Adede	(Kenya)	1995 to 1997
- Agwu Ukiwe Okali	(Nigeria)	1997 to 2001
- Adama Dieng	(Senegal)	2001 to 2012
- Bongani Majola	(South Africa)	2012 to 2015

Although the Tribunal was established as an independent and impartial criminal court, the UN Secretary-General, UN General Assembly and UN Security Council played an important role in the selection of all staff members holding leadership positions, but also in the establishment of the ICTR itself, along with the creation of its Statute and Rules of Procedure and Evidence (RPE). This oversight and influence played both a positive and negative role in the legitimacy of the ICTR, which is further examined in Chapters 4, 5 and 6.

To understand the importance of legitimacy for the ICTR, in line with the first sub-question of this research – *why was legitimacy important for the ICTR?* – the next section examines the dynamics of legitimacy in a post-conflict environment, particularly in relation to the work of international criminal courts. The section then focuses on organisational legitimacy and introduces the concept of legitimisation, describing how legitimisation activities enable organisations to gain, maintain and/or repair their legitimacy when faced with a legitimacy challenge.

1.2 Legitimacy

'Legitimacy' is a term mainly associated with two disciplines: law and political science. From a legal perspective, legitimacy is defined as *"conformity to the law or to rules; the recognition of law"*;[69] while in political science, the term legitimacy is often associated with other concepts such as power, authority or conformity, and is often used to explain the dynamics between individuals, governments, state-run institutions and organisations. In this context, the term is defined as *"the ability to be defended with logic or justification; validity"*.[70]

According to both the legal and political interpretations of the term, the concept of legitimacy is used to describe the consenting relationship between an authority and those who accept this authority in a relatively stable environment. In this setting, research typically focuses on the relationship between established governing bodies or organisations and

69 Oxford Dictionary, 'legitimacy'. Retrieved from: https://www.lexico.com/definition/legitimacy.
70 *ibid.*

their stakeholders, and is based on the shared values and norms of a particular community or society.[71]

The picture is very different when examining the concept of legitimacy in a (post-)conflict environment, where power dynamics are likely to be fragmented and a variety of individuals or groups compete for the power to govern, while seeking allegiance from divided communities.[72] Research conducted by Whalan demonstrates that attempts to legitimise individuals or groups operating in a (post-)conflict environment are as much about horizontal relationships between those competing for legitimate power, as they are about hierarchical relationships between the incoming government and the people that they will lead.[73]

In a war-torn environment and among a population that has experienced extreme violence, exercising power that is perceived as legitimate plays an important role in the transition to a peaceful society. People behave differently towards legitimised power than when confronted with brute force, which is why those in power strive to legitimise their authority.[74] Indeed, Arendt goes so far as to say that "*no government exclusively based on the means of violence has ever existed*",[75] and Dogan claims that "*even the most tyrannic rulers try to justify their reign*".[76] Legitimate power is therefore considered more efficient as it allows for resources to be used for other activities.[77] It has also been shown to be more resilient as it "*withstands shock and failure because a solid level of support from its subordinates can be guaranteed*".[78]

In line with this, ensuring that transitional justice mechanisms operating in post-conflict environments are perceived as legitimate is a prerequisite for individuals and communities (many of whom have experienced violations of their human rights) to restore their trust in society: "*strengthening people's perceptions of legitimacy should be of concern to all those*

71 David Beetham, *Political Legitimacy*, Malden and Oxford: Blackwell, 2001, pp. 107-116; Max Weber, *Economy and Society: An Outline of Interpretive Sociology*, Berkeley: University of California Press, 1978, pp. 212-213.

72 Florian Weigand, *Investigating the Role of Legitimacy in the Political Order of Conflict-torn Spaces*, Security in Transition Working Paper Series, 2015, 4, p. 4.

73 Jeni Whalan, *The Local Legitimacy of Peacekeepers*, Journal of Intervention and Statebuilding, 2017, 11(3), p. 309.

74 Marjo Hoefnagels, *Political Violence and Peace Research*, in: *Repression and Repressive Violence*, Amsterdam: Swets & Zeitlinger, 1977, pp. 29-39; Weigand, 2015, pp. 14-15.

75 Hannah Arendt, *Reflections on violence*, Journal of International Affairs, 1969, p. 10.

76 Mattei Dogan, *Conceptions of Legitimacy*, Encyclopedia of Government and Politics, 1992, 1, p. 116.

77 Anthony Bottoms and Justice Tankebe, *Beyond Procedural Justice: A Dialogic Approach to Legitimacy in Criminal Justice*, The Journal of Criminal Law and Criminology, 2012; Tom R. Tyler, *Why People Obey the Law*, Princeton University Press, 2006; Tom R. Tyler, *Enhancing Police Legitimacy*, The ANNALS of the American Academy of Political and Social Science, 2004, 593(1).

78 David Beetham, *Revisiting Legitimacy, Twenty Years On*, Legitimacy and Criminal Justice: An International Exploration, 2013, p. 33.

involved in these institutions".[79] The legitimacy of these mechanisms is particularly important for their acceptance in post-conflict environments and influences their potential to contribute to peace and justice.[80] Research has shown how organisational legitimacy can affect the post-conflict environment by promoting compliance and cooperation, which then enhances collective social order and stability.[81]

Research conducted by Oomen identifies five factors that enhance the legitimacy of transitional justice mechanisms operating in post-conflict environments. These mechanisms should:

i. demonstrate no apparent bias, ensuring that all the perpetrators of human rights violations are subject to prosecution or are invited to confess in front of a non-judicial forum;
ii. be rooted in the local context, by representing the collective norms, values and practices derived from customary and/or state law;
iii. be *accessible to all* through the language(s) spoken, the physical proximity to the survivors of the conflict, and the provision of clear explanations of the proceedings;
iv. comprise a comprehensive procedure at the national and local level by: punishing the perpetrators, recognising and compensating the survivors, honouring the memory of the dead, establishing some form of truth of what happened, and promoting reconciliation; and
v. include socio-economic justice by, for example, providing children with access to education, adults a means of securing a livelihood, and rebuilding homes.[82]

In line with Oomen's findings, other scholars emphasise the need to adhere to values and norms, which are explicitly communicated to all the stakeholders and which are locally accepted or acknowledged, to ensure the legitimacy of organisations operating in a (post-)conflict environment.[83] Transparency is also mentioned as important for organisational legitimacy, regardless of the environment in which the organisation operates.[84]

---

79 Oomen, 2009, p. 175.

80 Pierre Hazan, *Measuring the impact of punishment and forgiveness: a framework for evaluating transitional justice,* International Review of the Red Cross, 2006, 88(861), p. 46; Barbara Oomen, *Transitional Justice and Its Legitimacy: The Case for a Local Perspective,* Netherlands Quarterly of Human Rights, 2007, 25(1), p. 144.

81 Hazan, 2006, pp. 31-38; Oomen, 2007, pp. 142-148; Whalan, 2017, pp. 310-313.

82 Oomen, 2007, pp. 146-148.

83 David Beetham, *The Legitimation of Power,* Basingstoke: Macmillan, 1991, pp. 15-20; Hazan, 2006, p. 46; Mark C. Suchman, *Managing Legitimacy: Strategic and Institutional Approaches,* Academy of Management Review, 1995, 20(3), p. 574.

84 Julia Black, *Constructing and contesting legitimacy and accountability in polycentric regulatory regimes,* Regulation & Governance, 2008, 2(2), p. 154; Jessica Lincoln, *Transitional Justice, Peace and Accountability Outreach and the Role of International Courts after Conflict,* Taylor & Francis, 2011, p. 51.

An organisation that is considered legitimate is perceived as more meaningful and predictable, and is consequently considered as trustworthy, which is especially important for organisations operating in a (post-)conflict environment.[85] This reflects both Suchman and Beetham's work on organisations operating in stable environments: Suchman's research demonstrates how organisational legitimacy influences the way stakeholders respond to an organisation's services and products;[86] while Beetham's findings illustrate how legitimacy helps to promote compliance and cooperation, which then enhances the stability and effectiveness of an organisation.[87]

1.2.1 *The Legitimacy of International Criminal Courts*

International criminal courts and tribunals have a mandate to investigate and prosecute the political and/or military leaders involved in committing the worst crimes known to mankind. They therefore play a key role in post-conflict environments where local communities have experienced gross violations of their human rights.[88] A critical factor in ensuring the fulfilment of an international criminal court's mandate is ensuring that it is also perceived as a legitimate legal instrument within the post-conflict environment.[89]

However, the nature of an international criminal court's work may lead to its legitimacy being challenged, for example, due to: the physical distance between an international criminal court and the crime scenes and/or the witnesses or survivors of international crimes;[90] the years, sometimes decades, that have passed since the crimes took place and the start of the criminal trials, which may hinder criminal investigations;[91] the involvement of the international community, which may invoke a post-colonial sentiment in some post-conflict environments;[92] and the language and/or cultural barriers between those

85 Oomen, 2007, pp. 144-145.

86 Suchman, 1995, pp. 574-575.

87 Beetham, 2013, p. 20.

88 Cryer et al., 2019, pp. 30-43; Hazan, 2006, p. 28; Lincoln, 2011, pp. 116-118; Peskin, 2008, pp. 7-9.

89 Sara Darehshori, *Lessons for Outreach from the Ad Hoc Tribunals, the Special Court for Sierra Leone, and the International Criminal Court*, New England Journal of International and Comparative Law, 2007, 14, pp. 300-306; Hazan, 2006, pp. 33-34; Oomen, 2007, pp. 141-148.

90 Cryer et al., 2019, p. 43.

91 Nancy A. Combs, *Fact-Finding without Facts: The Uncertain Evidentiary Foundations of International Criminal Convictions*, Cambridge University Press, 2010; Patricia M. Wald, *To Establish Incredible Events by Credible Evidence: The Use of Affidavit Testimony in Yugoslavia War Crimes Tribunal Proceedings*, Harvard International Law Journal, 2001b, 42.

92 Brendon Cannon, Dominic Pkalya and Bosire Maragia, *The International Criminal Court and Africa: Contextualizing the Anti-ICC Narrative*, African Journal of International Criminal Justice (2017), no. 1-2, 2016, pp. 24-25; Cryer et al., 2019, pp. 44-45 & 551; Tim Murithi, *The African Union and the International Criminal Court: An Embattled Relationship?* Institute for Justice and Reconciliation, Policy Brief, 2003, (8), p. 5.

prosecuting the crimes and those accused of committing crimes, and/or the survivors or witnesses of the crimes.[93]

Furthermore, international criminal law is a specialised and technical area of the law, given that it has multiple sources (namely, customary international law and treaties) and refers to the judicial decisions of different courts.[94] Additionally, the same act (for example, the act of killing) can be classified as a crime against humanity, a genocidal act or a war crime depending on the contextual elements of the crime, rather than on the act itself.[95]

When the ICTR and the ICTY were established in the early 1990s, international criminal law was still in its infancy, with the most recent international military trials in Nuremberg and Tokyo having taken place almost 50 years earlier. As a result, the Chambers, OTP and defence teams working at both the ICTR and the ICTY did not have a recent body of case law to draw on for the definitions and elements of war crimes, crimes against humanity or genocide, resulting in extensive debates on the interpretation of the law within the courtroom.[96]

Moreover, international criminal trials are factually complex compared to most domestic criminal cases: the crimes were often committed by hierarchical groups working together, rather than by a single individual, and may have taken place in multiple locations and over different periods of time. As Wald's research demonstrates, conducting an international criminal trial *"[...] is usually more akin to documenting an episode or even an era of national or ethnic conflicts rather than proving a single discrete incident".*[97] Some of the facts considered in international criminal proceedings are highly technical, particularly those relating to mass grave exhumations or the use of specific weapons or military tactics, which require the assistance of expert witnesses to help interpret the evidence.[98]

These are just some of the factors that may prevent stakeholders, including legal practitioners and government officials, from accepting or fully comprehending the work

---

93 Besmir Fidahić, *Linguistic justice: Translation and interpretation at the International Criminal Tribunal for the former Yugoslavia*, Maastricht University, 2018; ICTR, *Prosecutor v. Jean-Paul Akayesu*, Judgment, ICTR-96-4-T, 2 September 1998, para. 145-154.

94 Mohamed Elewa Badar, *Drawing the Boundaries of Mens Rea in the Jurisprudence of the International Criminal Tribunal for the former Yugoslavia*, International Criminal Law Review, 2006, 6(3), pp. 346-348; Elies van Sliedregt and Sergey Vasiliev (eds.), *Pluralism in International Criminal Law*, Oxford: Oxford University Press, 2014, p. 68.

95 Antonio Cassese, *The Nexus Requirement for War Crimes*, Journal of International Criminal Justice, 2012, 10(5), p. 1395; John R. Cencich, *International Criminal Investigations of Genocide and Crimes Against Humanity: A War Crimes Investigator's Perspective*, International Criminal Justice Review, 2009, 19(2), p. 179; Cryer et al., 2019, p. 230; William A. Schabas, *State Policy as an Element of International Crimes*, The Journal of Criminal Law and Criminology, 2008a, pp. 960-964.

96 Cryer et al., 2019, pp. 207, 227-229 & 263-265; interviewees A2, A9, T4, T22 & T24; van Sliedregt & Vasiliev, 2014, pp. 60-69.

97 Wald, 2001b, pp. 536-537.

98 Ziggy MacDonald, *Official Crime Statistics: Their Use and Interpretation*, The Economic Journal, 2002, 112(477), pp. 89-90; Smeulers & Grünfeld, 2011, pp. 25-27.

of an international criminal court. As a result, international criminal courts run the risk of becoming inaccessible or irrelevant to stakeholders, reducing their ability to fulfil their mandates, especially in terms of reconciliation and the restoration or maintenance peace in a post-conflict environment.[99]

Furthermore, international organisations, including international criminal courts, operate in a very different social, political and legal sphere from national organisations, making them particularly vulnerable to questions related regarding their legitimacy:[100]

> "All social systems must confront what we might call the problem of social control – that is, how to get actors to comply with society's rules – but the problem is particularly acute for international relations, because the international social system does not possess an overarching center of political power to enforce rules."[101]

Several international criminal courts have seen their legitimacy challenged due to the nature of their establishment and due to debates over the hierarchy of sources associated with international law,[102] given that there is a lack of *"[...] centralized and hierarchically structured law-making and law-enforcing authority"*.[103] This is further challenged by the numerous stakeholders who have a vested interest in the activities of an international criminal court, for example UN member states or state parties to a treaty that establish and support the work of the court; individual states involved in the conflict and/or the post-conflict transition process; the survivors and perpetrators of the conflict; and the groups or organisations representing the perpetrators or survivors of the conflict.[104]

---

99 Varda Hussain, *Sustaining Judicial Rescues: The Role of Outreach and Capacity-Building Efforts in War Crimes Tribunals*, Virginia Journal of International Law, 2004, 45, pp. 549 & 580-583; Victor Peskin, *Courting Rwanda: The Promises and Pitfalls of the ICTR Outreach Programme*,Journal of International Criminal Justice, 2005a, 3(4), p. 951; Martien Schotsmans and François-Xavier Nsanzuwera, *Victims in the Balance: Challenges Ahead for the International Criminal Tribunal for Rwanda*. International Federation for Human Rights, 2002, pp. 8-10.

100 Black, 2008, pp. 140-141; Ian Hurd, *Legitimacy and Authority in International Politics*, International Organization, 1999, 53(2), pp. 379-408; Sergey Vasiliev, *Between International Criminal Justice and Injustice: Theorising Legitimacy,* in: Nobuo Hayashi and Cecilia M. Bailliet (eds.), *The Legitimacy of International Criminal Tribunals*, Cambridge University Press (2016), 2015, p. 5; Armin von Bogdandy and Ingo Venzke, *In Whose Name? An Investigation of International Courts' Public Authority and Its Democratic Justification*, European Journal of International Law, 2012, 23(1), pp. 7-41.

101 Hurd, 1999, p. 379.

102 Darehshori, 2007, p. 301; Hazan, 2006, pp. 30-34; ICTR, *Prosecutor v. Joseph Kanyabashi*, Decision on the defence motion on jurisdiction, ICTR-96-15-T, 18 June 1997; Murithi, 2003; Vasiliev, 2015, p. 5.

103 Mario Prost, *Hierarchy and the Sources of International Law: A Critique*, Houston Journal of International Law, 2017, 39, p. 286.

104 Cryer et al., 2019, pp. 446-448 & 551-553; ICTR website, 'Defence and Detention'; ICTR website, 'Registry'; Vasiliev, 2015, pp. 5-7.

In order to gain and maintain legitimacy, an international criminal court must act impartially and limit the influence, or interference, of its key stakeholders.[105] However, this poses a challenge in itself, as each stakeholder will have *"[...] different expectations regarding what constitutes proper behaviour"*[106] in relation to its interactions with the international court.

The need for *"proper behaviour"*[107] is especially important in the case of international criminal courts, as they embody the international rule of law; an international criminal court has the responsibility to render impartial judgments, demonstrate its commitment to procedural justice, and ensure strict adherence to the rule of law.[108] However, stakeholders will instinctively refer to their own traditions, values, customs and culture to assess the legitimacy of an international court.[109] The challenges for international criminal courts are therefore great, especially since they also play a key role in contributing to the success of transitional justice in a post-conflict environment, which aims to restore peace, fight impunity and promote reconciliation in a post-conflict environment.[110]

1.2.2 Organisational Legitimacy

Although studies on legitimacy originally focused on legal, political and societal systems, the emergence of institutional theories and organisational studies in the late 1970s offered a new perspective from which to examine the notion of legitimacy.[111] In 1995, Suchman conducted an extensive literature review that focused specifically on organisational legitimacy. His findings show that that most organisations, especially commercial organisations, are well aware of the importance of legitimacy and have various mechanisms in place to manage their legitimacy.[112] According to Suchman's study, organisational legitimacy can be divided into three different categories:

105 Dinah Shelton, *Form, Function, and the Powers of International Courts*, Chicago Journal of International Law, 9, pp. 543-544.

106 Michael Barnett and Martha Finnemore, *Rules for the World: International Organizations in Global Politics*, Cornell University Press, 2004, p. 171.

107 Barnett & Finnemore, 2004, p. 171.

108 Laurence Helfer and Anne-Marie Slaughter, *Toward a Theory of Effective Supranational Adjudication*, Yale Law Journal, 1997, 107, pp. 389-391; Vasiliev, 2015, p. 6.

109 Oomen, 2007, pp. 146-148; Benjamin Schiff, *Lessons from the ICC for ICC/R2P Convergence*, The Finnish Yearbook of International Law 2010, 21(1), p. 42.

110 Yuval Shany, *Assessing the Effectiveness of International Courts: A Goal-Based Approach*, American Journal of International Law, 2012, 106(2), p. 253; Vasiliev, 2015, p. 6.

111 John W. Meyer and Brian Rowan, *Institutionalized Organizations: Formal Structure as Myth and Ceremony*,American Journal of Sociology, 1977, 83, pp. 340-363; Lynne G. Zucker, *The Role of Institutionalization in Cultural Persistence*, American Sociological Review, 1977, 42, pp. 726-743.

112 Suchman, 1995, pp. 573-577.

- *Pragmatic* legitimacy is achieved when the needs and interests of the organisation's stakeholders are met, and refers to the organisation's performance and its ability to produce desired and/or expected results.[113] For example, a school is expected to provide a certain level of education, and a restaurant is expected to serve a certain quality and/or type of food. If these organisations do not meet these expectations, they may lose pragmatic legitimacy.
- *Moral* legitimacy is attributed to an organisation when its actions and/or behaviour are consistent with the ethics and values of its environment, namely the environment of its stakeholders.[114] If stakeholders are aware that a business has been set-up in a way that allows it to evade taxes, or if it is known that its staff are known to be poorly paid, the business is at risk of losing its moral legitimacy.
- *Cognitive* legitimacy is conferred on an organisation when its broader goals are deemed appropriate and socially acceptable; support for the organisation is not linked to the self-interest of its stakeholders (*pragmatic* legitimacy) nor to their value assessments (*moral* legitimacy), but rather to the character of the organisation as a whole and to its position in its environment. This form of legitimacy is most often associated with institutions such as schools, religious institutions, courts, and hospitals.[115] Challenges to an organisation's *cognitive* legitimacy are rare because they question the existence of the organisation as a whole, rather than its actions or activities. The performance of a school (*pragmatic* legitimacy) or the behaviour of its staff (*moral* legitimacy) may be scrutinised, but the existence of the school itself is rarely questioned (*cognitive* legitimacy).

Suchman's research found that the decision to grant an organisation pragmatic or moral legitimacy was usually made following discussions and deliberations among stakeholders, while cognitive legitimacy was recognised through unspoken assumptions about the organisation.[116] The environment in which an organisation operates and where the stakeholders are located therefore plays a critical role when it comes to organisational legitimacy. Suchman's definition of legitimacy underlines the need to take into consideration an organisation's environmental factors: "*[...] a generalized perception or assumption that the actions of an entity are desirable, proper, or appropriate within some socially constructed system of norms, values, beliefs, and definitions*".[117] This definition suggests that legitimacy

113 *idem.*, pp. 578-579.
114 *idem.*, pp. 579-582.
115 *idem.*, pp. 582-583.
116 *idem.*, p. 585.
117 *idem.*, p. 574.

is shaped by the reaction of stakeholders to an organisation's activities, which are in line with the accepted norms and values of a specific environment.[118]

1.2.3 Gaining, Maintaining and Repairing Legitimacy

In an effort to manage organisational legitimacy, especially when faced with legitimacy challenges, organisations, including international criminal courts, will engage in legitimisation activities.[119] Legitimisation[120] is the act of gaining, maintaining and/or repairing legitimacy: it is the process of making something legitimate (or acceptable) to a society, a specific group or an individual. The process of legitimisation is achieved by providing arguments that explain the actions, ideas or decisions of an individual or organisation in order for them to gain support and approval.[121] Legitimisation activities may take the form of rhetorical claims or justifications, communicated, for example, in advertising campaigns, and/or through specific actions, such as the establishment of an ethics or oversight committee, or the restructuring of certain organisational processes or procedures.[122]

Suchman's research provides an overview of the management of organisational legitimacy, specifically the legitimisation activities that organisations undertake to gain, maintain or repair their legitimacy.[123] When an organisation is first established, or when it hires a new director or launches a new product, it faces the task of *gaining* legitimacy for the organisation as a whole, or for the new employee or product, or possibly even to confirm the validity of the leadership that made the decision to establish the organisation or hire the new director.[124] In general, all organisations invest a significant amount of time and effort to proactively establish their legitimacy vis-à-vis their environment, especially if the organisation itself lacks *"the support of traditions and norms and so suffers the 'liability of newness'"*.[125] According to Suchman, an organisation will engage in legitimisation

118 *ibid.*

119 Blake E. Ashforth and Barrie W. Gibbs, *The Double-Edge of Organizational Legitimation*, Organization Science, 1990, 1(2), pp. 177-194; David Deephouse, Jonathan Bundy, Leigh Plunkett Tost and Mark Suchman, *Organizational Legitimacy: Six Key Questions*, The SAGE Handbook of Organizational Institutionalism, 2017, pp. 17-19.

120 Also referred to as 'legitimation'.

121 Ashforth & Gibbs, 1990, pp. 177-194; Deephouse et al., 2017, pp. 17-19.

122 Honorata Mazepus, Wouter Veenendaal, Anthea McCarthy-Jones and Juan Manuel Trak Vásquez, *A comparative study of legitimation strategies in hybrid regimes*, Policy Studies, 2016, 37(4), p. 354.

123 Suchman, 1995, pp. 585-599.

124 Suchman, 1995, p. 586.

125 Ashforth & Gibbs, 1990, p. 182.

activities to counter this *"liability of newness"*,[126] which involves selecting, conforming to, or manipulating its environment.[127]

Legitimacy-*repairing* activities are similar to those used to gain legitimacy. However, they constitute the reaction of an organisation to its environment, often in response to an unforeseen crisis related to the organisation's activities, or employee behaviour, or when questions arise related to the very existence of the organisation.[128] The two main approaches to repairing legitimacy can be categorised as either symbolic or substantive legitimisation activities.[129]

Maintaining legitimacy is generally considered easier than gaining or repairing legitimacy, since the organisation is not proactively or reactively responding to its environment and therefore does not need to invest the same level of effort in legitimisation.[130] However, attention is still paid to maintaining organisational legitimacy, especially if the organisation operates in an environment that is continuously evolving and/or caters to a diverse set of stakeholders. In these cases, an organisation's legitimisation activities can be categorised as either risk mitigation by *"perceiving future changes"* or as protecting and/or promoting the organisation's past accomplishments.[131]

Several studies show how discourse and/or actions can be framed in specific ways to promote the legitimacy of organisational practices.[132] However, there is also a risk that the narrative put forward by an organisation about a particular event or activity may lead to different interpretations, which could either legitimise or de-legitimise the event or activity in question – depending on the perspective of the organisation's stakeholders.[133] Given the importance of *"legitimate structures for the peaceful settlement of disputes and the fair administration of justice"*[134] in post-conflict environments, there is a need for a better understanding of the legitimisation activities implemented by international criminal courts.

Furthermore, international criminal courts require strong relationships and collaboration with states, and good communication and understanding among all

---

126 *ibid.*

127 Suchman, 1995, pp. 587-588

128 *idem.*, pp. 597-598.

129 Ashforth & Gibbs, 1990, pp. 178-182.

130 Suchman, 1995, pp. 593-596.

131 *idem.*, pp. 593-596.

132 Ashforth & Gibbs, 1990; Douglas W. Creed, Maureen A. Scully and John R. Austin, *Clothes Make the Person? The Tailoring of Legitimating Accounts and the Social Construction of Identity*, Organization Science, 2002, 13(5), 475-496; Antonio Reyes, *Strategies of legitimization in political discourse: From words to actions*, Discourse & Society, 2011, 22(6), 781-807.

133 *ibid.*

134 United Nations Security Council, *Rule of law and transitional justice in conflict and post-conflict societies.* Report of the Secretary-General, S/2004/616, 23 August 2004, para. 2. Retrieved from: https://www.securitycouncilreport.org/atf/cf/%7B65BFCF9B-6D27-4E9C-8CD3-CF6E4FF96FF9%7D/PCS%20S%202004%20616.pdf.

stakeholders involved in their work, in order to fulfil their mandate and address the complexities of conducting trials in a post-conflict environment. Legitimacy therefore plays an important role in managing these relationships, allowing international criminal courts to function as "*legitimate structures*"[135] by providing much-needed resources, infrastructure, support and recognition.[136]

1.3 The Importance of Legitimacy for the ICTR

The previous section has demonstrated the importance of organisational legitimacy, more specifically the legitimacy of international criminal courts established to assist a region or country in the transition from a period of conflict in which gross human rights violations have taken place, to a more cohesive and stable society, in which reconciliation is promoted and accountability for past abuses is recognised and addressed.

Over the past two decades, there has been an increased recognition by diplomats and those working within international criminal courts that external relations, communication and outreach programmes are key to ensuring the legitimacy of international criminal courts, rather than being merely auxiliary.[137] Darehshori, a former prosecutor at the ICTR, advocates for strong communication and outreach efforts to ensure that international criminal courts can have a positive impact on the populations directly affected by the crimes they investigate.[138]

Yet the development and implementation of appropriate outreach activities is just as important. A study conducted by Zacklin highlights the negative consequences of the ICTY's outreach programme, which led to misunderstandings about the ICTY's work and created tensions among certain communities within the former Yugoslavia.[139] Other studies examined the external communication and outreach programmes conducted by the Special Court for Sierra Leone (SCSL) and concluded that although the SCSL's programmes were innovative, the Sierra Leonean population remained poorly informed about the activities

---

135 *ibid.*

136 Janine Natalya Clark, *International War Crimes Tribunals and the Challenge of Outreach*, International Criminal Law Review, 2009, 9(1), pp. 99-116; Mahmoud Cherif Bassiouni, *Former Yugoslavia: Investigating Violations of International Humanitarian Law and Establishing an International Criminal Tribunal*, Fordham International Law Journal, 1994, 18, pp. 1192-1193 & 1197; Antonio Cassese, *On the Current Trends towards Criminal Prosecution and Punishment of Breaches of International Humanitarian Law*,European Journal of International Law, 1998, 9(1), pp. 12-13; Drumbl, 2007, pp. 144-148.

137 Paige Arthur (ed.), *Identities in Transition: Challenges for Transitional Justice in Divided Societies*, Cambridge University Press, 2010, p. 168; Chuck Sudetic and Carla Del Ponte, *Madam Prosecutor: Confrontations with Humanity's Worst Criminals and the Culture of Impunity*, New York: Other Press, 2011, p. 376.

138 Darehshori, 2007.

139 Ralph Zacklin, *The Failings of Ad Hoc International Tribunals*, Journal of International Criminal Justice, 2004, 2, pp. 541-545.

of the Court. Although most Sierra Leoneans were aware of the existence of the SCSL, very few understood its mandate and activities.[140]

These findings are problematic, as the basic understanding of the work of an international criminal court is critical in building perceptions of its legitimacy, and legitimacy has been shown to have an impact on organisational success.[141] This is confirmed by Oomen's research, which concludes that strengthening perceptions of legitimacy should be the primary concern of all those involved in transitional justice institutions.[142]

Research conducted by Wierda, Nassar and Maalouf examined the legitimacy challenges faced by the Special Tribunal for Lebanon (STL), given the selective nature of its jurisdiction and fears that the Tribunal could act as an instrument for foreign powers.[143] The authors demonstrate how these legitimacy challenges could have been addressed by raising awareness of the process used to select the Tribunal's judges and senior officials, as well as the importance of securing funding from a wider range of states.[144] Similarly, Danner's study of the International Criminal Court (ICC) also highlighted the importance for the OTP to provide insight into its impartial, transparent decision-making processes, thereby strengthening its legitimacy and emphasising the ICC's adherence to international values and norms.[145]

In line with Danner's work, Ford's literature review concludes that the legitimacy of international criminal courts is largely dependent on the individuals selected to be indicted by the court.[146] Research by Glasius echoes Ford's findings by demonstrating that international criminal courts are often criticised for being undemocratic, arguing that they should pursue broader social goals developed in dialogue with stakeholders working and

140 Stuart Ford, *How Special is the Special Court's Outreach Section? The Sierra Leone Special Court and Its Legacy: The Impact for Africa and International Criminal Law* (Charles Chernor Jalloh ed.), Cambridge University Press (2014), 2012b; Rachel Kerr and Jessica Lincoln, *The Special Court for Sierra Leone: Outreach, Legacy and Impact*, Department of War Studies, King's College London: War Crimes Research Group, 2008; Lincoln, 2011, p. 95.

141 Ruby Dagher, *Legitimacy and post-conflict state-building: the undervalued role of performance legitimacy*, Conflict, Security & Development, 2018, 18(2), pp. 98-99; Robert D. Lamb, *Rethinking Legitimacy and Illegitimacy: A New Approach to Assessing Support and Opposition Across Disciplines*. Lanham, MD: CSIS and Rowman & Littlefield, 2014; Suchman, 1995, pp. 578-579.

142 Oomen, 2007, pp. 141-143.

143 Marieke Wierda, Habib Nassar and Lynn Maalouf, *Early Reflections on Local Perceptions, Legitimacy and Legacy of the Special Tribunal for Lebanon*, Journal of International Criminal Justice, 2007, 5(5), pp. 1065-1081.

144 *idem.*, p. 1076.

145 Allison Marston Danner, *Enhancing the Legitimacy and Accountability of Prosecutorial Discretion at the International Criminal Court*, American Journal of International Law, 2003, pp. 523-524 & 536-552.

146 Stuart Ford, *A Social Psychology Model of the Perceived Legitimacy of International Criminal Courts: Implications for the Success of Transitional Justice Mechanisms*, Vanderbilt Journal of Transnational Law, 2012a, 45, p. 405.

living in the post-conflict environment in which they operate.[147] Henham also emphasises the importance of delivering justice within a more "*socially inclusive*"[148] framework, illustrating how international criminal courts could be seen as more legitimate if their decisions and judgments were more understandable to all stakeholders involved, leading to social rehabilitation and reconciliation, especially in contexts where divisions in the post-conflict society persist.[149]

While the studies conducted by the scholars mentioned in this section examine the importance of legitimacy for international criminal courts,[150] underline the need for courts to be perceived as legitimate instruments of law,[151] explore the outreach activities carried out by international courts,[152] and/or identify a link between the legitimacy of international criminal courts and the implementation of outreach programmes,[153] no studies were found that examine the legitimisation activities carried out by an international criminal court, when faced with legitimacy challenges, in order to gain, maintain or repair its legitimacy.[154]

1.3.1 Why the ICTR?

The ICTR closed its doors on 31 December 2015, leaving behind a rich legacy for international criminal law,[155] while Rwanda is seen as a success story following its rapid recovery since the 1994 genocide.[156] With this in mind, it is worth looking back at the actions and activities of the UN-established Tribunal based in Arusha to examine how the ICTR operated during its 20-years of existence, whether its legitimacy fluctuated over time, and if so, whether – and how –it overcame any legitimacy challenges.

---

147 Marlies Glasius, *Do International Criminal Courts Require Democratic Legitimacy?* European Journal of International Law, 2012, 23(1), pp. 43-66.

148 Ralph Henham, *Sentencing and the Legitimacy of Trial Justice*, Routledge, 2013, p. 70.

149 Henham, 2013, pp. 118-123.

150 Nienke Grossman, Harlan Grant Cohen, Andreas Føllesdal and Geir Ulfstein (eds.), *Legitimacy and International Courts*, Cambridge University Press, 2018; Vasiliev, 2015.

151 Robert J. Chaskin, *Fostering Neighborhood Democracy: Legitimacy and Accountability within Loosely Coupled Systems*, Nonprofit and Voluntary Sector Quarterly, 2003, 32(2), pp. 161-189; Sunshine & Tyler, 2003.

152 Danner, 2003; Darehshori, 2007; Wierda, Nassar & Maalouf, 2007.

153 Donna E. Arzt, *Views on the Ground: The Local Perception of International Criminal Tribunals in the former Yugoslavia and Sierra Leone*, The ANNALS of the American Academy of Political and Social Science, 2006, 603(1), pp. 226-239; Clark, 2009, pp. 99-116.

154 Suchman, 1995, p. 600.

155 Cisse, 1998, pp. 161-188; Cryer et al., 2019, pp. 207-208; ICTR website, 'Cases': https://unictr.irmct.org/en/cases.

156 Bloomberg, *Africa's Would-Be Switzerland Shows Economic Clout With WEF*, 10 May 2016. Retrieved from: https://www.bloomberg.com/news/articles/2016-05-09/africa-s-would-be-switzerland-flaunts-economic-prowess-with-wef.

According to studies by Beetham, the first condition for legitimacy is that it is obtained and exercised in accordance with established rules.[157] In the case of the ICTR, the Tribunal was established by the UN – an intergovernmental organisation with 193 member states governed by the UN Security Council and the UN General Assembly[158] – through the adoption of UN Security Council Resolution 955. The establishment of the Tribunal through a UN resolution, together with its founding documents – including the ICTR Statute and the ICTR RPE – provided a solid basis for the ICTR's legitimacy, and the conformity of its activities with the mandate defined in its founding documents provided a basis against which the legitimacy of the Tribunal could be measured.[159]

Yet despite the support of 193 UN member states and the adoption of UN Resolution 955, the ICTR's connection with the UN can be viewed as both a strength and a weakness. On the one hand, the UN's resources, infrastructure and network helped the Tribunal to set up courtrooms and offices at the AICC in Tanzania, allowed it to attract qualified staff members, and required all UN member states to contribute to its operations. On the other hand, the ICTR was founded following a genocide that took place in full view of the world, while the UN – established to "*maintain international peace and security*"[160] – failed to intervene, prevent or stop the atrocities that took place on Rwandan soil. As a result, some scholars have argued that the Tribunal was established to redress the UN's failure to address the escalating violence in 1994, and not as part of a deliberate policy to promote peace and reconciliation in Rwanda and the Great Lakes region.[161]

Other potential threats to the ICTR's legitimacy might have been its location, based in Arusha rather than in Kigali, and the temporal jurisdiction of the Tribunal, both of which created friction with the Rwandan government.[162] Furthermore, by the time the Tribunal closed its doors, on 31 December 2015, the failure to indict any members of the RPF gave rise to claims that the Tribunal was exercising 'victor's justice'.[163]

Taking into consideration the political sensitivities that surrounded the establishment of the ICTR, the complexity of international criminal law – which was magnified by the location of the Tribunal in Tanzania rather than near the crime scenes and witnesses in Rwanda – and the cultural and linguistic hurdles it encountered, it appears that the Tribunal

157 Beetham, 1991, pp. 15-20.
158 UN website, 'About us': https://www.un.org/en/about-us/.
159 Cryer et al., 2019, p. 137.
160 UN Charter, 24 October 1945, Article 1.
161 Bouka, 2013a; Moghalu, 2005, p. 24; Peskin, 2008, p. 159.
162 Cryer et al., 2019, p. 137; United Nations Security Council, *The Situation Concerning Rwanda*. Provisional Report of the 3453rd Meeting, S/PV.3453, 8 November 1994, pp. 14-16.
163 Yolande A. Bouka, *(Oral) History of Violence: Conflicting Narratives in Post-Genocide Rwanda*, in: *Oral History Forum d'histoire orale*, 2013b, 33, p. 3; Human Rights Watch, *Rwanda: Tribunal Risks Supporting 'Victor's Justice', Tribunal Should Vigorously Pursue Crimes of Rwandan Patriotic Front*, 1 June 2009. Retrieved from: https://www.hrw.org/news/2009/06/01/rwanda-tribunal-risks-supporting-victors-justice; Straus & Waldorf, 2011, p. 174.

faced a number of challenges during its 20-year existence that threatened its reputation as a legitimate court of law. The need for the ICTR to address these concerns and to promote itself as a legitimate Tribunal should therefore have been a top priority.

As a result, this study takes a closer look at various legitimacy challenges that the ICTR faced to examine how the Tribunal initially gained legitimacy and whether stakeholders viewed it as a legitimate organisation. It then identifies specific legitimacy challenges that the ICTR faced and how it overcame them; and investigates the day-to-day activities that the Tribunal undertook to maintain its legitimacy, and the influence that these activities had on the Tribunal's mandate.

1.3.2 Key Objectives of This Study

In light of the information provided thus far, this research focuses on the following three objectives. First and foremost, it examines the importance of organisational legitimacy, in particular for the ICTR. In examining the concept of legitimacy, this study looks at how perceptions of organisational legitimacy are formed and the impact that these perceptions have on the functioning of an international criminal court. For the purpose of this research, organisational legitimacy is defined as: *"[...] the perceived appropriateness of an organization to a social system in terms of rules, values, norms, and definitions".*[164]

The second objective is to identify and examine the legitimacy challenges that the ICTR faced, which provides insights into the post-conflict environment in which the ICTR was working and highlights the variety of challenges experienced by the Tribunal over the years. The diversity of the Tribunal's stakeholders, each with their own specific needs and expectations, is also examined, highlighting how the ICTR's broad mandate and the diversity of its stakeholders increased the complexity of its operations in both Rwanda and in Tanzania.

The third and final objective of this research is to examine the Tribunal's response to the legitimacy challenges it faced, using legitimisation activities aimed at gaining, maintaining and repairing its organisational legitimacy. In exploring the ICTR's response to its legitimacy challenges, this third objective provides information on: what legitimisation activities the Tribunal implemented; how they were implemented; and where the Tribunal chose to focus its resources and attention, and the reasoning behind these choices. In doing so, the study also exposes some of the challenges that the ICTR chose to ignore or not to address.

The main objective of this study is to emphasise the critical importance of organisational legitimacy for international criminal courts, particularly with respect to their work in

164 Deephouse et al., 2017, p. 9.

(post-)conflict environments, and to inform the development and/or revision of their legitimisation activities. In recognising of the importance of organisational legitimacy, this study seeks to overcome the notion that an international criminal court is legitimate solely by virtue of its legal status and the nature of its work. This assumption risks detracting from the important work of these courts.

1.4 Outline of This Book

This book consists of seven chapters, with the first chapter serving as an introduction to the research topic and the objectives of this study. Chapter 2 presents the theoretical framework used for the research by first examining the concept of legitimacy and why legitimacy is important for an organisation, especially for organisations operating in a (post-)conflict environment. Different forms of organisational legitimacy are described by focusing on the importance of the relationship between an organisation and its key stakeholders. Making use of research conducted by Suchman, Deephouse, Bundy and Tost,[165] the chapter describes how an organisation may engage in legitimisation activities to gain, maintain and repair its pragmatic, moral and/or cognitive legitimacy, especially when faced with legitimacy challenges. The third and final part of Chapter 2 presents the theoretical framework designed for this research in order to examine the ICTR's legitimisation actions and to better understand the focus and key priorities of the Tribunal over the course of its 20-year existence.

Following the theoretical framework, Chapter 3 provides information on the research approach used to answer the main research question and sub-questions. The chapter describes the empirical research that took place and the ethical considerations that were taken into account, as well as the limitations of this study, including a discussion about the validity and generalisability of the research findings.

Chapters 4, 5 and 6 present the findings of the empirical research. Chapter 4 examines whether the ICTR was perceived as legitimate, and if so, how it gained its legitimacy. The chapter provides interviewees' interpretations of the concept of legitimacy and compares them with the findings from the literature review, the archival research and the theoretical framework presented in Chapter 2. Furthermore, the chapter describes how perceptions of legitimacy are formed and how this is related to the concept of legitimisation. By examining the activities of the ICTR, the chapter also explores the legitimacy of the UN (which created and supported the ICTR), as well as the relationship between these two organisations – in particular how the Tribunal's link with the UN affected its own legitimacy vis-à-vis its other stakeholders.

165 Deephouse, et al., 2017; Suchman, 1995.

Chapter 5 focuses in on eight categories of legitimacy challenges that the Tribunal faced and the legitimisation activities undertaken in response to each of these challenges. The chapter is divided into eight sections that cover the ICTR's 20-year lifespan, while also examining how legitimacy challenges may continue to threaten the Tribunal's legitimacy even after closing its doors in December 2015. In doing so, this chapter demonstrates the importance of legitimacy for the ICTR and highlights the specific legitimisation activities that were undertaken to gain, maintain and repair the pragmatic, moral and cognitive legitimacy of the Tribunal, particularly in relation to two of its key stakeholders: the UN and the Rwandan government.

Chapter 6 takes a broader approach in examining whether – and how – the Tribunal maintained its legitimacy over the years. Specifically, this chapter focuses on how the Tribunal managed its legitimacy in relation to its mandate, using its existing legitimacy to garner support and interest from certain stakeholders, sometimes at the expense of other stakeholders. First, the ICTR's mandate and key short- and long-term objectives are identified through speeches and documents presented by the UN and the ICTR. The chapter then examines the relationship between the Tribunal's legitimisation activities and these short- and long-term objectives. Given the ad hoc nature of the Tribunal, there was a certain pressure to ensure that its short-term objectives were met while promoting its long-term objectives, which were related to the mission and societal values of the UN. However, in pursuing certain objectives – related to pragmatic, moral and cognitive legitimacy – the relationship between the ICTR and its two key stakeholders may have created unforeseen legitimacy challenges, which are further explored in this chapter.

The concluding chapter of this book presents and reflects on the key findings of the empirical research, and makes recommendations for existing and future international criminal courts. The first part revisits the central research question and sub-questions to highlight the main conclusions of this study. Taking into account the research findings, the second part of the chapter provides general recommendations related to enhancing the legitimacy of international criminal courts, demonstrating the importance of recognising and managing organisational legitimacy, while also ensuring that international criminal courts interact with their stakeholders. The importance of acknowledging all three legitimacy types (pragmatic, moral and cognitive) is also highlighted in this section, as is the need to understand the local environment in which an international criminal court operates. The chapter ends by identifying avenues for further research.

2 Legitimacy: Theoretical Framework

Numerous terms are used interchangeably with the words *legitimate* or *legitimacy*; the comparison to other concepts depends principally on the discipline or the approach taken by the author. Yet legitimacy is an everyday word, which is used and understood by all, so why is it such a difficult notion to explain? The answer may lie in the fact that legitimacy is a concept that develops and interacts with other social phenomena, and may be used synonymously with the notions of authority, accountability, power, consent and judgement.[1]

Legitimacy has long been recognised as a core element in political and governance systems as a means to explain the relationship between the societal acceptance of regimes and organisations, and their ability to exercise power and authority effectively.[2] In the case of organisations, such as international criminal courts and tribunals, assessments of legitimacy can be based on: the way in which an organisation is established, its legality and its underlying values; the experience, expertise and integrity of the organisation's staff; and/or the efficiency and effectiveness of its operational procedures.[3] These forms of assessment can follow an organisation from its inception throughout its lifespan and may even continue once its operations have come to an end.[4]

The concept of organisational legitimacy is influenced by a multitude of internal and external factors, which justifies an organisation's role in society, and helps attract resources and support from its stakeholders.[5] Legitimacy is therefore considered an important resource in its own right: it carries a weight that can make or break an organisation. However, perceptions of an organisation's legitimacy may differ among various

1 Julia Black, *Constructing and contesting legitimacy and accountability in polycentric regulatory regimes,* Regulation & Governance, 2008, 2(2), pp. 137-164; Andreas Føllesdal, Johan Karlsson Schaffer and Geir Ulfstein (eds.), *The Legitimacy of International Human Rights Regimes: Legal, Political and Philosophical Perspectives*, Cambridge University Press, 2013, pp. 16-21; Ian Hurd, *Legitimacy and Authority in International Politics,* International Organization, 1999, 53(2), pp. 379-408; Jean-Jacques Rousseau, *Rousseau: 'The Social Contract' and Other Later Political Writings*, Cambridge University Press, 1997; Tom R. Tyler, *Why People Obey the Law,* Princeton University Press, 2006.

2 Black, 2008, pp. 137-164; Mattei Dogan, *Conceptions of Legitimacy*, Encyclopedia of Government and Politics, 1992, 1, pp. 116-126; Max Weber, *Economy and Society: An Outline of Interpretive Sociology*, Berkeley: University of California Press, 1978.

3 Derick W. Brinkerhoff, *Organizational Legitimacy, Capacity, and Capacity Development*, University of Kansas, Public Management Research Association (PMRA), 2005.

4 Daniel Bodansky, Jeffrey L. Dunoff and Mark A. Pollack, *Legitimacy in International Law and International Relations,*Interdisciplinary Perspectives on International Law and International Relations: The State of the Art, 2013, pp. 321-341.

5 Alex Bitektine, *Toward a Theory of Social Judgments of Organizations: The Case of Legitimacy, Reputation, and Status,* Academy of Management Review, 2011, 36(1) pp. 151-179.

stakeholders; perceptions can be contradictory, evolve over time and be difficult to manage.[6] Legitimisation activities aimed at gaining, maintaining and (if needed) repairing organisational legitimacy are therefore crucial for the management of an organisation's legitimacy.[7]

Aside from the definitional questions, identifying the factors that influence assessments of legitimacy often take a normative or an empirical approach.[8] The normative approach identifies the societal standards used to gauge legitimacy and, rather than addressing the individual or collective response to such standards, examines whether the standard for legitimacy has been achieved and whether the sources used to assess legitimacy should be respected.[9] In contrast, the empirical approach explores legitimacy as a belief, and legitimisation as a social process; studies that use the empirical approach often associate legitimacy with a social value such as consent, acceptance, reputation or status.[10]

The aim of this chapter is to describe the concept of organisational legitimacy and how the theoretical framework used for this research was constructed. The chapter starts by describing different forms of organisational legitimacy, as well as the role of stakeholders in assessing an organisation's legitimacy. Referring to the research conducted by Suchman, Deephouse et al. and Ashforth and Gibbs,[11] the second part of this chapter examines the notion of legitimisation and the circumstances in which this process is performed by organisations. The section describes the ways in which an organisation seeks to gain, maintain and repair its legitimacy[12] using legitimisation activities, examining how these actions can be analysed in order to better understand an organisation's focus and objectives. The third and final section presents the theoretical framework of this research, designed to examine the legitimisation activities implemented by the ICTR when faced with legitimacy challenges over the course of its 20-year lifespan.

---

6 Blake E. Ashforth and Barrie W. Gibbs, *The Double-Edge of Organizational Legitimation*, Organization Science, 1990, 1(2), 177-194; Douglas W. Creed, Maureen A. Scully and John R. Austin, *Clothes Make the Person? The Tailoring of Legitimating Accounts and the Social Construction of Identity*, Organization Science, 2002, 13(5), pp. 475-496; Antonio Reyes, *Strategies of legitimization in political discourse: From words to actions*, Discourse & Society, 2011, 22(6), pp. 781-807.

7 David Deephouse, Jonathan Bundy, Leigh Plunkett Tost and Mark Suchman, *Organizational Legitimacy: Six Key Questions*, The SAGE Handbook of Organizational Institutionalism, 2017.

8 Sergey Vasiliev, *Between International Criminal Justice and Injustice: Theorising Legitimacy*,in: Nobuo Hayashi and Cecilia M. Bailliet (eds.), *The Legitimacy of International Criminal Tribunals*, Cambridge University Press (2016), 2015, pp. 12-13.

9 Bodansky et al., 2013.

10 Allen E. Buchanan, *Justice, Legitimacy, and Self-Determination: Moral Foundations for International Law*, Oxford University Press, 2007; Vasiliev, 2015.

11 Ashforth & Gibbs, 1990; Deephouse et al., 2017; Suchman, 1995.

12 Suchman, 1995, pp. 585-599.

2.1 LEGITIMACY

"Legitimacy is known more readily when it is absent than when it is present."[13]

The term legitimacy originates from the Latin word *lex* (and its root word *leg-*) meaning *law*: with the Latin noun *legitimitas* directly translating to *legitimacy*; the verb *legitimo* means "*to make legal*"; while the adjective *legitimus* translates to "*lawful*" or "*right*".[14] In line with this, the English word *legitimate* is defined as a verb that means *"conforming to the law or to rules"*,or as an adjective meaning *"able to be defended with logic or justification; valid."*[15]

Due to the legal roots of the term legitimacy - as described above - the distinction between the terms *legitimacy*and *legality* is still hotly debated. Indeed, in the legal sphere, legitimacy is often connected to the notion of legality given that normative assessments of legitimacy often make use of the legal standards of the rule of law. As such, legal scholars have argued that if the government or an organisation complies with the rule of law, it can essentially be considered legitimate.[16] Furthermore, legality and legitimacy are both defined as *"being in accordance with the law"*,[17] so it is understandable that there may be confusion or debate over their use.

Yet, despite the legal origins of the term, scholars have demonstrated that not all legal acts are necessarily perceived or recognised as legitimate, and a legitimate act is not necessarily considered legal. Indeed, it has been argued that conceptually it is better to keep the two terms separate.[18] Clark illustrates the relevance of nuances when determining legitimacy, explaining that while *"what is legitimate is what the law ordains"*,[19] the general public's interpretation regarding the legitimacy of the law also needs to be taken into consideration.[20] Beetham also highlights the need for the law - including traditional law or unwritten rules - to be recognised as legitimate by the collective group,[21] as does Weber,

---

13 Gerald R. Salancik and Jeffrey Pfeffer, *The External Control of Organizations: A Resource Dependence Perspective*, New York: Harper & Row, 1978, p. 194.

14 Oxford Dictionary, 'legitimacy'. Retrieved from: https://www.lexico.com/definition/legitimacy.

15 *idem.*, 'legitimate'. Retrieved from: https://www.lexico.com/definition/legitimate.

16 Clark, 2005; Ian Hurd, *Torture and the politics of legitimation in international law*, in: Føllesdal et al., 2013, pp. 165-168; Joanna Nicholson, *Strengthening the Effectiveness of International Criminal Law through the Principle of Legality*, International Criminal Law Review, 2017, 17(4) (2017), pp. 656-681; Benjamin Schiff, *Lessons from the ICC for ICC/R2P Convergence*, The Finnish Yearbook of International Law 2010, 21(1); Vasiliev, 2015.

17 Oxford dictionary, 'legality'. Retrieved from: https://www.lexico.com/definition/legality; Oxford Dictionary, 'legitimacy'. Retrieved from: https://www.lexico.com/definition/legitimacy.

18 Vasiliev, 2015, pp. 9-11.

19 Ian Clark, *Legitimacy in International Society*, Oxford: Oxford University Press, 2005, p. 210.

20 Clark, 2005, pp. 210-211.

21 David Beetham, *The Legitimation of Power*, Basingstoke: Macmillan, 1991, p. 22.

through his definition of *"traditional legitimacy"*, which describes how rules are deemed legitimate when they align with socially accepted values and norms.[22] The rule of law, therefore, requires an additional element of acceptance - or consent - from a population in order to be considered legitimate.

Furthermore, Vasiliev explains how the two terms legality and legitimacy can be distinguished and recognised in their own right: *"legality is a definitive finding which may be controverted by an expert argument or reversed by a competent (e.g. judicial) finding to the contrary. By contrast, legitimacy is a dynamic, relative, and variable value, and is subject to constant renegotiation."*[23] As such, legality refers to a legal framework, and defines what fits within the limits of that framework, while legitimacy reflects society's acceptance of such a framework. More specifically, *legality* consists of two concepts: *nulla crimen sine lege* (there is no crime without law) and *nullum poena sine lege* (there is no punishment without law); while*legitimacy* explains why an individual, group and/or society will comply with the law. However, legality can influence - or indeed play a role in - the construction or definition of legitimacy and vice versa.[24]

2.1.1 An Evolving Concept

Aside from the legal roots of the term legitimacy, the seeds for the concept were sown in political philosophy. In describing the optimal social structure, Plato believed that the *"ideal polity"*[25] should be run by a council of philosophers or kings that *"have the spirit and power of philosophy"*.[26] These leaders would start their rule at the age of fifty, once they had gained essential experience in the world: *"let those who still survive and have distinguished themselves in every action of their lives and in every branch of knowledge come at last to their consummation."*[27] The legitimacy of a society's leader was therefore based on age.

As a student of Plato, Aristotle continued to examine the notion of an ideal society in his essays collected in a volume titled *Politics* (written between 335-323 BCE), in which he describes humans as social animals that are helpless unless they live in a community, with governments that manage and oversee these communities in the pursuit of the common good. Aristotle accentuates the role of justice in ensuring that humans act appropriately and conform to public life.[28] Unlike Plato, who believes that experienced

22 Weber, 1978, p. 266.
23 Vasiliev, 2015, p. 10.
24 Nicholson, 2017, pp. 658-659.
25 Plato and Benjamin Jowett, *The Republic*, Waiheke Island: Floating Press, 2009, p. 444.
26 *idem.*, p. 382.
27 *idem.*, p. 530.
28 Aristotle, Ernest Barker and R. F. Stalley, *Politics*, Oxford University Press, 1998, pp. 9-12.

"*philosopher kings*" should rule society,[29] Aristotle argues that humans possess different skills and qualities, and that those deemed most competent should be the legitimate leaders.[30] Legitimate rule therefore shifts from an assessment based on age and experience, to an assessment of skill and competence.

Building on these earlier works, Hobbes (1651) explored the idea of a social agreement,examining how moral obligations are formed between individuals through a mutual contract, which form the basis for a society in which individuals agree to collectively live together.[31] This social agreement was later examined by Locke (1689), who focused on the idea of *consent,* examining the dynamics behind the commitments that individuals make to one another when forming a society or social group: *"all men are naturally in the state of nature, and remain so until they* ***consent*** *to make themselves members of some political society".*[32]

In a similar vein, Rousseau (1762) examined why individuals work towards a *"harmony of interests"* instead of fighting for their own interests, and how the emergence of a ruling power is dependent on the *"general will"* of a community of individuals.[33] Given that a society depends on the collective agreement or social consent of its citizens, Rousseau stated that only democratic or *"republic"* rule can be legitimate, while an autocracy or dictatorship is by default illegitimate;[34] while according to Locke consent is only achieved through majority rule.[35]

Weber built on these earlier works in his essay *The Three Types of Legitimate Rule* published in 1922,[36] in which he named and described the notion of legitimacy as the acceptance and recognition of the authority of a government or state actor by the general public: legitimacy occurs when authority (or political power) is obtained through consent and mutual understandings, rather than through coercion. As such, organisations or individuals that hold positions of power need to justify their authority in some shape or form in order to achieve legitimacy, especially during times of hardship or crisis.[37]

---

29 Plato & Jowett, 2009, p. 530.

30 Aristotle et al., 1998, p. 100.

31 Russell Hardin, *Compliance, Consent, and Legitimacy,* The Oxford Handbook of Comparative Politics, 2007, pp. 241-243; Thomas Hobbes, *Leviathan,* John C. A. Gaskin (ed.), Oxford University Press, Oxford, 1998, p. 89.

32 John Locke, *Second Treatise of Government: An Essay Concerning the True Original, Extent and End of Civil Government,* John Wiley & Sons, 2014, p. 7 – *original emphasis.*

33 Jean-Jacques Rousseau, *Rousseau: 'The Social Contract' and Other Later Political Writings,* Cambridge University Press, 1997, p. 60.

34 *idem.,* pp. 138-139.

35 Locke, 2014, pp. 24-25.

36 Max Weber, *Economy and Society: An Outline of Interpretive Sociology,* Berkeley: University of California Press, 1978. Original title: *Die drei reinen Typen der legitimen Herrschaft,* 1922.

37 *idem.,* pp. 212-213.

There are a wide variety of factors that might give an individual or an organisation the legitimacy to govern over others: legality, democratic process, religion, experience, expertise, integrity etc.; all of which could be considered as factors that influence the recognition of an individual's or an organisation's legitimacy.[38] Moreover, Weber's explanation of legitimacy embodies Locke's philosophical viewpoint, which prescribes that legitimacy can only exist through the establishment of consent: *"[...] if you and I consent to a certain arrangement as to how we shall treat each other, then surely that arrangement is legitimate"*.[39]

Through his research, Weber offers three types of legitimacy (described as *"pure types of authority"* or *"legitimate domination"*) to examine the way in which legitimacy develops and operates within different social contexts:[40]

i) *rational* (or legal) legitimacy is created through pre-established laws and rules, which also hold accountable those who establish the laws and hold positions of authority. The use of the term *rational* for this category refers to *"rational calculation"*,which accentuates that the rules cannot change at the discretion of the individual in power, nor can the laws be applied retroactively;[41]
ii) *traditional* legitimacy originates from social customs and norms, and is formed through historically accepted practices that are rarely questioned: *"legitimacy is claimed for and believed in by virtue of the sanctity of age-old rules"*;[42]
iii) *charismatic* legitimacy refers to the charisma of the individual in power. Legitimacy is awarded to charismatic leaders, who are often appointed in times of crisis when a society faces a period of transformation, which leads to the selection of a persuasive and captivating leader who can take charge and establish new rules.[43]

Weber viewed these three types of legitimacy as interchangeable over time within any given society, presenting the idea that societies are cyclical: a society might transform from a legitimate charismatic government to a government that rules with rational or traditional legitimacy.[44]

The interpretation of legitimacy described by Locke, Hobbes and Rousseau, and articulated by Weber, therefore focuses on the characteristics of, and relationships between, different stakeholders in a society. Their interpretations encompass the legal interpretation

38 Daniel Bodansky, Jeffrey Dunoff and Mark Pollack, *Legitimacy in International Law and International Relations,* Interdisciplinary Perspectives on International Law and International Relations: The State of the Art, 2013, p. 324.
39 Samantha Besson and John Tasioulas (eds.), *The Philosophy of International Law,* Oxford University Press, 2010, p. 91; Locke, 2014, p. 7.
40 Weber, 1978.
41 *idem.*, pp. 217-219.
42 *idem.*, p. 226.
43 *idem.*, pp. 241-245.
44 *idem.*, pp. 213-215.

of legitimacy, which focuses on the acceptance (or lack thereof) of the rule of law, and involves the public recognition that society needs a system of rules to ensure that it can operate in an orderly manner, while also respecting the rights of each individual.[45]

To better understand the distinction between the legal and philosophical interpretations of legitimacy, Weber's work (1922) offers an argument that reconceptualises legitimacy as a social phenomenon, detaching the term from its normative legacy.[46] Weber puts forward an approach that recognises legitimacy as a baseline from which to identify the factors that incentivise a community or society to consent to the authority of an individual or organisation (demonstrating an empirical or descriptive approach), echoing the insights shared by Locke, Hobbes and Rousseau. In contrast, socially created standards, such as the rule of law, provide a normative assessment as to whether a situation, an action, an individual or an organisation is legitimate or not (the normative approach).[47] Both empirical and normative legitimacy are therefore used as a means to evaluate or assess the legitimacy of someone or something, using different criteria.[48]

However, an overlap between normative and empirical legitimacy does remain. The empirical take on the dynamics of legitimacy reflects the legal, political and philosophical debates surrounding the concept, by demonstrating that legitimacy is as much about perceptions and interactions as it is about the normative validity of a given rule or law. As explained by Vasiliev: *"legitimacy denotes the sociological fact of acceptance of the authority of a norm or institution by the relevant population or constituency, as an empirical matter."*[49]

For example, in order for the legal standards of the rule of law to be considered legitimate, both the structure that creates the law and law enforcement mechanisms must be perceived as legitimate.[50] The rule of law is established through legal interpretations made by judges; yet the validity of judges lies not only in their legal analyses, but also through their behaviour and actions: a judge must issue fair, unbiased, and balanced opinions when resolving disputes, since a judge, and the legal system itself, must be perceived as legitimate. This is vital to ensure that society is ruled by legal codes, rather than through shifting politics or financial influences. Several studies have demonstrated

---

45 Sergey Vasiliev, *Between International Criminal Justice and Injustice: Theorising Legitimacy*,in: Nobuo Hayashi and Cecilia M. Bailliet (eds.), *The Legitimacy of International Criminal Tribunals*, Cambridge University Press (2016), 2015, pp. 9-10.

46 Weber, 1978, pp. 31-38.

47 Vasiliev, 2015, pp. 12-13.

48 *ibid.*

49 Vasiliev, 2015, p. 9.

50 Anthony Bottoms and Justice Tankebe, *Beyond Procedural Justice: A Dialogic Approach to Legitimacy in Criminal Justice*, The Journal of Criminal Law and Criminology, 2012, pp. 119-170; Justice Tankebe, Michael D. Reisig and Xia Wang, *A Multidimensional Model of Police Legitimacy: A Cross-Cultural Assessment,* Law and Human Behavior, 2016, 40(1), pp. 11-22; Tom R. Tyler, *Enhancing Police Legitimacy*, The ANNALS of the American Academy of Political and Social Science, 2004, 593(1), pp. 84-99; Tom R. Tyler, *Why People Obey the Law*, Princeton University Press, 2006.

connections between the perceived legitimacy of law enforcement mechanisms (ex. the police force or the courts) and public compliance,[51] which results in "*appropriate social behaviour*".[52]

Taking another approach, Scharpf explains that the empirical approach to assessing political legitimacy rests on two normative criteria: input legitimacy, which relates to the system or structure that selects political leaders or the government in power (for example through elections), and output legitimacy, which uses political standards (the mandate, ideology or manifesto of a politician or political party) to assess the performance of the political leader or government.[53] Research by Schmidt provides a third normative criterion to the equation, namely throughput legitimacy, which focuses on the processes that shape how decisions are made.[54]

The empirical approach to legitimacy is also adopted by psychologist and sociologists examining the factors that influence the manner in which individuals consent to authority and recognise legitimacy. Studies by Tyler concentrate predominantly on how and why individuals conform to (or question) authority:[55] "*the roots of legitimacy lie in people's assessments of the fairness of the decision-making procedures used by authorities and institutions*".[56] Rather than focus on the substantial elements of the decisions made by organisations, Tyler's interest lies in the procedures through which decisions are made (also known as throughput legitimacy)[57] which contribute to the construction of legitimacy.[58]

The work of criminologists Bottoms and Tankebe emphasises the importance of a two-dimensional dialogue through which legitimacy is constructed,[59] a dynamic that is

51 Bottoms & Tankebe, 2012; Margaret Levi, Audrey Sacks and Tom R. Tyler, *Conceptualizing Legitimacy, Measuring Legitimating Beliefs*, American Behavioral Scientist, 2009, 53(3), pp. 354-375; Tankebe et al., 2016; Tyler, 2004.Tyler, 2006.

52 Tyler, 2004, p. 96.

53 Fritz W. Scharpf, *Problem Solving Effectiveness and Democratic Accountability in the EU*, Max-Planck-Institut für Gesellschaftsforschung (MPIfG) working paper, 2003, 3(1), pp. 4-6.

54 Vivian A. Schmidt, *Democracy and Legitimacy in the European Union Revisited: Input, Output and 'Throughput'*, Political Studies, 2013, 61(1), pp. 2-22.

55 Tom R. Tyler, *The Psychology of Legitimacy: A Relational Perspective on Voluntary Deference to Authorities*, Personality and Social Psychology Review, 1997, 1(4), pp. 323-345; Tyler, 2001; Tom R. Tyler, *Enhancing Police Legitimacy*, The ANNALS of the American Academy of Political and Social Science, 2004, 593(1), pp. 84-99; Tyler, 2006.

56 Tom R. Tyler, *A Psychological Perspective on the Legitimacy of Institutions and Authorities*, in: John T. Jost and Brenda Major (eds.), *The Psychology of Legitimacy: Emerging Perspectives on Ideology, Justice, and Intergroup Relations*, Cambridge: Cambridge University Press, 2001, p. 416.

57 Vivian A. Schmidt, *Democracy and Legitimacy in the European Union Revisited: Input, Output and 'Throughput'*, Political Studies, 2013, 61(1), pp. 2-22.

58 Tyler, 1997; Tyler, 2001; Tyler, 2004; Tyler, 2006.

59 Anthony Bottoms and Justice Tankebe, *Beyond Procedural Justice: A Dialogic Approach to Legitimacy in Criminal Justice*, The Journal of Criminal Law and Criminology, 2012.

reflected in studies conducted by both Beetham and Suchman.[60] The model proposed by Bottoms and Tankebe provides four conditions that distinguish between legitimate and illegitimate authority; according to the authors, all four conditions are necessary in order for legitimacy to be accepted:[61]

i) *"lawfulness"*, which concerns the source of power or authority and whether it is exercised in a manner that conforms to a society's established laws and/or rules;[62]
ii) *"distributive justice"*, which explores whether resources are allocated fairly among groups or individuals that have different needs;[63]
iii) *"procedural justice"*, which describes the fairness of the processes and procedures employed to reach specific outcomes or decisions;[64] and
iv) *"effectiveness"*, which identifies how the authority establishes and maintains rightful power (for example, how legal authorities respond to the security and safety needs of their citizens).[65]

This model encapsulates the multidimensional nature of legitimacy and demonstrates that legitimacy is not a standalone notion, but rather a concept that is developed over time through continuous interactions.

Understanding the complexity of the notion of legitimacy and examining the concept from the perspective of different disciplines, therefore highlights the important role of individual interpretations of this term. Legitimacy has a chameleon like nature: changing in relation to its context. Weber's research highlights two predominant approaches (normative and empirical) that can be used to assess legitimacy, while additional research has identified different normative criteria that can be used to evaluate empirical legitimacy (input, throughput and output). These developments have increased the opportunities for research related to legitimacy, primarily in terms of the relationship between this concept and the functioning of organisations.

2.1.2 Organisational Legitimacy

Legitimacy is an important concept in organisational theory for multiple reasons: it is a resource that provides access to other vital organisational resources such as capital, personnel and technology, and it can also be used as a means to collaborate with other

60 Beetham, 1991; Suchman, 1995.
61 Justice Tankebe, Michael D. Reisig and Xia Wang, *A Multidimensional Model of Police Legitimacy: A Cross-Cultural Assessment,* Law and Human Behavior, 2016, 40(1), pp. 5-8.
62 Bottoms & Tankebe, 2012, pp. 122-123.
63 *idem.*, p. 123.
64 *ibid.*
65 *ibid.*

organisations. The role of legitimacy in resource exchange, networking and communications between an organisation and its environment is summarised by Hybels, who explains that:

> "Legitimacy often has been conceptualized as simply one of many resources that organizations must obtain from their environments. But rather than viewing legitimacy as something that is exchanged among organizations, legitimacy is better conceived as both part of the context for exchange and a by-product of exchange. Legitimacy itself has no material form. It exists only as a symbolic representation of the collective evaluation of an organization, as evidenced to both observers and participants perhaps most convincingly by the flow of resources."[66]

Furthermore, research by Deephouse and Carter demonstrates that most stakeholders within society will only engage with legitimate organisations,[67] and organisational theorists from a variety of academic fields describe the notion of legitimacy as an essential ingredient for the continuity and growth of an organisation.[68]

Knoke, one of the first scholars to examine organisational legitimacy, describes the legitimacy of an organisation as "*the acceptance by the general public and by relevant elite organizations of an association's right to exist and to pursue its affairs in its chosen manner*".[69] The notion that legitimacy provides an organisation with a certain amount of freedom to do as it wishes is similar to the "*strategic choice perspective*" proposed by Child, which demonstrates how organisations that are considered legitimate receive a certain degree of autonomy to choose the stakeholders they wish to engage with, and the quality and quantity of the products that they source and produce, while also enjoying the freedom to decide on their own management style and organisational structure.[70]

---

66 Ralph C. Hybels, On Legitimacy, Legitimation, and Organizations: A Critical Review and Integrative Theoretical Model, Academy of Management Proceedings, Briarcliff Manor, NY 10510: Academy of Management, 1995, p. 243.

67 David L. Deephouse and Suzanne M. Carter, *An Examination of Differences Between Organizational Legitimacy and Organizational Reputation*, Journal of Management Studies, 2005, 42(2), pp. 329-360.

68 Black, 2008, pp. 141-144; Hybels, 1995, pp. 241-245; Michael Meyer, Renate Buber and Anahid Aghamanoukjan, *In Search of Legitimacy: Managerialism and Legitimation in Civil Society Organizations*, Voluntas: International Journal of Voluntary and Nonprofit Organizations, 2013, 24(1), pp. 169-171; Suchman, 1995; Monica A. Zimmerman and Gerald J. Zeitz, *Beyond Survival: Achieving New Venture Growth by Building*,Academy of Management Review, 2002, 27(3), p. 414.

69 David Knoke, *The Political Economies of Associations*, Research in Political Sociology, 1985, 1(1), p. 222.

70 John Child, *Organizational Structure, Environment and Performance: The Role of Strategic Choice*, Sociology, 1972, 6(1), pp. 1-22.

Indeed, several studies demonstrate that organisational legitimacy is a way for an organisation to avoid enquiries or confrontations with its stakeholders, or even from the general public.[71] As explained by Meyer and Scott:

> "We take the view that organizational legitimacy refers to the degree of cultural support for an organization – the extent to which the array of established cultural accounts provide explanations for its existence, functioning, and jurisdiction, and lack or deny alternatives [...] A completely legitimate organization would be one about which no question could be raised."[72]

In other words, a legitimate organisation has the freedom to manage itself and pursue its activities as it sees fit; as Brown explains: *"legitimate status is a sine qua non for easy access to resources, unrestricted access to markets, and long term survival"*.[73] Yet when it comes to framing or examining the notion of organisational legitimacy, Pfeffer and Salancik argue that this concept, especially with regard to an established organisation, is only relevant if or when there is a reason for the organisation's legitimacy to be questioned.[74] Likewise, Meyer and Rowan believe that the concept of legitimacy rests on either the absence or the presence of questioning.[75]

2.1.3 *Sources of Organisational Legitimacy*

When exploring how organisational legitimacy comes into being – what the source of legitimacy is – a number of organisational theorists suggest that there are three key factors to take into consideration: the environment of the organisation, the characteristics of the organisation and the actions of the organisation, particularly with regard to activities linked to legitimisation.[76] In a first instance, the environment of an organisation plays an important role as it consists of all the stakeholders of an organisation, as well as the cultural and societal context of an organisation.[77] Research by Gutterman examines how perceptions

71 Andrew D. Brown, *Narrative, Politics and Legitimacy in an IT Implementation,* Journal of Management Studies, 1998, 35(1), pp. 35-58; David L. Deephouse, *Does Isomorphism Legitimate?* Academy of Management Journal, 1996, 39(4), pp. 1024-1039; Suchman, 1995.

72 John W. Meyer and W. Richard Scott, *Organizational Environments: Ritual and Rationality,* Beverly Hills, CA: Sage, 1983, p. 201

73 Brown, 1998, p. 35.

74 Salancik & Pfeffer, 1978, p. 194.

75 John W. Meyer and Brian Rowan, *Institutionalized Organizations: Formal Structure as Myth and Ceremony,* American Journal of Sociology, 1977, 83, p. 349.

76 Brinkerhoff, 2005, pp. 5-6; Brown, 1998; Deephouse, 1996; Schiff, 2010.

77 Ashforth & Gibbs, 1990, p. 183; Brinkerhoff, 2005, p. 5; Salancik & Pfeffer, 1978, pp. 228-230; Suchman, 1995, pp. 573-576.

of legitimacy are constructed in different societies in relation to governance structures. In patrimonial societies, for example, Gutterman found that assessments of legitimacy are based on the collective interests and needs of social groups (family, professional, religious or ethnic affiliations);[78] while in democracies legitimacy is based on the needs and interests of individuals, which are represented through social institutions and a political system that ensures social stability.[79]

The ethos or nature of an organisation also influences organisational legitimacy: this not only covers organisational culture and structure, which are vast components in their own right, it may also encompass different departments or divisions within the organisation, which may include sub-cultures and sub-structures.[80] These divisions and departments may themselves be connected with other entities that may be internal or external to the organisation.[81] Likewise, the actions or activities of an organisation, and any divisions or departments within the organisation, often mirror the complexities of an organisation's culture. Schiff's research emphasises the need to break down the different components of an organisation in order to assess its legitimacy. The three areas mentioned by Schiff for particular focus are: *design*, which relates to the establishment of an organisation; *operations*, referring to the internal workings of an organisation; and *consequential*, which refers to the impact of the organisation's output.[82]

The organisational activities linked specifically to legitimisation involve the continuous testing and redefinition of the organisation's legitimacy through ongoing interaction with its environment.[83] Designing, developing and implementing legitimisation activities to promote or enhance organisational legitimacy become particularly challenging in an international setting, since both the organisation and the environment may lack the information and background required to understand, interpret, and evaluate each other. Yet, scholars have shown that in most situations the perception of organisational legitimacy can broadly be categorised as *instrumental* (shared needs) and *substantive* (shared values).[84]

- *Instrumental* legitimacy denotes the extent to which the governance structure of an organisation responds to the needs and expectations of its stakeholders. Studies that focus on instrumental legitimacy examine the way in which an authority effectively

78 Ellen Gutterman, *Banning Bribes Abroad: US Enforcement of the Foreign Corrupt Practices Act*, Osgoode Hall Law Journal, 2015, 53, pp. 57-58.

79 Gutterman, 2015, p. 37; Mitchell A. Seligson, *The Impact of Corruption on Regime Legitimacy: A Comparative Study of Four Latin American Countries*, The Journal of Politics, 2002, 64(2), pp. 412-413.

80 Ashforth & Gibbs, 1990, p. 191; Brinkerhoff, 2005, pp. 11-14; Salancik & Pfeffer, 1978, pp. 229-232.

81 Brinkerhoff, 2005, p. i & 1.

82 Schiff, 2010, pp. 101-105.

83 Brinkerhoff, 2005, p. 10; Suchman, 1995, pp. 596-597.

84 Margaret Levi, Audrey Sacks and Tom R. Tyler, *Conceptualizing Legitimacy, Measuring Legitimating Beliefs*, American Behavioral Scientist, 2009, 53(3), pp. 356-359; Henri Tajfel (ed.), *Social Identity and Intergroup Relations*, Cambridge University Press, 2010, p. 255.

and efficiently uses resources to satisfy the needs of its stakeholders. Legitimacy is therefore constructed using *instrumental* means.[85]

- *Substantive* legitimacy is an assessment based on shared values.[86] This concept relates to the "*social identity theory*",[87] which explains how the identity of an individual is comprised of shared norms and values that are associated with their membership to a specific social group.[88] Groups or communities offer a social identity that provides a framework for the interactions that take place within a specific environment, for example, the affiliation with a sports club, a school or university, and/or within family life, at school or work, and/or with a religion or an ethnic group.

In relation to substantive legitimacy, Seligson's research offers additional factors that determine how legitimacy may be assessed, including age, education, and gender. Seligson demonstrates how legitimacy is constructed based on the interaction between these specific social identities and the authority in question, within particular cultural settings.[89] If an organisation is perceived as going against the shared values of the group, all the activities or services provided by that organisation may be regarded as irrelevant, and the organisation itself may be perceived as illegitimate.[90] The social identity of stakeholders is therefore key when examining the actions of an organisation, or an equivalent authority, as it plays an important role in assessing whether decisions taken are fair, and to ensure that the social group is respectfully represented.[91]

Organisational legitimacy may therefore be considered as a relational agreement between an organisation and its stakeholders. In many ways it is similar to the social contract theory, which examines how social order is created, while also examining the relationship of consent between political authority and the individual.[92] Social agreements are made as a means to an end; they benefit both sides, and remain legitimate as long as both sides fulfil

85 Cord Schmelzle, *Evaluating Governance: Effectiveness and Legitimacy in Areas of Limited Statehood*, SFB-Governance Working Paper, 2012, 26, pp. 13-16; Levi et al., 2009, pp. 356-359.

86 *ibid.*

87 John T. Jost and Brenda Major (eds.), *The Psychology of Legitimacy: Emerging Perspectives on Ideology, Justice, and Intergroup Relations*, Cambridge University Press, 2001, p. 333.

88 Jost & Major, 2001, pp. 207-209; Tajfel, 2010, p. 255.

89 Seligson, 2002, pp. 422-423 & 450; Tajfel, 2010, p. 255.

90 Levi et al., 2009, p. 355.

91 Jason Sunshine and Tom R. Tyler, *The Role of Procedural Justice and Legitimacy in Shaping Public Support for Policing*, Law and Society Review, 2003, 37(3), pp. 513-548; Tom R. Tyler, *A Psychological Perspective on the Legitimacy of Institutions and Authorities*, in: John T. Jost and Brenda Major (eds.), *The Psychology of Legitimacy: Emerging Perspectives on Ideology, Justice, and Intergroup Relations*. Cambridge: Cambridge University Press, 2001; Tom R. Tyler and Yuen Huo, *Trust in the Law: Encouraging Public Cooperation with the Police and Courts*, Russell Sage Foundation, 2002.

92 Hobbes, 1998; McKinsey Global Institute, *The Social Contract in the 21st Century. Outcomes so far for workers, consumers and savers in advanced economies*, February 2020; Rousseau, 1997.

their part of the agreement.[93] Yet the ability for stakeholders to legitimise (or delegitimise) an organisation is one of the most powerful resources that they possess. Organisations therefore need to carefully decide which stakeholders to focus on when designing strategies that promote or enhance their legitimacy, which becomes an exercise in stakeholder analysis.[94]

Legitimacy is awarded by the organisation's stakeholders, who make an assessment – consciously or not – regarding an organisation's legitimacy by evaluating the organisation's behaviour and activities against particular criteria or standards associated with the agreed mandate or purpose of the organisation.[95] The effort and resources put into legitimisation activities therefore depend to some extent on what the organisation aims to accomplish.[96] If the goods or services that the organisation produces are already recognised as valued and desirable, the organisation is unlikely to invest time and resources to promote its organisational legitimacy. However, if the organisation is engaged in contentious activities or if it departs sharply from its original operating structure or activities, the promotion of its legitimacy, targeting key stakeholders, will become much more important.[97]

Early research related to organisational legitimacy focused on the importance of the government or state-run bodies in granting legitimacy, given that most organisations are routinely assessed by some form of regulation: taxation authorities, auditors, or financial watchdogs.[98] Other studies focused on the importance of public opinion as a reflection of social values that can be measured by surveys or through media analysis.[99] Yet it is questionable whether the media reflects public opinion or whether it influences it.[100] Since the early 2000s, social media has played a predominant role in influencing perceptions: one tweet can challenge the legitimacy of the most well-established organisation. Civil society organisations also play an important role in influencing public opinion, and play an active part in establishing or challenging organisational legitimacy.[101] They actively

---

93 Samantha Besson and John Tasioulas (eds.), *The Philosophy of International Law*, Oxford University Press, 2010, p. 91; Locke, 2014, p. 7.

94 Brinkerhoff, 2005; McKinsey Global Institute, 2020, pp. 117-127.

95 Martin Ruef, and W. Richard Scott, *A Multidimensional Model of Organizational Legitimacy: Hospital Survival in Changing Institutional Environments*, Administrative Science Quarterly, 1998, p. 880.

96 McKinsey Global Institute, 2020, pp. 31-34.

97 Derick W. Brinkerhoff and Benjamin Crosby, *Managing Policy Reform: Concepts and Tools for Decision-makers in Developing and Transitioning Countries*, Kumarian Press, 2002, pp. 143-146.

98 Black, 2008, pp. 137-139; Deephouse, 1996, p. 1025; Deephouse et al., 2017, p. 29; John Dowling and Jeffrey Pfeffer, *Organizational Legitimacy: Social Values and Organizational Behavior*, Pacific Sociological Review, 1975, 18(1), p. 133.

99 Bitektine, 2011, p. 155; Dowling & Pfeffer, 1975, p. 134.

100 Bitektine, 2011, p. 159; Deephouse, 1996, pp. 1027-1028.

101 Brinkerhoff, 2005, pp. 11-14.

demand the legitimisation of (public) organisations and governmental policies, and also present their arguments through (social) media channels.[102]

In order to better understand organisational legitimacy and how it is shaped through the interactions between an organisation and the organisational environment, the following section presents three different types of legitimacy, and the influence that they have on both an organisation and the organisation's environment.

2.1.4 Pragmatic, Moral and Cognitive Legitimacy

When studying organisational legitimacy, many scholars[103] refer to a paper written by Suchman,[104] which provides an overview of definitions and research related to organisational legitimacy, while also examining how legitimacy influences an organisation's operations and behaviour. Suchman became interested in the concept of organisational legitimacy when researching the influence of law firms and venture capitalists on the design and development of California's Silicon Valley.[105] This study led him to examine how these law firms and venture capitalists had gained legitimacy in the region.[106] Both research projects formed the basis of Suchman's comprehensive literature review that examined other studies related to this notion of organisational legitimacy, and how different types of legitimacy influence the activities of an organisation and the perceptions and acceptance of its stakeholders. As a result, Suchman provides a framework that describes three general types of organisational legitimacy - pragmatic, moral and cognitive - in relation to the interaction between the organisation and its stakeholders and/or the organisational environment.[107]

---

102 Alex Bitektine and Patrick Haack, *The "Macro" and the "Micro" of Legitimacy: Toward a Multilevel Theory of the Legitimacy Process*, Academy of Management Review, 2015, 40(1), pp. 49-75.

103 For example: Howard E. Aldrich and Martin Ruef, *Organizational Evolution and Entrepreneurship*, Sage Publications, 2006; David L. Deephouse and Suzanne M. Carter, *An Examination of Differences Between Organizational Legitimacy and Organizational Reputation*, Journal of Management Studies, 2005, 42(2), 329-360; Mark Easterby-Smith and Marjorie A. Lyles, The Evolving Field of Organizational Learning and Knowledge Management, *Handbook of Organizational Learning and Knowledge Management*, 2011, 2, 1-20; Honorata Mazepus, Wouter Veenendaal, Anthea McCarthy-Jones and Juan Manuel Trak Vásquez, *A comparative study of legitimation strategies in hybrid regimes*, Policy Studies, 2016, 37(4); Sergey Vasiliev, *Between International Criminal Justice and Injustice: Theorising Legitimacy*,in: Nobuo Hayashi and Cecilia M. Bailliet (eds.), *The Legitimacy of International Criminal Tribunals*, Cambridge University Press (2016), 2015.

104 Suchman, 1995.

105 Mark C. Suchman, *On the Role of Law Firms in the Structuration of Silicon Valley*, Disputes Processing Research Program, Institute for Legal Studies, University of Wisconsin-Madison Law School, 1994a.

106 Mark C. Suchman, *On Advice of Counsel: Law Firms and Venture Capital Funds as Information Intermediaries in the Structuration of Silicon Valley*, Thesis (Ph.D.) Stanford University, 1994b.

107 Suchman, 1995, pp. 577-585.

2.1.4.1 Pragmatic Legitimacy

Pragmatic legitimacy relates to the immediate needs and expectations of the organisation's stakeholders: the organisation must provide the services and products that are expected of it, while its actions and behaviours are also assessed by its stakeholders in relation to these requirements. If the organisation fulfils its stakeholders' needs, it receives their support and its legitimacy is endorsed. The relationship between the organisation and its stakeholders could be described as one of give and take.[108]

This type of legitimacy comes in three forms: exchange, influence and dispositional. *Exchange* legitimacy refers to the support an organisation receives from its stakeholders in exchange for behaviour, policies and/or products that benefit, or address the direct needs, of the stakeholders. The assessment of the organisation is immediate and its fate is in the hands of its stakeholders as they have the ability to give or take legitimacy from an organisation in response to its actions and/or behaviour.[109]

Influence legitimacy is more abstract than exchange legitimacy, as it is awarded when the consequences of the organisation's activities or policies reflect the interests and needs of its stakeholders. This form of pragmatic legitimacy is hard to quantify as it may be difficult to connect the organisation's actions to specific outcomes experienced by its stakeholders, and to assess the direct link between the influence of an organisation's products, behaviour, and/or policies on the needs and interests of its stakeholders.[110]

Dispositional legitimacy is awarded to an organisation when its stakeholders believe that it has their best interests at heart.[111] This assessment is usually based on previous interactions between the organisation and its the stakeholders, or when certain organisational activities that are well received are then generalised and implemented within the organisation as a whole.[112] Dispositional legitimacy also contains an element of exchange that is present within all forms of pragmatic legitimacy, yet this exchange is not specific to an action or a set of policies; there is rather a general acceptance of the organisation's legitimacy based on the experiences of the interactions with the organisation.[113]

2.1.4.2 Moral Legitimacy

Moral legitimacy refers to legitimacy that is awarded to an organisation when its actions are considered ethical and socially acceptable by its stakeholders and/or the environment. In this context, a legitimate organisation reflects the desired norms and values of a given

108 *idem.*, pp. 578-579.
109 *idem.*, p. 578.
110 *ibid.*
111 *ibid.*
112 Suchman, 1995, p. 572; Walter Powell, *Expanding the Scope of Institutional Analysis*, The New Institutionalism in Organizational Analysis, Chicago, 1991, p. 197.
113 Suchman, 1995, p. 578.

society, and its activities and/or products meet socially accepted standards. Stakeholders therefore use normative standards to assess the organisation, rather than evaluating the legitimacy of the organisation in relation to their own interests and needs.[114] Suchman's study identifies four forms of moral legitimacy: consequential, procedural, structural and personal.[115]

Consequential legitimacy refers to assessments made by stakeholders with regard to the outputs and outcomes of an organisation's activities, and can be summarised as an evaluation as to whether the organisation is '*doing the right thing*'. The assessment is often made in comparison with other, similar organisations, and – in a similar fashion to (pragmatic) exchange legitimacy – relies on tangible, measurable outputs. Organisations that do not produce quantifiable results may sometimes see their consequential legitimacy questioned.[116]

Procedural legitimacy refers to the processes, systems, and practices used by an organisation, and could be compared to Schmidt's description of throughput legitimacy, which focuses on the processes that shape how decisions are made within an organisation.[117] While consequential legitimacy refers to '*doing the right thing*', procedural legitimacy relates to the organisation '*doing things right*'. If an organisation is unable to demonstrate measurable results, its moral legitimacy can be assessed by examining the way in which it works. This assessment is usually achieved through some form of socially recognised accreditation or external regulation.[118]

Structural legitimacy refers to assessments regarding the operational capacity or the function of the organisation, and is awarded when the organisation is deemed suitably equipped for the mandate that it has been given, or the services that it provides. Rather than evaluating the organisation's processes or its products, its legitimacy is assessed by examining whether the organisation has the capacity to perform a specific job, and whether it is the right fit for the task at hand. In contrast to procedural legitimacy, which examines individual processes, structural legitimacy looks at the organisation's competence as a whole[119]

Personal legitimacy derives from the personal characteristics, reputation and charisma of individual members of an organisation's board, its management team, the CEO and/or its staff. Historically, this was a fairly common way to award moral legitimacy to an organisation.[120] Indeed, this type of legitimacy remains prevalent in countries where

114 *idem.*, p. 579.
115 *idem.*, pp. 580-582.
116 *idem.*, p. 580.
117 Schmidt, 2013, pp. 2-22.
118 Deephouse, 1996, p. 1025; Suchman, 1995, p. 580.
119 Suchman, 1995, p. 581.
120 For example Weber's "charismatic legitimacy", 1978, pp. 241-245.

traditions of paternalism define organisations by the characteristics of those who lead them.[121] Personal legitimacy is therefore awarded when the leader, board or management, or indeed department or section heads, are deemed competent for the task that they have been assigned.

2.1.4.3 Cognitive Legitimacy

Cognitive legitimacy refers to a type of organisational legitimacy that remains largely unchallenged. The organisation is often fully integrated within its environment and pursues activities that fit with the broader social understandings of what is appropriate and necessary. Selznick describes organisations with cognitive legitimacy as having become *"infused with value beyond the technical requirements at hand"*.[122] Support for the organisation is not related to self-interest, but rather to its accepted status within society. While Suchman's description of moral and pragmatic legitimacy involves some form of stakeholder assessment, cognitive legitimacy does not: the organisation is considered part of society, and may even be regarded as indispensable.[123] This form of legitimacy stems from the idea that the organisation is relatable and coherent in one of two ways, according to Suchman: through comprehensibility and/or due to its "*taken-for-grantedness*".[124]

A legitimacy based on *comprehensibility* refers to an organisation that is aligned with the culture of its environment, and/or the cultural background of its stakeholders.[125] Different cultures have different expectations for organisations. For example, certain cultures favour indirect communication or a reactive response style, in contrast to interactive communication with stakeholders. Similarly, some cultures emphasise the importance of procedures and regulations, while this may be less prominent in societies where the culture of uncertainty is high and it is widely accepted that organisations make decisions on emerging issues as and when they arise.[126] In general, it appears that an organisation is awarded cognitive legitimacy when it demonstrates an ability to produce socially acceptable and meaningful results that are deemed appropriate and relevant within the culture of its environment.[127]

---

121 Suchman, 1995, pp. 581-582.

122 Philip Selznick, *Leadership in Administration: A Sociological Interpretation*, Berkeley: University of California Press, 1957, p. 17.

123 Suchman, 1995, pp. 582-583.

124 *ibid.*

125 *idem.*, p. 582.

126 Michael Barnett and Martha Finnemore, *Rules for the world: International organizations in global politics*, Cornell University Press, 2004, p. 171; Narjess Boubakri, Omrane Guedhami, Chuck CY Kwok and Walid Saffar, *National culture and privatization: The relationship between collectivism and residual state ownership*, Journal of International Business Studies, 2016, 47(2), pp. 170-190.

127 Suchman, 1995, p. 582.

The second form of cognitive legitimacy relates to an organisation's "*taken-for-grantedness*",[128] which is when an organisation's environment and/or its stakeholders accept it – including its structures, procedures and activities – as completely necessary, and it is unimaginable that another organisation could take its place. In this case, the organisation's legitimacy is embedded in the social structure of everyday life, where the same cultural knowledge and understanding is shared widely among stakeholders and influenced by the organisation's environment. This shared social reality may relate to a single organisation, or to certain sectors within society, such as education or healthcare. The "*taken-for-grantedness*" of the organisation is not dependent on the activities or behaviour of the organisation, but rather on the assumptions projected by its stakeholders and/or by the environment, which relate to the organisation's function within society, or the sector in which it finds itself.[129] It is hard to picture society without this type of organisation.

2.1.4.4 A Summary of the Typology

In summary, cognitive and moral legitimacy are perhaps the most widely recognised types of legitimacy found in the literature. Cognitive legitimacy is awarded to an organisation that is largely integrated within society; while moral legitimacy may be compared to normative legitimacy: the organisation abides by socially accepted standards or regulations. Pragmatic legitimacy relates to an organisation's capacity to achieve specific outputs and outcomes for its stakeholders. This type of legitimacy has been rejected by some organisational theorists, who argue that this activity refers rather to organisational learning, whereby an organisation adjusts its actions in response to the reaction of its stakeholders.[130] However, including pragmatic legitimacy to this typology provides an additional level of stakeholder assessment, which some authors believe is just as relevant for an organisation's legitimacy, even if it is based on short-term assessments of an organisation's performance.[131]

Although there are clear differences between the three types of legitimacy, cultural and social influences are important factors for all three: cognitive legitimacy concentrates on the actions of an organisation in a broader cultural context; while moral legitimacy focuses on the appropriateness of an organisation's actions measured against an existing framework of societal values and norms (rules and regulations); and pragmatic legitimacy responds

128 *idem.*, p. 583.

129 Deephouse et al., 2017, pp. 19-20; Suchman, 1995, p. 583.

130 Howard E. Aldrich and Martin Ruef, *Organizational Evolution and Entrepreneurship*, Sage Publications, 2006; Mark Easterby-Smith and Marjorie A. Lyles, The Evolving Field of Organizational Learning and Knowledge Management, *Handbook of Organizational Learning and Knowledge Management*, 2011, 2, pp. 1-20.

131 Ashforth & Gibbs, 1990, p. 184; Bitektine, 2011; p. 159; Deephouse et al. 2017, pp. 19-20; Suchman, 1995, pp. 584-585.

directly to the needs, interests and expectations of its stakeholders. Suchman summarises all three legitimacy types of organisational legitimacy as: *"a generalized perception or assumption that the actions of an entity are desirable, proper, or appropriate within some socially constructed system of norms, values, beliefs, and definitions".*[132]

A summary of these three types of legitimacy can be found in the following table:

Table 1 Legitimacy types: pragmatic, moral and cognitive.[133]

Type	Sub-Type	Definition	Stakeholder Relationship
Pragmatic legitimacy	Exchange Influence Dispositional	Organisation fulfils the needs and interests of its stakeholders.	Organisation provides goods and services, in exchange for legitimacy.
Moral legitimacy	Consequential Procedural Structural Personal	Organisation reflects socially acceptable and desirable norms, standards and values.	Organisation meets the accepted social criteria regarding: its outputs/results, its procedures, its structure, and/or its management and staff.
Cognitive legitimacy	Comprehensibility Taken-for-Granted	Organisation pursues goals and activities that fit with broad social understandings of what is deemed appropriate and desirable.	Organisation "makes sense" within a certain culture and/or is 'taken for granted' according to socially constructed realities.

While conceptual distinctions between these three types of legitimacy can be made, in practice pragmatic, moral and cognitive legitimacy tend to merge with one another. Recognising that the boundaries between the types of legitimacy are fluid allows for strategies that gain, maintain or repair legitimacy through legitimisation activities that take into account the organisation's pragmatic, moral and cognitive legitimacy at different times or in different situations.[134] As Thirkell-White explains *"legitimacy is always a matter of degree but strengths in one area can compensate for weaknesses in another".*[135]

For example, an organisation that demonstrates consistent transparency and accountability, solidifying its moral legitimacy with stakeholders, may retain its

132 Suchman, 1995, p. 574
133 Suchman, 1995, pp. 577-585.
134 *idem.*, p. 585.
135 Ben Thirkell-White, *Institutional Legitimacy and the International Financial Architecture*, European Consortium for Political Research, Joint Sessions of Workshops, Edinburgh, March 2003, p. 7.

organisational legitimacy when faced with questions regarding the quality of its performance (pragmatic legitimacy). Likewise, when an organisation displays excellent results, or high quality products, validating its pragmatic legitimacy, its stakeholders may be less likely to raise concerns regarding the organisation's ethical standards (moral legitimacy).[136]

As such, although categorising legitimacy into types helps to provide an understanding of the interplay between legitimacy and an organisation's activity and/or behaviour – and assists in creating a theoretical framework for research purposes – it is important to acknowledge that such categories are not strictly separate empirical phenomena. This typology offered by Suchman is useful in providing clarity regarding the notion of legitimacy, which allows academics to debate, replicate, and refine certain theories or ideas regarding a certain topic or dynamic.[137] Furthermore, it acts as a resource from which practitioners can measure and assess the legitimacy of their organisation.[138]

In order to understand the dynamics of organisational legitimacy, this study focuses on the act of legitimisation: how legitimacy is managed. Examining the process of legitimisation implemented at the ICTR reveals the Tribunal's relationship with the concept of legitimacy – namely how challenges to the Tribunal's legitimacy were addressed – providing insights into the focus and key priorities of the Tribunal over the course of its 20-year existence.

2.2 MANAGING LEGITIMACY: LEGITIMISATION[139]

Legitimisation is the process of gaining, maintaining and/or repairing legitimacy. In the case of organisational legitimacy, both the organisation and its environment are involved in legitimisation.[140] On the one hand, the organisation has to make sense of the legitimacy requirements of its environment by observing, interpreting and even influencing those requirements. On the other hand, the environment has to make sense of the organisation and assess whether it meets the socially acceptable norms and values, and/or the needs and expectations of its stakeholders. Legitimisation is, therefore, as complex and multifaceted as legitimacy itself. The process of legitimisation is further complicated in the case of international organisations, given that both the organisation and the environment(s) in which it operates may lack the information necessary to understand, interpret and assess one another.[141]

136 Ashforth & Gibbs, 1990, p. 184.
137 Roy Suddaby, *Challenges for Institutional Theory*, Journal of Management Inquiry, 2010, 19(1), pp. 14-20.
138 McKinsey Global Institute, 2020, pp. 3-4.
139 Also referred to as *legitimation*.
140 Hybels, 1995, p. 241; Suchman, 1995, p. 573.
141 Bitektine, 2011, pp. 151-179.

Organisations make use of legitimisation activities to promote their legitimacy, including the legitimacy of its leadership and/or management, its products or services, and/or its operational structures.[142] The techniques organisations use to enhance their legitimacy may include donating to charities, setting up corporate social responsibility programmes, obtaining (and advertising) external endorsements, and demonstrating transparent operating and management structures.[143] Techniques may also involve setting up, or hiring, a public relations firm or department that can provide specific explanations for an organisation's actions or behaviour in order to gain or maintain the support and approval of its stakeholders.[144]

Managing organisational legitimacy is important at all times, but different phases of an organisation's existence may call for different types of legitimisation activities.[145] Suchman describes these phases as moment when legitimisation strategies are put into place to gain, maintain and/or repair organisational legitimacy.[146]

Due to the particular characteristics of these three legitimisation strategies, they may be used to identify the specific legitimacy challenges faced by an organisation and to categorise the different legitimisation activities implemented in order to gain, maintain or repair an organisation's legitimacy. The following sections describe these three legitimisation strategies in more detail.

2.2.1 *Gaining Legitimacy*

When an organisation is first established – or when an existing organisation introduces a new division, a new product, or a new staff member (for example, a new director or chief executive) – it has to gain legitimacy.[147] The act of gaining legitimacy is usually a proactive endeavour, especially when the organisation's establishment, or one of its activities, is new to its environment and/or stakeholders and suffers from a *"liability of newness"*.[148]

There are usually two distinct legitimacy challenges to this "*newness*": organisations need to distinguish themselves from similar organisations that exist in the same environment, to demonstrate that they are unique and necessary, highlighting their

142 Reyes, 2011, pp. 781-807; Suchman, 1995, pp. 573-577.
143 Ashforth & Gibbs, 1990, p. 181; Bitektine & Haack, 2015, pp. 54-57; Peter K. Manning, *Organizational Communication*, Transaction Publishers, 1992, pp. 149-162; McKinsey Global Institute, 2020, pp. 1-10.
144 Ashforth & Gibbs, 1990, pp. 180-181; Reyes, 2011, p. 782.
145 Deephouse et al., 2017, pp. 21-22.
146 Suchman, 1995, p. 585.
147 *idem.*,p. 586.
148 Ashforth & Gibbs, 1990, p. 182.

competitive advantage, while at the same time they need to convince the existing organisations to recognise and support them as 'one of them'.[149]

In order to gain legitimacy and address these two legitimacy challenges, an organisation usually acts proactively by adopting legitimisation activities that fall into one of three categories: conforming, selecting or manipulating the environment.[150] Within each of these categories, the choice of legitimisation activity illustrates whether the organisation seeks primarily to gain its pragmatic, moral or cognitive legitimacy.

The two legitimacy challenges associated with gaining legitimacy, and the three types of legitimisation activity implemented to address these challenges, are summarised in the following table:

Table 2 Gaining legitimacy: legitimacy challenges and legitimisation activities.[151]

Challenge	Legitimisation Activity	
Emphasise their Differences Gain Support	Conform Select Manipulate	Environment

The organisation therefore needs to navigate its new environment, finding the right balance between aligning with pre-existing organisations, while demonstrating the different services and/or products that it brings to the environment, in order to promote its legitimacy to its stakeholders. The three legitimisation activities implemented to gain legitimacy are further described below.

2.2.1.1 Conforming to the Environment

According to research, the most straightforward legitimisation activity linked to gaining legitimacy is to position the organisation within a pre-existing sector.[152] Gaining legitimacy by conforming to the environment consists in the organisation demonstrating its fit within the regulatory standards, the moral values and the cultural norms of its environment. This task can be achieved by *"presenting their innovation broadly enough to encompass existing knowledge and to invoke familiar cognitive categories"*.[153] Conformist activities also symbolise

149 Deephouse et al., 2017, p. 22; Suchman, 1995, p. 586.
150 Suchman, 1995, pp. 587-593.
151 *ibid.*
152 Bitektine, 2011, p. 158; Deephouse et al., 2017, p. 22.
153 Bitektine, 2011, p. 165.

the organisation's commitment to the established societal order by demonstrating its desire to fit in rather than ruffle feathers.[154] An organisation will adopt certain legitimisation activities in order to conform to its environment, which reflects the legitimacy type - pragmatic, moral or cognitive - that it is aiming to promote.

In promoting its *pragmatic* legitimacy, organisations use one of three legitimisation activities, or a combination of two or three. In a first instance the organisation can demonstrate that it will meet the needs and expectations of its stakeholders by delivering a certain product or service as expected. Another legitimisation activity involves including a select group of stakeholders in some of the organisation's decision-making processes, for example, with regard to how the organisation produces a particular product or how it provides a particular service, or how it chooses to interact with its environment. The third legitimisation activity implemented by organisations involves slowly building trust and gaining a reputation with its stakeholders and/or within the environment. This may be achieved by demonstrating positive behaviour or providing additional services or special products to its stakeholders. This technique is called *"co-opting constituents",*[155] which is known as an effective way for an organisation to assimilate into its new environment. A good example of this is the fast-food restaurant McDonald's, which adapts its menu to reflect local tastes, conforming to the needs and expectations of its stakeholders in over 100 countries worldwide.[156]

Organisations may also adopt a conformist stance in pursuit of*moral* legitimacy. In doing so, they must conform to the regulations and ethical standards assigned by the environment. Three legitimisation activities have been recognised as central for organisations wishing to gain moral legitimacy. In a first instance, the organisation may focus on producing outcomes that receive reward or praise. This is similar to achieving pragmatic legitimacy as the organisation provides its stakeholder with a desirable outcome in exchange for legitimacy; however, in this case the organisation aims to satisfy its stakeholders' conscience, as opposed to their direct needs, which relates rather to pragmatic legitimacy.[157] Energy suppliers delivering 'clean' or 'green' energy provide a good example of this.[158]

Concrete moral outcomes are, however, difficult to attain. As such, organisations usually opt for less direct approaches. One of the most common legitimisation activities implemented by organisations is to become affiliated, in some shape or form, with

154 Deephouse et al., 2017, p. 22; Suchman, 1995, p. 587.

155 Suchman, 1995, p. 587.

156 McDonald's website, 'FAQs': https://www.mcdonalds.com/gb/en-gb/help/faq/18812-why-is-the-mcdonalds-menu-different-in-different-countries.html.

157 Suchman, 1995, p. 588.

158 Rolf Wüstenhagen and Michael Bilharz, *Green energy market development in Germany: effective public policy and emerging customer demand*, Energy Policy, 2006, 34 (13), 1681-1696.

recognised regulatory bodies, or other organisations recognised for their moral legitimacy located in the same environment. An organisation may seek to join respectable networks or align its products, services and/or processes with those of other reputable organisations; for example, the 'fair trade' label used on consumer goods indicates that the organisation behind the product adheres to sustainable and equitable trade relations.[159] Alternatively, the organisation may also hire or associate itself with an individual that is considered to hold a high moral standing within the environment or set up a corporate social responsibility department. The actions taken in this regard may be purely symbolic, whereby the organisation in question does not need to make any substantial changes to any of its operational procedures or internal structures, but merely emphasises its association with particular individuals or a certain social agenda.[160]

The third legitimisation activity observed in this category relates the organisation's goals which are used to justify the organisation's existence. Given that the goals are not necessarily linked directly to the organisation's operations, they too can be tweaked to give an impression of conforming to the societal ideals of its environment. This activity is sometimes requested by the organisation's stakeholders in order to further their own political or cultural objectives.[161] Research shows that even superficial changes to an organisation's communicated objectives or mandate can prove to have a profound impact on its environment, as cognitive dissonance and self-selection can gradually produce a new generation of employees who start to adhere to, or strive to achieve, the ideal goals.[162] This suggests that legitimisation activities related to promoting an organisation's moral legitimacy have the capacity to shift the organisation's mandate or overarching goals.[163]

Organisations therefore seek to gain pragmatic legitimacy by conforming to the needs and expectations of their stakeholders, while moral legitimacy is gained by conforming to the environment's ethical principles and/or regulatory standards. With regard to gaining cognitive legitimacy, an organisation aims rather to conform to established organisational models that are already rooted in society. Along these lines, research has shown that organisations seeking to gain legitimacy will often pursue cognitive legitimacy by mimicking the most prominent and highly-esteemed organisations that are present in their new environment.[164] This is known as "*mimetic isomorphism*".[165]

159 Homaira Semeen and Muhammad Azizul Islam, *Social impact disclosure and symbolic power: Evidence from UK fair trade organizations*, Critical Perspectives on Accounting, 2020, 102181.
160 Suchman, 1995, p. 588.
161 *ibid.*
162 Jost & Major, 2001, p. 159.
163 Jost & Major, 2001, pp. 159-160; Suchman, 1995, p. 588.
164 Suchman, 1995, p. 589.
165 Deephouse et al., 2017, p. 19.

If an organisation is created in a new sector, or in an environment that lacks similar organisations, legitimacy may be gained by establishing protocols and procedures that mirror those used by organisations that possess cognitive legitimacy, even if these organisations incomparable. Alternatively, an organisation may also seek to professionalise its activities ("*professionalisation*") by highlighting its relevance within the environment by demonstrating certain competences, capabilities and/or skills.[166]

There may well be overlap between the legitimisation activities used within each legitimacy type; however, as a typology they are organised as follows:

Table 3 Conforming to the environment: legitimacy type and legitimisation activity.[167]

Legitimacy Type	Legitimisation Activities
Pragmatic	Conform to demands - Respond to needs - Co-opt constituents - Build reputation
Moral	Conform to ideals - Produce proper outcomes - Embed in institutions - Offer symbolic displays
Cognitive	Conform to models - Mimic standards - Formalise operations - Professionalise operations

2.2.1.2 Selecting the Environment

In order to avoid moulding an organisation to the requirements of its environment, the legitimisation activities categorised as *selecting the environment* take a different approach. The simplest of these is selecting an environment that will consider the organisation as

166 Suchman, 1995, p. 589.
167 *idem.*, pp. 587-589.

legitimate without demanding many changes in return: rather than simply conforming to the demands of a specific environment, the organisation will locate to a more suitable venue.[168]

For organisations aiming to achieve pragmatic legitimacy, selecting a favourable environment is simply a matter of market research. The organisation must identify and attract stakeholders that value the products or services that the organisation is equipped to provide. Additionally, or alternatively, the organisation may choose to offer an important organisational role to an individual who is perceived as credible or trustworthy to the organisation's stakeholders, yet who is unlikely to demand dramatic changes to the organisation's operations or activities.[169] The sportswear company Nike provides an example of this by paying top athletes to promote their brand (for example Cristiano Ronaldo, Serena Williams and Michael Jordan), thereby associating their product with sporting excellence in a variety of sports (in this case football, tennis and basketball) without making changes to their product or operational structure.[170]

In selecting the environment, organisations promoting their moral legitimacy adopt activities that reflect the cultural concerns of their stakeholders and their environment. Generally speaking, organisations are more limited in their choice of moral standards than in their decision regarding which products or services to offer (related to the pragmatic legitimacy type). That said, the decision regarding which regulations or ethical standards an organisation chooses to abide by depends largely on its own goals, and on the range of activities that these organisational goals require in order to be perceived as ethical and morally acceptable to the environment.[171]

By adjusting its organisational goals, an organisation has the flexibility of choosing from a range of moral criteria, such as accountability, confidentiality, efficiency, reliability, responsiveness etc. The organisation can select the terms that best fit with the norms and values recognised by its environment and insert them into its mission statement or mandate, and communicate this to its environment and stakeholders.[172] Interestingly, research shows that organisations tend to face higher scrutiny when the environment perceives their services to be particularly challenging (for example, hospitals or the police), or if their products are of particular importance (for example, the medical labs producing the COVID-19 vaccine).[173] Likewise, organisations appear to face higher levels of scrutiny

---

168 *idem.*, p. 589.
169 *ibid.*
170 Bassant Eyada, *Brand Activism, the Relation and Impact on Consumer Perception: A Case Study on Nike Advertising*, International Journal of Marketing Studies, 2020, 12(4).
171 Suchman, 1995, p. 589.
172 *idem.*, p. 590.
173 Bitektine, 2011, pp. 156, 162-164.

related to their core activities, as opposed to the peripheral activities or services that they may offer.[174]

In general, gaining cognitive legitimacy will depend on the sector in which the organisation finds itself (for example, healthcare, education, consumer goods etc.). Selecting an appropriate organisational environment is therefore one of the more productive ways of gaining cognitive legitimacy: often centrally regulated sectors provide the most welcoming environment for organisations that conform to the established sectoral standards, while unregulated sectors are better suited to unconventional or innovative organisations.[175]

Yet some organisations find it difficult to operate in one particular organisational environment. If this challenge occurs, an organisation may attempt to manage its environmental constraints by dividing up organisational activities and dispersing them among favourable environments. This may involve adopting a multi-organisational structure or separating the more general operations from the technical parts of the organisation.[176] Alternatively, legitimacy may be achieved by dividing the different organisational activities in order for them to reflect the legitimacy standard assigned or recognised by different environments.[177]

An organisation may otherwise prefer to focus on its stakeholders by dividing them into separate stakeholder groups and catering to one or two groups – sometimes at the expense of other stakeholders – or by combining stakeholder groups and demonstrating that organisational behaviours are legitimate under a particular shared standard of practice. The desired cognitive legitimacy of its environment may prevent an organisation from being perceived as a preferred alternative to other dominant organisations within a particular sector; however, often the fragmented nature of a larger cultural environment can create gaps in which an emerging organisation may get the chance to select a favourable environment in order to gain legitimacy.[178]

174 *ibid.*
175 Black, 2008, pp. 152-153; Suchman, 1995, p. 590.
176 Suchman, 1995, p. 572.
177 Powell, 1991, p. 197.
178 Suchman, 1995, p. 590.

Table 4 Selecting the environment: legitimacy type and legitimisation activity.[179]

Legitimacy Type	Legitimisation Activities
Pragmatic	Select markets - Locate friendly stakeholders - Recruit friendly co-optees
Moral	Select domain - Define goals
Cognitive	Select labels - Seek certification

2.2.1.3 Manipulating the Environment

This category involves an organisation influencing the structure of its environment by creating new stakeholders and new standards for legitimacy. Even though most organisations gain legitimacy primarily by selecting or conforming to their environment, these legitimisation activities are sometimes not enough. The act of manipulating the environment involves the most action from the organisation as it must understand and interfere with its environment in order to develop specifically tailored services or products. This proactive manipulation is less controllable, less common, and appears to be far less understood than either conforming to or selecting the environment.[180]

Pragmatic legitimacy reflects a relationship of direct exchange between an organisation and its stakeholders. It is therefore considered the easiest form of legitimacy to manipulate. In gaining legitimacy, the organisation may manipulate its environment through advertising campaigns, in order to persuade new stakeholders to engage with its work, and emphasising the value of a particular product or service. Alternatively, the organisation may attempt to develop a sense of need for a particular service or product, and then offer itself as the one that can fulfil that need.[181] Online platforms such as Facebook or Amazon are good

179 *idem.*, pp. 589-591.
180 Ashforth & Gibbs, 1990, p. 188; Suchman, 1995, p. 591.
181 Suchman, 1995, p. 591.

examples of this, or products like the smartphone, which now seem to be indispensable.[182] In addition to influencing stakeholder tastes, organisations may use advertising campaigns to promote the image of the organisation itself, while also directing the stakeholder's attention to the services and products that they offer.[183]

Establishing new grounds for moral legitimacy is a slightly greater challenge for organisations. Research has shown that organisations may attempt to build their moral legitimacy by accumulating and promoting success stories, particularly related to their structure or processes. These procedural activities and/or the structural set-up of an organisation are shown to have an influence on the stakeholder's perception of "*consequential legitimacy*",[184] which in turn influences the organisation's moral legitimacy.[185] This is known as the *"demonstration effect"*,whereby the success of an organisation's operational capacities directly impacts the organisation's credibility.[186] In addition to this, an organisation may draw its stakeholders' attention to positive performance indicators, while excluding less favourable or unimportant outcomes. Given that success is considered a socially constructed phenomenon, the organisation can manipulate the lens through which the stakeholder perceives the success of the organisation.[187]

However, demonstrating isolated procedural successes does not represent the quickest nor the most effective route to gaining moral legitimacy, especially when linked to an organisation's alternative operating processes and/or structure. A good example of this is Tony's Chocolonely's message regarding slavery in the chocolate industry, whereby the organisation ensures that no child labour or modern slavery is used at any point in the production of their chocolate bars.[188] Suchman's research explains that this form of legitimisation often works best when a group of organisations work together in order to convince stakeholders of the legitimate nature of a certain output, organisational structure and/or specific procedures.[189] In this way, the link between an organisation's success and its structure and/or procedures becomes more convincing, providing the organisation with recognised moral legitimacy. This is often achieved through lobbying or advertising campaigns, or even through the funding of scientific research. Once accomplished, these legitimisation activities may exert pressure on the accepted norms and standards within

182 Luca Pancani, Emanuele Preti and Paolo Riva, *The Psychology of Smartphone: The Development of the Smartphone Impact Scale (SIS)*, Assessment, 2020, 27(6), 1176-1197.
183 Suchman, 1995, pp. 591-592.
184 Schiff, 2010, p. 101; Suchman, 1995, p. 580.
185 Ashforth & Gibbs, 1990, pp. 185-186; Suchman, 1995, p. 592.
186 Laurence R. Helfer and Anne-Marie Slaughter, *Toward a Theory of Effective Supranational Adjudication*, Yale Law Journal, 1997, 107, p. 273.
187 Jeffrey Pfeffer, *Management as Symbolic Action: The Creation and Maintenance of Organizational Paradigm*, Research in Organizational Behavior, 1981, 3, p. 30.
188 See Tony's Chocolonely's mission statement. Retrieved from: https://tonyschocolonely.com/uk/en/our-mission/.
189 Suchman, 1995, pp. 592.

an environment, which can convince stakeholders of the value of such organisational activity.[190]

When the focus of environment manipulation turns from moral to cognitive legitimacy, the need for collective action (as mentioned above) becomes more apparent. Research into legitimisation activities in this area have identified three general activities: "*persistence*", "*promoting new models*" and "*standardising new models*".[191] Indeed, individual organisations may find ways to gain cognitive legitimacy by using techniques of persistence; however, often persistence alone cannot compete with the power of collective action, which usually takes one of two forms: "*popularisation*" or "*standardisation*".[192]

When an organisation chooses "*popularisation*" as an approach to gaining legitimacy, it may choose legitimisation activities such as lobbying, advertising, event sponsorship or scientific research to promote its way of working, or the focus of its work.[193] As mentioned, these forms of activity are generally more effective when executed by a group of organisations, or the organisational sector as a whole.[194] Pfeffer suggests that organisations can enhance the significance of a new perspective "*through continually articulating stories which [illustrate] its reality*".[195]

Alternatively, an organisation may promote "*standardisation*", which entails "*organisational isomorphism*", whereby organisations facing similar constraints will imitate or influence each other when developing new organisational procedures and/or structures,[196] or as Hannan and Freeman explain, the "*simple prevalence of a form tends to give it legitimacy*".[197] Organisations can therefore enhance their significance in an environment by shaping similar organisations in the same sector, or in the wider environment, into their own image. This may be achieved either through modelling or through coercion and regulation.[198]

Literature offers few details as to exactly how organisations influence or persuade their stakeholders and environment into awarding them with cognitive legitimacy through manipulation; however, the legitimisation activities implemented to manipulate the environment for cognitive legitimacy are described using the notion of institutionalisation, which is the process of embedding an organisation – or a new concept – within a particular

---

190 *idem.*, pp. 591-592.
191 Suchman, 1995, p. 592.
192 *ibid.*
193 Marc A. Mamigonian, *Academic Denial of the Armenian Genocide in American Scholarship: Denialism as Manufactured Controversy*, Genocide Studies International, 2015, 9(1), pp. 61-82.
194 Suchman, 1995, pp. 592.
195 Pfeffer, 1981, p. 23.
196 Deephouse, 1996, pp. 1024-1025.
197 Michael T. Hannan and John Freeman, *Organizational Ecology*, Harvard University Press, 1989, p. 132.
198 Deephouse, 1996, p. 1025; Deephouse et al., 2017, p. 19.

organisational sector or environment.[199] The process of institutionalisation often takes on a life of its own: it may reflect organisational activities, yet contradict the organisation's agreed mandate or objectives. These transitions within a sector or environment are therefore difficult to predict, and the process is difficult to identify, even after the fact.[200]

To conclude, the legitimisation activities that aim to gain legitimacy through manipulating the environment may be summarised as follows:

Table 5 Manipulating the environment: legitimacy type and legitimisation activity.[201]

Legitimacy Type	Legitimisation Activities
Pragmatic	Advertise - Advertise product - Advertise image
Moral	Persuade - Demonstrate success - 'Spread the word'
Cognitive	Institutionalise - Persist - Popularise new models - Standardise new models

2.2.2 *Maintaining Legitimacy*

Maintaining the legitimacy of an organisation involves promoting the organisation as an entity that continues to adhere to the ethics and norms of its environment.[202] According to Suchman, there are three legitimacy challenges that may arise related to maintaining

199 Meyer & Rowan, 1977, pp. 360-361; Suchman, 1995, p. 593.
200 *ibid.*
201 *idem.*, pp. 591-593.
202 Ashforth & Gibbs, 1990, p. 183.

legitimacy: "*stakeholder heterogeneity*", "*organisational homogeneity*" and (linked to gaining legitimacy) "*institutionalisation*".[203]

The stakeholders of any single organisation often have a wide, diverse range of needs and expectations. This is known as "*stakeholder heterogeneity*". Given that legitimacy represents the relationship between an organisation and its stakeholders, "*stakeholder heterogeneity*" is an important legitimacy challenge that any organisation must remain aware of and, if needed, address. Satisfying, or even recognising, all of an organisation's stakeholders is virtually impossible for any organisation. Over time, this problem may expose the organisation to unanticipated needs and expectations that may be difficult for an organisation to address.[204]

Another legitimacy challenge for an organisation is related to complacency, which may result in the organisation becoming rigid or inflexible regarding the adjustment of its policies or practices. This is known as "*organisational homogeneity*" and describes the scenario whereby the continuous, smooth operations of an organisation affect its ability to respond to developments in its internal or external environment. If an organisation stays in this homogeneous state while its environment is heterogeneous, the organisation may lose its stakeholders to smaller, more versatile organisations offering similar services.[205]

The final legitimacy challenge linked to maintaining legitimacy is "institutionalisation", which relates to the activity of gaining legitimacy by embedding an organisation within a particular organisational sector or environment.[206] This same process can also result in a legitimacy challenge, when a particular organisation, or group of similar organisations, comes under attack for the actions of a comparable organisation.[207] For example, the deregulation of the financial industry in the United States impacted the legitimacy of financial institutions around the world.[208] Alternatively, the organisation may be targeted on ideological grounds if it is perceived as redundant, or because it symbolises an unpopular or undesirable societal issue or event.[209] Even if the legitimacy challenge does not directly address the organisation in question, it does require attention as inactivity in this case may be the organisation's greatest downfall.[210]

Despite these three types of legitimacy challenge, maintaining legitimacy is generally easier than gaining or repairing legitimacy. According to Suchman's research, organisations

203 Suchman, 1995, p. 594.
204 *ibid.*
205 *ibid.*
206 Meyer & Rowan, 1977, pp. 360-361; Suchman, 1995, p. 593.
207 Suchman, 1995, p. 594.
208 Luiz Carlos Bresser-Pereira, *The Global Financial Crisis and a New Capitalism?* Journal of Post Keynesian Economics, 2010, 32(4), pp. 499-534; Erik Jones, *Output Legitimacy and the Global Financial Crisis: Perceptions Matter*, JCMS: Journal of Common Market Studies, 2009, 47(5), pp. 1085-1105.
209 Sunshine & Tyler, 2003.
210 Suchman, 1995, p. 594.

do not invest the same level of effort or attention into maintaining legitimacy as they do in gaining and repairing legitimacy. It does not involve the same level of urgency. The legitimisation activities implemented to maintain organisational legitimacy focus on either mitigating risk – *"perceiving a future crisis"* – or *"protecting past accomplishments"*.[211]

Table 6 Maintaining legitimacy: legitimacy challenge and legitimisation activity.[212]

Legitimacy Challenge	Legitimisation Activity
Stakeholder Heterogeneity Organisation Homogeneity Institutionalisation	i) Perceive Future Crisis ii) Protect Past Accomplishments

2.2.2.1 Perceiving a Future Crisis

This legitimisation activity aims to mitigate the risks to the organisation's legitimacy by enhancing the organisation's *"ability to recognise stakeholder reactions and foresee emerging challenges."*[213] The need for this legitimisation activity is best summed up by Hinings and Greenwood, who explain that "*a common theme in the [organisational] decline literature is that decision-makers often delude themselves into believing that a problem does not exist or that it is not serious*".[214] Organisations need to remain alert and aware of external developments that might bring their status as a legitimate organisation into question.

In order to manage its legitimacy, the organisation needs to ensure that it remains aligned with its environment, notably the environment that is most closely affiliated to its stakeholders. This legitimisation activity involves monitoring any changes in the organisation's environment, while ensuring that the essential environmental norms and values are taken into account during any organisational decision-making process. Legitimisation activities aiming to mitigate risks may also involve employing staff members that represent specific stakeholder groups, from which the organisation can learn about its stakeholders' values, beliefs and reactions.[215]

As demonstrated with the legitimisation strategy aimed at gaining legitimacy: in identifying the legitimisation activity that an organisation chooses to implement, when

211 *idem.*, pp. 594-597.
212 *ibid.*
213 *idem.*, p. 595.
214 Royston Greenwood and Christopher Robin Hinings, *Organizational Design Types, Tracks and the Dynamics of Strategic Change*, Organization Studies, 1988, 9(3), p. 308.
215 Ashforth & Gibbs, 1990, p. 183; Suchman, 1995, p. 595.

faced with a challenge linked to maintaining its legitimacy, the legitimacy type – pragmatic, moral or cognitive – that the organisation is seeking to promote or protect can be identified.[216]

In the case of the pragmatic legitimacy type, an organisation will focus its efforts on monitoring any emerging stakeholder demands. It may ask stakeholders directly about their needs or expectations by including them in certain parts of the organisational decision-making, or by making use of focus groups. Alternatively, the organisation may decide to establish a research and development team to study stakeholder behaviour or identify any changing needs. For example, in the summer of 1980 a team at Coca-Cola was asked to address the increasing health concerns connected to sugary soft-drinks and two years later Diet Coke was launched. The new product enabled Coca-Cola to maintain its legitimacy by delivering the Coca-Cola taste to those looking for a healthier option.[217] An organisation may also turn to its own employees, who may be able to provide cultural insights into a specific stakeholder's way of thinking.[218]

With regard to moral legitimacy, the organisation needs to be aware of any changes to its environment's values systems. The legitimisation activities relate mainly to the organisational culture and the manner in which it interacts with both internal and external stakeholders. The organisation may, for example, decide to establish an ethics committee or oversight team to monitor internal and external developments, or turn to its employees to make sure that adequate training is provided to ensure that certain normative principles are adhered to within the organisation itself.[219] An example of this is the #MeToo movement from 2018, which resulted in an increase in gender diversity within organisational management and the introduction of new employment and harassment policies.[220]

In the case of cognitive legitimacy, the organisation must keep a track of any cultural or societal developments that may influence the organisation's existence, its activities, or the sector in which the organisation finds itself. The organisation may directly address those who are questioning the organisation's presence or who are sceptical of the organisation's activities. The legitimacy challenges linked to the significance of the organisation are the most subtle, and identifying these challenges may occur when it is already too late, so here too the organisation must find a link with its environment in order to keep in touch with any changes that may impact its existence.[221]

---

216 Suchman, 1995, p. 596.

217 Ella Chorazy, *Coke and health*, in: Robert Crawford, Linda Brennan and Susie Khamis (eds.), *Decoding Coca-Cola: A Biography of a Global Brand*, Routledge, 2020, pp. 207-225.

218 Suchman, 1995, p. 596.

219 *idem.*, p. 596.

220 Joan MacLeod Heminway, *Me, Too and #MeToo: Women in Congress and the Boardroom*, George Washington Law Review, 2019, 87, pp. 1079-109; Elizabeth C. Tippett, *The Legal Implications of the MeToo Movement*, Minnesota Law Review, 2018, 103(1), pp. 229-302.

221 Suchman, 1995, p. 596.

Significantly, the adoption of bridge building activities is used with all the legitimacy types in this category. Rather than manipulating its environment, the organisation must take the role of observer by monitoring any changes related to the needs, the interests and the values of its stakeholders, as well as the wider environment in which it finds itself.[222]

Table 7 Perceiving a future crisis: legitimacy type and legitimisation activity.[223]

Legitimacy Type	Legitimisation Activities
Pragmatic	Monitor tastes - Consult opinion leaders
Moral	Monitor ethics - Consult professions
Cognitive	Monitor outlooks - Consult doubters

2.2.2.2 Protecting Past Accomplishments

An organisation may otherwise choose to maintain its legitimacy by strengthening and promoting "*the legitimacy they have already acquired*".[224] Ashforth and Gibbs note that "*having adjudged the organisation credible, constituents tend to relax their vigilance and content themselves with evidence of ongoing performance vis-a-vis their interests and with periodic assurances of 'business-as-usual'*".[225] Consequently, organisations should avoid unexpected events that might reawaken scrutiny from their stakeholders. This can be achieved by regulating internal operations to prevent any unfavourable situations, and using (subtle) legitimisation activities "*whereby management can occasionally deviate from social norms without seriously upsetting the organisation's standing*".[226] Indeed, it is

222 *idem.*, p. 595.
223 *ibid.*
224 *ibid.*
225 Ashforth & Gibbs, 1990, p. 183.
226 *idem.*, p. 189.

important for organisations to weigh the direct benefits of any new legitimisation activities against the scrutiny that these activities might attract.

Suchman identifies two types of legitimisation action under the category of "*protecting accomplishments*:" "*communication*" and "*stockpiling*".[227] When examining the legitimisation activities used to protect the legitimacy of an organisation through communication, it is possible to identify which legitimacy type the organisation is aiming to protect.[228]

With regard to pragmatic legitimacy, all exchanges between the organisation and its stakeholders are consistent and predictable; communication is therefore frank and honest. The organisation does not only meet stakeholder needs, it also removes any uncertainties they may have and instils the message that the stakeholders are in control.[229] In the case of moral legitimacy, the legitimisation activities implemented by an organisation emphasise its position of responsibility and authority. The communication style of the organisation takes an authoritative tone with its stakeholders; it takes ownership of any challenges related to its legitimacy, while downplaying substantial concerns, and refuting any claims of improper behaviour.[230]

When the organisational legitimacy type is cognitive in nature, any overt attention – including supportive attention – may confuse or disrupt the common "*taken-for-granted*" existence of the organisation within its environment. As such, an organisation will take a matter-of-fact approach with explanations that are "*supposedly of common knowledge*".[231] The organisation's legitimisation activities are simple, and may even come across as banal; its communication style is straightforward and rational in nature. The organisation's aim is to seamlessly explain its organisational behaviour by emphasising organic developments that are inevitable, and which remain aligned with societal or cultural norms.[232]

In addition to using communication to shield itself from any unforeseen challenges and to protect its legitimacy, an organisation may attempt to increase its legitimacy status by converting short-term legitimacy to long-term recognition and acceptance. This legitimisation activity is evident within all three organisational legitimacy types and is referred to as "*stockpiling*".[233]

In the case of pragmatic legitimacy, an organisation can stockpile legitimacy by demonstrating its consistent, dependable nature. Trust is built between the stakeholders and the organisation through the organisation's constant ability to deliver the goods and services that stakeholders need or expect, proving itself to be a reliable, trustworthy

---

227 Suchman, 1995, pp. 596-597.
228 *ibid.*
229 *idem.*, p. 596.
230 *ibid.*
231 Pfeffer, 1981, p. 15.
232 Suchman, 1995, p. 596.
233 *ibid.*

partner.[234] Organisations that wish to underline their moral legitimacy aim to build a relationship with their stakeholders based on mutual respect. The reputation of the organisation is key. An organisation will emphasise a strong values-based *modus operandi* and consistently demonstrate socially accepted, proper behaviour towards its stakeholders and its own employees.[235]

Organisations may also stockpile cognitive legitimacy, primarily by constructing communication links between the organisation and its social environment. Frequent and intense interaction between the organisation and its stakeholders creates a dense web of organisational significance within its environment that can resist, survive and repair any misunderstandings or legitimacy challenges that might occur.[236] Consequently, the more tightly the organisation is woven into the fabric of its environment, the more likely it is that belief in the organisation will approach a "*homeostatic ideal*".[237]

The link between the organisation's legitimacy type and the legitimisation activities it adopts through protecting past accomplishments are summarised in this table:

Table 8 Protecting past accomplishments: legitimacy type and legitimisation activity.[238]

Legitimacy Type	Legitimisation Activities
Pragmatic	Protect exchanges - Communicate honestly - Stockpile trust
Moral	Protect propriety - Communicate authoritatively - Stockpile esteem
Cognitive	Protect assumptions - Speak matter-of-factly - Stockpile interconnections

234 *ibid.*
235 *ibid.*
236 *ibid.*
237 *idem.*, p. 597.
238 *idem.*, pp. 595-597.

2.2.3 Repairing Legitimacy[239]

Of the three legitimisation activities, actions aimed at repairing legitimacy usually require the most attention from an organisation. Although legitimisation activities linked to repairing legitimacy are similar to those used to gain legitimacy, they represent activities that provide *"a reactive response to an unforeseen crisis"*,[240] in contrast to the proactive actions taken by an organisation to gain legitimacy.

In line with the multiple interpretations of the concept of legitimacy, and the variety of factors that influence perceptions of legitimacy, it is no surprise that the challenges to organisational legitimacy are just as diverse and can occur at all stages of an organisation's lifespan. Challenges related to ethics and values are distinctly different from challenges regarding performance and functionality. Hirsch and Andrews considered two types of challenges to an organisation's legitimacy: *performance*challenges occur when organisations are perceived as having failed to execute their mandate (linked to Suchman's pragmatic legitimacy type); and *value* challenges occur when the organisation's integrity is in question, regardless of how well it has fulfilled its agreed mandate or activities (Suchman's moral legitimacy type).[241]

All organisations are expected to provide a certain service or product, and are therefore susceptible to performance challenges. However, organisations that request or require a certain level of trust are particularly vulnerable to value challenges. This applies especially to organisations whose work is underpinned by certain societal values (for example social services, faith-based organisations and courts) and/or involves high levels of trust (for example schools, hospitals, banks and the police). In general, performance challenges are easier to regulate, yet both types of challenge need to be addressed equally in order to ensure the organisation's continued existence.[242]

While performance challenges are directly related to actions (pragmatic legitimacy), and value challenges relate to integrity and ethics (moral legitimacy), legitimacy challenges may also relate to failures of *meaning* (cognitive legitimacy).[243] Challenges related to meaning go deeper than the performance and values challenges, as they touch on the

239 Deephouse et al. propose the term *"responding"* instead of repairing legitimacy (Deephouse et al., 2017, p. 23); however, the original term *"repair"* (Suchman, 1995, p. 597) has been kept here as it implies that legitimacy needs to be restored following a challenge to the organisation's legitimacy. Furthermore, it can be argued that all three legitimisation actions - gaining, maintaining and repairing – require the organisation to *respond* to its environment.

240 Suchman, 1995, p. 597.

241 Deephouse et al., 2017, p. 23; Paul M. Hirsch, and John Andrews, *Administrators' Response to Performance and Value Challenges – Or, Stance, Symbols and Behavior in a World of Changing Frames*, in: *Leadership and Organizational Culture: New Perspectives on Administrative Theory and Practice*, 1984, pp. 173-174; Suchman, 1995, pp. 597-598.

242 Ashforth & Gibbs, 1990, p. 184; Deephouse et al., 2017, p. 23.

243 Ashforth & Gibbs, 1990, p. 180; Deephouse et al., 2017, p. 23; Suchman, 1995, pp. 597-598.

validity of an organisation's existence. For example, stakeholders may begin to suspect that the structure of the organisation is in fact a façade, or that the organisation's outputs may actually be harmful, or that so-called efficient procedures are an illusion.[244]

As a result, unlike challenges linked to gaining and maintaining legitimacy, challenges related to repairing legitimacy are directly connected to the organisation's legitimacy type, as demonstrated in the table below.

Table 9 Repairing legitimacy: legitimacy challenges and legitimacy types.[245]

Legitimacy Challenge	Legitimacy Type
Performance	Pragmatic
Value	Moral
Meaning	Cognitive

With regard to repairing legitimacy, the initial – and most important – task in mending a breach of trust in an organisation is to swiftly communicate a narrative that separates the legitimacy challenge from a more general assessment of the organisation as a whole.[246] Two categories of legitimisation action used to repair the organisational legitimacy are identified as "*formulating a normalising account*" and "*strategic restructuring*"[247] or, as defined by Ashforth and Gibbs, "*symbolic*" and "*substantive*"actions.[248]

2.2.3.1 Symbolic Action

Rather than change its activities or organisational behaviour, an organisation may decide to portray its activities in a manner that is consistent with social values and expectations.

244 Deephouse et al., 2017, pp. 16-17; Suchman, 1995, pp. 597-598.
245 Ashforth & Gibbs, 1990, p. 180; Deephouse et al., 2017, p. 23; Suchman, 1995, pp. 597-598.
246 Suchman, 1995, p. 598.
247 *idem.*, pp. 597-598.
248 Ashforth & Gibbs, 1990, p. 178.

Similar to the five neutralisation techniques proposed by Sykes and Matza in 1957,[249] these symbolic legitimisation activities aim to *"transform the meaning of acts"*[250] and Ashforth and Gibbs provide six separate categories of action.

In a first instance, the organisation may *"promote socially acceptable goals"* while pursuing less acceptable ones. Many organisations formulate and publicise ethical policies but do not establish procedures for monitoring compliance or imposing sanctions.[251] Similarly, the organisation might simply suppress information regarding activities or outcomes likely to undermine organisational legitimacy; Ashforth and Gibbs label this symbolic action as *"denial and concealment"*.[252] Alternatively (or additionally), the organisation may attempt to recast the meaning of its goals or objectives by *"redefining objectives and goals"*. This form of symbolic action demonstrates legitimisation as a retrospective process, given that the organisation will frame its past illegitimate action(s) in line with the current, acceptable social values.[253]

"Providing excuses and justifications" is when an organisation offers certain explanations for its behaviour, in an attempt to remove itself from a situation that threatens its legitimacy:[254] *"excuses"* are used to deny or minimise an organisation's responsibility for a given event, alternative explanations will be provided, or the causality of the event or situation is deflected to another party or event; while *"justifications"* describe the situation in which an organisation will take responsibility for the situation or event in question, but will refrain from expressing any regret, with the aim of minimising the backlash of a legitimacy challenge, while demonstrating some authority and control over the situation.[255]

"Offering apologies" is another symbolic action that may prevent or minimise the loss of organisational legitimacy. Apologies involve an acknowledgement of (some) responsibility for a negative event or situation, and include an expression of remorse. This legitimisation activity serves to convey the organisation's understanding and concern regarding the consequences of a legitimacy challenge related to a certain situation or event, in order to receive understanding from its stakeholders. This legitimisation activity may be implemented to reaffirm an appearance of control, and send a message that the organisation has learnt from the event, while also attempting to maintain some credibility. However, by accepting responsibility and apologising for a situation in which its legitimacy

---

249 The neutralisation techniques proposed by Sykes and Matza consist of the: denial of responsibility, denial of injury, denial of the victim, condemnation of the condemners and appeal to higher loyalties (Gresham M. Sykes and David Matza, *Techniques of Neutralization: A Theory of Delinquency*, American Sociological Review, 1957, 22(6), pp. 667-669).

250 Ashforth & Gibbs, 1990, p. 180.

251 *ibid.*

252 *ibid.*

253 *ibid.*

254 *idem.*, p. 181.

255 *ibid.*

is in question, the organisation exposes itself to potential charges of incompetence or corruption, which may lead to financial or reputational damages. As such, organisations do not tend to apologise except in the most obvious or insignificant cases.

The sixth, and final, symbolic action described by Ashforth and Gibbs sees an organisation adopt certain highly visible practices that are consistent with its environment's social expectations, while leaving the essential operational procedures of the organisation intact. Meyer and Rowan coined this symbolic action as "*ceremonial conformity*".[256] Organisations may opt to establish a complaints office, an ethics committee or a task force to investigate particular issues, all of which provide the appearance of action without the substance.

These six categories of symbolic action demonstrate how organisations utilise a variety of practices in order to legitimise the activities of their organisations. They may be used interchangeably or in combination, and may also be carried out together with substantive actions.

2.2.3.2 Substantive Action

Legitimisation activities described by Ashforth and Gibbs as "*substantive action*" involve a significant change in the policies, the structure(s), the objectives, and/or the activities of an organisation in response to a legitimacy challenge. Ashforth and Gibbs provide four categories of substantive action.[257]

The first category, "*role performance*", describes the response of an organisation that simply does what it is expected to do, or what its stakeholders tell it to do (particularly if the stakeholders provide the organisation with critical resources). This substantive action follows the exchange theory (related to Suchman's pragmatic legitimacy type), whereby stakeholders provide their support in exchange for the expected organisational behaviour. Regardless of whether role performance is determined by a response to the market, or legal or political ideals, the assessment of its stakeholders' needs and expectations is a necessary condition for survival of most organisations seeking to repair their legitimacy.[258]

The second category of substantive action is "*coercive isomorphism*", which refers to a situation whereby the organisation is pressured into conforming to the norms and expectations of its stakeholders. This is a coercive measure, meaning that the organisation does not necessarily change its behaviour because it believes it to be better, but rather because it is forced to align with its stakeholders' expectations. This action relates to the core values of the organisation: why it exists and how it should function. Legitimacy may be repaired by simply conforming to certain ethical standards or regulations that are

256 Meyer & Rowan, 1977, p. 341.
257 Ashforth & Gibbs, 1990, p. 178.
258 *ibid.*

recognised by the organisation's environment. This practice is especially significant when stakeholders are unfamiliar with the organisation or its activities, or, vice-versa, if the stakeholders' expectations are not clear to the organisation.[259]

The following two types substantive actions provide a way for the organisation to gain some control regarding the perceptions of legitimacy that its stakeholders hold, and also demonstrate an attempt to reduce the power that stakeholders have over the organisation. The first, "*altering resource dependencies*", provides the organisation with a certain degree of freedom and leverage by tapping into a variety of resources and networks, rather than being dependent on any one particular stakeholder. Aside from the added flexibility that this provides the organisation, it also reduces the need for the organisation to adhere to the expectations and requirements of any specific stakeholder.[260]

The second is "*altering socially institutionalized practices*", which involves the organisation flipping the tables and attempting to make its environment conform to its own actions and practices.[261] This legitimisation activity may include intensive lobbying against government legislation, pushing certain ideals through advertising campaigns, negotiating with regulators, and awarding research grants to influence stakeholder and even the public's perception of their work. A good example of this is the work of the tobacco industry in the 1960s, when the health risks associated with smoking cigarettes became a huge threat to the legitimacy of the product.[262]

In addition to these substantive and symbolic actions, most legitimacy activities implemented to gain legitimacy can also serve to repair the legitimacy of an organisation following a crisis, provided that the organisation continues to enjoy some credibility with relevant stakeholders.[263] Generally speaking, research shows that effective legitimisation activities appear to depend less on conforming to any single set of stakeholder expectations, than on determining which stakeholders care about which standards, and constructing a viable collection of reassurances that satisfy enough stakeholders on enough standards for as long as possible.[264]

The following table provides a summary of legitimisation actions implemented to repair legitimacy following a challenge to an organisation's legitimacy:

259 *ibid.*
260 *ibid.*
261 *ibid.*
262 Mamigonian, 2015, pp. 61-82.
263 Suchman, 1995, p. 599.
264 Ashforth & Gibbs, 1990, p. 182; Suchman, 1995, pp. 585-586.

Table 10 Symbolic and substantive actions.[265]

Symbolic Actions	Substantive Actions
Promote Socially Acceptable Goals Denial and Concealment Redefine Objectives and Goals Provide Excuses and Justifications Offer Apologies Ceremonial Conformity	Role Performance Coercive Isomorphism Alter Resource Dependencies Alter Socially Organisational Practices

Having examined how organisational legitimacy may be managed, and making use of research conducted by Suchman, Deephouse et al., and Ashforth and Gibbs,[266] the following section presents the theoretical framework designed for the purpose of this research, which brings together the elements involved in gaining, maintaining and/or repairing legitimacy in order to examine the legitimisation activities implemented by the ICTR.

2.3 Operationalising the Framework

The ICTR faced a number of legitimacy challenges from the day of its inception, through UN Resolution 955, to its closure on 31 December 2015. In order to manage its legitimacy, the Tribunal implemented legitimisation activities designed to gain, maintain and/or repair its legitimacy. However, the ICTR could not respond to all legitimacy challenges nor did it have the capacity to direct its legitimisation efforts towards all of its stakeholders. The choices made with regard to which legitimacy challenges to respond to, what legitimisation activities to implement, and which stakeholders to engage with, provide an insight into the way in which the ICTR operated with regard to managing its legitimacy.

The aim of this research is to examine the legitimisation activities implemented by the ICTR when faced with certain legitimacy challenges, to better understand which legitimacy type the Tribunal sought to gain, maintain and /or repair (pragmatic, moral or cognitive), and why, while also identifying the stakeholders that were targeted by these legitimisation activities, and why.

For the purpose of this study, and in line with the research conducted by Suchman, Deephouse et al., and Ashforth and Gibbs,[267] five main components have been identified as being part of the legitimisation process. These consist of: a *legitimacy challenge*, which

265 Ashforth & Gibbs, 1990, pp. 178, 180-181; Suchman, 1995, pp. 597-599.
266 Ashforth & Gibbs, 1990; Deephouse, et al., 2017; Suchman, 1995.
267 Ashforth & Gibbs, 1990; Deephouse, et al., 2017; Suchman, 1995.

refers to any event or situation that threatened the legitimacy of the Tribunal; a *legitimisation strategy* that has the aim of gaining, maintaining and/or repairing legitimacy;[268] a *legitimisation activity*, which is linked to each of the legitimisation strategies (to gain, maintain and/or repair legitimacy) and is implemented as an action intended to respond to a legitimacy challenge; a *legitimacy type*, which refers to Suchman's categorisation of organisational legitimacy as either pragmatic, moral or cognitive;[269] and the *stakeholder*, which, for this research, refers to any individual, group, organisation or system that had an interest in the Tribunal, and could either affect or be affected by the activities of the ICTR.

Starting with *legitimacy challenges*, *legitimisation strategies* and *legitimisation activities*: according to the research conducted by Suchman and Deephouse et al., legitimacy challenges and legitimisation activities are intrinsically linked by one of the three legitimisation strategies – gaining, maintaining and repairing legitimacy.[270]

When an organisation is faced with a *legitimacy challenge*, it will make use of one of three *legitimisation strategies* identified through Suchman's literature review in order to gain, maintain or to repair its legitimacy.[271] Within each of these strategies, there are various *legitimisation activities* that an organisation will adopt in order to respond directly to a specific legitimacy challenge.

Figure 1 Legitimisation when faced with a legitimacy challenge.

Furthermore, when an organisation aims to gain or maintain its legitimacy, the *legitimisation activity* implemented corresponds to a certain *legitimacy type* (pragmatic, moral and cognitive). It may therefore be argued that when deciding on which legitimisation activity to use in order to *gain* or *maintain* its legitimacy, an organisation will also make a choice as to whether to gain or maintain its pragmatic, moral or cognitive legitimacy.

268 Suchman, 1995, p. 585.
269 *idem.*, pp. 577-585.
270 Deephouse et al., 2017, pp. 4-6; Suchman, 1995, pp. 586-598.
271 Suchman, 1995, p. 585.

For example, if an organisation is establishing itself in a new environment, it may face a challenge in gaining trust or interest in its products or services (*legitimacy challenge*); in order to gain legitimacy (*legitimisation strategy*) the organisation may therefore choose to conform to certain regulations that are required by its environment (*legitimisation activity*). By conforming to the regulatory standards set by its environment, the organisation adopts a legitimisation activity that corresponds to moral legitimacy (*legitimacy type*).[272]

Legitimisation Strategy → Legitimisation Activity → Legitimacy Type

In responding to one or more legitimacy challenges, an organisation may use a collection of legitimisation activities that could be categorised under each of the three legitimacy types – pragmatic, moral and cognitive. However, usually there is one dominant legitimacy type that an organisation will lean towards, and that it will invest more effort and resources in achieving.[273] As such, this study proposes that the legitimisation activities implemented by the ICTR may shed light on the legitimacy type that the Tribunal most commonly adhered to.

In addition to providing an insight into the Tribunal's preferred legitimacy type, the legitimisation activities of an organisation are directed towards certain stakeholders. As a result, this study also submits that when identifying the legitimisation activities implemented by the ICTR, it will become clear which stakeholders the ICTR focused its resources on during the legitimisation process.

According to this approach, the theoretical framework of this research suggests that: with information regarding the *legitimacy challenges* faced by the Tribunal, and the *legitimisation activities* implemented by the Tribunal in response to these challenges, this study can identify (a) whether the Tribunal implemented a specific *legitimacy type* (pragmatic, moral and/or cognitive) and (b) which *stakeholders* it engaged with.

It is also important to note that the ICTR may have implemented several legitimisation activities in response to one legitimacy challenge:

272 See table 4: Selecting the environment.

273 Suchman, 1995, p. 586.

Figure 2 Different legitimisation activities implemented in response to a legitimacy challenge.

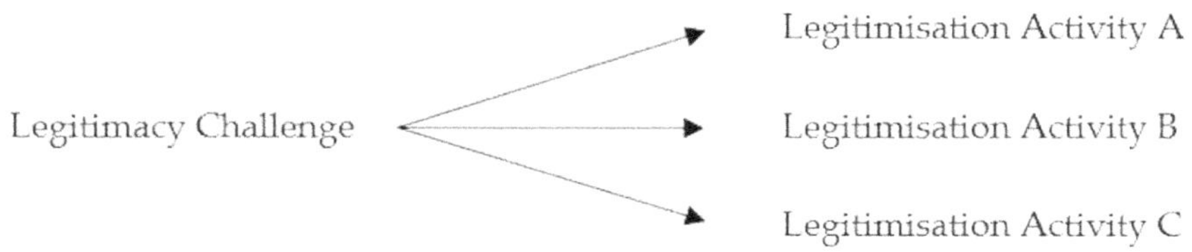

Given that different legitimisation activities can be implemented to address one legitimacy challenge, it is also possible that different legitimisation activities were implemented by the Tribunal to engage different stakeholders:

Figure 3 Different legitimisation activities targeting different stakeholders.

The situation is slightly different when examining legitimisation activities implemented to repair the Tribunal's legitimacy. When an organisation is faced with legitimacy challenges related to repairing its legitimacy, the legitimacy challenge is directly linked to a legitimacy type: challenges that are related to the *performance* of the organisation directly impact *pragmatic* legitimacy, challenges that relate to *value* or *ethics* influence the *moral* legitimacy of an organisation, while challenges related to the fundamental *meaning* or *significance* of an organisation are connected to *cognitive* legitimacy.

Table 11 Repairing Legitimacy: legitimacy challenge and legitimacy type.[274]

Legitimacy Challenge	Legitimacy Type
Performance	Pragmatic
Value	Moral
Meaning	Cognitive

As a result, while the legitimisation activities still provide information regarding which stakeholders are targeted, it is the legitimacy challenge that informs the legitimacy type that the organisation is managing.

Legitimacy Challenge → Legitimacy Type

Legitimisation Activity → Stakeholder

The way in which to uncover the legitimacy type(s) and the stakeholder(s) associated with any particular legitimisation activity therefore varies slightly between the strategies aimed at gaining and maintaining legitimacy, and strategies implemented to repair legitimacy. However, this study proposes that in all situations – in which gaining, maintain and repairing legitimacy are required – both the *legitimacy type* and the targeted *stakeholder* can be identified by first uncovering the *legitimacy challenge* and the subsequent *legitimisation activity* implemented by the ICTR to address this challenge.

In order, therefore, to better understand the nature and characteristics of both the legitimacy challenges and the legitimisation activities (which may then be used to identify the legitimacy type and targeted stakeholders), the framework proposed here suggests that first the legitimacy challenge faced by the ICTR needs to be identified, and then categorised

274 Ashforth & Gibbs, 1990, p. 180; Deephouse et al., 2017, p. 23; Suchman, 1995, pp. 597-598.

as a challenge linked to either gaining or maintaining legitimacy, or as a challenge that requires a strategy to repair the Tribunal's legitimacy.

Once the legitimacy challenge has been identified under one of the three legitimacy strategies (gain, maintain or repair), the challenge itself can be labelled according to the categorisation described by Suchman:[275]

Table 12 Connecting a legitimacy challenge with a legitimisation strategy.[276]

Legitimacy Challenge		Legitimisation Strategy
Emphasising their difference Gaining support	⇒	Gaining
Stakeholder heterogeneity Organisation homogeneity Institutionalisation	⇒	Maintaining
Performance Value Meaning	⇒	Repairing

Once the legitimacy challenge has been categorised as a challenge in gaining, maintaining or repairing legitimacy, the legitimisation activity implemented by the Tribunal to address the challenge can then be identified, again using the categories described in Suchman's study:[277]

275 Suchman, 1995, pp. 586-598.
276 Ashforth & Gibbs, 1990, p. 180; Deephouse et al., 2017, p. 23; Suchman, 1995, pp. 586-599.
277 Suchman, 1995, pp. 586-599.

Table 13 Legitimisation strategies: linking legitimacy challenges with legitimisation activities.[278]

Legitimacy Challenge	Legitimisation Strategy	Legitimisation Activities
Emphasising their difference Gaining support	Gaining	Conform Select Manipulate
Stakeholder heterogeneity Organisation homogeneity Institutionalisation	Maintaining	Perceive Future Crisis Protect Past Accomplishments
Performance Value Meaning	Repairing	Symbolic Actions Substantive Actions

By identifying the legitimisation strategy – which provides information regarding the nature of the legitimacy challenges faced by the ICTR, and the characteristics of legitimisation activities implemented to address these challenges – the legitimacy type and the targeted stakeholders prioritised by the ICTR can then be identified. The following sections provide more detail regarding how this information is examined for each of the legitimatisation strategies: gaining, maintaining and repairing.

2.3.1 Gaining Legitimacy

The legitimacy challenges faced by the ICTR in relation to gaining legitimacy may be categorised as either a challenge in *"emphasising their difference"* or in *"gaining support"*. Once the challenge has been determined, the legitimisation activities implemented by the ICTR to address this challenge can be identified: conforming to the environment, selecting the environment and/or manipulating the environment.

278 *ibid.*

Table 14 Gaining legitimacy: legitimacy challenge and legitimisation activity.[279]

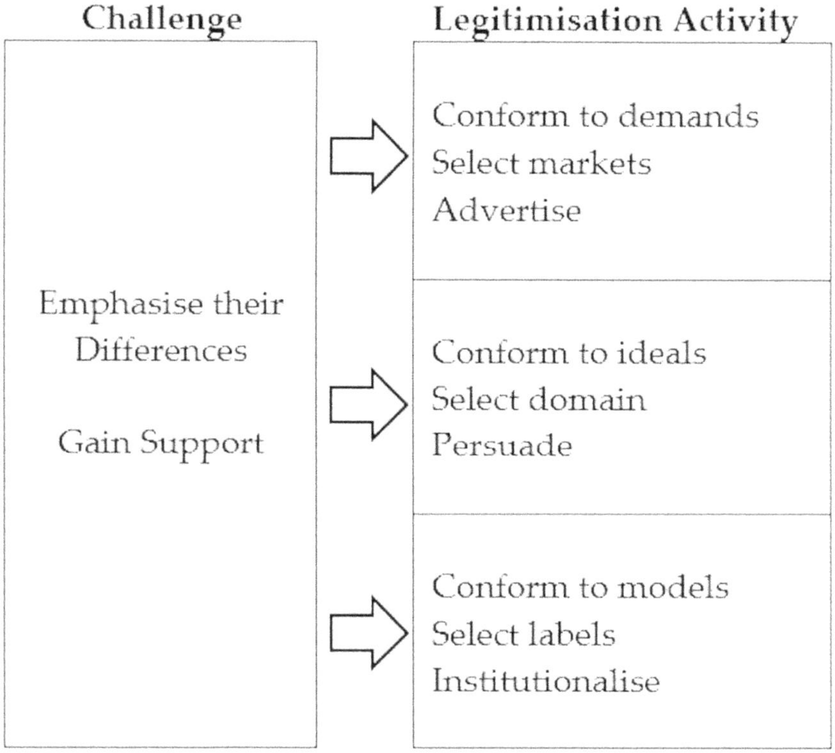

The manner in which the ICTR conformed, selected and/or manipulated its environment provides an insight into whether its aim was to promote its pragmatic, moral and/or cognitive legitimacy.

279 *idem.*, pp. 587-593.

Table 15 Gaining legitimacy: discovering legitimacy type(s).

Challenge	Legitimisation Activity	*Legitimacy Type*
Emphasise their Differences Gain Support	Conform to demands Select markets Advertise	*Pragmatic?*
	Conform to ideals Select domain Persuade	*Moral?*
	Conform to models Select labels Institutionalise	*Cognitive?*

In addition to providing information regarding the legitimacy type(s), the legitimisation activity also indicates the stakeholder(s) that were targeted during this legitimisation process.

Table 16 Gaining legitimacy: discovering legitimacy type(s) and stakeholder(s).

Challenge	Legitimisation Activity	*Legitimacy Type*	*Stakeholder*
Emphasise their Differences Gain Support	Conform to demands Select markets Advertise	*Pragmatic?*	
	Conform to ideals Select domain Persuade	*Moral?*	?
	Conform to models Select labels Institutionalise	*Cognitive?*	

A very similar process of analysis takes place when examining the activities implemented to maintain the legitimacy of the ICTR.

2.3.2 Maintaining Legitimacy

Legitimacy challenge(s) related to maintaining legitimacy are categorised under one of the following three legitimacy challenges: "*stakeholder heterogeneity*", which relates to challenges in recognising or addressing the interests and needs of all of its stakeholders; "*organisation homogeneity*", which reflects an organisation's inability to respond to developments in its internal or external environment due to the rigidity of its policies and/or procedures; and the challenge related to "*institutionalisation*", which refers to the situation whereby an organisation that is associated with an unpopular or undesirable societal issue or event, or, on the contrary, that it is considered as redundant to its environment.

An organisation may respond to these challenges by either mitigating any future risks ("*perceive future crisis*") and/or by protecting its past accomplishments;[280] and the legitimisation activity implemented by the organisation aims to either promote its pragmatic, moral and/or cognitive legitimacy (legitimacy type).

Table 17 Maintaining legitimacy: discovering legitimacy type(s).

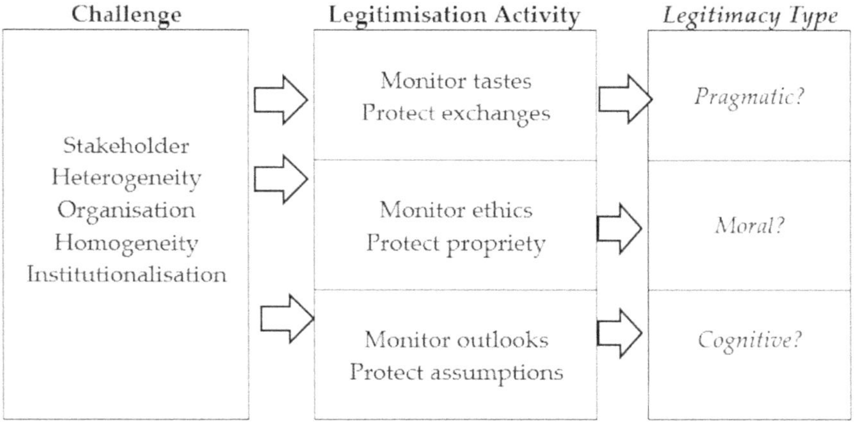

As with gaining legitimacy, in addition to providing an insight as to which legitimacy type the ICTR was seeking to promote (pragmatic, moral and/or cognitive), the legitimisation activities implemented by the Tribunal, also sheds light as to which stakeholder(s) the ICTR was focusing its legitimisation activities on.

280 Tables 7 and 8.

Table 18 Maintaining legitimacy: discovering legitimacy type(s) and stakeholder(s).

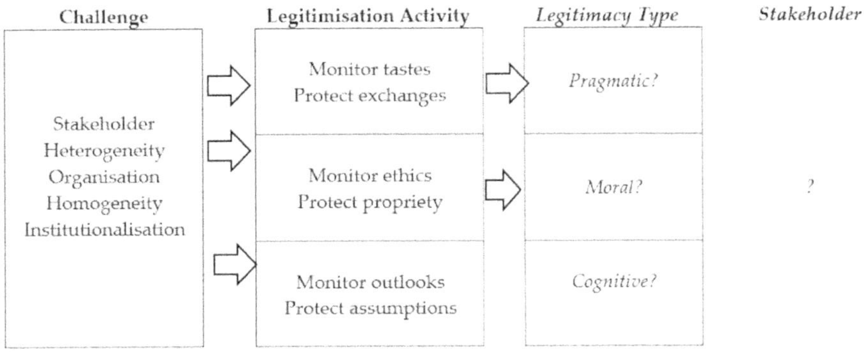

2.3.3 *Repairing Legitimacy*

A different scheme is used to identify the legitimacy type(s) and stakeholder(s) that are targeted in relation to legitimacy challenges that required the ICTR to repair its legitimacy. In the case of repairing legitimacy, the legitimacy challenge identified by the Tribunal provides an indication as to which legitimacy type it was concerned with protecting and promoting. Studies have identified three legitimacy challenges that are directly linked to three corresponding legitimacy types:[281]

Table 19 Repairing legitimacy: legitimacy challenges and legitimacy types.[282]

Challenge	Legitimacy Type
Performance	Pragmatic
Value	Moral
Meaning	Cognitive

Once the legitimacy challenge has been identified and classified as either a performance, value or meaning challenge – thereby indicating whether the challenge is linked to

281 Deephouse et al., 2017, p. 23; Suchman, 1995, pp. 597-598.
282 Ashforth & Gibbs, 1990, p. 180; Deephouse et al., 2017, p. 23; Suchman, 1995, pp. 597-598.

pragmatic, moral or cognitive legitimacy – the legitimisation activity implemented by the Tribunal can be identified,[283] which provides an insight as to which stakeholder(s) were targeted by the Tribunal in relation to its legitimisation process.

Table 20 Repairing legitimacy: legitimisation activity and stakeholders.

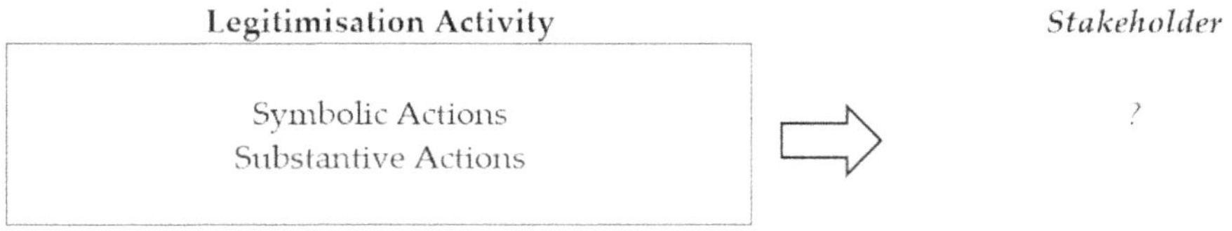

As a result, although the process of identifying the legitimacy type promoted and/or protected by the ICTR, and the stakeholder(s) most frequently targeted through legitimisation activities, is different when examining situations in which the Tribunal sought to repair its legitimacy – as opposed to gaining and maintaining legitimacy – it is possible to obtain the same information in all situations, when the legitimacy challenge and legitimisation activity is known.

Despite the clear lines that exist between legitimisation strategies and legitimisation activities, there is a possibility that the Tribunal demonstrated different priorities – in terms of its target stakeholders and its most dominant legitimacy type – when seeking to gain, maintain or repair its legitimacy. Alternatively, the ICTR may demonstrate consistency when managing its legitimacy, with regard to both in the legitimacy type(s) and the stakeholder(s) it addressed through the legitimisation activities it implemented. Furthermore, the Tribunal may have faced legitimacy challenges that it chose not to respond to. Chapters 4, 5 and 6 make use of the theoretical framework presented here in order to identify and analyse the legitimacy challenges faced by the ICTR and the responses it took towards these challenges.

The following chapter, Chapter 3, describes how this theoretical framework was put into action in order to examine the activities of the Tribunal based in Arusha, Tanzania. One limitation to this approach is that the ICTR is being considered as a single unified organisation. Indeed, often the job of an external relations department is to emphasise a united front to the external world: one coherent voice. However, the reality is often different, especially for organisations with multiple departments and diverse personalities. This is demonstrated in the following chapters. Although the complexity of the ICTR, with its

283 Ashforth & Gibbs, 1990, p. 178.

different organs and sections, has been taken into account in this research, the ICTR, for the purpose of this initial analysis, is regarded as one single entity.

3 Methodology

The legitimacy of an international criminal court has been demonstrated to be crucial for its acceptance in a post-conflict environment. With this in mind, this research examines the measures taken by the ICTR to promote its legitimacy, especially when faced with certain legitimacy challenges. Yet, as described in Chapter 2, there are many different definitions to the term legitimacy, and, as a result, there are several approaches that can be used to study and understand the notion of legitimacy. This research adopts an empirically oriented approach to examine how the ICTR gained, maintained and/or repaired its legitimacy. Legitimacy – in this empirical sense – examines the factors that incentivise stakeholders to consent to the legitimacy of an organisation.[1]

The objective of this chapter is to explain how this research was operationalised. It is split into four sections. The first section describes the research approach adopted to answer the main research question, explaining why the choice was made to examine the ICTR as a single case study using qualitative methods, namely the exploratory approach.[2] The second section of this chapter describes the way data was collected, which comprised of a literature review, archival research, and semi-structured interviews that were conducted during field trips to Rwanda and Tanzania, as well as by telephone, and online via Skype and Zoom. Aside from facilitating face-to-face interviews, the field trips also provided a way to better understand of the context of the research topic, with the trip to Arusha in Tanzania offering the possibility to consult the ICTR's archive and to visit the town in which the ICTR was located. The section concludes with a review of the ethical considerations taken for this research, particularly with regard to the interviews conducted.

The third section of this chapter describes how the primary data obtained through the archival research and interviews was triangulated with secondary data obtained through the desk research consisting predominantly of reports produced by media outlets and civil society organisations, and a review of academic literature.[3] All data was analysed using an open coding method facilitated through the ATLAS.ti software.[4] Finally, the limitations

1 Mark C. Suchman, *Managing Legitimacy: Strategic and Institutional Approaches*, Academy of Management Review, 1995, 20(3), pp. 573-577; Max Weber, *Economy and Society: An Outline of Interpretive Sociology*, Berkeley: University of California Press, 1978.

2 Laura Beth Nielsen, The Need for Multi-Method Approaches in Empirical Legal Research, in: Peter Cane and Herbert M. Kritzer (eds.), The Oxford Handbook of Empirical Legal Research, Oxford Handbooks in Law, 2010, p. 955; Robert K. Yin, Case Study Research: Design and Methods, Sage: London, 2009.

3 Uwe Flick, *Triangulation in Qualitative Research*, A Companion to Qualitative Research, 2004, pp. 178-179.

4 Brigitte Smit, *Atlas.ti for qualitative data analysis*, Perspectives in Education, 2002, 20(3), p. 69; Juliet Corbin and Anselm Strauss, *Grounded Theory Research: Procedures, Canons, and Evaluative Criteria*, Qualitative Sociology, 1990, 13(1), pp. 12-13.

of this study are presented, alongside a discussion regarding the validity and generalisability of this research.

3.1 Research Approach

Given the legal and political nature of the post-conflict environment, which uses judicial and non-judicial means to redress gross human rights violations in politically volatile settings,[5] this research turned to tools that could examine the efforts made by the ICTR, which was itself established through legal and political means – as a product of UN Security Council Resolution 955.[6] The term legitimacy has been employed to understand the activities of the ICTR as it too carries strong ties to both law and political science.[7]

While political and legal scholars have established various criteria to define and understand the notion of legitimacy, the empirical approach used in this study examines the construction of legitimacy through interactions between an organisation and its stakeholders.[8] Organisations will adopt certain activities to justify their existence, their actions and behaviour to their stakeholders, while stakeholders may challenge the legitimacy of an organisation by contesting the justifications presented to them. This evaluative interaction between an organisation and its stakeholders, which relates to strategies aimed at gaining, maintaining and repairing legitimacy, is conducted through legitimisation actions.[9]

Unlike quantitative research methods, which are used for testing or confirming hypotheses to provide generalisable facts about a topic, qualitative research is used to explain or better understand patterns of behaviour or developments within a particular process. Exploratory and descriptive studies usually make use of qualitative and inductive research methods, whereas explanatory studies are more often quantitative and deductive in nature.[10] This research takes an explorative case study approach as it investigates the interaction between an organisation and its stakeholders within a particular context that

5 Pierre Hazan, *Measuring the impact of punishment and forgiveness: a framework for evaluating transitional justice*, International Review of the Red Cross, 2006, 88(861), p. 46; Barbara Oomen, *Transitional Justice and Its Legitimacy: The Case for a Local Perspective*, Netherlands Quarterly of Human Rights, 2007, 25(1), pp. 141-148.

6 United Nations Security Council, *The Situation Concerning Rwanda*. Provisional Report of the 3453rd Meeting, S/PV.3453, 8 November 1994.

7 See Chapter 2.

8 David Beetham, *The Legitimation of Power*, Basingstoke: Macmillan, 1991; Bottoms & Tankebe, 2012, p. 124; Suchman, 1995, p. 574.

9 David Deephouse, Jonathan Bundy, Leigh Plunkett Tost and Mark Suchman, *Organizational Legitimacy: Six Key Questions*, The SAGE Handbook of Organizational Institutionalism, 2017, pp. 17-19; Suchman, 1995, pp. 585-599.

10 Matthew David and Carole D. Sutton (eds.), *Social Research: An Introduction*, Sage, 2011, pp. 165-166.

has not been studied or thoroughly investigated in the past. This approach begins with a general idea that is refined through a series of stages, often referred to as primary and secondary research, which include a range of data collection methods such as a literature review, interviews and observation.[11]

In order to examine the fluid, multifaceted nature of empirical legitimacy in relation to international criminal courts, a single case study was considered as a way in which to provide a certain degree of depth, detail and understanding of the subject matter. The exploratory case study approach is often used to explain relationships that may be too complex for surveys or experimentation, and has been defined as *"an empirical enquiry that investigates a contemporary phenomenon in depth and within its real-life context, especially when the boundaries between phenomenon and context are not clearly evident"*.[12] This definition is fitting for the topic of legitimacy as it presents an approach that allows for the thorough analysis of the complex nature of this concept when applied to the actions of one international criminal court in particular, the ICTR.

Although there has been criticism of the case study approach, given that the results may be difficult to generalise, this form of research has *"the potential to contribute to the process of knowledge accumulation in a given field or in a society"*.[13] In this research, the single case study approach offers an opportunity to examine the activities of the ICTR in relation to its legitimacy, providing additional data and a different perspective to the theories related to organisational legitimacy, while offering insights for existing and future international criminal courts that may identify similar legitimacy challenges.

3.2 Data Collection

Following the exploratory case study approach, this research is comprised of two research stages in order to refine its focus, while also providing a more nuanced understanding of the subject matter.[14] Firstly, a literature review was conducted, which examined the notion of legitimacy and identified a large number of legitimacy challenges faced by the ICTR during its 20 years of existence. Secondly, semi-structured interviews took place by telephone, online via Skype or Zoom, or face-to-face during field trips to Rwanda and Tanzania; archival research was also conducted at several institutions in Rwanda and at the International Residual Mechanism for Criminal Tribunals (IR-MCT) in Arusha. In collecting data through different methods and using diverse sources, the information

11 Nielsen, 2010, p. 955; Smit, 2002, pp. 66-68; Corbin & Strauss, 1990, pp. 12-13.
12 Robert K. Yin, Case Study Research: Design and Methods, Sage: London, 2009, p. 14.
13 Bent Flyvbjerg, *Five Misunderstandings About Case-study Research*, Qualitative Inquiry, 2006, 12(2), p. 227.
14 Nielsen, 2010, p. 955.

received can be triangulated, which is crucial in obtaining a rich description of the phenomenon being studied.[15]

3.2.1 Literature Review

A literature review provides the foundations from which to gain knowledge of a particular topic, develop ideas, advance certain theories and compare research findings to existing knowledge. With the wealth of information available through the internet, and the fast-paced nature of developments in international criminal law, as well as an increasing number of researchers publishing reports, articles and blogs on a wide variety of issues linked to specific issues, it is also challenging to keep up with the latest research, while assessing all the data associated with a particular research area. This is why the literature review, as a research method, is more relevant than ever, providing a systematic way to collect and synthesise information available on any given topic.[16]

The literature review for this research was focused on three specific areas: defining and understanding legitimacy, the history and social context of Rwanda, and the creation and operations of the ICTR. In a first instance, a review of the literature related to the development of the notion of legitimacy was conducted, examining how perceptions of legitimacy are formed and the influence of legitimacy on the functioning of organisations or individuals in positions of authority or power. Given this research's focus on the ICTR, various studies were consulted that had focused on understanding how legitimacy is constructed through the interactions between stakeholders and (international) organisations; and the analysis of literature soon turned to organisational legitimacy, which immediately touched on the research – and the oft-used definition of organisational legitimacy – conducted by Mark Suchman.[17]

The literature review then turned to the history of Rwanda, focusing in particular on the dynamics that led the conflict that took place from 1990 to 1994, culminating in the 1994 genocide. The analysis of the information related to this topic stretched from the arrival of the Tutsi, Hutu and Twa ethnic groups on the land that is now known as Rwanda, to the personal anecdotes of those that experienced the genocide first hand. It was also important to examine the creation of the ICTR and other transitional justice mechanisms established following the 1994 genocide. Here too, the literature review examined reports related to the transitional justice efforts that took place in Rwanda, through Rwanda's national courts and the gacaca court system, while documents related to the creation of

15 Nielsen, 2010, p. 955; Smit, 2002, p. 66; Flick, 2004, pp. 178-179.

16 Hannah Snyder, *Literature review as a research methodology: An overview and guidelines*, Journal of Business Research, 2019, 104, p. 333.

17 Suchman, 1995, pp. 571-610.

the international tribunal in Arusha were also consulted, as were the more personal accounts of those that worked for the ICTR or who observed the trials that took place in Arusha.

The UN and IR-MCT websites were consulted for information regarding the ICTR. The ICTR's annual reports, financial audits, newsletters, press releases, completion strategies, founding documents and case files, were among the most relevant documents consulted for this research. Furthermore, 49 interviews were conducted with ICTR staff members in 2008 as part of the Tribunal's legacy project *"Voices from the Rwandan Tribunal"*,[18] which were recorded, transcribed and made available online, providing additional valuable insights for this research.

In order to access certain documents that were not available online, the IR-MCT was contacted directly. One such instance was to gain access to the original ICTR website, which was taken off-line during the course of this research: a link to a web-archive was made available with the help of staff based at the IR-MCT in The Hague.[19] Most other information related to the ICTR was found through internet searches, using key words entered in both French and English.

Many of the books consulted for this study, notably those related to organisational management and legitimacy, were retrieved through Maastricht University's library collection, which also gave access to other Dutch libraries through the inter-library loan system. Books that could not be borrowed locally were otherwise bought; on the whole these books consisted of first-hand accounts of the genocide, or personal reflections of those that had observed the (inner) workings of the ICTR.

Another key source of information came from reports written by civil society organisations, which were accessed online. The majority of these reports provided detailed insights into the unfolding of the genocide in 1994 and the aftermath, describing the situation in Rwanda as it developed from a post-conflict, fragile state towards its current state. Newspaper reports, those available online, offered a picture of these developments from a more immediate angle and provided precise dates that allowed for a narrative to form between the press releases or decisions issued by the ICTR and the reactions reported in the news. More recent accounts and opinion pieces were also consulted through blogs: these items allowed for the Kinyarwanda voice to be heard as translation tools could be applied to the text.[20] The accounts were more recent than the media reports from the 1990s and early 2000s, yet they also offered the views of Rwandans living in Rwanda, and those who had settled elsewhere, regarding political issues and the transitional justice mechanisms that had been established following the divisive conflict of the early 1990s.

18 Voices from the Rwanda Tribunal Project, website 'Tribunal Voices': http://www.tribunalvoices.org/.

19 Web archive for the original ICTR website: https://web.archive.org/web/20070729015547/; http://www.unictr.org/default.htm.

20 For example, Justice4Survivors: https://justice-survivors.com/.

Given the broad scope of the topics for this research – (organisational) legitimacy, the history of Rwanda and the ICTR – a selection had to be made in order to ensure a systematic review of the most relevant literature for this study. The process was fairly organic, with the reading of material on (organisational) legitimacy taking place almost simultaneously with the analysis of documents pertaining to the ICTR, and the activities taking place in Arusha. As ideas formed for the theoretical framework, regarding legitimisation activities and the importance of the interactions that take place between the stakeholder(s) and an organisation, the selection of documents related to the ICTR, its activities and its communication with its key stakeholders, also came to the fore. It is also important to note that although the literature review took a central role in the first two years of the research, the review of documents, reports and books was crucial throughout the entire research process.

Yet, despite the exploratory nature of this research, the literature review process carries the unavoidable risk of selection bias.[21] By choosing to study a particular topic, using tools that are easily available – for example Maastricht University's library – and submitting selected key words into internet search tools, this research was prone to selection bias. As such, the choice of certain books, articles, reports, media coverage and blogs could, by default, lead to certain conclusions. The scale of information now available thanks to the internet and the digitalisation of books may reduce the selection bias linked to location, and searching for and reading text in both English and French – the two languages used at the ICTR (official UN languages) and in Rwanda – also allowed for a wider access to information. Yet, the selection process remains in the hands of the researcher, from the initiation of the idea and research proposal to the search criteria (especially through the selection of key words) and the choice of literature.

In order to mitigate some of the risks associated with selection bias, this study turned to interviews in order to give more insight into the context and to provide a deeper understanding of the topics being examined. Although this approach clearly did not remove all the selection bias, as interview partners were also selected for this research, the semi-structured nature of the interviews allowed for new topics and themes to emerge during discussions that had not transpired during the literature review. Additionally, through snowballing techniques and haphazard meetings not all interviewees interviewed for this study featured on the original interview list. Furthermore, gaining access to the archives of the ICTR and other organisations that had worked with, or reported on the activities of, the Tribunal also provided another perspective regarding the research matter. A field trip to Tanzania was organised to consult the ICTR archive and interview former ICTR staff members living or working in Arusha; and a trip to Rwanda was also planned

21 Roger Gomm, Social Research Methodology: A Critical Introduction, Macmillan International Higher Education, 2008, p. 347.

in order to better understand the Rwandan context, to visit libraries and archives, and to meet and interview the representatives of other organisations that had worked with or alongside the ICTR, as well as former ICTR staff members living in Rwanda.

3.2.2 *Field Trips*

While an extensive literature review provided information on legitimacy types, legitimisation activities, the behaviour of (international) organisations striving to be perceived as legitimate, and information regarding the success of transitional justice mechanisms in post-conflict environments, the field trip to Rwanda and Tanzania served to bring these elements together by examining how the ICTR developed and implemented legitimisation activities in order to gain, maintain and/or repair its legitimacy. The visit provided an opportunity to gain a better understanding of the local context and also provided the chance to access data that was unavailable online or within Europe, notably the ICTR's archive located in Arusha. Travelling between Arusha and Kigali also gave a better idea of the distance (both literally and symbolically) between these two locations.

The fieldwork in Rwanda consisted of semi-structured interviews with government officials, journalists, academics, lawyers and judges, and the representatives of civil society organisations that were associated with the work of the ICTR. Additionally, interviews were conducted with former employees of the Tribunal living in Rwanda, notably those involved in the outreach programmes, the Witness and Victims Support Section, translators, investigators and lawyers (for both the OTP and defence teams). There was also an opportunity to visit and consult the archives and libraries of the National Commission for the Fight against Genocide (CNLG), the University of Rwanda (Butare campus), the New Times (Rwandan newspaper), IBUKA, the Institute of Legal Practice and Development (ILPD), the Legal Aid Forum (LAF) and the Kigali Genocide Memorial.

Given that several interviews had been organised prior to arriving in Rwanda and language was not considered an issue as French and English are widely spoken, it appeared that employing a research assistant would not be necessary. However, it was soon clear that all meetings required not only a research permit, but also an officially stamped letter requesting an interview and explaining the purpose of the research being conducted. The letters needed to be presented in person and stamped at each location prior to each interview. The same process was repeated for follow-up interviews, and also applied when visiting libraries and accessing archives.

During the first days in Kigali, informal meetings had been organised with contacts provided by researchers and interviewees based in Belgium, the Netherlands and the United Kingdom (UK), a few of whom had offered to serve as research assistants during the field trip. Following a couple of unsuccessful research days in Kigali, the choice was soon made to employ an experienced research assistant, who had worked with researchers from Germany, the UK, the United States of America (USA) and the universities of Tilburg and Maastricht in the Netherlands. Furthermore, although motorbike taxis can be found everywhere in Kigali, and buses and car services are readily available for longer trips, hiring a driver for the one-month research period in Rwanda also proved to be the most time- and cost-efficient way to travel both within Kigali and throughout the country.

A contract was signed (including a confidentiality clause) by the research assistant and the driver to ensure that the names of interviewees and the content of the interviews were not divulged to third parties. Although impossible to check on this, the recommendations from previous researchers provided some reassurance that the identities of interviewees would not be compromised. Providing a list of contacts to the driver and the research assistant ensured not only a swifter research process (interviews were grouped by location as far as possible), it also led to the addition of names and institutions that had not initially featured on the interview list. The addition of a research assistant and a driver to the 'research team' also allowed for impromptu meals with family members, visits to milk bars and hidden buffet-lunch spots, language and etiquette classes, and a trip to visit the driver's cow – an important commodity in Rwanda. The conversations in the car, including debriefs following each interview, also provided additional background information on life in Rwanda prior to, during and after the 1994 genocide.

Aside from a few ad hoc meetings with friends or family looking for advice on study or work opportunities (or coffee export) in Europe, at no point did the research assistant or the driver take control of the interview list or redirect the course of the research. This sentiment was, however, experienced in five other interviews, during which the list of all interviewees for this research was asked for (but not provided) and the topic of the study was questioned. In two cases the interviewees explained that the research would yield much better results if it addressed the gacaca court system rather than the ICTR.

There was no need to employ a research assistant in Tanzania as all interviews took place in Arusha and meetings were easily organised with interviewees, without the need to provide a research permit or a stamped letter.

The trip to Arusha in Tanzania was organised in order to visit the former location of the ICTR at the AICC and to consult the ICTR archive housed in a purpose-built facility at the Arusha branch of the IR-MCT. The IR-MCT is located just outside the town of Arusha, where approximately 20 former ICTR staff members were employed at the time of the visit (September 2019). The review hearing for Ngirabatware's case was also underway at the time, which meant that a number of former ICTR staff members had been recalled to assist in the proceedings, namely staff from the Witness and Victims Support Section, and former ICTR judges now working for the IR-MCT; it was therefore an opportune time to meet with a variety of former ICTR staff, and to conduct interviews. The IR-MCT canteen also provided the chance to meet with IR-MCT staff members and visitors who did not feature on the original interview list.

Additionally, a handful of former ICTR staff members that had stayed on to work for other institutions based in Arusha also agreed to be interviewed. Three interviewees acted as guides over the course of the stay, explaining the changes to the town of Arusha over the past 20 years, with one providing a tour of the former ICTR location at the AICC.

In addition to taking notes during the interviews, a diary was kept to record observations and experiences during the trips to both Rwanda and Tanzania. The diary provided an opportunity to digest the day's events and more closely consider certain ideas or thoughts. On returning to the Netherlands, the diary also served as a way to revisit some of the discussions that took place during the trips or impressions of events that had taken place, and to reflect on themes that transpired during the interviews.

3.2.2.1 Archival Research

During the trip to Rwanda, opportunities arose to visit and consult archives located at CNLG and IBUKA that could shed light on the workings of the ICTR, particularly in relation to its interactions with these two organisations. There was also a chance to view the archive of The New Times, an English language newspaper established in Rwanda in 1995, which provided an insight into the news coverage of the Tribunal (and other transitional justice mechanisms operating in Rwanda) from 1995 to 2015, through news articles that are not accessible online. As well as archives, the libraries held by CNLG, LAF, ILPD, the University of Rwanda and the Kigali Genocide Memorial gave access to a range of books that had not featured during the initial literature review, while also shedding light on which books were available in Rwanda regarding the ICTR, international criminal law and other topics related to transitional justice.

The archival research in Arusha focused on the ICTR's administrative archive, rather than the judicial section of the archive, as the aim of the visit was to uncover any policy papers or internal memorandum related to legitimisation activities, specifically communications and/or outreach strategies. Both the judicial and the administrative archives are housed in a large, tailor-made facility located opposite the IR-MCT courtroom. The ICTR's judicial records are extremely well organised and also contain active dossiers, given that the IR-MCT continues to work on certain cases. The ICTR's administrative archive is, unfortunately, not at all organised, aside from a simple (also disorganised)[22] categorisation of boxes labelled as classified and unclassified. The boxes generally contained a large number of press clippings, often accompanied with annotations written by ICTR

22 Despite the labelling of classified and unclassified boxes, certain documents in the unclassified boxed were reported to the archivist as containing sensitive information. The boxes appeared to have been filled randomly, as they contained a variety of documents from various departments and different years.

staff members, or stapled to a paper highlighting some key points. The majority of the documents appeared to originate from the Registry as speeches, conference presentations and internal 'housekeeping' documents were found; however, there were also internal memos documenting the interactions between the various organs of the Tribunal.

Although the archival research at the IR-MCT did not uncover any documents linked to a communication or outreach strategy, the information held in the administrative archive did provide an insight into the workings of the Tribunal, and gave voices to the various ICTR staff members that had played a key role either behind the scenes or in front of the cameras.

A selection process therefore also took place when reviewing documents from the ICTR's administrative archive, however, given that the initial aim was to uncover documents that were not present (for example policy papers linked to a communications strategy or an external relations plan), the archival research resulted in an open assessment of all the documents that were accessible. Additionally, given that there was no order to the papers placed in the boxes, every sheet of paper was consulted in order to ensure that valuable information was not put aside.

The archival research also provided an unexpected way to break the ice with former ICTR staff members (some of whom were then working for the IR-MCT). Interviewees were keen to know what information was being uncovered and whether anything relevant to their current work had been found: budget sheets from previous years, information related to certain visits that had taken place, or conference papers on certain topics etc.; others were interested in the content of the archive for nostalgic reasons; and those working at the IR-MCT library hoped that the research would stimulate funding to organise the administrative records.[23]

It should also be noted that gaining access to archives in both Rwanda and Arusha required jumping through a variety of bureaucratic hoops. While it is understandable that organisations require information about which records need to be consulted for purely practical reasons, CNLG and IBUKA requested additional details on the purpose of the research and the need for specific information related to the Tribunal, while the IR-MCT in Arusha asked for an exact list of the documents that were to be consulted, which was challenging given that they themselves did not know what was available in the ICTR's administrative records. In both cases, the luxury of time – and in Rwanda with the guidance of a research assistant – provided the possibility to deliver the documentation requested and to contact the appropriate persons in order to gain access. This was, however, not the

---

23 N.B. no information was shared at the time, but a general description of the documents that were being held was provided. Any access to the archive was strictly regulated and a staff member was present for the duration of the archival research, which took place in a room by the archive. Boxes were brought out at the start of every day and replaced at the end of the day. All photocopies taken were checked before they left the premises. There is still no inventory regarding the contents of the administrative archive (August 2021).

case at The New Times, where verification of the research permit was enough to grant access to the documents required.

3.2.2.2 Semi-Structured Interviews

The aim of conducting semi-structured interviews was to obtain additional, anecdotal data to compliment and add to the literature review and the archival research. The interviews provided a manner in which to interact with the topic through discussions with individuals that had worked at the Tribunal or in organisations that were operating alongside the ICTR. The interviews provided a space to experiment with certain ideas and assumptions concerning the subject matter, and to uncover topics that had not been addressed or uncovered during the literature review. The discussions with interviewees proved to be determinative to the research by exposing a narrative regarding legitimacy and the work of the Tribunal that started emerging over the course of the two field trips.

Qualitative interviews are designed to further understand and unravel the subject of a research, and to provide insights into a particular phenomenon, while also offering information regarding the general context in which certain events occur.[24] Reading about events or hearing certain thoughts regarding perceptions is insightful but may remain two-dimensional, while discussing an individual's perceptions or thoughts regarding a particular topic during an interview allows for a wider exploration as to when and why certain perceptions were formed, identifying elements that may be important in understanding a particular event or activity.[25] Yet perceptions of legitimacy may be influenced by a multitude of factors, especially in the context of international criminal courts operating in transitional, post-conflict environments. Given the personal, anecdotal nature of interviews, they need to be validated against other sources, which, in this case, was provided through the literature review and archival research, including newspaper articles and civil society reports.[26]

In order to gain insights into the Tribunal and its legitimacy, interviews were conducted with the representatives of organisations that had worked with or alongside the ICTR at some point during its 20 years of existence, including news agencies that had covered the trials in Arusha or that were established in Rwanda at the time. In setting up the interviews, contact was made with organisations that were associated with the work of the ICTR, during which the research objectives were explained and a time for an interview was requested. A representative for each organisation was selected and contacted via email, based on their position and connection with the work of the ICTR. In five cases, another

24 Lisa Webley, *Qualitative Approaches to Empirical Legal Research*, in: Peter Cane and Herbert M. Kritzer (eds.), The Oxford Handbook of Empirical Legal Research, Oxford Handbooks in Law, 2010, p. 937.

25 Todd Landman, *Social Science, Methods and Human Rights*, The Sage Handbook of Human Rights, 2014, pp. 194-195.

26 Gomm, 2008, p. 242; Flick, 2004, pp. 178-179.

representative of the organisation with more experience or knowledge of the work of the ICTR was proposed by the original contact person, either in addition to, or instead of, the individual initially contacted. Staff members from the ICTR that had been involved in external relations, including the outreach programmes, were also contacted for an interview via email. In one case an interview was conducted with a lawyer with the same name as a former ICTR staff member, who had worked at the same law firm in Kigali. Despite the mistaken identity, the interview went ahead, providing another perspective on the ICTR's work.

A total of 71 interviews took place between July 2019 and April 2020. The interviews varied in length from 40 to 120 minutes. The majority of the interviews took place during the field trips to Rwanda and Tanzania in August and September 2019; interviews also took place in the Netherlands, Belgium, the UK and also by telephone and online via Skype or Zoom. The interviewees consisted of independent journalists and researchers, and representatives of the following organisations:

- Aegis Trust
- African Court on Human and Peoples' Rights
- Association des Veuves du Genocide Agahozo (Avega)
- Caritas Rwanda
- Communauté des Potiers du Rwanda (COPORWA)
- Court of Appeal (Rwanda)
- East African Community (EAC)
- Genocide Fugitive Tracking Unit (GFTU)
- Great Lakes Initiative for Human Rights Development (GLIHD)
- IBUKA
- International Criminal Tribunal for Rwanda (ICTR)
- International Residual Mechanism for Criminal Tribunals (IR-MCT)
- La Fondation Hirondelle
- Legal Aid Forum (LAF)
- National Commission for the Fight Against Genocide (CNLG)
- National Public Prosecution Authority (Rwanda)
- National Unity and Reconciliation Commission (NURC)
- Never Again Rwanda
- Norwegian People's Aid
- RCN Justice & Démocratie
- Solace Ministries
- The New Times
- University of Rwanda

All interviewees were asked for an interview via telephone, e-mail or in person, during which information was shared regarding the research project and the purpose of the interview. Once the interviewee agreed to participate in the study, an interview was scheduled. At the beginning of the interview, information about the research project was provided again and questions were answered, if the interviewees had any. Prior to the interview, some interviewees asked for the list of questions and, given the semi-structured nature of the interviews, they were sent an overview of the topics that would be addressed. Interviews took place in French and in English, with one conducted in Kinyarwanda with the research assistant providing the translations.

The interviews conducted were semi-structured in nature. As such, the topic of the interview was introduced to the interviewee and general questions were asked during the course of the interview, to guide the flow of the conversation. The objective of this form of interview is to provide interviewees with the freedom to raise any points that they find relevant to the topic in question. The conversation therefore develops organically and provides a range of insights that may otherwise be overlooked.[27] A follow-up interview, conversation and/or communication via telephone or email took place with 24 of the original 71 interviewees.

Both anonymity and consent were guaranteed prior to the interview. Consent to be interviewed was asked during the initial contact with the interviewee, following a short introduction to the research. All interviewees were contacted prior to the interview in order to invite them for the interview and to inform them of the nature of the interview. Furthermore, as stated in the consent form (provided in French or in English) presented at the start of the interview, the participants were informed that they could withdraw from the research at any time. Consent was asked to ensure that the participant understood the nature and purpose of taking part in the research, and to ensure that they agreed to the use of the information provided during the interview.

No audio or visual recordings were made during the interviews for two reasons: firstly, to allow interviewees to respond more freely, without worrying about the recording of the discussion; secondly, recording was not deemed necessary, as the main objective of the interviews was to validate findings from the literature review and to identify additional information that might provide insights regarding the activities of the ICTR. Instead a request was made for written notes to be taken. In Rwanda, the research assistant was present and took notes during almost all the interviews. Each interviewee was informed of the possible presence of a research assistant and their consent to his presence was requested again at the start of each interview.

Although some interviewees agreed to be cited with their full name and the name of their affiliated organisation, anonymity was granted to all interviewees to protect the

27 *idem.*, p. 229.

identity of those who preferred to remain anonymous. All interviewees agreed to be referred to in the context of their organisation; however, given that some of the organisations were small and that there were always several witnesses who were aware of who was being interviewed, each interviewee was coded under one of the following six categories – the government (G), civil society (CS), academia (A), the Rwandan judiciary (J), the media (M), and those that had worked at the ICTR (T) – rather than listed as a representative of a specific organisation.

In order to further ensure the anonymity of each interviewee, all the dates of the interviews have also been removed from this research: in both Rwanda and Tanzania there is a requirement to sign in and out when visiting an organisation, and to state the reason for the visit, even if just to request an interview, or to consult a library or an archive. It would therefore be incredibly easy to trace an interviewee using the date of the interview. Although offering full anonymity has consequences for the accountability of this research – preventing the possibility of reviewing some of the research findings – providing a comprehensive list of the organisations that were represented for the interviews, together with details on the subject matter, provides the information required to repeat this study.[28] Offering anonymity gave interviewees the chance to talk freely during the interviews without thinking about any possible repercussions.

Individuals that were contacted for an interview occasionally provided the contact details of another potential interviewee. This phenomenon is known as snowball sampling and is a common practice in empirical research; however, this sampling method runs the risk that more interviewees with similar points of view are interviewed, representing a one-sided approach to a topic.[29] This bias is similar to the selection bias, whereby the research may be skewed towards a particular conclusion.

Besides contacting the representatives of organisations involved in some way with the ICTR's work in Arusha, the accommodation chosen during the trips to Rwanda and Tanzania played a larger role than initially anticipated. Both places were chosen for their location and the possibility of conducting interviews in a private corner of the lobby area, with good access to a stable internet connection and reasonable rates. In Rwanda, these criteria were met by the Onomo Hotel in Kigali, which opened its doors in December 2018, just a few months prior to the scheduled research visit. This not only allowed for excellent rates and good services, including a large lobby area that allowed for private conversations, it also meant that the hotel – part of a chain of African hotels – was in full promotion mode: organising conferences, networking evenings and brunch meetings. The various events organised by the hotel provided an excellent opportunity to meet with the

28 *idem.*, p. 386.
29 *idem.*, p. 152.

representatives of organisations and government bodies that had not featured on the initial interview list.

Likewise, albeit in a different fashion, the Sundown Carnival Hotel located at the foot of the hill where the IR-MCT was located, just outside Arusha, had turned into a mini-outpost for those working on the review hearing for Ngirabatware's case. This also offered an opportunity to meet with individuals that had not featured on the original interview list. Furthermore, although a car service was offered by the hotel for the short 2 kilometre trip to the gates of the IR-MCT, there was often an offer of a lift by someone driving to or from the premises, which provided the chance to speak to more people involved with the work of the IR-MCT, the former ICTR and/or international criminal law in general, forming another way in which to diversify the conversation with regard to the perceptions of the ICTR's legitimacy. The meal times in both countries, and road trips in Rwanda, also provided the chance to speak with various people from different walks of life that had not initially been contacted or connected with this study.

As such, in addition to the 71 'official' interviews, numerous informal conversations took place that were related in some way to the research topic, transitional justice or international criminal law. These conversations are not considered interviews as they were not conducted in the formal setting of an interview, and consent forms were not signed. Among these conversation partners were former members of the RPF, young Rwandans that were born after the genocide, staff working at the IR-MCT, refugees from both sides of the conflict that had since returned home or who are still based in Europe, Europeans that had lived in Rwanda prior to the 1994 genocide, and Rwandan farmers, some of whom were keen to direct the research focus towards the economic developments taking place in Rwanda or to discuss export opportunities, rather than to discuss the tragic events of the past. Although all of these informal conversations have not been directly referred to in this book, they provide contextual background that was key to this research.

Additionally, several individuals were also informally consulted during the literature review that took place at the start of this research, which assisted in focusing the objectives of the study and provided background information related to the inner workings of the ICTR; these conversations continued throughout the research. Yet there were also conversations that did not take place. During the trip to Rwanda, two individuals that had initially agreed to an interview decided that they did not want to go on-record to discuss the research topic; these two interviews therefore transformed into an informal conversation, which remained off-record. Finally, one Rwandan individual, who was contacted due to his work at the ICTR, did not want any connection at all with research addressing the 1994 genocide nor the work of the Tribunal in Arusha.

3.2.2.3 Ethical Considerations

The section above details some of the main ethical considerations taken into account in the design of this study: consent was requested from interviewees at two stages of the research, in requesting and scheduling an interview and at the start of the interview itself; the participation of interviewees was voluntary; and all interviewees were guaranteed confidentiality and anonymity.

Given that human subjects were involved in the study, the research design was presented to the Ethics Review Committee Inner City faculties (ERCIC) at Maastricht University. This provided an opportunity to refine the research design in order to ensure that all ethical considerations had been taken into account before commencing the empirical part of the study. A second ethical review of the research design was conducted by the University of Rwanda's Ethics Committee in relation to the empirical research taking place in Rwanda, which formed part for the process of receiving a Rwandan research permit.

In order to obtain a permit to conduct research in Rwanda, researchers must be affiliated with an academic institution within the country. For the purpose of this study, Dr. Denis Bikesha, Dean of the School of Law at the University of Rwanda (UR), agreed to supervise this research for the duration of the field trip in Rwanda. In order to be affiliated with the UR, the research needed to be approved by the UR's Ethics Committee. Once these steps had been taken, the application for a research permit could be submitted to the National Council for Science and Technology (NCST). Following its approval, the research permit was then collected in person upon arrival in Kigali. This research permit was required in order to schedule all the interviews in Rwanda, and was checked by the interviewee at the start of every interview. The permit was also required in order to access archives and some of the libraries located in Rwanda. The process was simpler for Tanzania, as a C1 study visa was applied for using an online form, together with an invitation letter issued by the IR-MCT.

Despite the affiliation with both UR and the IR-MCT, there were no constraints imposed on this research by either organisation, nor was there any request for remuneration, apart from a € 60 administration fee from UR for processing the research permit requirements.

3.2.2.4 Temporal Concerns

As demonstrated in Chapter 2, time plays an important role in the perception of legitimacy. The literature review demonstrated that the ICTR's legitimacy was questioned throughout its lifetime and the interviews conducted for this research aimed to gain more information regarding these legitimacy challenges and the legitimacy of the Tribunal. However, interviewees could only be expected to provide recollections of their general perception of the Tribunal's legitimacy and/or its legitimacy in connection to certain events, rather than offer an accurate account of what they had thought at a particular moment in time.

The interviewees were asked to describe instances when they questioned the legitimacy of the Tribunal, or viewed it as a legitimate organisation, which in most cases they were able to do. Yet, the information provided involved asking the interviewees to recount certain memories, which could easily have been distorted by more recent events, or tainted by media reports or discussions within the community, for example.

Furthermore, the ICTR was created in a particular moment in time, which is easy to forget due to the fast-paced development of international criminal law. The challenges associated with creating an international criminal court and the issues related to a lack of infrastructure are difficult to visualise when visiting the modern and vibrant city of Kigali and town of Arusha. Also, progress in communications (internet and social media) has made giant strides, even since 2015 when the ICTR closed its doors. These general developments already project a very different image (almost incomprehensible) of the legitimacy challenges faced by the ICTR from 1994 to 2015, especially in comparison to the international courts working in today's world.

In line with this, the needs and expectations associated with the work of the ICTR also changed over the course of the Tribunal's 20-year lifespan. During the first years of the ICTR's activities in Arusha, Rwanda was recovering from a devastating conflict that had taken the lives of approximately 10% of its population, and the process of rebuilding the country had started in earnest;[30] while in the final years of the Tribunal's operations, Rwanda's economy was strong, and its social development and infrastructure was considered among the most developed on the African continent.[31] The role of the Tribunal therefore also changed within this rapidly evolving context, while the wider geo-political landscape also transformed over the years, from 1994 to 2015, influencing the way in which the Tribunal's legitimacy was defined.

One way to address this limitation was to consult personal accounts written by journalists and ICTR staff members, reports published by civil society organisations and newspaper articles, in order to capture a snapshot of the Tribunal's legitimacy written at a certain point in time. These accounts were then triangulated with the information shared during the interviews.[32]

The archival research at the IR-MCT also provided an opportunity to examine the internal and external communications produced by the Tribunal on specific dates and

---

30 Alison L. Des Forges, *Leave None to Tell the Story: Genocide in Rwanda*, Human Rights Watch, 1999, pp. 15-16; United Nations Security Council (1999). *Report of the Independent Inquiry into the actions of the United Nations during the 1994 genocide in Rwanda*, S/199/1257, 15 December 1999; Marijke Verpoorten, *The Death Toll of the Rwandan Genocide: A Detailed Analysis for Gikongoro Province,* Population, 2005, 60(4), pp. 332-333.

31 Bloomberg, *Africa's Would-Be Switzerland Shows Economic Clout With WEF*, 10 May 2016. Retrieved from: https://www.bloomberg.com/news/articles/2016-05-09/africa-s-would-be-switzerlands-flaunts-economic-prowess-with-wef.

32 Nielsen, 2010, p. 955; Smit, 2002, p. 66; Flick, 2004, pp. 178-179.

related to certain topics. The ICTR archive consisted of numerous clippings of newspaper articles collected by the Tribunal staff, together with handwritten notes, which also gave an indication as to the events and topics that were on the Tribunal's radar.

Yet, regardless of the number of documents available and the accuracy of the interviewees' recollections, there is no doubt that a longitudinal study conducted from the time of the deliberations at the UN Security Council in late 1994 to the closure of the Tribunal in December 2015 would have produced a more accurate account of the ICTR's legitimacy over the course of its lifespan, including the changes in perceptions associated with the Tribunal's actions.

3.3 Data Analysis

In qualitative research, data analysis is based on language, images and observations often involving some form of textual analysis. For the purpose of this study an analysis of the themes arising from the literature review, the archival research, the interviews and the interactions that took place during the research all played a role in examining the activities of the ICTR in relation to its legitimacy and legitimisation activities. Content analysis was used as a way to categorise the meaning of words, phrases and sentences in line with the theoretical framework described in Chapter 2.[33] The coding of all the text, including the notes taken during the interviews and all the documents copied during the archival research, brought to light new themes that had not surfaced during the field trip.

All data that was available in word or PDF was analysed using ATLAS.ti software; the documents that had been photocopied were coded by hand.[34] In line with the exploratory approach taken for this study, the coding of the text took an inductive approach, which consists of utilising an open coding technique: highlighting and coding certain phrases using labels that categorised the text into various themes. The coding allowed for a reflective process to take place, with new themes arising, and different codes introduced or removed. The coding structure was therefore continuously refined over the course reading and re-reading the texts.[35] At the end of the process, a total of 37 codes were used to tag 804 quotations in the documents uploaded to the ATLAS.ti software.

With the codes in place, the data could be analysed to show any patterns, ambiguities and/or inconsistencies within the text of the transcribed interviews, or in the various communications produced by the ICTR. In some cases, interviewees were contacted via

33 Smit, 2002, pp. 66-67.

34 Scanning of documents was not possible in January 2020 due to the cyber-attack experienced by Maastricht University, followed by the COVID-19 measures put in place from 12 March 2020. Most of the documents that had been photocopied during the archival research were therefore not uploaded to ATLAS.ti.

35 Smit, 2002, p. 69; Corbin & Strauss, 1990, pp. 12-13.

email, Zoom or Skype in order to clarify a point that had been made, or to request more information on a particular topic.

The triangulation of the different data sources offered a way in which to validate the conclusions that were drawn regarding certain topics.[36] This was especially important when examining legitimacy challenges that had occurred in the early years of the Tribunal's existence, which relied predominantly on speeches, press releases and reports written at the time, and which were also coloured by the memories of interviewees. Indeed, although the semi-structured interviews provided data that may not be generalisable beyond the sample group or the case study chosen for this research, they did provide a more in-depth understanding of the events and actions that had taken place at specific times over the course of the Tribunal's history.

Even though the closure of the ICTR in December 2015 prevented an examination of the Tribunal in action, it did provide an advantage of looking back at the activities of the ICTR from start to finish, and gave an opportunity to examine the legacy of the organisation. The chosen scope of this research was therefore based on both theoretical and practical reasons, which relate to specificity of the research project and its feasibility.[37] That said, the following section will take a closer look at the limitations of this study and the research design.

3.4 LIMITATIONS

In addition to the selection bias previously mentioned, this section examines other limitations related to conducting empirical research. The main challenge linked to empirical research, in particular when conducting interviews, is the effect of the interviewer and the interview setting. The behaviour of an individual will immediately change when in an interview setting, being asked questions, and in this case the interviewee was being asked to respond as a representative of their current or former organisation. As a result, the unnatural situation created by the interview setting may well cause an interviewee to respond differently than they would in another, neutral or more informal setting.[38] This interview effect was one reason why it was decided not to record any interviews, and rather to take notes. Furthermore, complete anonymity was guaranteed. Yet this does not mean that an interviewee will not respond differently to questions asked in a formal interview setting. Indeed, there were several occasions during which the interviewee spoke more freely about the topics discussed during the interview the moment the 'official' interview

36 Gomm, 2008, pp. 241-243; Flick, 2004, pp. 178-179.
37 Flyvbjerg, 2006, pp. 224-226.
38 Gomm, 2008, p. 222.

was over; for example, interviewees would disclose important information on the way to their car or the lift.

In line with this, the topic and/or the location of the interview may influence the information that is shared. For the purpose of this study, the interviewee had the option to choose the location of the interview: the interview usually took place at the interviewee's place of work, but also took place in hotel lobbies, in cafés or in restaurants. In one case an interviewee chose a busy restaurant, where a large number of the other patrons were known to him and came to the table to say hello. These various settings not only have an influence on the interviewee, and inform the capacity in which the interview is taking place, they also impact the interviewer.

Remaining an impartial, unbiased, neutral interviewer is also a challenge, and a limitation in empirical studies.[39] Maintaining the same professional behaviour in each interview and holding back any signs of agreement, disagreement or surprise during the interaction is imperative. Yet, gaining the trust of an interviewee while refraining from divulging any personal expectations or opinions is a fine balance, especially when broaching sensitive topics. Several interviewees asked specific questions at the start of the interview in order to gauge any assumptions that might be held, and the angle of the research being conducted by a European researcher, while three interviewees attempted to change the topic of the research, which they considered was of little importance. Responding to these questions in an objective fashion, without disclosing any personal views was one way of minimising any interviewer effects, yet it is near impossible to remove the bias of both the interview situation and the interviewer asking questions.

Additional factors such as gender, ethnicity, nationality and age also play a role in the interaction between the interviewer and interviewee.[40] Indeed, age and status plays an important role in Rwanda and was evident during the interviews: with the younger or junior level interviewees seemingly eager to engage, while more senior interviewees seemed wary of yet another researcher asking questions, with one interviewee asking whether they would ever see the results of the discussion or hear of this research again. Indeed, with a large number of researchers interested in Rwanda (in particular the Rwandan genocide), there seemed to be a sense of interview fatigue with some interviewees (including the three mentioned above) keen to discuss another topic.[41]

In line with the interviewer bias, the personal bias is a challenge that is also difficult to remove from empirical research. There is no doubt that the content and the manner in which the interviews were conducted changed over the weeks spent in Rwanda and Tanzania. There is a better understanding of the topic, the culture and the environment,

39 *idem.*, pp. 221-222.
40 *ibid.*
41 David & Sutton, 2011, p. 266.

the acquisition of some phrases in Kinyarwanda and Swahili (in Tanzania), and a familiarity starts to form with both the country and the interview setting. Furthermore, through the series of discussions with different interview partners, opinions start to form along with a better understanding of the context. The organic change in a researcher is undoubtedly apparent during an interview, and may indeed make the interviewer better equipped to ask the right questions. However, the familiarity and ease of subsequent interviews may also divulge forming ideas that influence the answers or behaviour of the interviewee.[42]

Comprehension bias was another limitation experienced during some of the interviews, where the words and context were understood but the message sometimes came across as confusing, or interviewees appeared to contradict themselves. This often related to cultural or linguistic misunderstandings.[43] For this the presence of a Rwandan research assistant was incredibly helpful. A debriefing meeting was held after every interview, which served as a moment to test ideas and compare notes. Yet, the cultural disparities remained even with the research assistant, which is why conversations with Rwandans that (had) lived in Europe for several years, and Europeans who (had) lived in Rwanda, also helped in gaining a better understanding of the data that had been collected.

The comprehension bias is, however, impossible to completely remove, especially as a foreign researcher with a different cultural background. The specificity of having lived, or been raised, in a country that has experienced genocide made the field trip to Rwanda indispensable. Yet, as stated by one interviewee "*if you haven't lived it, you will never understand it*".[44] During some interactions there was a sense that an underlying tension or code was influencing the conversation, and there were clearly cultural sensitivities and nuances that were lost during the interactions, or indeed moments that were impossible to understand. In one case, the research assistant had disclosed having worked closely with an interviewee, yet there were no signs of recognition between the two from the start to the end of the interview. This was questioned during the debriefing directly after the interview, to which the research assistant explained that he had followed the lead of the interviewee – a person of more seniority – and given that they had shown no sign of recognition the research assistant had done the same.

Indeed, there was also a risk of bias in bringing a research assistant to the interviews. On the one hand the assistant opened many doors by acting as a guide to the distinctive research protocols that had to be followed in order to schedule an interview – even if an appointment had been made by email, a formal request needed to be made by hand delivering a letter to the office of the person in question. On the other hand, the assistant also bore witness to all the interviews and was himself Rwandan; the social or cultural

42 Gomm, 2008, p. 243.
43 *idem.*, pp. 242-243.
44 Interviewee CS3.

associations made between the interviewee and the research assistant, who was affiliated to the research, may have had an influence on the interview. A confidentiality agreement had been signed as a condition of working as an assistant to the research, and this was explained prior to the start of each interview. Furthermore, there was not one occasion in which an interviewee asked to meet without the research assistant, or where more information was asked about the research assistant or even the driver. However, the political undertones and lack of cultural awareness may have prevented any nuances, non-verbal communication or discomfort on the part of the interviewee from being recognised.

In addition to the cultural differences, there was also a chance of a comprehensibility bias through language. Although just one interview required translation as it was conducted in both Kinyarwanda and English, the use of French and English in interviews may have given a false sense of understanding, especially with regard to implicit communication. Certain nuances may well have been missed or misunderstood due to cultural disparities, yet given that the same language was being spoken, this could very well have been overlooked. Throughout the trip in Rwanda it was also clear that etiquette and non-verbal communication played an important role in all interactions. Although guided by a research assistant, it would have been impossible to catch a moment in which a misspoken word or action may have changed the course of the interview. Furthermore, despite the relationship of trust built with the research assistant, there remained an imbalance due to the payment for his work, which may also have impeded him from pointing out any mistakes made during an interview.

On a more personal note, while health and safety issues did not raise any concerns in the planning of the trips to Tanzania and Rwanda, the historical sensitivities that have played out between the French and the Rwandan governments were taken into account when organising the trip to Rwanda. Deciding not to travel to Rwanda with a French passport was a conscious decision, and no mention of French nationality was disclosed during the trip. It is near impossible to assess whether possessing the French nationality would have had any impact on the data collection for this research, even though the potential risk of influencing the interviews or access to archives was perceived as great enough to withhold this information.

The final limitation to be addressed in this section is the generalisability of this research. The in-depth, exploratory approach of this single case study research has produced findings that are specific to the particular case in question. Any conclusions regarding the ICTR and its legitimisation activities may therefore be difficult to generalise to the conditions or situation of another international criminal court. Indeed, the following chapters will demonstrate that the ICTR operated under particular conditions, different even to the ICTY operating at the same time. However, by examining the notion of legitimacy in relation to the ICTR, the importance of this concept and the role it plays in the functioning of an international criminal court is already a significant finding. Furthermore, there are general lessons that can be learnt from the interactions between the ICTR's key stakeholders, which reflect the dynamics experienced by current day international courts.[45]

Although it is clear that examining the actions of a specific international criminal tribunal – with a complex governance structure, working in a politically sensitive geopolitical environment – through the lens of legitimisation activities runs the risk of losing the broader context, or even missing out on the intricate layers of organisational management or international relations. Yet focusing on one organisation and observing its relationship with the notion of legitimacy also allows for a deeper understanding of the complexities of running an international organisation within this multifaceted environment. In many ways, choosing to examine just one international criminal tribunal, focusing on one conflict that took place in one country, is a means to simplify and understand an already complex subject matter.

45 Flyvbjerg, 2006, p. 227.

4 Looking Back: A Legitimate Tribunal?

The aim of this research is to understand how the Tribunal sought to establish itself as a credible court of law, operating in the emerging environment of international criminal law and working within a post-conflict environment. Before examining the legitimisation activities implemented to address specific legitimacy challenges (Chapter 5), this chapter examines whether the ICTR was perceived as legitimate, and if so, how it gained its legitimacy. The chapter makes use of the interviews and documents uncovered during the archival research to better understand the relationship between the Tribunal and the perceptions of its legitimacy. In doing so, this chapter touches on the three sub-questions of this research:

- Why was legitimacy important for the ICTR?
- What challenges did the ICTR face that threatened its legitimacy?
- How did the ICTR respond to the threats to its legitimacy?

In line with the first and second sub-questions, the first section of this chapter examines how the concept of legitimacy is defined, focusing particularly on how the term is interpreted alongside the term legality by highlighting the similarities and differences between these two concepts. In doing so, this first section highlights an initial legitimacy challenge faced by the Tribunal, related to its legality, providing an insight into the legitimisation activities implemented by the ICTR, which are examined in more detail in Chapter 5.

Understanding how the term legitimacy is interpreted leads to the second section of this chapter, which examines how the ICTR may have gained legitimacy, namely how and why perceptions of the Tribunal's legitimacy emerged. A key factor in providing the ICTR with legitimacy was explained through its recognition of the 1994 genocide and its ability to arrest and prosecute senior military and political figures, while other interviewees emphasise its affiliation with the UN as being a defining factor in the Tribunal's legitimacy.

The third and final section of this chapter examines the concept of legitimisation,[1] which refers to the third sub-section for this research – *how did the ICTR respond to threats to its legitimacy* – by providing an insight into the actions and activities implemented by the Tribunal in order to manage its organisational legitimacy. The section also demonstrates that the Tribunal was aware of the importance of its legitimacy – although it is the ICTR's

1 Also known as *legitimation* (Blake E. Ashforth and Barrie W. Gibbs, *The Double-Edge of Organizational Legitimation*, Organization Science, 1990, pp. 177-194; David Deephouse, Jonathan Bundy, Leigh Plunkett Tost and Mark Suchman, *Organizational Legitimacy: Six Key Questions*, The SAGE Handbook of Organizational Institutionalism, 2017, pp. 17-19).

image that is most commonly referred to – and in 2003 established an *External Relations and Strategic Planning Section* that focused specifically on all external communications. Given that various words are used interchangeably to describe the concept of legitimacy, the chapter starts by examining how certain interviewees define legitimacy.

4.1 Legitimacy versus Legality

As discussed in Chapter 2, there are numerous interpretations of the term legitimacy. The Latin roots of the word provide an affiliation with law, yet there is also an association with philosophy, politics and sociology.[2] Legitimacy is connected to the notions of consent, authority and social order – originally presented through the works of Hobbes (1651), Locke (1689) and Rousseau (1762), and later by Weber (1922) [3] – while studies also link the term to concepts of accountability and regulation.[4] The scope of this notion of legitimacy was encapsulated by the director of a Rwandan civil society organisation, who was initially hesitant to offer a definition given that his background was in the social sciences and not in law:[5]

> "Legitimacy comes from lex, which is the Latin for law, so legitimate means something is recognised as legal. But legitimacy can go above and beyond the law. Everything that is acceptable, that is recognised socially can be called legitimate."[6]

---

2 Mattei Dogan, *Conceptions of Legitimacy*, Encyclopedia of Government and Politics, 1992, 1, pp. 116-126; Ian Hurd, *Legitimacy and Authority in International Politics*, International Organization, 1999, 53(2), pp. 379-408; Oxford dictionary, 'legitimacy'. Retrieved from: https://www.lexico.com/definition/legitimacy; Tom R. Tyler, *Why People Obey the Law*, Princeton University Press, 2006; Sergey Vasiliev, *Between International Criminal Justice and Injustice: Theorising Legitimacy*, in: Nobuo Hayashi and Cecilia M. Bailliet (eds.), *The Legitimacy of International Criminal Tribunals*,Cambridge University Press (2016), 2015.

3 Thomas Hobbes, *Leviathan*, John C. A. Gaskin (ed.), Oxford University Press, Oxford, 1998; John Locke, *Second Treatise of Government: An Essay Concerning the True Original, Extent and End of Civil Government*, John Wiley & Sons, 2014; Jean-Jacques Rousseau, *Rousseau: 'The Social Contract' and Other Later Political Writings*, Cambridge University Press, 1997; Max Weber, *Economy and Society: An Outline of Interpretive Sociology*, Berkeley: University of California Press, 1978.

4 Julia Black, *Constructing and contesting legitimacy and accountability in polycentric regulatory regimes*, Regulation & Governance, 2008, 2(2), pp. 137-164; Jason Sunshine and Tom R. Tyler, *The Role of Procedural Justice and Legitimacy in Shaping Public Support for Policing*, Law and Society Review, 2003, 37(3), pp. 513-548.

5 This may have been due to the research focus on the ICTR, and an assumption that the question on legitimacy was focused on a legal definition; however no mention of law was given prior to this question, and other interviewees that did not have a legal background did not make this connection to the Latin root of the word.

6 Translated from French: "*La légitimité vient de lex, qui est le latin pour la loi, donc légitime signifie que quelque chose est reconnu comme légal. Mais la légitimité va au-delà de la loi. Tout ce qui est acceptable, qui est reconnu socialement peut être qualifié de légitime.*" (CS11).

Indeed, aside from this interviewee, most interviewees that referred to the Latin origins of the term did have a legal background and they too made the distinction between legality and legitimacy: the link between the rule of law and the need for legitimacy. As one government official explained:

> "Legitimacy is linked to sovereignty. Courts are made by law, but it is the legitimacy of those who make the law that is important. The key issue with law is how it is put in place, how it is adopted. The law needs to be legitimate. This ties in with the legitimacy of the government, which is considered sovereign, that makes the law."[7]

In the literature, the legitimacy of a government is dependent on certain factors, namely the manner in which it was established, the actions that it takes, and the behaviour of its officials.[8] This statement illustrates how legitimacy is linked to the sovereignty or authority of the government, which is then projected through the justice system. In Rwanda, judges are appointed by the government, and the government decides on the laws, hence the need for "*the legitimacy of the government*".[9] Following their appointment, by a legitimate government, the legitimacy of a judge is based on their own behaviour and actions, and on their legal analyses.[10] A judge is expected to issue unbiased, balanced opinions when resolving disputes: there is a "*need for the legitimacy of those that both write the law and those that implement it*".[11] This demonstrates the connection between legality and legitimacy: the rule of law must itself be considered legitimate in order to be effective.[12]

In this sense, legality and legitimacy are intertwined, with both concepts requiring the other in order to exist: "*Legitimacy is the 'raison d'être' of the court. It is rooted in international norms to try violations of human rights and to try the international crime of genocide, therefore it is legitimate*".[13] This statement, provided by the representative of a civil society organisation when discussing the ICTR's legitimacy, as a court of law, was echoed by others, namely those working within the Rwandan justice system: "*It demonstrated an effective, good use of law. So yes, it was legitimate*".[14] In fact, the need to

---

7 Interviewee G3.

8 Weber, 1978, pp. 217-245.

9 Interviewee G3.

10 Tyler, 2006, pp. 135-139.

11 Interviewee G3.

12 Daniel Z. Epstein, Rationality, *Legitimacy, & the Law*, Washington University Jurisprudence Review, 2014, 7, p. 6; Lisa Hilbink, *The Origins of Positive Judicial Independence*, World Politics, 64(4), 2012, pp. 592-595.

13 Translated from French: "*La légitimité est la raison d'être de la cour. C'est enraciné dans les normes internationales de juger les violations des droits de l'homme et de juger le crime international de génocide, donc c'est légitime.*" (CS18).

14 Interviewee J1.

distinguish between the two terms, in the case of the ICTR, was perceived as redundant by some:

> "Legitimate? Yes, it was legal. Did it even seek legitimacy? Distinguish between legality and legitimacy. They did not mean to be legitimate. Was it their priority? They believed that their legitimacy came from their legality. They were legitimate through legality; that's how they saw it."[15]

Indeed, legal scholars have argued that if an organisation complies with the rule of law, it can essentially be considered legitimate.[16] Yet from its inception, the ICTR did not receive universal acceptance that it had legitimate legal authority: as an international criminal court, addressing the crimes that occurred in the sovereign state of Rwanda, the legality of the Tribunal was questioned.[17] The Tribunal's authority was not based on treaty law, but rather on a resolution created by the UN Security Council based on Chapter 7 of the UN Charter.[18] This was a clear challenge in gaining legitimacy for the newly established ICTR.

Prior to the establishment of the ICTY, there was no precedent for creating an international criminal tribunal or court through UN Chapter 7; referring specifically to Article 41, the Charter states that:

> "The Security Council may decide what measures not involving the use of armed force are to be employed to give effect to its decisions, and it may call upon the Members of the United Nations to apply such measures. These may include complete or partial interruption of economic relations and of rail, sea, air, postal, telegraphic, radio, and other means of communication, and the severance of diplomatic relations."[19]

Imposing sanctions is one thing, establishing a court of law is another. However, the UN Charter gives the UN Security Council primary responsibility to maintain peace and

---

15 Translated from French: "*Légitime? Oui, c'était légal. At-il même cherché la légitimité? Faites la distinction entre légalité et légitimité. Ils ne voulaient pas être légitimes, est-ce-que c'était leur priorité? Ils croyaient que leur légitimité venait de leur légalité. Ils étaient légitimes par la légalité; c'est ainsi qu'ils l'ont vu.*" (CS20)

16 Joanna Nicholson, *Strengthening the Effectiveness of International Criminal Law through the Principle of Legality*, International Criminal Law Review, 2017, 17(4) (2017), pp. 656-681; Benjamin Schiff, *Lessons from the ICC for ICC/R2P Convergence*, The Finnish Yearbook of International Law 2010, 21(1); Vasiliev, 2015, pp. 19-20.

17 ICTR, *Prosecutor v. Joseph Kanyabashi*, Decision on the defence motion on jurisdiction, ICTR-96-15-T, 18 June 1997, p. 3.

18 United Nations, *Charter of the United Nations*, 24 October 1945, Chapter 7.

19 United Nations, *Charter of the United Nations*, 24 October 1945, Article 41.

security; this is clearly stated under Articles 24 and 39 of the UN Charter.[20] Furthermore, Article 41 does not exclude establishing a tribunal; the list of measures is not exhaustive.

Yet the legality of the Tribunal was raised in 1997, during one of the first trials held in Arusha. In his opening statement, Evans Monari – a defence lawyer for Joseph Kanyabashi – argued that the UN Security Council had no authority to establish the Tribunal, given that the conflict in Rwanda did not pose any threat to international peace and security.[21] A further objection by Monari claimed that the Tribunal was infringing on the sovereignty of states following the principle of *jus de non evocando*, which offers the accused the right to be tried in a domestic court.[22] Monari claimed that this principle had not been respected and that the ICTR did not have the authority to exercise primacy over Rwanda's national courts.[23] Furthermore, Monari highlighted that the UN was established to focus on states rather than on individuals, and that the trials taking place at the ICTR were politically motivated.[24]

In response to the legitimacy challenge, the Trial Chamber adopts a legitimisation activity related to *conforming to the environment* using established models that are rooted and recognised in society:[25] on 18 June 1997, judges Sekule, Khan and Pillay agreed to examine the motion presented by the defence.

> "Notwithstanding the fact that some of the questions raised by the Defence Counsel have already been addressed in the decision rendered on 2 October 1995 by the Appeals Chamber for the Former Yugoslavia, the Trial Chamber finds that, in view of the issues raised regarding the establishment of this Tribunal, its jurisdiction and its independence and in the interests of justice, that the Defence Counsel's motion deserves a hearing and full consideration."[26]

---

20 Article 24: "*In order to ensure prompt and effective action by the United Nations, its Members confer on the Security Council primary responsibility for the maintenance of international peace and security, and agree that in carrying out its duties under this responsibility the Security Council acts on their behalf.*" (United Nations, *Charter of the United Nations*, 24 October 1945, Article 24(1)); and
Article 39: "*The Security Council shall determine the existence of any threat to the peace, breach of the peace, or act of aggression and shall make recommendations, or decide what measures shall be taken in accordance with Articles 41 and 42, to maintain or restore international peace and security.*" (United Nations, Charter of the United Nations, 24 October 1945, Article 39).

21 ICTR, *Prosecutor v. Joseph Kanyabashi*, Decision on the defence motion on jurisdiction, ICTR-96-15-T, 18 June 1997, para. 7(ii), 9 & 25.

22 *idem.*, para. 7(i), 7(iii), 9, 30 & 31.

23 *idem.*, para. 7(iii) & 31.

24 *idem.*, para. 7(i), 33, 37 & 45.

25 Suchman, 1995, p. 589.

26 ICTR, *Prosecutor v. Joseph Kanyabashi*, Decision on the defence motion on jurisdiction, ICTR-96-15-T, 18 June 1997, para. 6.

Following a full hearing on the matter, addressing each point raised by Monari, the motion was finally dismissed:

> "The Trial Chamber simply reiterates that, pursuant to Article 1 of the Statute, all persons who are suspected of having committed crimes falling within the jurisdiction of the Tribunal are liable to prosecution. The Trial Chamber is not persuaded by the arguments advanced by the Defence Counsel that the Tribunal is not impartial and independent and accordingly rejects this contention."[27]

The Trial Chamber enforces the Tribunal's cognitive legitimacy by referring to protocols and procedure,[28] and the message is delivered by elected judges within one of the Tribunal's courtrooms, emphasising "*professionalisation*" which further demonstrates the authority and competence of the ICTR.[29] Subsequently, the argument regarding the legality of the ICTR was never raised again. A member of the Rwandan judiciary provides a reason as to why they think this is the case:

> "The ICTR was created through the UN Charter. This had never been done before. Does the UN Security Council have the power to create a tribunal? It is not forbidden, so that means that it is allowed. It was a great idea to create a tribunal through the Security Council. This is power that Nuremberg did not have. Power provides the autonomy to rule. But there are different angles to take. Those tried by the ICTR say that the ICTR is not legitimate. They challenged the court from the beginning, but then they accepted the legitimacy of the ICTR. They did this because norms come from law. The ICTR was a UN institution. The UN established it. It was therefore legitimate."[30]

In addition to the UN's legal basis for establishing the Tribunal, through Chapter 7 of the UN Charter, it was the Rwandan government that approached the UN Security Council with regard to establishing a criminal court.[31] Yet was this legal standard, and the request for a tribunal from the Rwandan government, enough to solidify the ICTR's position as a legitimate international criminal court? The following section takes a closer look at the various factors that might have provided the Tribunal with its legitimacy.

---

27 *idem.*, para. 49 & 50.

28 Suchman, 1995, p. 589.

29 *ibid.*

30 Interviewee J4.

31 United Nations Security Council, *Letter dated 94/09/28 from the Permanent Representative of Rwanda to the United Nations addressed to the President of the Security Council*, S/1994/1115, 29 September 1994. Retrieved from: https://digitallibrary.un.org/record/197773?ln=en.

4.2 Gaining Its Legitimacy

One could argue that facts are formed through the perception of a particular event or situation; likewise, one may deem something or someone to be legitimate, or to speak the truth, while another may have a different opinion. Although legitimacy is intertwined with the notion of legality, which reflects the *normative approach* to assessing legitimacy,[32] the recognition of the ICTR as a legitimate international criminal tribunal can also be assessed using the *empirical approach*, which associates assessments of legitimacy with a social value such as consent or acceptance.[33]

This second approach (empirical) provides another perspective to the normative approach – which makes use of societal or legal standards to assess the legitimacy of the ICTR as a court of law[34] – as it is based on contextual or cultural definitions (or perceptions) of legitimacy and may even be contingent on the social identity (age, gender, socio-economic background or education) of the individual or group making the legitimacy assessment.[35]

This empirical approach is helpful in understanding the different 'levels' of legitimacy that were sometimes described by the interviewees: *"The ICTR was legitimate. It was better than the Nuremberg trials, which were also legitimate, but not as legitimate as the ICTR. The international community needed to do something for Rwanda"*.[36] When pressed to explain the difference in legitimacy between the Nuremberg Military Tribunal and the ICTR, the interviewee explained that the war was over when the Nuremberg trials took place, which was not the case in Rwanda, as the former regime had simply left the country; the Tribunal was therefore needed to address the crimes committed in order to prevent another conflict from erupting.[37] Rwanda had experienced a continuous cycle of violence – or *"(smaller) genocides"*[38] – between the Hutu and Tutsi ethnic groups since the

32 Daniel Bodansky, Jeffrey L. Dunoff and Mark A. Pollack, *Legitimacy in International Law and International Relations*,Interdisciplinary Perspectives on International Law and International Relations: The State of the Art, 2013, pp. 321-341.

33 Allen E. Buchanan, *Justice, Legitimacy, and Self-Determination: Moral Foundations for International Law*, Oxford University Press, 2007; Vasiliev, 2015.

34 Daniel Bodansky, Jeffrey L. Dunoff and Mark A. Pollack, *Legitimacy in International Law and International Relations*,Interdisciplinary Perspectives on International Law and International Relations: The State of the Art, 2013, pp. 321-341.

35 Mitchell A. Seligson, *The Impact of Corruption on Regime Legitimacy: A Comparative Study of Four Latin American Countries*, The Journal of Politics, 2002, 64(2), pp. 422-423 & 450; Henri Tajfel (ed.), *Social Identity and Intergroup Relations*, Cambridge University Press, 2010, p. 255.

36 Interviewee CS12.

37 *ibid.*

38 Scott Straus and Lars Waldorf (eds.), *Remaking Rwanda: State Building and Human Rights After Mass Violence*, University of Wisconsin Press, 2011, p. 50.

country's independence in 1959.[39] The ICTR was therefore regarded as a way to put an end to the tensions within the country and to restore peace in the region.[40]

Furthermore, the trials conducted by the ICTR also served as a means to documenting the conflict in Rwanda: *"There is a genocide history in all the regions. If you want to know what happened in various parts of the country, it is all on file"*.[41] The murder of approximately six million Jews by the Nazi regime during World War II was a notoriously well-documented genocide, which facilitated the task of prosecuting those most responsible during the Nuremberg trials.[42] This was not the case in Rwanda, where the genocide was effectively organised through word of mouth[43] and, for a large part, coordinated through radio broadcasts.[44] The use of witness testimony was therefore key in establishing events that had taken place in Rwanda in 1994.[45] When asked about the Tribunal's legitimacy, a former ICTR staff member alluded to this when explaining importance of the ICTR archive, which holds the historical records of the events of 1994: *"Did it legitimate itself? Look at how it acted, what did it do? It acknowledged the genocide. It contributed to the history of the genocide, look at all the testimonies we collected"*.[46]

4.2.1 Recognition of the Genocide

The assessment of the ICTR's legitimacy demonstrated up to this point are largely based on the actions of the Tribunal. The very establishment of the ICTR recognised the genocide in Rwanda, and subsequent trials recognised other events that had taken place in Rwanda, which also provided the ICTR with legitimacy. According to a journalist who covered the trials in Arusha:

---

39 Interviewees CS12, CS13, J4 & A10; Straus & Waldorf, 2011, p. 50.

40 Interviewee CS12.

41 Interviewee T24.

42 Zygmunt Bauman, *The Uniqueness and Normality of the Holocaust*, in: *Modernity and the Holocaust*, Cambridge: Polity Press, 1991, p. 98; Nancy A. Combs, *Fact-Finding without Facts: The Uncertain Evidentiary Foundations of International Criminal Convictions*, Cambridge University Press, 2010, pp. 11-12.

43 Rwanda's "*thousand hills*" assist in the administrative organisation of the country, which is divided into five provinces (North, East, South, West and Kigali City), 30 districts and 416 sectors. Within these sectors, the country is divided into cells (2,148 in total) and villages (14,837). This administrative system has traditionally revolved around the '*hill*', which consists of a collection of families who live together (interviewees G1 & CS3; Rwandan government website, 'administrative structure'. Retrieved from: https://www.gov.rw/government/administrative-structure#c4493; Taraku & Karlsen, 2002, p. 18).

44 Jose E. Alvarez, *Crimes of States/Crimes of Hate: Lessons from Rwanda*, Yale Journal of International Law, 1999, 24, p. 392; ICTR, *Prosecutor v. Ferdinand Nahimana*, Jean-Bosco Barayagwiza and Hassan Ngeze (Media Case), Judgment and Sentence, ICTR-99-52-T, 3 December 2003.

45 Mohamed Othman, *The 'Protection' of Refugee Witnesses by the International Criminal Tribunal for Rwanda*, International Journal of Refugee Law, 2002, 14(4), p. 495.

46 Interviewee T10.

> "The good of the ICTR is as follows: the genocide against the Tutsi was recognised by the international community; rape was recognised as a weapon of war; and the world woke up. It was time to end impunity. International criminal law restarted. Waking up consciousness."[47]

Indeed, going back to Suchman's definition of organisational legitimacy, the emphasis is on *"the actions"* taken by an organisation: *"Legitimacy is a generalised perception or assumption that* ***the actions***[48] *of an entity are desirable, proper, or appropriate within some socially constructed system of norms, values, beliefs, and definitions"*.[49] Connecting legitimacy to the actions of the organisation is demonstrated by the following list of accomplishments that the director of a civil society organisation provided when asked about the Tribunal's legitimacy:

> "The ICTR was legitimate because one, it recognised genocide; two, it recognised rape as a weapon for the genocide; three, the archives are collections of important documents for the future; four, the ICTR made efforts to disseminate their activities, what they accomplished; and five, Jean Kambanda accepted his role in the genocide as a representative of the government. This demonstrated the government's active role."[50]

Indeed, a reoccurring theme linked to the ICTR's legitimacy was that of recognition:

> "Rwandans were very happy when the international community established the court. It was established early on, not too late, and recognised genocide against Tutsi. This was important for the survivors as important people were arrested. The Tribunal also recognised rape as a crime of genocide and there was the Karemera trial. Recognising the genocide was a turning point."[51]

Several interviewees explained that the recognition of the genocide against the Tutsi was the first indication for them that the Tribunal was a legitimate criminal court; this was

---

47 Interviewee M2.
48 Bold font added.
49 Suchman, 1995, p. 574.
50 Translated from French: *"Le TPIR était légitime parce que, un, il reconnaissait le génocide; deux, il a reconnu le viol comme une arme du génocide; trois, les archives sont des collections de documents importants pour l'avenir; quatre, le TPIR s'est efforcé de diffuser ses activités, ce qu'il a accompli; et cinq, Jean Kambanda a accepté son rôle dans le génocide en tant que représentant du gouvernement. Cela démontre le rôle actif du gouvernement."* (CS6).
51 Interviewee CS7.

sometimes followed by the recognition of rape as a crime of genocide, as mentioned above[52] and by the employee of another civil society organisation, who had worked closely with witnesses who took part in trials at the Tribunal:

> "The ICTR had an important role because it recognised the facts. It made sure there was no impunity. It recognised rape of women as a crime and the fear here [Rwanda] has now gone. This is important. People, Rwandans are coming back. The génocidaires[53] are no longer in power."[54]

This way of allocating legitimacy to an organisation can also be labelled as *output legitimacy*, which assesses legitimacy based on the results - or output - of an organisation, or the impact of actions that are considered effective in addressing certain issues. This form of legitimacy increases when the needs of individuals in society are met.[55] The notion of output legitimacy was also aptly described by another interviewee:

> "You ask whether the ICTR was legitimate? Did it deliver? This would be output legitimacy. Delivery and necessity. Objectively, what was the issue? The genocide. If this issue calls for such a tribunal you can decide whether it is legitimate or not. Corruption may affect the delivery. Is it worth it? It is worthwhile if the delivery, the output is achieved. This is the same as for a marriage, people enter it for different reasons, for love or for babies. They will judge the legitimacy of the marriage based on whether their expected outcome is delivered."[56]

In response to this interviewee, it appears that the very establishment of the Tribunal and the recognition that atrocious crimes were committed was a key indicator in assessing the legitimacy of the Tribunal: *"It was important. It was legitimate. In the Nyiramasuhuko case there were victims of sexual violence. This was recognised as a genocidal act by the*

52 Interviewee CS7.

53 *Génocidaire* is the Rwandan term used to refer to a perpetrator of genocide (in French this term would be referred to as *génocideurs*). In the context of the Rwandan genocide, the term is used to describe both those that have been convicted of committing an act of genocide and those alleged to have committed an act of genocide (Thierry Cruvellier, *Court of Remorse Inside the International Criminal Tribunal for Rwanda*, University of Wisconsin Press, 2010, pp. 4-5).

54 Interviewee CS22.

55 Fritz W. Scharpf, *Problem Solving Effectiveness and Democratic Accountability in the EU*, Max-Planck-Institut für Gesellschaftsforschung (MPIfG) working paper, 2003, 3(1), pp. 4-5; Vivian A. Schmidt, *Democracy and Legitimacy in the European Union Revisited: Input, Output and 'Throughput'*, Political Studies, 2013, 61(1), p. 3.

56 Interviewee A8.

international community."[57] Indeed, the acknowledgement by the international community is key, and was also mentioned as an important factor in the fight against the denial of genocide:

> "The ICTR was an important contribution. So many genocides have happened in this world, but only three are recognised. Rwanda's genocide is recognised, this is incredible. The establishment of the court demonstrates recognition worldwide. This is especially important for the deniers, also those in Europe."[58]

The need to establish the fact that a genocide did take place in 1994 was emphasised by several interviewees, especially given the history of conflict in Rwanda and the denial of the genocide "*which has been present since 1959*".[59] This appears to be reflected in the response of another interviewee, the director of a civil society organisation based in Rwanda, when asked about the legitimacy of the ICTR: "*it is the truth, legitimacy means the truth*".[60] Through its jurisprudence the ICTR – and by default the UN and the international community – acknowledged the genocide of 1994, which was especially important, given that the international community failed to label the gross human rights violations taking place in Rwanda as genocidal acts during the conflict itself.[61] Indeed, as stated by another interviewee "*What is needed for legitimacy is agreeing on the facts and understanding the context*".[62] According to the majority of the interviewees, the creation of the ICTR put an end to any doubt regarding the 1994 genocide in Rwanda.

The ICTR therefore gained legitimacy by conforming to its environment, in this case responding to the needs and expectations of its stakeholders.[63] These actions reflect both pragmatic and moral legitimacy: the Tribunal delivers the outcomes that are expected (the Tribunal was established to prosecute those responsible for the crime of genocide),[64] which reflects pragmatic legitimacy; while the recognition of a genocide in Rwanda also satisfies the moral and ethical conscience of its stakeholders in line with moral legitimacy.[65]

57 Interviewee CS21.
58 Interviewee G4.
59 Interviewee A10.
60 Translated from French: "*c'est la vérité, la légitimité signifie la verité.*" (CS13).
61 Luke Glanville, *Is "genocide" still a powerful word?* Journal of Genocide Research, 2009, 11(4), pp. 467-474; Barbara Harff, *No Lessons Learned from the Holocaust? Assessing Risks of Genocide and Political Mass Murder since 1955*, American Political Science Review, 2003, 97(01), pp. 58, 64.
62 Translated from French: "*Si c'est la légalité contre la légitimité. Ce qu'il faut pour la légitimité, c'est de s'entendre sur les faits et de comprendre le contexte.*" (CS19).
63 Suchman, 1995, pp. 587-588.
64 United Nations Security Council, *Resolution 955*, S/RES/955, 8 November 1994, preamble; United Nations Security Council, *Statute of the International Criminal Tribunal for Rwanda* (as amended on 31 December 2010), 8 November 1994, Article 1.
65 Suchman, 1995, pp. 587-588.

4.2.2 *Apprehending the 'Big Fish'*

In addition to the recognition of the crimes of genocide that had taken place in Rwanda, and the documentation of witness testimony, another key factor in assessing the Tribunal's legitimacy was its ability to apprehend those most responsible for planning, instigating, and aiding and abetting the genocide against the Tutsi in 1994, otherwise referred to as the 'big fish'.[66] The relevance of this was not lost on those working for the Tribunal at the time: *"At first there was quite some resistance, but over time the Rwanda government softened its stance towards the ICTR. Especially at the beginning, when all the 'big fish' were seen to be arrested. The ICTR had resources that the Rwanda government did not have"*.[67] The resources that came with the international criminal tribunal appear to have played an important role in measuring the legitimacy of the ICTR:

> "To assess its legitimacy you must look at the creation, implementation and completion. Was there a failure to comply with international criminal law? Was there impact to justice? The ICTR did what national courts could not do. Rwanda did not have human resources, there was no capacity in Rwanda then, the ICTR brought a level of diplomacy."[68]

This sentiment is echoed by another interviewee, who refers back to the legal footprint of the Tribunal as well as its ability to prosecute those most responsible for crimes committed in 1994: *"The ICTR was legitimate and has played a big role in international norms. It tried those who planned, incited and lead the genocide"*.[69] Indeed, when discussing the importance of international courts for transitional justice, a Rwandan academic made reference to the impact that arresting and prosecuting senior government officials had on those living in Rwanda: *"Although many were against the ICTR here, it was important in addition to the national courts and the gacaca. Of all the cabinet ministers of the former government, only two escaped justice. If it weren't for the ICTR they would all be free. Living outside of Rwanda"*.[70]

Despite the Tribunal's capacity to apprehend key players involved in the 1994 genocide, the early release and acquittals of some of the individuals prosecuted in Arusha had an adverse effect on the Tribunal's legitimacy – a topic which will be further developed in

66 In international criminal law, 'big fish' refers to those most responsible for the commission of international crimes (Hitomi Takemura, *Big Fish and Small Fish Debate–An Examination of the Prosecutorial Discretion*, International Criminal Law Review, 2007, 7(4), pp. 677-685).

67 Interviewee T3.

68 Interviewee T24.

69 Interviewee CS21.

70 Interviewee A5.

Chapter 5.[71] Yet, as one government official stated: *"Also of importance are the cases that were judged. Although there were too few, this also is recognition of the acts of people. Even if they were acquitted, they were there in the courtroom"*.[72]

However, not all interviewees were impressed with the Tribunal's ability to apprehend the 'big fish', as a Rwandan journalist explained: *"The strategy of ICTR was to get the 'big fish' but this was their own interpretation. Some big fish were not convenient to catch and are still free"*.[73] This reference to the Tribunal's strategy raises the question regarding the origins of the ICTR's legitimacy. Rather than providing the ICTR with legitimacy it could be argued that the arrest of the 'big fish' was only possible due to the legitimacy of the ICTR.

This same logic could also apply to the Tribunal's recognition of the genocide: the only reason that the Tribunal's judgments regarding the crimes of genocide mattered was because of the ICTR's affiliation with the UN.[74] It is therefore not the ICTR's output, or results, that provided the Tribunal with legitimacy, but rather it was due to the ICTR's existing legitimacy that such actions, or output, were possible:

> "Catching the big fish, which was impossible for the Rwandan government to do. Not just because of resources, but the principle of sovereignty: the government can't go to other countries to arrest a fugitive, they need State cooperation. The link with the UN really helped with this. Also the fact that they stood trial. This was an important message for Rwanda and for the international community. Regardless of the length of sentence, it was important to see them there. It was a relief to see the Prime Minister and Bagasora stand trial."[75]

Indeed, apprehending the 'big fish' provided a means from which to gain (and maintain) legitimacy, yet these actions were also possible due to the ICTR's affiliation with the UN, which provided the Tribunal with legitimacy by default (a guarantee of sorts), while also providing resources in the form of funding and networks, which also enabled the arrests and prosecution of these 'big fish': *"It is clear that things went wrong at the ICTR, but the court was able to stop important people. The powerful people had to go to court. Regardless*

71 Section 5.7.
72 Interviewee G4.
73 Interviewee M2.
74 See Section 2.3.
75 Interviewee T21.

of how much time the ICTR took to try cases, and even the acquittals, the fact that the court was there and operational was enough".[76]

This balancing act between gaining legitimacy through actions, and making use of existing organisational legitimacy in order to act, is further examined in Chapter 5.[77] Although Suchman's initial definition of legitimacy clearly highlights that the actions of an entity can assist organisation in gaining legitimacy[78] – reflecting pragmatic legitimacy[79] – a later definition described by Suchman and his colleagues provides a broader definition of organisational legitimacy as being: *"the perceived appropriateness of an organization to a social system in terms of rules, values, norms, and definitions"*.[80] This definition does not focus on the actions of the organisation, but rather on an assessment of the organisation based on the social norms of its environment – reflecting moral and cognitive legitimacy.[81] The ICTR was regarded as a legitimate organisation given that it had been established by the UN, and as such the Tribunal was endorsed by 193 UN member states.[82] In line with this, the establishment of the ICTR sent a strong message that Rwanda and Rwandans were finally being recognised and acknowledged by the international community:

> "The UN hasn't changed, but at least they are doing something. They now accept Rwanda as more of an equal. It takes part in peacekeeping and conflict resolution in other countries. The UN's recognition of Rwanda is important. Also Bill Clinton confessing that he did not do enough to help is important. Even the Pope confessed to the Church's involvement. These actions help to reduce the issue of denial. It's time for Rwanda to move on from victimisation to active citizenship."[83]

The form of legitimacy demonstrated here may be regarded as input legitimacy, which focuses on the systems or structures that have established or selected the individual or

76 Translated from French: *"Il est clair que les choses ont mal tourné au TPIR, mais le tribunal a pu arrêter des personnes importantes. Les gens puissants ont dû aller au tribunal. Quel que soit le temps que le TPIR a mis pour juger les affaires, et même les acquittements, le fait que le tribunal était là et opérationnel était suffisant."* (CS13)

77 Section 5.8.

78 Suchman, 1995, p. 574.

79 *idem.*, p. 378.

80 Deephouse et al., 2017, p. 9.

81 Suchman, 1995, pp. 579-583.

82 United Nations website, 'About Us': https://www.un.org/en/about-us/.

83 Interviewee CS22.

organisation.[84] The most common example for input legitimacy is an election. The way in which an election is conducted and those that take part in the election play a role in deciding the legitimacy of the election result; input legitimacy generally increases if more people are able to take part in the election.[85] Yet, in line with this measure of legitimacy, it is surprising that not one interviewee raised Rwanda's veto of UN resolution 955; the resolution adopted by the UN Security Council to establish the ICTR.

4.2.3 The Legitimacy of the UN

Rwanda's temporary position on the UN Security Council from 1994 to 1995 provided the government with a seat at the negotiating table to discuss the establishment of an international criminal tribunal for Rwanda.[86] During discussions, the Rwandan delegation raised seven objections concerning the jurisdiction, location and structure of the proposed international tribunal.[87] These objections were, arguably, the first legitimacy challenges faced by the Tribunal, emerging before the ICTR had actually been created.

The first objection related to the temporal jurisdiction of the court: the Rwandan delegation argued that the Tribunal should address crimes committed from 1 October 1990, when the civil war in Rwanda began – this would also account for crimes committed during the civil war and any activities associated with the planning and incitement of genocidal acts.[88] Secondly, the delegation considered the resources allocated to the structure and composition of the Tribunal as insufficient to address the magnitude of the crimes committed on Rwandan soil.[89]

A third objection raised by the Rwandan delegation related to the court's authority to prosecute the three international crimes – war crimes, crimes against humanity and genocide – which the delegation insisted was a waste of resources given that the Tribunal only needed to focus on prosecuting the crime of genocide.[90] The fourth objection raised was directed at how the judges would be selected for the Tribunal, at which the Rwandan delegation insisted the countries that *"took a very active part in the civil war in Rwanda"* should not be permitted to propose candidates for such a position.[91] The commutation

84 Scharpf, 2003; Tom R. Tyler, *A Psychological Perspective on the Legitimacy of Institutions and Authorities*, in: John T. Jost and Brenda Major (eds.), *The Psychology of Legitimacy: Emerging Perspectives on Ideology*, Justice, and Intergroup Relations, Cambridge: Cambridge University Press, 2001, p. 416.

85 Scharpf, 2003.

86 David P. Forsythe, *Encyclopedia of Human Rights*, Oxford University Press, 2009, 1, p. 121.

87 United Nations Security Council, *The Situation Concerning Rwanda*. Provisional Report of the 3453rd Meeting, S/PV.3453, 8 November 1994, pp. 14-16.

88 *idem.*, p. 14.

89 *idem.*, p. 15.

90 *ibid.*

91 *ibid.*

and enforcement of sentences was raised as the fifth objection to UN Resolution 955, as the Rwandan delegation insisted that these decisions should be left to Rwandans alone to decide; and, in line with this, the delegation also objected to the absence of capital punishment, a sentence that was used in the Rwandan judicial system at the time.[92] Finally, the location of the tribunal was raised as the seventh, final, objection as the Rwandan delegation insisted that such a court should be located in Rwanda.[93]

The head of the delegation, Mr. Bakuramusta, summed up Rwanda's position regarding the establishment of an international court by stating: "my delegation considers that the establishment of so ineffective an international tribunal would only appease the conscience of the international community rather than respond to the expectations of the Rwandese people and of the victims of genocide in particular".[94]

In its capacity as member of the UN Security Council at the time, the Rwandan delegation to the UN Security Council eventually voted against UN Resolution 955, while the 13 other member states voted in favour of the resolution, and China abstained.[95] The Rwandan veto of Resolution 955 was raised by Kingsley Moghalu, a spokesperson for the ICTR, during a conference in 2000:

> "In the early years of the ICTR, the situation of open scepticism about the tribunal existed among Rwandan citizens. There were several reasons for this state of affairs, chief among them problems and delays the tribunal experienced in getting started, and initial disappointment that the ICTR could not impose the death penalty."[96]

Rwanda's opposition to UN Resolution 955 signalled a bad start for the Tribunal, certainly with regard to its legitimacy, and indeed the legitimacy of the international criminal law project as a whole, as explained by Oomen: *"an international court has the greatest chance of being perceived as legitimate if it involves the people concerned in its set-up".*[97] This

---

92 *idem.*, p. 16.

93 *ibid.*

94 *idem.*, p. 15.

95 China considered the events that occurred in Rwanda in 1994 as an internal conflict and therefore a matter for Rwanda, rather than the UN, to address (United Nations Security Council, *The Situation Concerning Rwanda*, Provisional Report of the 3453rd Meeting, S/PV.3453, 8 November 1994, pp. 3 & 11).

96 Kingsley Chiedu Moghalu, *The International Criminal Tribunal for Rwanda and the development of an effective international criminal law – legal, political and policy dimensions*, International Conference on Replacing the law of force with the force of law – African conflicts and the International Criminal Court, organised by the Committee for an Effective International Criminal Law in Konstanz, Germany, 5 April 2000, p. 13.

97 Barbara Oomen, *Justice Mechanisms and the Question of Legitimacy. The Example of Rwanda's Multi-layered Justice Mechanisms*, in: Kai Ambos, Judith Large, and Marieke Wierda (eds.), *Building a Future on Peace and Justice*, Springer Berlin Heidelberg, 2009, p. 184.

sentiment was shared by the UN Secretary-General in 2006 in a speech regarding the ICTR and the ICTY, who stated that: *"a key lesson learned from those experiences was that the interested State should be associated in the establishment of the tribunal".*[98]

Yet this set back was not mentioned during any of the interviews. On the contrary, interviewees spoke largely of the sense of relief felt when the news came that an international tribunal would be established for Rwanda: *"Rwandans were very happy when international community established the court".*[99] When asked about the Rwandan delegation's veto of Resolution 955, interviewees did not recall the veto, nor was it raised as a possible legitimacy challenge faced by the Tribunal. On the contrary, a former ICTR staff member – a Rwandan lawyer based in Kigali – explained the necessity of the Tribunal's location in Arusha, far from Rwanda, by stating that:

> "The Tribunal allowed for an independence of ideas and held a high level of impartiality. There was equality of arms. The prosecution also had to work. This is not like in the national system. There was no interaction between judges and lawyers outside of chambers. The building in Arusha had three wings. Judges and lawyers only met in court."[100]

This answer may be one indication of the influence of time on the perceptions of the ICTR's legitimacy.[101] Indeed, despite the seven objections raised by the Rwandan delegation in November 1994, assessments of the Tribunal's legitimacy appeared to refer either to the short term outputs of the Tribunal – recognising the genocide and arresting the 'big fish' – and/or its long-term impact: *"If you ask about legitimacy, how many people are satisfied by this exercise? The first choice should be Rwanda. Show society, show that there is a change."*[102] As a member of Rwanda's judiciary explains:

> "The ICTR faced some challenges, as did other international courts. But they achieved what they sought to do. It was an incredibly difficult mandate, and international criminal law was new and a number of challenges also impacted the task at hand. The Tribunal also had an impact on the legal system in Rwanda: genocide and international crimes were adopted into national legislation; the suspect now has certain rights. We have everything to do with

98 United Nations Security Council, *Report of the Secretary-General pursuant to paragraph 6 of resolution 1644 (2005)*, S/2006/176, 21 March 2006, para. 2
99 Interviewee CS7.
100 Interviewee T24.
101 Section 3.2.2.4.
102 Interviewee T24.

international crimes. The Tribunal helped with the capacity building of the legal sector. Lawyers, judges and students of law all had training there."[103]

For many, it was therefore the international community's recognition of the crimes committed in 1994 and the support received in arresting and prosecuting the 'big fish', while also strengthening Rwanda's own criminal justice system, that provided the ICTR with its legitimacy. The interviewees highlight how, in their eyes, the Tribunal therefore gained legitimacy by conforming to its environment: following accepted procedures and protocols, demonstrating moral values and adhering to the societal norms of an international criminal court. All three legitimacy types (pragmatic, moral and cognitive) played a role in enabling the ICTR to gain its legitimacy.[104]

The establishment of the ICTR, through UN Resolution 955, and its output, thanks to the support of the international community, was therefore key in determining its legitimacy: *"Legitimacy, yes. The UN created the Tribunal for the objective of prosecuting the génocidaires, which gives legitimacy to the court. It was also a way to stop crime. This was achieved, which makes it legitimate."*[105] The mission and objectives of the Tribunal were also key, as explained by an official from the Rwandan government: *"Yes, the ICTR was legitimate. It was established by a credible institution and its purpose was to establish the truth. Regardless of whether it was perfect or not, it had all the required needs for a legitimate court".*[106]

The affiliation to the UN therefore clearly played an important role in providing the Tribunal with its legitimacy, as explained by the director of a civil society organisation: *"The ICTR was legitimate because of the UN, there's nothing we can do about it. The UN is an internationally recognised institution."*[107] The same sentiment was shared by another interviewee: "*Legitimacy? Who started, created the mandate? This is important. It was established by the UN and the law. It was created after an international survey showing the security situation, made by the UN Security Council. This provides the ICTR with legitimacy."*[108]

In fact, the Tribunal's affiliation with the UN was of paramount importance, as a member of Rwanda's judiciary explained:

103 Interviewee J2.

104 Suchman, 1995, pp. 587-589.

105 Translated from French: *"Légitimité, oui. L'ONU a créé le Tribunal dans le but de poursuivre les génocidaires, ce qui donne une légitimité au tribunal. C'était aussi un moyen d'arrêter le crime. Cela a été réalisé, ce qui le rend légitime."* (T9).

106 Interviewee G4.

107 Translated from French: "*Le TPIR était légitime à cause de l'ONU, on ne peut rien y faire. L'ONU est une institution internationalement reconnue.*" (CS6).

108 Interviewee CS22.

> "The ICTR was evidently legitimate as it was a branch of the UN. This is the problem with the current ICC, which is treaty based. It can't work. It is not effective as States can decide to ratify or not, and they can leave if they wish. The connection with the UN is the best. [...] The link to the UN means that a country has no choice but to comply."[109]

Although in line with other interviewees, the last sentence of this response was surprising, given that the UN had failed to take action in stopping the genocide occurring in Rwanda. On the 20th anniversary of the start of the genocide the UN Secretary-General expressed regret for the UN's failure in both preventing and stopping the genocide that took place in Rwanda in 1994.[110] Indeed, having failed to prevent or intervene while mass killings took place in Rwanda, some remain convinced that the establishment of an international criminal tribunal was a way in which the UN member states tried to appease their guilt of inaction.[111] The political complexities of the UN's role and responsibility with regard to Rwanda and the genocide was raised during another interview:

> "France and Belgium supported the Hutu regime. This is clear. France has veto powers at the UN Security Council. It is due to the guilt and shame of the international community that the ICTR was established, but this turned bad to good, as the Tribunal recognised genocide in Rwanda for the first time. This is the most important factor."[112]

In March 1999, the UN Secretary-General established an independent inquiry into the events surrounding the UN's response (or lack thereof) to the 1994 genocide in Rwanda.[113] The subsequent report highlighted several key areas of miscommunication and inaction, including the UN's failure to respond to a cable – the 11th January Cable – sent by UNAMIR's Forces Commander, Canadian Lieutenant General Romeo Dallaire, in January

---

109 Interviewee J2.

110 United Nations Secretary General, *Commemoration in Kigali – Rwanda*,7 April 2014. Retrieved from: https://www.un.org/en/preventgenocide/rwanda/commemorations-2014.shtml.

111 United Nations Security Council, *The Situation Concerning Rwanda*, Provisional Report of the 3453rd Meeting, S/PV.3453, 8 November 1994, pp. 15-16; Sara Kendall and Sarah M. H. Nouwen, *Speaking of legacy: toward an ethos of modesty at the International Criminal Tribunal for Rwanda*, American Journal of International Law, 2016, 110(2), p. 215; Victor Peskin, *Beyond Victor's Justice? The Challenge of Prosecuting the Winners at the International Criminal Tribunals for the Former Yugoslavia and Rwanda*, Journal of Human Rights, 2005b, 4(2), p. 215.

112 Interviewee CS21.

113 United Nations Security Council, *Report of the Independent Inquiry into the actions of the United Nations during the 1994 genocide in Rwanda*, S/199/1257, 15 December 1999. Retrieved from: https://www.un.org/en/ga/search/view_doc.asp?symbol=S/1999/1257.

1994. The cable had issued a stark warning of the risk of a genocide in Rwanda.[114] Yet the report directs most of its criticism at the UN Security Council's reaction to the first reports of the killings. UNAMIR had been operational in Rwanda on a peacekeeping mission since October 1993, and had provided regular updates on the gravity of the situation. Despite this, the report indicates that the UN Security Council was reluctant to authorise a more robust peacekeeping force, together with the necessary additional resources, in order to assist the troops on the ground.[115] Indeed, following the death of ten Belgian peacekeepers on 7 April 1994, Belgium immediately withdrew its troops from Rwanda, and there was little interest from other UN member states to contribute to UNAMIR in Rwanda, much less strengthen its mandate.[116]

The UN report states that the inaction of the international community *"has led to widespread bitterness in Rwanda."*[117] UN staff faced a hostile atmosphere in Rwanda in the years following the genocide, with Rwandans disheartened by the UN's failure to intervene and Rwandan authorities calling for answers for the lack of international action.[118] This sentiment was echoed by another interviewee:

> "The UN was here. People felt protected and some who had fled even returned because they felt safe. Some of the victims sheltered in a school because it was being guarded by the UN. But when the Interahamwe arrived the UN fled and all those in the school were killed. [...] The génocidaire government was also supported by foreign governments. Those that are also part of the UN Security Council. It felt at the time like the country did not have the weight, the importance to be protected. Even Mitterand said it was a tribal war, a different type of conflict. These superpower countries were only interested in protecting themselves."[119]

114 *idem.*, pp. 10 & 33.

115 United Nations Security Council, *Report of the Independent Inquiry into the actions of the United Nations during the 1994 genocide in Rwanda*, S/199/1257, 15 December 1999, pp. 31-33.

116 *idem.*, pp. 36-37; David Scheffer, *All the Missing Souls: A Personal History of the War Crimes Tribunals*, Princeton University Press, 2013, 11, p. 56.

117 United Nations Security Council, *Report of the Independent Inquiry into the actions of the United Nations during the 1994 genocide in Rwanda*, S/199/1257, 15 December 1999, p. 37.

118 Cruvellier, 2010, p. 17; Global Policy Forum, *UN Chief Leaves Rwanda after Unhappy Visit*, 8 May 1998. Retrieved from: https://www.globalpolicy.org/component/content/article/190/39200.html; New York Times, *As Crowds Vent Their Rage, Rwanda Publicly Executes 22*,25 April 1998. Retrieved from: https://www.nytimes.com/1998/04/25/world/as-crowds-vent-their-rage-rwanda-publicly-executes-22.html; New York Times, *Ugly Reality in Rwanda*, 10 May 1998. Retrieved from: https://www.nytimes.com/1998/05/10/world/ugly-reality-in-rwanda.html.

119 Interviewee CS22.

Yet, while acknowledging the failure of the UN to intervene during the 1994 conflict, another interviewee from the Rwandan judiciary[120] reiterated a sentiment from the director of a civil society organisation, who stated that *"the guilt [...] turned bad to good"*:[121]

> "The UN failed their mission in Rwanda in 1994, but it failed due to the mandate, which was impossible. The UN has learnt that it can't make that mistake again. Now they need to think about the civilians without hesitation, whether it is part of their mandate or not. They must go beyond their mandate if civilians are in harm's way."[122]

Furthermore, the director of another civil society organisation explained that regardless of the UN's past actions, justice was needed in Rwanda*"to help people move on. Not only emotionally, but socially and economically, the country needed to move forward"*.[123] The interviewee explained that during the genocide in 1994, there had been no indication or knowledge of what would come next, "*the concept of justice seemed far*away".[124] As a result, the very existence of the ICTR was an acknowledgment that the international community recognised that heinous crimes had been committed in Rwanda.

Given the complex situation in which the Tribunal was created – following the inaction of the UN during the conflict in 1994 and the Rwandan delegation's veto of UN Resolution 955 – the ICTR was off to a troubling start; and various challenges to the Tribunal's legitimacy continued throughout its 20-year existence. The following section describes how structures designed to manage legitimacy were implemented within the Tribunal, before examining specific legitimisation activities that were carried out in relation to legitimacy challenges in Chapter 5.

4.3 IMPLEMENTING A STRUCTURE FOR LEGITIMISATION

Research has shown that organisations often manage their legitimacy by promoting a favourable image of their activities or their staff by donating to charities and/or actively seeking external endorsements[125] – conforming to, selecting or manipulating its

120 Interviewee J2.

121 Interviewee CS21.

122 Interviewee J2.

123 Translated from French: *"[...] pour aider les gens à avancer. Non seulement émotionnellement, mais aussi socialement et économiquement, le pays avait besoin d'aller de l'avant."* (CS13).

124 Translated from French: *"[...] certainement le concept de justice semblait loin."* (CS13).

125 John Dowling and Jeffrey Pfeffer, *Organizational Legitimacy: Social Values and Organizational Behavior*, Pacific Sociological Review, 1975, 18(1), pp. 122-136; Joseph Galaskiewicz, *Professional Networks and the Institutionalization of a Single Mind Set*, American Sociological Review, 1985, pp. 639-658; Gerald R.

environment, and/or protecting past accomplishments.[126] When it comes to the work of an international criminal court, however, this process is not as straightforward as it may sound, as explained by a former ICTR staff member:

> "It was very difficult to keep people interested in the Tribunal's activities. Trials were so long and people are only interested in the outcome. So yes, keeping people interested and informed was a challenge. There is not much to say about the everyday activities of a court. At least, not what the general public is interested in."[127]

The responsibility for handling all matters related to public information and external relations was allocated to the Registry,[128] which was responsible for the Tribunal's administration, including both judicial and non-judicial support.[129] In 2003, all external relations tasks were assigned to the newly established *External Relations and Strategic Planning Section* (ERSPS), which was also charged with policy development and fundraising for the ICTR.[130] The ERSPS was, therefore, designated the task of communicating the developments and functioning of the ICTR, specifically with regard to its UN mandate.[131]

As a result, the ERSPS was in regular contact with the media, ensuring the wide dissemination of information about the activities of the ICTR through press meetings and press releases, as well as developing and updating the Tribunal's own website, producing newsletters and distributing information brochures in English, French and Kinyarwanda. Not only did the ERSPS seek to inform and raise awareness regarding the Tribunal's activities, it was bound by the *Principle of Publicity*,[132] which required the Registry to make

---

Salancik and Jeffrey Pfeffer, *The External Control of Organizations: A Resource Dependence Perspective*, New York: Harper & Row, 1978.

126 Suchman, 1995, pp. 587-593 & 595.

127 Interviewee T18.

128 All press related matters were managed under the *Press and Information Section*, renamed the *Press and Public Affairs Unit* in 2001.

129 United Nations Security Council, *Statute of the International Criminal Tribunal for Rwanda* (as amended on 31 December 2010), 8 November 1994, Article 16; United Nations Security Council, *ICTR Rules of Procedure and Evidence* (as amended on 13 May 2015), 29 June 1995, rule 33.

130 The UN General Assembly sent auditors to the ICTR in 2002. One of their recommendations (to enhance the efficiency of the Tribunal) was to establish the ERSPS within in the Office of the Registrar, to coordinate all the external matters particularly in the area of cooperation, judicial assistance, protocol and external liaising with stakeholders (ICTR, *8th Annual Report*, A/58/140-S/2003/707, 11 July 2003, p. 5; ICTR, *7th Annual Report*, A/57/163-S/2002/733, 2 July 2002, p. 16; United Nations General Assembly, *Resolution 56/248 A*, A/RES/56/248, 24 December 2001).

131 UN Resolution 955, S/RES/955, 8 November 1994; Roland Kouassi G. Amoussouga, Interview conducted by Tribunal Voices (video 89), 29-30 October 2008. Retrieved from: http://www.tribunalvoices.org/voices/video/89.

132 ICTR Statute, 2010, Article 20.

all of the ICTR documents publicly available: all motions and requests filed by the parties (defence and prosecution), any decisions or judgments, transcripts and recordings of public hearings, and the minutes of proceedings. When asked whether some of the ERSPS's activities might be (explicitly or implicitly) linked to promoting the ICTR's legitimacy, one former ICTR staff member explained that such legitimisation activities or documents did not exist: *"There was no strategy regarding legitimacy. [...] We monitored all information regarding the Tribunal. [...] We were keen to show all the work that was being done. It was hard to contend with the other news at the time"*.[133]

Yet, although *"there was no strategy regarding legitimacy"*[134] and promoting the Tribunal's legitimacy was considered a redundant task by some former ICTR staff members – *"It was a court of law, an international criminal tribunal. Yes it was legitimate"*[135] – it became clear that the ERSPS was focused on building a positive image of the Tribunal, while increasing awareness and interest in the ICTR's work – *"My main job was to promote the activities of the Tribunal."*[136] Promoting new services and influencing the opinion of stakeholders is a key component to gaining legitimacy by *"manipulating the environment"* according to Suchman; it also requires the most effort on the part of the organisation.[137] In this case, the ICTR created a whole new section within the Registry to address its external image.

The ERSPS also served as a means to maintain the Tribunal's legitimacy by monitoring any emerging stakeholder demands.[138] As mentioned above, the ERSPS staff *"monitored all information regarding the Tribunal"* and they *"were keen to show all the work that was being done"* as part of their mandate to obtain the cooperation from government institutions and civil society organisations, both worldwide and in Rwanda itself.[139] Indeed, according to a presentation given by the ICTR registrar, Adama Dieng, it appeared to be one of the main functions of the Section: *"Under the leadership of the Registrar, the External Relations and Strategic Planning Section contributes to the building of a positive image of the Tribunal"*.[140]

Despite the perception that the Tribunal had absolute legitimacy by some former ICTR staff,[141] the importance of the ICTR's image was evident through the documents reviewed

133 Interviewee T5.
134 *ibid.*
135 Interviewee T25.
136 Interviewee T11.
137 Suchman, 1995, p. 591.
138 *idem.*, p. 595.
139 Interviewee T5.
140 Adama Dieng, *The Challenges of Administration of International Criminal Tribunals with Specific Reference to ICTR*, Prosecutor's Colloquium on the Challenges of International Criminal Justice, Arusha, Tanzania, 25 November 2004, p. 7.
141 Interviewees T10, T16, T17 & T19.

during archival research, and during the interviews with individuals that had worked at the ICTR. For example, in May 2000 the ICTR registrar called a general staff meeting in Arusha following an incident that had taken place at the ICTR's Kigali office, during which he stated: "*We cannot have the image of the Tribunal tarnished at this critical phase of our completion strategy as a result of misconduct of some staff members*".[142] This same message was repeated in 2005 during a conference with the registrars of other international criminal tribunals where Dieng reiterated the key objectives of the ERSPS, one of which was "*Building a positive image of the Tribunal*".[143] Even those working on the defence teams emphasised the importance of image for their work at the Tribunal:

> "Our image was very important. We were conscious of this. We wanted to prevent people thinking that we were not impartial, so we were careful about how we portrayed ourselves. [...] the environment was tense. This entered into of our private life. We had to be on good behaviour at all times. We could not have parties for example, or invite big groups around, because it would easily give a negative image."[144]

The ICTR's focus on its external image was obvious to a journalist who had worked in the ICTR's press room in Arusha: "*It was more concerned with its image for the outside world. Setting a precedent. It was an academic exercise to grow, to develop international criminal law*".[145] However, when it came to communicating this positive image, another journalist was sceptical:

> "There was no communication strategy. As with all big institutions. People working there didn't know what they were supposed to communicate or how, so they just made sure to promote the ICTR in any way possible. They always aimed to place it in good light. There was certainly not a problem with lack of resources."[146]

---

142 Adama Dieng, *Registrar's special address to staff members on their ethical duties and obligations*, Simba Hall, Arusha, 20 May 2000, p. 8.

143 Adama Dieng, *The Registrar's presentation on the UNICTR's Public Information & Outreach Programme*. Meeting of the Registrars of the International Criminal Tribunals, Arusha, 8 February 2005, p. 1.

144 Translated from French: "*Notre image était très importante. Nous en étions conscients. Nous voulions empêcher les gens de penser que nous n'étions pas impartiaux, nous avons donc fait attention à la façon dont nous nous représentions. [...] L'environnement était tendu. Cela faisait partie de note vie privée. Nous devions toujours avoir un bon comportement. Nous ne pouvions pas organiser de fêtes par exemple, ni inviter de grands groupes, car cela donnerait facilement une image négative.*" (T23).

145 Interviewee M2.

146 Translated from French: "*Il n'y avait pas de stratégie de communication. Comme toutes les grandes institutions. Les gens qui y travaillaient ne savaient pas ce qu'ils étaient censés communiquer ou comment, alors ils*

According to a third journalist, a Rwandan who reported on behalf of an international media outlet, the Tribunal's legitimisation activities, or the promotion of its image, did not reach the Rwandan public: "*Rwandans were not interested, including the Rwandan government. This was a major flaw. If anything the ICTR retained a negative image throughout and didn't do much to improve their image.*"[147] This overtly negative image of the Tribunal was not evident in the newspaper articles consulted in the ICTR's archive, nor during archival research at The New Times in Rwanda.[148] However, with regard to external relations, a former ICTR employee explained that the official communication channels were conducted through the Rwandan government and the governments of UN member states: "*The link with Rwanda was through the Ministry of Justice and with States was through the Ministry of Foreign Affairs*".[149]

The responses given by these three journalists do, however, raise questions regarding the ICTR's legitimisation activities. The implications of losing legitimacy poses a serious threat to all organisations, whether public or private in nature: there may be economic, political, legal, reputational consequences, or other social sanctions. Likewise, an increase in the perception of legitimacy is beneficial for an organisation for the same reasons: it may lead to more partnerships, more funding, etc. Legitimacy is therefore key for the existence and development of an organisation.[150] Regardless of whether a strategy to promote the Tribunal's legitimacy was in place, or indeed whether activities were implemented to improve the image of the Tribunal – rather than viewed as legitimisation – the actions of the ICTR provide an insight into both the legitimacy type promoted by the Tribunal (pragmatic, moral or cognitive), and the stakeholders that were targeted through these legitimisation activities implemented by the Tribunal to gain, maintain and/or repair its legitimacy.

4.4 Conclusion

The different interpretations of legitimacy and the assessments of the ICTR's legitimacy described in this chapter demonstrate the fluidity of this notion. Although the concept of legitimacy is clear and recognisable to all, as it is examined there are different facades that

s'assuraient simplement de promouvoir le TPIR de toutes les manières possibles. Ils ont toujours cherché à le placer sous un bon éclairage. Le manque de ressources n'était certainement pas un problème." (M3).

147 Translated from French: "*Les Rwandais n'étaient pas intéressés, y compris du gouvernement rwandais. C'était un défaut majeur. En fait, le TPIR a conservé une image négative tout au long et n'a pas fait grand-chose pour améliorer leur image.*" (M1).

148 The New Times is an English language newspaper established in Rwanda in 1995: https://www.newtimes.co.rw/.

149 Interviewee T18.

150 Meyer et al., 2013, pp. 169-171.

begin to emerge, which provide interesting nuances to this unassuming word. The complexity of the term was highlighted through the discussions with interviewees, some of whom viewed the ICTR as both legitimate and illegitimate at the same time, as demonstrated by this statement given by an interviewee:

> "The legitimacy of the ICTR. It was legitimate. It had to be there, even if results weren't there. There were huge expectations for the court. The ICTR was necessary. The operational errors were regretful. The repercussions were terrible for survivors. This is a big lesson for the future."[151]

Other interviewees appeared to struggle between recognising the legitimacy of the Tribunal and the positive actions that it took, while explaining that certain actions, or some individuals working at the ICTR, were not legitimate:

> "Legitimacy of international treaties come from established bodies, like the UN. [However] it is emotionally difficult when there are people acquitted even though they did it. It is the same as the corrupt police officer, who, when he is arrested, he protests against the system. At the ICTR, look at the court and the judgments, who made these decisions? How could there be acquittals?"[152]

Similarly, the source of the ICTR's legitimacy also appeared to overlap, according to interviewees. Certain factors clearly helped the Tribunal increase its legitimacy in the eyes of its stakeholders, yet it could also be argued that it was due to the ICTR's legitimacy that it was able to achieve certain milestones. For example, prosecuting those most responsible for crimes committed in 1994 provided the ICTR with legitimacy; yet, apprehending the 'big fish' was only possible due to the Tribunal's legitimacy. As a result, it is unclear whether the actions of the ICTR provided the Tribunal with legitimacy (output legitimacy), and/or whether it was the Tribunal's affiliation with the UN, itself considered a legitimate entity, that provided the ICTR with legitimacy (input legitimacy). If the latter is the case – that the UN provided the ICTR with unconditional, *cognitive* legitimacy – it is unclear how or why the survivors of the Rwandan genocide continue to consider the UN a legitimate organisation, given that it failed to prevent and intervene in the 1994 genocide. Furthermore, the fact that Rwanda vetoed the establishment of the Tribunal, as a temporary member of the UN Security Council in 1994, was not raised in any of the interviews.

---

151 Translated from French: *"La légitimité du TPIR. Il devait être là, même si les résultats n'étaient pas là. Les attentes du tribunal étaient énormes. Le TPIR était nécessaire. Les erreurs opérationnelles étaient regrettables. Les répercussions ont été terribles pour les survivants. C'est une grande leçon pour l'avenir."* (CS6).

152 Interviewee CS23.

The answer may, however, lie in the recognition of the 1994 genocide, which the UN presented to Rwanda through the creation of the ICTR, and the survivors of the genocide: *"The ICTR was an important contribution. So many genocides have happened in this world, but only three are recognised. Rwanda's genocide is recognised, this is incredible."*[153] Several interviewees emphasised the Tribunal's recognition of the 1994 genocide in Rwanda, and the labelling of acts of sexual violence as crimes of genocide, as incredibly important for both the country as a whole and the survivors of the genocide. In this case, the Tribunal successfully gained legitimacy by *conforming* to the needs and expectations of its stakeholders.[154] Furthermore, the fact that this recognition came from the UN – an organisation consisting of 193 member states – provided the Tribunal and its decisions with additional significance.

Yet, although the ICTR was generally perceived as legitimate, it was concerned about its image and implemented various legitimisation activities in order to gain and maintain its legitimacy, especially with regard to certain stakeholders. The Tribunal's legitimacy was not absolute, and over the course of its 20-year lifespan the ICTR experienced numerous legitimacy challenges that threatened its very existence. In order to delve deeper into this complex concept of legitimacy in relation to the ICTR, and to examine how the Tribunal managed its legitimacy in the post-conflict environment of Rwanda and the re-emerging realm of international criminal law, the following chapter describes specific legitimacy challenges that were identified through the literature review and discussed during the interviews, and examines the legitimisation activities implemented by the ICTR when faced with these challenges.

153 Interviewee G4.
154 Suchman, 1995, p. 587.

5 LEGITIMISATION IN PRACTICE

Legitimacy is an important factor in the management of an organisation for multiple reasons: it is used as a means to collaborate with other organisations and to gain access to resources such as qualified staff and infrastructure.[1] Given that the ICTR operated on an annual budget, it was obliged to demonstrate its legitimacy to UN member states in order to receive funding for its staff and operations on a yearly basis.[2] Information regarding its activities, the management of each organ, the number of indictees arrested and/or prosecuted, etc. was largely provided through the ICTR's annual report presented at UN General Assembly meetings.[3]

The legitimacy of the Tribunal was also important for its relationship with the Rwandan government. In order to run investigations within the post-conflict state of Rwanda and fly witnesses in from Kigali for trials taking place in Arusha, the ICTR needed to obtain visas, permits, and flight permissions from both the Rwandan and Tanzanian governments. Yet, starting from the Rwandan delegation's veto of UN Resolution 955 in November 1994, relations between the Tribunal and the Rwandan government remained fragile throughout the ICTR's 20-year existence.[4]

This fragility, and the influence of the Rwandan government on the ICTR's operations, was highlighted during an interview with a Rwandan judge: *"The Rwandan government clashed with the ICTR. This demonstrated that the ICTR was not as powerful as it thought it was"*.[5] The interview provided an insight into the psychological, political and sociological factors that shape the manner in which individuals recognise legitimacy.[6] Given that

1 Monica A. Zimmerman and Gerald J. Zeitz, *Beyond Survival: Achieving New Venture Growth by Building*,Academy of Management Review, 2002, 27(3), pp. 414-431; Michael Meyer, Renate Buber and Anahid Aghamanoukjan, *In Search of Legitimacy: Managerialism and Legitimation in Civil Society Organizations*, Voluntas: International Journal of Voluntary and Nonprofit Organizations, 2013, 24(1), pp. 169-171.

2 Starting in 2002 (for the years 2002 and 2003) budgets were provided every two years (ACABQ (2001). *Financing of the International Criminal Tribunal for the Prosecution of Persons Responsible for Genocide and Other Serious Violations of International Humanitarian Law Committed in the Territory of Rwanda and Rwandan Citizens Responsible for Genocide and Other Such Violations Committed in the Territory of Neighbouring States between 1 January and 31 December 1994 (ICTR)*, A/56/666, 29 November 2001).

3 United Nations Security Council, *Resolution 955*, S/RES/955, 8 November 1994, para. 4; United Nations General Assembly, *Resolution 52/218*, A/RES/52/218, 3 February 1998. ICTR Annual Reports (1996-2015) can be found at: https://unictr.irmct.org/en/documents/annual-reports.

4 Peskin, 2008, pp. 151-153.

5 Interviewee J4.

6 Margaret Levi, Audrey Sacks and Tom R. Tyler, *Conceptualizing Legitimacy, Measuring Legitimating Beliefs*, American Behavioral Scientist, 2009, 53(3), pp. 354-375; Matthew Lister, *The Legitimating Role of Consent in International Law*, Chicago Journal of International Law, 2010, 11, pp. 663-691.

legitimacy reflects the acceptance of an organisation within any given environment, tension between the Tribunal and the Rwandan government could harm the ICTR's legitimacy in Rwanda and reflect badly on the wider international community, namely the UN and each individual member state.

To examine the ICTR's legitimacy further, this chapter is divided into eight sections that represent legitimacy challenges that were identified through the literature review and highlighted during the interviews conducted for this research. The aim of these sections is to present *legitimisation in practice* by describing the legitimacy challenges faced by the ICTR and the legitimisation activities implemented to address these challenges. Each section demonstrates that the management of an organisation's legitimacy is multifaceted, and that a challenge to organisational legitimacy may be dealt with in different ways depending on when the challenge is perceived by the organisation, who perceives the challenge, and how is it perceived. Furthermore, the legitimacy challenge itself may be comprised of other challenges, or indeed act as a catalyst for additional legitimacy challenges.

In order to examine *legitimisation in practice,* the chapter applies the theoretical framework developed in Chapter 2, which connects the legitimacy challenges faced by the ICTR to the legitimisation activities implemented in order to gain, maintain and repair its legitimacy.[7] An overview of this framework is summarised in the following table:

Table 21 Gaining, maintaining and repairing legitimacy: legitimacy challenges and legitimisation activities.[8]

Objective	Challenge	Legitimisation Activity
Gain Legitimacy	Emphasise their Differences Gain Support	Conform to Environment Select the Environment Manipulate the Environment
Maintain Legitimacy	Stakeholder Heterogeneity Organisation Homogeneity Institutionalisation	Perceive Future Crisis Protect Past Accomplishments
Repair Legitimacy	Performance (pragmatic) Value (moral) Meaning (cognitive)	Symbolic Action Substantive Action

7 Section 2.3.
8 Suchman, 1995, pp. 586-599.

As explained in Chapter 2, the legitimisation activity (or activities) implemented by the ICTR, in order to address the legitimacy challenges it faced, provides information regarding the type of legitimacy (pragmatic, moral or cognitive) that was promoted by the Tribunal, and also enables the identification of the stakeholders that were at the receiving end of each legitimisation activity.[9]

The eight sections in the chapter provide an insight into the legitimacy challenges and the legitimisation activities that were uncovered during the literature review, the interviews and the archival research conducted for this research. The eight sections represent legitimacy challenges that were grouped into eight different categories using the codes created in the ATLAS.ti software.

Section 1 examines legitimacy challenges related to the ICTR's location in Tanzania. The establishment of the Tribunal in Arusha created a distance between the survivors of the genocide and the work of the ICTR; it hindered its access to witnesses and crimes scenes located in Rwanda; and also appeared far from the eyes of the world, which appeared to be focused on the ICTY based in The Hague. Section 2 examines challenges connected to the management and human resources of the ICTR, especially when reports of underqualified staff and nepotism surfaced in 1996. This category of challenges links to Section 3, which describes the legitimacy challenge faced by the ICTR when alleged *génocidaires* were found to be working within its walls in Arusha.

Challenges related to the context, referring to cultural and linguistic differences between the ICTR's courtroom and Rwanda, are addressed in Section 4. This category of challenges also relates to the location of the ICTR in Tanzania, rather than Rwanda, and addresses additional legitimacy challenges faced by the Tribunal, particularly with regard to the involvement of witnesses during trials. Section 5 describes how the Tribunal's legitimacy was also questioned by the Twa community, who were not represented during any of the trials that took place in Arusha, despite their involvement in the 1994 genocide. Addressing the concerns of this community appears to have been out of the scope of the ICTR's legitimisation activities.

The establishment of the Rwandan gacaca court system in 2002 also highlighted the distance between the Tribunal and the survivors of the 1994 genocide. Section 6 examines the legitimacy challenges that arose due to comparisons between these two justice mechanisms, notably related to the costs and duration of trials. Two additional legitimacy challenges are categorised under the heading "*the politics of justice*" in Section 7, as they demonstrate the sensitive political environment in which the Tribunal was operating. The acquittals and early release of those prosecuted by the ICTR created waves of anger and disbelief in Rwanda, notably the acquittal of Jean Bosco Barayagawiza, which created legitimacy challenges within the Tribunal itself. Similarly, the removal of the ICTR

9 *ibid.*

prosecutor, Carla Del Ponte, related to investigations into crimes that may have been committed by members of the RPF, also raised questions regarding the Tribunal's legitimacy. The inability to arrest and prosecute all the Tribunal's fugitives was also discussed as a legitimacy challenge for the ICTR and is addressed in Section 8, the final section of this chapter.

5.1 The Location: Arusha, Tanzania

When the UN Security Council adopted Resolution 955 in November 1994, the location of the Tribunal was still uncertain.[10] Establishing the ICTR in Kigali was considered an unfavourable option given that the infrastructure in Rwanda – devastated after four years of conflict – could not have accommodated the Tribunal. Furthermore, the UN Secretary-General also considered the security risks in bringing leaders from the previous regime back into Rwanda, and the need for the International Tribunal to be perceived as a just and fair court, with complete impartiality and objectivity. This led to the conclusion that trial proceedings would be best held outside Rwanda in a neighbouring, neutral country, with an investigative unit based in Kigali.[11]

The decision to locate the ICTR in Tanzania was made by the UN Security Council in February 1995,[12] following the Tanzanian government's offer to accommodate the Tribunal in the Arusha International Conference Centre – AICC.[13] The conference centre in Arusha held symbolic relevance, given that the building had previously hosted the negotiations between the Rwandan government and the RPF, which culminated in the signing of the peace agreement, the Arusha Accords, in 1993. Furthermore, the layout and space available at the AICC could readily house an international criminal tribunal.[14]

Yet, based in Arusha, the Tribunal faced a challenge in addressing crimes that had been committed over a thousand kilometres away, in the neighbouring state of Rwanda. This

---

10 United Nations Security Council, *Resolution 955*, S/RES/955, 8 November 1994, para. 5.

11 United Nations Security Council, *Letter dated 1 October 1994 from the Secretary-General addressed to the President of the Security Council*, S/1994/1125, 4 October 1994, para. 136-138; United Nations Security Council, *Report of the Secretary-General pursuant to paragraph 5 of Security Council resolution 955*, S/1995/134, 13 February 1995, para. 37-38 & 42-45.

12 United Nations Security Council, *Resolution 977*, S/RES/977, 22 February 1995; United Nations Security Council, S/1995/134, 13 February 1995, para. 37-38 & 42-45.

13 ICTR, *1st Annual Report*, A/51/399, S/1996/778, 24 September 1996, Appendix, p. 20.

14 George Andreopoulos, Rosemary Barberet and James P. Levine (eds.), *International Criminal Justice: Critical Perspectives and New Challenges*, Springer Science & Business Media, 2010, p. 171; Erik Møse, *The ICTR: Experiences and Challenges*, New England Journal of International and Comparative Law, 2005, 12, pp. 1-2; Victor Peskin, *International Justice in Rwanda and the Balkans: Virtual Trials and the Struggle for State Cooperation*, Cambridge University Press, 2008, p. 167.

point was raised early on by the Rwandan delegation during negotiations with the UN Security Council:

> "We requested the establishment of this Tribunal to teach the Rwandese people a lesson, to fight against the impunity to which it had become accustomed since 1959 and to promote national reconciliation. It therefore seems clear that the seat of the International Tribunal should be set in Rwanda; it will have to deal with Rwandese suspects, responsible for crimes committed in Rwanda against the Rwandese. Only in this way can the desired effects be achieved."[15]

Not only did this physical distance impede access to witnesses and crime scenes – *"the ICTR should have been in Rwanda. This would have made it much easier to meet survivors. It would have had a presence in Rwanda. Easier to get the facts."*[16] – the Tribunal was wholly dependent on the Rwandan government's cooperation in facilitating the collection of evidence and access to witnesses by providing visas and flight permits.[17] The distance also impacted the accessibility of the Tribunal to the Rwandans, many of whom had experienced gross human rights violations during the 1994 genocide:[18] *"Few people could go to Arusha. The whole process was too far from the people."*[19] Indeed, the frustration regarding the Tribunal's location in Tanzania was made clear during a discussion with a journalist: *"It would have been much better to have ICTR here [Rwanda]. An aircraft came to Rwanda two or three times a week for investigators and witnesses. But Rwanda should have seen things through its own eyes."*[20]

A former president of the ICTR, Judge Vagn Joensen, mentions some of the challenges related to the ICTR's location in Arusha during his interview with a Rwandan radio station in February 2016:

> "There are advantages and disadvantages of international courts compared to domestic courts and one of these disadvantages is that we are not sitting as a domestic court. We are not sitting on the location where the crimes happened. In a domestic court, you can go to the court house and see what happened,

15 United Nations Security Council, *The Situation Concerning Rwanda.* Provisional Report of the 3453rd Meeting, S/PV.3453, 8 November 1994, p. 16.

16 Interviewee CS5.

17 Kingsley Moghalu, *Rwanda's Genocide: The Politics of Global Justice*, Palgrave Macmillan, 2005, pp. 136-143; Oosterveld and John McManus, *The Cooperation of States with the International Criminal Court,* Fordham International Law Journal, 2002, 25(3), p. 822.

18 Victor Peskin, *Courting Rwanda: The Promises and Pitfalls of the ICTR Outreach Programme,*Journal of International Criminal Justice, 2005a, 3(4), p. 951.

19 Interviewee CS22.

20 Interviewee M2.

> listen to the witnesses and get a full impression of everything. It's your own judges that are handling cases and very often you also have media participating, in some systems at least. An international court can't aggregate in that way for logistical and security reasons, and a number of other reasons. We often sit far away from the place where the event happened and where the victims and the affected society are, but we have done our best to compensate for that. Of course Tanzania is not far from Rwanda, but if you have to pay a flight to get there it's only a few people who can afford that and have the time to do it. This is certainly not the case for the majority of Rwandans."[21]

Locating the Tribunal would clearly have been more visible to Rwandans had it been based in Kigali: "*The situation was very, very delicate after the genocide. For survivors, justice had to be seen to be done. For them. Some people recognised that they had done wrong. Some fled, others asked for forgiveness and turned themselves in.*"[22] However, as addressed in the UN Secretary-General's report,[23] it was also clear that for reasons of efficiency, security and impartiality Kigali was not a viable option for the International Criminal Tribunal, as explained by an interviewee who was involved in discussions with the Rwandan government regarding criminal justice in Rwanda following the genocide:

> "Practical issues were not great, but the ICTR needed to exist. If organised here [Rwanda] the security and impartiality would have been compromised. It would not have worked. It was legitimate also because they could work independently. The legal system in the West is legitimate. It is an organised legal system. People here [Rwanda] were morally and physically destroyed. It was better to take the justice to another country. Also, it allowed the gacaca to do its work here."[24]

Yet, one interviewee, a former ICTR staff member, claimed that the concerns related to the safety and security of those accused of committing acts of genocide were unfounded given that "*even ministers, former government officials involved in the genocide now live peacefully in Rwanda. They were tried in Rwanda. This makes a difference. They are*

21 Jambonews, *Closing interview with the President of the International Criminal Tribunal for Rwanda (ICTR) – Part I*,4 February 2016. Retrieved from: https://www.jambonews.net/en/actualites/20160204-closing-interview-with-the-president-of-the-international-criminal-tribunal-for-rwanda-ictr-part-i/.

22 Translated from French: "*La situation était très très délicate après le génocide. Pour les survivants, il fallait voir que justice était faite. Pour eux. Certaines personnes ont reconnu qu'elles avaient mal agi. Certains ont fui, d'autres ont demandé pardon et se sont rendus.*" (CS11).

23 United Nations Security Council, *Report of the Secretary-General pursuant to paragraph 5 of Security Council resolution 955*, S/1995/134, 13 February 1995, para. 37-38 & 42-45.

24 Interviewee CS12.

remorseful".[25] The interviewee also suggested that feelings of guilt and shame experienced by certain defendants may have made it impossible for their trials to take place in Rwanda:

> "The accused could not be tried in Rwanda because of the shame they felt for their actions. The security in Rwanda was good, just as good as here in Arusha. It would however have been difficult for these people to stand trial in front of their people."[26]

Aside from security issues, it may well have been difficult for the leaders of the former regime to stand trial in Rwanda, for political reasons or possibly even due to their shame. Regardless of their reasoning, interviewees were split in their opinion regarding the location of the Tribunal, with the majority expressing their regret that the Tribunal was not located in Rwanda, while others explained that trials in Kigali would not have been possible. However, the decision to locate the Tribunal in Arusha was made in 1995, over 25 years ago, and Rwanda is in a very different state today. The observations made during the interviews may therefore reflect the time that has passed since the establishment of the Tribunal, when the country was slowly emerging from a four-year civil war, and also the gift of hindsight, following the ICTR's 20 years of work, operating from Arusha.

From its inception, therefore, the Tribunal faced a legitimacy challenge related to its location in Arusha, which was far from the survivors of the genocide who could not observe the trials taking place, and also created logistical issues related to the access to crime scenes and witnesses that were vital for the ICTR's operations, which also meant that the Tribunal was wholly dependent on the Rwandan government's cooperation. Furthermore, this was the first international criminal court established on the African continent, and the second international criminal tribunal to emerge since the Nuremberg and Tokyo trials that took place following World War II. The legitimisation strategy used by the Tribunal therefore related to gaining legitimacy.[27]

5.1.1 *Gaining Legitimacy*

When an organisation is first established it has to gain legitimacy, which involves two distinct challenges: gaining support from the environment[28] and emphasising its differences

25 Interviewee T21.

26 *ibid.*

27 Suchman, 1995, p. 586.

28 The organisational environment is composed of stakeholders or institutions that affect the operations, resources and performance of an organisation (John M. Bryson, *Strategic Planning for Public and Nonprofit Organizations: A Guide to Strengthening and Sustaining Organizational Achievement*, John Wiley & Sons, 2018, pp. 45-46).

with pre-existing organisations.[29] On the one hand, the new organisation emphasises the similarities it has with comparable, pre-existing organisations;[30] while on the other, the organisation needs to distinguish itself from these pre-existing organisations, to demonstrate its uniqueness, its necessity and its competitive advantage.[31] In the case of the ICTR, there were no other international criminal tribunals in the world at the time of its establishment, apart from the ICTY, which was established in 1993. Yet, despite the relative newness of the ICTY, the Tribunal in The Hague had already built a strong reputation regarding the necessity of an international criminal tribunal to bring security and peace to a region. In September 1994, the Rwandan government wrote to the UN Security Council asking for similar assistance, by *"Setting up as soon as possible an international tribunal to try the criminals"*.[32]

As with the ICTY, the ICTR was established to achieve positive, long-term outcomes, albeit in a different part of the world: the ICTY addressed crimes being committed in the Balkans during the early 1990s, while the ICTR focused on crimes committed in Rwanda in 1994. Despite the different temporal and territorial jurisdictions, the ICTY and ICTR shared several similarities: both tribunals were established by the UN and worked in parallel: they shared a prosecutor (until 2003), appellate judges and an Appeals Chamber (all based in The Hague), and – perhaps most importantly – they were both funded by the UN General Assembly and relied on the full cooperation of individual UN member states to track, arrest and transfer indicted individuals. These mutual resources appear to have added an element of competition between the two tribunals, with the older of the two – the ICTY – demonstrating a slight advantage.[33]

Unlike the ICTR based in Arusha, the ICTY was located in The Hague – an international city of justice and peace[34] – a little over a kilometre away from the Peace Palace and the seat of the International Court of Justice. In addition to its physical location, the ICTY was presiding over an ongoing conflict in the former Yugoslavia, which involved political actors from both Europe and North America, including NATO. Given that politicians and the armed forces of numerous states were directly linked to the events being covered during the proceedings at the ICTY, the media and public interest (and opinion) were quick to

29 *ibid.*; Deephouse et al., 2017, p. 22.

30 Deephouse et al., 2017, p. 22; Suchman, 1995, p. 586.

31 *ibid.*; Blake E. Ashforth and Barrie W. Gibbs, *The Double-Edge of Organizational Legitimation*, Organization Science, 1990, 1(2), p. 182.

32 United Nations Security Council, *Letter dated 94/09/28 from the Permanent Representative of Rwanda to the United Nations addressed to the President of the Security Council*, S/1994/1115, 29 September 1994. Retrieved from: https://digitallibrary.un.org/record/197773?ln=en.

33 Interviewees T11, T13, T15 & T18; Varda Hussain, *Sustaining Judicial Rescues: The Role of Outreach and Capacity-Building Efforts in War Crimes Tribunals*, Virginia Journal of International Law, 2004, 45, pp. 561-565; Moghalu, 2005, pp. 127-130.

34 International cities of peace. Retrieved from: http://www.internationalcitiesofpeace.org/cities-listing/.

follow. Perhaps for these reasons, the ICTY experienced continuous global media coverage throughout its existence. On 12 February 2002, over 500 journalists from across the globe were in The Hague to cover the first day of Slobodan Milosevic's trial;[35] while the largest number of journalists to attend a trial day at the ICTR amounted to approximately 80 journalists, who travelled to Arusha on 2 September 1998 to cover the judgment of Akayesu's trial, which involved the first decision ever made by a criminal court with regard to the crime of genocide.[36]

In an attempt to gain its legitimacy, the challenge faced by the ICTR was to both identify with the ICTY in order to *gain support*, while also to distinguish itself from its sister Tribunal, by *emphasising the differences* between the two tribunals.[37] Although the structure and administration of the two tribunals was managed by two separate registrars, the organisation of the ICTR and ICTY remained very similar: their judges and prosecutors were elected by the UN Security Council and UN General Assembly; they shared the same substantial jurisdiction in relation to international crimes; they were both *ad hoc* in nature, with a limited life-span; and they were both established in the early 1990s.[38]

Furthermore, both tribunals played an important role in reviving international criminal law, following the International Military Tribunal (IMT) located in Nuremberg and the International Military Tribunal for the Far East (IMTFE) based in Tokyo, which were established following World War II:[39] "*The ICTR and ICTY were the mothers of international criminal law. After such a long period of time from Nuremberg and Tokyo. From them the hybrid courts were born and of course the ICC*".[40] The key difference was, therefore, their territorial mandate: one tribunal was focused on Rwanda in the African Great Lakes region; while the other was created to prosecute international crimes committed in the territory of the former Yugoslavia, in Europe.

Another difference between the two tribunals was their start date: the ICTY was established in May 1993, almost a full year before the start of Rwanda's genocide (April 1994), while the ICTR was established in November 1994. The Tribunal in The Hague therefore had to overcome the initial teething problems associated with starting a completely

---

35 Michael Barratt Brown, Edward S. Herman and David Peterson, *The Trial of Slobodan Milosevic*, Spokesman Books, 2004, 2, pp. 143-154; Klaus Bachmann and Aleksandar Fatić, *The UN International Criminal Tribunals: Transition Without Justice?* Routledge, 2015, p. x; Chris Stephen, *Judgement Day: The Trial of Slobodan Milošević,* London: Atlantic Books, 2005, pp. 128.

36 Bachmann & Fatić, 2015, p. xi; ICTR, Prosecutor v. Jean-Paul Akayesu, Judgment, ICTR-96-4-T, 2 September 1998; Kinglsey Chiedu Moghalu, *Image and Reality of War Crimes Justice: External Perceptions of the International Criminal Tribunal for Rwanda*, Fletcher Forum of World Affairs, 2002, 26(2), pp. 25-26.

37 Deephouse et al., 2017, p. 22; Suchman, 1995, p. 586.

38 Robert Cryer, Darryl Robinson and Sergey Vasiliev, *An Introduction to International Criminal Law and Procedure*, Cambridge University Press, 2019, pp. 127-129 & 137-138.

39 *idem.*, p. 127.

40 Interviewee T21.

new form of organisation, certainly since the IMT and IMTFE established in the 1940s. In terms of gaining legitimacy, the ICTR could ride on the coattails of its big sister, effectively making use of the lessons learnt in the ICTY's first year and a half of existence. Indeed, throughout the ICTR's existence it experienced a "*liability of newness*"[41] due to the short-term, *ad hoc* nature of its mandate, and, as a result, demonstrated "*the support of traditions and norms*"[42] in order to highlight its position as a legitimate international criminal tribunal, while working hard to obtain the support of its stakeholders. The presence of the ICTY in The Hague therefore served as a helpful and necessary support, bolstering the recognition of international criminal law and the work of international criminal courts, and, later on, the arrival of the ICC – another new international criminal court – also helped to solidify the concept of international criminal law *in practice*.[43]

Having described the plight of the ICTR in emerging as a new international criminal court, the first on the African continent, and the need for the Tribunal to gain its legitimacy, especially working alongside its sister Tribunal based in The Hague, the following section examines the legitimisation activities implemented by the Tribunal to gain, maintain and/or repair its legitimacy. These legitimisation activities provide information regarding the legitimacy type favoured by the ICTR and also shed light on the stakeholders that were targeted by these legitimisation activities.

5.1.2 Pragmatic Legitimacy

When seeking to gain legitimacy, an organisation will use certain *legitimisation activities* related to its environment. In order to avoid moulding an organisation to the requirements of its environment, it may be located in a suitable or appropriate location, in line with the legitimisation activity of "*selecting its environment*".[44] The decision to locate the Tribunal for Rwanda on the African continent relates to this legitimisation activity as served to bring the Tribunal closer to Rwanda (while also distinguishing the mandate of the ICTR with that of the ICTY). As a former ICTR staff member explains: "*We would have had issues if it was all in The Hague. The African states wouldn't be happy. We [the ICTR] would not have had support.*"[45]

For an organisation to gain pragmatic legitimacy it may select an environment that welcomes or understands the value of its products and/or services.[46] The location chosen

41 Ashforth & Gibbs, 1990, p. 182.
42 *ibid.*
43 United Nations General Assembly, Fiftieth Session, 52nd plenary meeting, A/50/PV.52, 7 November 1995, New York, p. 7.
44 Suchman, 1995.
45 Interviewee T15.
46 Suchman, 1995, p. 589.

for the ICTR was Tanzania, a neighbouring country to Rwanda and also conveniently close to Nairobi, where the UN's African headquarters are located. Furthermore, the Tribunal was housed in the conference centre in Arusha, the AICC, a symbolic location known to many people living in the Great Lakes region given that this was where peace talks had been held during the Rwandan civil war, and where the Arusha Accords had been signed on 4 August 1993.

In addition to its location on the African continent, close to Rwanda and in the symbolic location of Arusha, the ICTR also hired staff from African countries, which is also in line with the pragmatic legitimacy type: if the organisation's objective is to gain influence in its environment, it may choose to offer key organisational roles to individuals (or a small group) that are considered as credible to its stakeholders. This technique is called *"co-opting constituents"*,[47] which is known as an effective way for an organisation to assimilate into its environment.

In contrast with the ICTY, established for a European conflict taking place in the former Yugoslavia – which employed three Dutch registrars and, in the final years, an Australian[48] – the ICTR focused on hiring staff from the African continent: the four ICTR registrars came from Kenya, Nigeria, Senegal and South Africa.[49] The first two presidents of the ICTR were also from Africa: Judge Laïty Kama was from Senegal and Judge Navanethem Pillay is from South Africa.[50]

Yet the efforts in selecting the environment for the ICTR were not enough for all its stakeholders, as demonstrated in an interview with a Rwandan government official:

> "Justice is important but it needs to be seen. The victims need to see that justice has been done to them. [...] For the criminal lawyer it has clearly been done. But not for victims. A different formula is needed for criminal law dealing with

---

47 *idem.*, p. 587.

48 ICTY registrars: Theo van Boven (February 1994 to December 1994), Dorothée de Sampayo Garrido-Nijgh (1995 to 2000), Hans Holthuis (2001 to 2009) – all from the Netherlands – and John Hocking from Australia (May 2009 to December 2017).

49 Andronico Adede was Kenyan and was appointed registrar from 1995 to 1997; Agwu Ukiwe Okali is Nigerian and was registrar from 1997 to 2001; Adama Dieng is Senegalese and was the registrar from 2001 to 2012; and Bongani Majola is South African and was ICTR registrar from 2012 to 2015.

50 Judge Laïty Kama from Senegal was president from 1995 to 1999, and Judge Navanethem Pillay from South Africa was president from 1999 to 2003.
No Rwandan national served as a judge at the ICTR, and no Rwandan nationals appeared on the UN Security Council list of candidates nominated to fill the position of judge (see ICTR Press Releases, for example: ICTR Press Release, *Security Council forwards to General Assembly 18 candidates for judges to ICTR*, 2 October 1998. Retrieved from: https://unictr.irmct.org/en/news/security-council-forwards-general-assembly-18-candidates-judges-ictr).

mass atrocities. Victims can't *understand the process. It is even harder when it comes to explaining the early releases and acquittals.*"[51]

Indeed, as explained by another interviewee, the location was a challenge for the ICTR: *"There was a double distance. Geographical, between Rwanda and the ICTR, and the time since the genocide. It was complex for the population. Outreach and training were needed*".[52] Furthermore, even a former ICTR staff member explained that *"having it based in Rwanda could have sped up the process of reconciliation*".[53] Faced with this legitimisation challenge regarding the distance of the Tribunal from the survivors of the genocide, the Tribunal implemented legitimisation activities in order to conform to its environment.[54]

These legitimisation activities are reported to be the most straightforward way in which to gain legitimacy.[55] *Conforming to the environment* consists in the organisation demonstrating its fit within the regulatory standards, the moral values and the cultural norms of its environment.[56] In a meeting between the ICTR's registrar and Rwandan authorities in August 1998, the Rwandan government voiced concerns that they were being left in the dark regarding certain activities at the Tribunal.[57] As a result, the ICTR agreed to provide a Rwandan government official with an office within the Tribunal. The *special representative of the Rwandan government* was appointed in October 1999 and given access to observe the judicial work of the Tribunal in Arusha on behalf of the Rwandan government.[58] The presence of the special representative facilitated communication between Kigali and Arusha in matters such as the transfer of witnesses, outreach and communication efforts, and the transmission of relevant court documents.[59]

In a further attempt to improve communication between Arusha and Rwanda, the Tribunal set up "*a sustained strategic communication program using a range of techniques to explain its work and relevance to audiences in Rwanda as well as to the international community*".[60] This comprised principally an information and documentation centre

---

51 Interviewee G3.

52 Translated from French: "*Il y avait une double distance. Géographique, entre le Rwanda et le TPIR, et le temps depuis le génocide. C'était complexe pour la population. La sensibilisation et la formation étaient nécessaires.*" (CS19).

53 Translated from French: "*l'avoir fondé au Rwanda aurait pu accélérer le processus de réconciliation.*" (T9).

54 Suchman, 1995, pp. 587-589.

55 *idem.*, p. 587.

56 *idem.*, pp. 587-589.

57 Interviewees CS12 & G3; David Scheffer, *A Personal History of the War Crimes Tribunals*, Princeton University Press, 2013, 11, p. 114.

58 ICTR Press Release, *Special representative of Rwandan government visits Tribunal*,13 October 1999. Retrieved from: https://unictr.irmct.org/en/news/special-representative-rwandan-government-visits-tribunal.

59 *ibid.*

60 Timothy Gallimore, *The Legacy of the of the International Criminal Tribunal for Rwanda (ICTR) and its Contributions to Reconciliation in Rwanda*, New England Journal of International and Comparative Law, 2007, 14, p. 260.

– locally known as *"umusanzu mu bwiyunge"* (*"contribution to reconciliation"*) – which was established in Kigali in 2000.[61] The Centre's main goal was to bridge the information gap between the Tribunal and the Rwandan population by providing a library, free internet access, and online legal research facilities.

Following the success of the Information Centre in Kigali, ten additional satellite centres were opened across Rwanda's five provinces in 2008 and 2009 thanks to funding from the European Union.[62] These provincial *umusanzu* centres were all equipped with internet access and television screens, which enabled those interested to follow ICTR court proceedings. They were located in or near court houses, and were managed by the ICTR information officers, all of whom where Rwandan, who assisted visitors in finding the information that they were looking for.[63] In this sense, the Tribunal effectively handed the responsibility of its outreach programmes to Rwandans, employed by the Tribunal, while keeping an overview of the activities that were taking place in Rwanda. This is another example of an organisation *conforming to its environment* with the intention of gaining pragmatic legitimacy: providing stakeholders with direct access to resources related to its work.[64]

5.1.3 *Moral and Cognitive Legitimacy*

The legitimisation activities mentioned previously are connected to pragmatic legitimacy and represent the ICTR's own efforts at legitimisation. When examining whether the ICTR implemented legitimisation activities aimed at gaining *moral* and/or *cognitive legitimacy*, the role of the UN, as founder and investor in the Tribunal, comes to the fore. These two legitimacy types – *moral* and *cognitive* – touch upon the very core of the Tribunal's existence, as an organisation established by the UN to perform a specific mandate in the name of the international community.[65]

---

61 ICTR Press Release, *ICTR Information Centre opens in Kigali*, 25 September 2000. Retrieved from: https://unictr.irmct.org/en/news/ictr-information-centre-opens-kigali.

62 ICTR, *14th Annual Report*, A/64/206–S/2009/396, 31 July 2009, para. 62; ICTR, *15th Annual Report*, A/65/188–S/2010/408, 30 July 2010, para. 61; ICTR Press Release, *ICTR Opens Two More Information Centres in Rwanda*, 23 February 2009. Retrieved from: https://unictr.irmct.org/en/news/ictr-opens-two-more-information-centres-rwanda. Funding was received from the European Instrument for Democracy and Human Rights (EIDHR) through the country-based support scheme. All the centres, including the main Information and Documentation Centre in Kigali, have since closed.

63 Interviewees T3, T6, T9 & T20; ICTR website, 'ICTR remembers': https://www.irmct.org/specials/ictr-remembers/index.html.

64 Suchman, 1995, p. 587.

65 United Nations Security Council, *Resolution 955*, S/RES/955, 8 November 1994, pp. 2-3.

In adopting "*conformist stances*" in pursuit of *moral legitimacy*, an organisation must follow the principles and ethical standards demonstrated by its environment.[66] A common legitimisation activity implemented by organisations entails associating itself, in some shape or form, with other legitimate organisations located within the same environment.[67] In this regard, the ICTR aligned itself with its sister Tribunal, the ICTY: the two tribunals organised joint workshops, seminars and conferences together, sharing best practices and learning new skills alongside their respective colleagues.[68] Furthermore, the registrars of both tribunals worked together on several operational matters, and from 2001 onwards they gave regular joint press briefings to highlight this collaboration:

> "[...] the two Registrars said that they were striving to achieve the common goal of completing the respective mandates of the two Tribunals by the year 2008, or as soon thereafter as possible. They said that there were several areas where each Tribunal could learn from the experience of the other and other areas where both Tribunals could pool resources together to enhance efficiency."[69]

---

66 Suchman, 1995, p. 588.

67 *ibid.*

68 ICTR Press Release, *The Prosecutor of the International Criminal Tribunals: ICTY and ICTR second workshop on crimes of sexual violence,* 3 October 1997. Retrieved from: https://unictr.irmct.org/en/news/prosecutor-international-criminal-tribunals-icty-and-ictr-second-workshop-crimes-sexual; ICTR Press Release, *ICTR and ICTY Harmonize their Goals,* 4 April 2003. Retrieved from: https://unictr.irmct.org/en/news/ictr-and-icty-harmonize-their-goals; ICTR Press Release, *Joint Statement on Implementation of Inter-Tribunal Co-operation Projects,* 15 March 2004. Retrieved from: https://unictr.irmct.org/en/news/joint-statement-implementation-inter-tribunal-co-operation-projects; ICTR Press Release, *International Criminal Tribunal Prosecutors Conclude Conference in Arusha,* 27 November 2004. Retrieved from: https://unictr.irmct.org/en/news/international-criminal-tribunal-prosecutors-conclude-conference-arusha; ICTR Press Release, *Second Colloquium of Prosecutors of International Tribunals held in Freetown, Sierra Leone,* 29 June 2005. Retrieved from: https://unictr.irmct.org/en/news/second-colloquium-prosecutors-international-tribunals-held-freetown-sierra-leone; ICTR Press Release, *The Office of the Prosecutor Completes Joint Advocacy Training Programme (25 - 30 January 2006),* 31 January 2006. Retrieved from: https://unictr.irmct.org/en/news/office-prosecutor-completes-joint-advocacy-training-programme-25-%E2%80%93-30-january-2006; ICTR Press Release, *16th Plenary Session of the Tribunal Meets in Arusha,* 10 July 2006. Retrieved from: https://unictr.irmct.org/en/news/16th-plenary-session-tribunal-meets-arusha; ICTR Press Release, *Roundtable Discussion on International Cooperation,* 28 November 2008. Retrieved from: https://unictr.irmct.org/en/news/roundtable-discussion-international-cooperation; ICTR Press Release, *International Criminal Justice: Lessons from the Past, Reflections on the Future,* 11 November 2009. Retrieved from: https://unictr.irmct.org/en/news/international-criminal-justice-lessons-past-reflections-future; ICTR Press Release, *Office of the Prosecutor to Host International Workshop on the Prosecution of Conflict-Related Sexual and Gender-Based Violence Crimes,* 15 November 2012. Retrieved from: https://unictr.irmct.org/en/news/office-prosecutor-host-international-workshop-prosecution-conflict-related-sexual-and-gender.

69 ICTR Press Release, *Registrars of ICTY and ICTR sign statement on co-operation,* 20 September 2001. Retrieved from: https://unictr.irmct.org/en/news/registrars-icty-and-ictr-sign-statement-co-operation.

Likewise, the organisational goals used to communicate the rationale for the organisation's existence were also aligned with the environment's societal ideals, giving a sense of conformity. This is evident from the two UN Resolutions adopted to establish the ICTY and ICTR. Certain passages in UN Resolution 955 (establishing the ICTR) are identical to UN Resolution 827, which established the ICTY, namely:

> "Determining that this situation continues to constitute a threat to international peace and security,
> Determined to put an end to such crimes and to take effective measures to bring to justice the persons who are responsible for them,
> Convinced that in the particular circumstances of Rwanda, the prosecution of persons responsible for serious violations of international humanitarian law would enable this aim to be achieved and would contribute to the process of national reconciliation and to the restoration and maintenance of peace,
> Believing that the establishment of an international tribunal for the prosecution of persons responsible for genocide and the other above-mentioned violations of international humanitarian law will contribute to ensuring that such violations are halted and effectively redressed."[70]

The ideological mission of these two tribunals was therefore the same. Yet, in order to conform to the environment, the ICTR needed to conform to a comparable, legitimate organisation within the same environment[71] and it is questionable as to whether the ICTY could be considered an established organisation, given that it was just a year and a half older than the ICTR. The additional year may not have afforded the ICTY its own *moral* and/or *cognitive* legitimacy, especially as it too was a completely new type of organisation, established 45 years after the closure of the IMTFE in Tokyo (1948). It appears, therefore, that both tribunals made use of their ties with the UN in order to gain legitimacy.

If an organisation is establishing itself in a new sector, or in an environment without any comparable organisation, legitimacy may be gained by establishing formal protocol and procedures under some form of officially recognised control. This approach to *conformity* relates to *cognitive legitimacy*, whereby an organisation strives to achieve certain societal standards that its environment expects from it.[72] Both the ICTR and ICTY were run as UN institutions. All protocols and management systems linked to human resources used the same operating systems as other UN offices; the department structures and

70 United Nations Security Council, *Resolution 827*, RES/1993/827, 25 May 1993, p. 1; United Nations Security Council, *Resolution 955*, S/RES/955, 8 November 1994, pp. 1-2.
71 Suchman, 1995, p. 588.
72 *ibid.*

logistical support also mirrored that of other UN institutions; and both tribunals reported to the UN Security Council and UN General Assembly on an annual basis.[73] In this way, the ICTR conformed not only to the ICTY, but also to the UN, and the standards expected of them by the UN member states. Indeed, as stated by an interviewee: "*The ICTR was evidently legitimate as it was a branch of the UN.*"[74]

Yet conforming to others also comes at a risk. While mimicking the positive traits of another 'legitimate' organisation provides some leverage in gaining legitimacy, it is also important for an organisation to distinguish itself, its goals and its mandate:

> "The ICTR has always been in the shadow of its sister institution, the ICTY, and perhaps only now, in view of the fact that the ICTY has secured all its suspects, becomes glaringly clear to many that there is still an important job to be finished for the ICTR."[75]

In order to achieve this, organisations can make use of the legitimisation activity: *selecting its environment*. Legitimisation activities that aim to *select* the environment take another perspective than those seeking to *conform* to the environment: they entail a more proactive approach.[76] In *selecting* the environment, an organisation promoting its *moral legitimacy* will adopt activities that reflect the cultural expectations and interests of its environment.[77] In this case, the *environment* appears to refer predominantly to the international community, represented by the UN, rather than to Rwanda or the African continent: first and foremost the Tribunal was a UN body and not an African court.[78] At the *pragmatic* level, the ICTR demonstrated its alliance with the African continent by hiring African employees and locating the seat of the Tribunal in Tanzania; however, at the *moral* and *cognitive* levels it seems that the legitimisation activities implemented by the ICTR emphasised this affiliation with the UN.

---

73 Bachmann & Fatić, 2015, pp. 36-53; Sarah M. Kilemi, *UNICTR Liquidation Report: Twenty Plus Years of Challenges, Achievements and Best Practices in Managing an International Criminal Tribunal*, Arusha, July 2016, p. 8; William A. Schabas, *The UN International Criminal Tribunals: The Former Yugoslavia, Rwanda and Sierra Leone*, Cambridge University Press, 2006, p. 507.

74 Interviewee J2.

75 Christophe Paulussen, *Arrest and Transfer*, in: Anne-Marie De Brouwer and Alette Smeulers (eds.), *The Elgar Companion to the International Criminal Tribunal for Rwanda*, Edward Elgar Publishing, 2016, p. 288.

76 Suchman, 1995, p. 588-589.

77 *idem.*, p. 589.

78 The African Union was established a few years later in 1999. The African Court of Justice and Human Rights (ACJHR) - also based in Arusha, Tanzania - was founded in 2004 following a merger of the African Court on Human and Peoples' Rights (established in 1998) and the Court of Justice of the African Union (established in 2003).

Although Rwanda initiated the request for an international court,[79] the Rwandan delegation vetoed the establishment of the ICTR based on several grounds,[80] while stating that "*an international tribunal would only appease the conscience of the international community rather than respond to the expectations of the Rwandese people and of the victims of genocide in particular*".[81] It appears that Rwanda felt that the ICTR was established as a court for the international community from the very start, rather than representing Rwanda and Rwandans.[82]

Furthermore, the terminology used in the ICTR Statute is identical to the language used in the ICTY Statute,[83] which aligns with the *selection process* used by organisations aiming to promote their *moral legitimacy*: the organisation will select the terms that best fit with the norms and values recognised by the environment; these terms are then inserted into the organisation's mandate, and communicated to its stakeholders.[84] The language and style used also relates to the UN Editorial Manual, which ensures that the approved UN terminology is employed by all UN institutions and that editorial standards, policies and practices are followed.[85]

These same arguments apply to gaining *cognitive legitimacy*. In this case, the cognitive legitimacy of an organisation will depend on the sector in which the organisation finds itself, *selecting* the appropriate environment is therefore a productive way of gaining legitimacy. The most common way of achieving this is to demonstrate that its organisational behaviours conform to the established sectoral standards.[86] Again, the UN provides a solid foundation from which to establish an international criminal tribunal. Indeed, despite the UN's failure to assist Rwandan during the 1994 genocide, the Rwandan government turned to the UN for assistance in arresting and prosecuting those responsible for the crimes committed on its territory: "*We request the international community to reinforce government efforts by: [...] (c) Setting up as soon as possible an international tribunal to try the criminals*".[87] It was therefore the UN's own cognitive legitimacy – as a recognised body established to maintain and ensure international peace and security – that led to the

79 United Nations Security Council, *Letter dated 94/09/28 from the Permanent Representative of Rwanda to the United Nations addressed to the President of the Security Council*, S/1994/1115, 29 September 1994.

80 United Nations Security Council, *The Situation Concerning Rwanda*. Provisional Report of the 3453rd Meeting, S/PV.3453, 8 November 1994, pp. 14-16.

81 *idem.*, p. 15.

82 Jean-Marie Kamatali, *From the ICTR to ICC: Learning from the ICTR Experience in Bringing Justice to Rwandans*, New England Journal of International and Comparative Law, 2005, 12, p. 93.

83 United Nations Security Council, *Statute of the International Criminal Tribunal for the former Yugoslavia* (as amended on 7 July 2009), 25 May 1993.

84 Suchman, 1995, p. 595.

85 United Nations Editorial Manual: http://dd.dgacm.org/editorialmanual/.

86 Suchman, 1995, p. 578.

87 United Nations Security Council, S/1994/1115, 29 September 1994, p. 4.

establishment of the ICTR, and assisted in the Tribunal gaining its own legitimacy through its affiliation to the UN.

In examining the legitimisation activities associated with gaining legitimacy, and the legitimacy challenges linked to the Tribunal's location in Arusha, it appears that *pragmatic legitimacy* was promoted at the local level and related to the daily functioning of the ICTR; while the *cognitive* and *moral legitimacy* of the ICTR were promoted through the Tribunal's affiliation to the UN, and indeed the path that was being carved by the ICTR's sister Tribunal – the ICTY – based in The Hague. It is therefore not surprising that the legitimisation activities implemented by the ICTR itself promoted *pragmatic* legitimacy; and the legitimisation activities used to promote the Tribunal's *moral* and *cognitive legitimacy* were endorsed by the Tribunal's founder – the UN – through the use of UN language, UN processes and UN regulation, which encapsulated the ICTR's very existence.

5.1.4 *Stakeholders*

Although the Rwandan government expressed its frustration regarding the location of the ICTR, the UN Security Council did eventually vote to establish the Tribunal in Tanzania,[88] a country to the east of Rwanda, rather than holding trials alongside proceedings taking place at the ICTY in The Hague, which had once been proposed as an option.[89] The location eventually chosen by the UN Security Council was the AICC in Arusha, which added symbolic significance to the seat chosen for the Tribunal, given that the conference centre had hosted the peace negotiations between the former Rwandan government and the RPF in 1993.[90] Furthermore, the Tribunal demonstrated that it was operating under the same UN standards as its sister Tribunal in The Hague, as requested by the Rwandan government;[91] and the Tribunal was established solely to prosecute those that had committed international crimes in 1994, at the end of the Rwandan civil war. Although Rwandans were not initially hired by the ICTR,[92] those holding leadership positions were citizens of African countries (namely, Kenya, Nigeria, Senegal and South Africa).

This messaging was also important for the UN member states supporting the work of these two international criminal tribunals, distinguishing the Tribunal in Arusha from the Tribunal in The Hague, while emphasising the similarities between the two, and their affiliation with the UN. However, the ICTY had the benefit of proximity to the UN's major

---

88 United Nations Security Council, *Resolution 977*, S/RES/977, 22 February 1995.

89 United Nations Security Council, *Letter dated 1 October 1994 from the Secretary-General addressed to the President of the Security Council*, S/1994/1125, 4 October 1994, para. 139; Scheffer, 2013, p. 69.

90 Andreopoulos et al., 2005, pp. 1-2; Peskin, 2008, p. 167.

91 *idem.*, p. 4.

92 Victor Peskin, *Courting Rwanda: The Promises and Pitfalls of the ICTR Outreach Programme*, Journal of International Criminal Justice, 2005a, 3(4), p. 959.

donors, both in physical distance and through media attention; and the conflict taking place in the former Yugoslavia involved several key UN member states. The ICTR therefore had to capitalise on the attention bestowed on the Tribunal in The Hague, while also demonstrating the uniqueness of the Tribunal based in Arusha, working to maintain peace in a completely different part of the world.

The two key stakeholders targeted by the Tribunal when gaining legitimacy, in the early years of its existence, therefore appear to have been the Rwandan government and the UN member states. The Rwandan government played an important role in providing access to both the crime scenes and the witnesses required for the execution of trials, while the UN member states were critical in providing funding for the ICTR's operations, as well as assistance in tracking and arresting the Tribunal's fugitives. In the case of this newly established UN institution, the legitimisation activities of *selecting* and *conforming to its environment* have both been used to gain all three legitimacy types: *pragmatic*, *moral* and *cognitive*.

Yet in examining these legitimisation strategies together with the legitimacy types, it is clear that the ICTR cannot be considered as a standalone organisation: the UN played an important role in not only establishing and funding the ICTR, but also in promoting the Tribunal's legitimacy, which adds an additional layer of complexity when examining legitimacy in relation to the ICTR.

5.2 Management and Human Resources

From the start, the *ad hoc* nature of the ICTR made it clear that the Tribunal in Arusha would have a limited lifespan. Although no specific closure date was set by the UN at the time of establishment, it was assumed that the ICTR would close its doors when all or most of those responsible for the serious violations of international humanitarian law that had occurred in Rwanda had been arrested and prosecuted.[93] The Tribunal therefore operated on a year-to-year basis, with annual budgets[94] and contracts allocated for a maximum period of one year.[95]

In order for the ICTR to implement its mandate and complete its work, the UN ensured that the necessary resources were provided, including adequate staffing. The number of staff employed by the ICTR increased gradually from 163 in 1995 to a peak of 1,100 from

93 Lise Bonvent, *Les Gens d'Arusha*. Paris: Cartouche, 2011, p. 61; Sara M. Kilemi, *ICTR Legacy: Administrative Achievements and Challenges*, ICTR Legacy Symposium in Arusha, Tanzania, 6-7 November 2014, p. 7; UN Resolution 955, S/RES/955, 8 November 1994.

94 In 2002 this changed to budgets for two years.

95 ICTR annual reports (1996 to 2015): https://unictr.irmct.org/en/documents/annual-reports; and financial reports and audited financial statements (1999 to 2016): https://www.un.org/ga/acabq/documents/all/611?order=title&sort=asc.

2004 to 2007; while the number decreased from 2008 to 2011 to 600, and further to 400 for the period covering 2012-2014, and by the second half of 2015 – the year the Tribunal eventually closed – the number of staff members was approximately 95.[96] At its peak, the staff members came from over 100 different countries.[97]

However, given that the ICTR's activities were funded on a provisional basis, only short-term contracts could be offered to its employees, making it difficult to recruit qualified personnel. As explained in the ICTR's final annual report: "*The ad hoc nature of the Tribunal as an organisation with a limited lifespan was an impediment to attracting and retaining qualified and dedicated professionals at the Tribunal*".[98] Additionally, when competent staff memebrs were found, it could take the UN up to a year to process their contracts and fly them out to Arusha:[99] "*In the beginning the administration was terrible. I had to apply for my salary several times. It took months.*"[100]

Finding suitable candidates was therefore not an easy task: "*despite efforts by the Tribunal to recruit more qualified staff, many sections still remain understaffed*".[101] Many candidates considered jobs offered by the ICTR to be insecure – due to the interim nature of their contract – so a position at the ICTR was often considered as a short-term opportunity to make ends meet – or to strengthen a resumé – while waiting to land a more secure job elsewhere: "*I had the impression that the ICTR was used as a career step. For young interns and UN bureaucrats. [...]. They used the job as a springboard for their future careers*".[102] It was therefore difficult for the Tribunal – given the limited job security for staff and no clear career path – to secure the core staffing requirements needed to complete its mandate.[103] Staff would often start searching for employment in other UN institutions immediately after starting their contracts with the ICTR; consequently, the pace of recruitment could not catch up with that of the resignations.[104] On 3 May 1995 the ICTR's prosecutor sent all UN member states a letter asking for cooperation:

96 *ibid.*

97 Kilemi, 2014, p. 3.

98 ICTR, *20th Annual Report*, A/70/218–S/2015/577, 31 July 2015, para. 53(a).

99 Bonvent, 2011, p. 20; United Nations General Assembly, *Audit and investigation of the International Criminal Tribunal for Rwanda*, Fifty-first Session, A/51/789, 6 February 1997, para. 17, 21 & 52.

100 Translated from French: "*Au début, l'administration était terrible. J'ai dû demander mon salaire plusieurs fois. Ça a pris des mois.*" (T2)

101 ICTR, *2nd Annual Report - Corrigendum*, A/52/582/Corr.1-S/1997/868/Corr.1, 2 December 1997, p. 2.

102 Translated from French: "*J'ai eu l'impression que le TPIR était utilisé comme une étape de carrière. Pour les jeunes stagiaires et les bureaucrates de l'ONU. [...]. Ils ont utilisé le travail comme tremplin pour leur future carrière.*" (M3).

103 Kilemi, 2014, pp. 8-9; Sylo Taraku and Gunnar M. Karlsen, *Prosecuting Genocide in Rwanda: The Gacaca System and the International Criminal Tribunal for Rwanda*, Oslo: Norwegian Helsinki Committee, 2002, p. 29.

104 Kilemi, 2014, p. 5; Møse, 2005, p. 9.

> "Recalling the terms of Security Council resolutions 955 (1994), this appeal calls on Governments to provide active assistance in the following areas: (1) recruitment of candidates for positions as investigators and interpreters; (2) secondment of personnel; (3) recruitment of liaison officers."[105]

An additional complication was the financial situation of the UN. The ICTR was established at a time when the UN was undergoing a serious financial crisis and was itself downsizing.[106] As such, many experienced and qualified staff members, who might normally have been willing to work at the ICTR, were reluctant to do so for fear of losing their then current jobs or being left out in the cold following their short-term assignment at the ICTR. Filling ICTR vacancies was also hampered by significant procedural red tape caused by the bureaucratic UN recruitment procedures, which resulted in significant delays during the recruitment process.[107]

The Tribunal was also located almost 300 kilometres from Nairobi and over 600 kilometres from Tanzania's largest city of Dar-es-Salem, and the town of Arusha lacked many of the facilities of a modern city, which did little to attract potential candidates. Indeed, at one point the ICTR prosecutor claimed that the deputy prosecutor for the Tribunal preferred to spend most of his time at his office in Kigali rather than to travel to the Tribunal in Arusha.[108] These challenges were even raised by the registrar during a staff assembly:

> "There have recently been some statements in the media by senior members of this Tribunal attacking the quality and commitment of staff members of the Tribunal. One such statement created the impression that, because of the remoteness of Arusha, the staff of the Tribunal are not of high quality because the best professionals would not want to come and live here."[109]

Appointing judges to the Tribunal in Arusha – rather than to the ICTY based in The Hague – also proved to be a challenge; with most judges opting to work in the Netherlands

---

105 ICTR, *1st Annual Report*, A/51/399-S/1996/778, 24 September 1996, para. 55.

106 Lise Morje Howard, *Sources of Change in United States–United Nations Relations*, Global Governance: A Review of Multilateralism and International Organizations, 2010, 16(4), pp. 491-492; David J. Scheffer, *International Judicial Intervention*, Foreign Policy, 1996, 102, p. 45.
UN Report, United Nations General Assembly, Forty-fourth Session, 84th Plenary Meeting, *Current financial crisis and financial emergency of the United Nations*, A/RES/44/195, 21 December 1989, p. 277.

107 Kilemi, 2014, p. 5; United Nations General Assembly, *Audit and investigation of the International Criminal Tribunal for Rwanda*, Fifty-first Session, A/51/789, 6 February 1997, para. 50-52.

108 Chuck Sudetic and Carla Del Ponte, *Madame Prosecutor: Confrontations with Humanity's Worst Criminals and the Culture of Impunity*, New York: Other Press, 2011, pp. 73-74.

109 Adama Dieng, *Registrar's Statement to ICTR Staff Assembly*, Arusha, 10 May 2002, p. 8.

rather than volunteer for a position in Tanzania.[110] The UN Security Council eventually decided to establish a pool of *ad litem* judges[111] through Resolution 1431, in order to increase the number of judges available to work in Arusha on a temporary basis.[112]

As a result of the challenges in recruiting staff, it appears that inexperienced personnel were hired at all levels of the organisation.[113] Furthermore, attempts to speed up the particularly slow UN recruitment system appeared to have led to the hasty employment of some staff members, without conducting appropriate background checks or a skills test.[114] As explained by a former ICTR staff member: *"There were elements of the ICTR that could be improved. The recruitment for example. There were three categories. It was aligned with the UN recruitment system. But there was nepotism. Expats were employing friends and family. People were not employed on merit."*[115]

In her autobiography, the former ICTR prosecutor, Carla Del Ponte, describes the struggles regarding inexperienced staff at the Tribunal.[116] In May 2001, seven senior staff members from the OTP were fired for *"professional incompetence"*[117] and from 2002 to 2003 the ICTR suffered a 20-month gap while waiting to hire a permanent deputy prosecutor to supervise the OTP in Arusha.[118] Furthermore, in an ironic turn of events, several lawyers who were found to be unqualified to work in Rwanda were able to get jobs as highly-paid lawyers at the ICTR.[119]

110 The Economist. *Judging Genocide: Arusha and the Hague*,14 June 2001. Retrieved from: https://www.globalpolicy.org/component/content/article/163/28719.html.

111 An *ad litem* judge is appointed to participate in a particular case or a limited set of cases.

112 United Nations Security Council, *Resolution 1431*, S/RES/1431, 14 August 2002, Articles 12*ter* & *quarter*; United Nations General Assembly, *Identical letters dated 4 March 2002 from the Secretary-General addressed to the President of the General Assembly and the President of the Security Council*, Fifty-sixth Session, A/56/861–S/2002/241, 8 March 2002.

113 United Nations General Assembly, *Audit and investigation of the International Criminal Tribunal for Rwanda*, Fifty-first Session, A/51/789, 6 February 1997, para. 20.

114 Christina M. Carroll, *An Assessment of the Role and Effectiveness of the International Criminal Tribunal for Rwanda and the Rwandan National Justice System in Dealing with the Mass Atrocities of 1994*, Boston University International Law Journal, 2000, 18, pp. 181-183; Cruvellier, 2010, p. 16; Sudetic & Del Ponte, 2011, p. 129.

115 Interviewee T24.

116 Sudetic & Del Ponte, 2011, pp. 127-130.

117 Amnesty International, *Annual Report 2002*, 27 May 2002 Retrieved from: https://www.amnesty.org/en/documents/pol10/0001/2002/en/.

118 All Africa News, Rwanda, *International Criminal Tribunal Chief Prosecutor to Appoint Deputy Next Month*, 31 July 2002. Retrieved from: https://allafrica.com/stories/200207310331.html; Human Rights Watch, *Rwanda and the Security Council: Changing the International Tribunal, Letter to Council Members on the International Criminal Tribunal for Rwanda*, 1 August 2003. Retrieved from: https://www.hrw.org/news/2003/08/01/rwanda-and-security-council-changing-international-tribunal; Moghalu, 2005, p. 129; Victor Peskin, *Beyond Victor's Justice? The Challenge of Prosecuting the Winners at the International Criminal Tribunals for the Former Yugoslavia and Rwanda*, Journal of Human Rights, 2005b, 4(2), 213-231, 2005, p. 224.

119 Taraku & Karlsen, 2002, p. 29.

Not only did the issues surrounding recruitment culminate in negative media coverage for the Tribunal – with reports of inexperienced personnel and ethical blunders – the lack of competent staff also influenced the organisational culture and the motivation of staff within the ICTR.[120]

> "It was very political. Emails between [name x] and [name y] were discovered by IBUKA, revealing corruption and he [name x] was suspended for two years. They made inquiries. The UN. [...] I was often left off the selection lists. My boss, [name z], put me forward for certain jobs. It was thanks to him that I got work. I was one of the few that could speak both French and English. This meant that I worked more hours, and worse hours. Weekends and nights. Most others could only speak one language, despite it being a requirement [to speak French and English]."[121]

It appears that the issues surrounding the recruitment could – in part – be due to the UN's lengthy recruitment procedures and a lack of managerial oversight: *"[Name] left for a year and a half. I was surprised he came back."*[122] The apparent lack of professionalism was also evident to the ICTR's external stakeholders, causing legitimacy challenges for the Tribunal:[123] *"The management at the ICTR was the problem"*;[124] and *"The management of the court was motivated by money. There was a gap. The leadership should have been Rwandan. There was a lack of commitment"*.[125] Despite working under UN conditions, the Tribunal in Arusha appeared to suffer from an absence of clear leadership:

> "There was no system. Everyone did their own thing. The rules were constantly changed. The rules of evidence and procedure changed all the time, you can

120 Adama Dieng, *Registrar's Statement to ICTR Staff Assembly*, Simba Hall, Arusha, 10 May 2002, p. 8; Adama Dieng, *Registrar's special address to staff members on their ethical duties and obligations*, Simba Hall, Arusha, 20 May 2005, pp. 1-2; interviewees T1 & T2; The Telegraph, *UNs special genocide tribunal for Rwanda a waste of time*, 4 February 2013. Retrieved from: https://www.telegraph.co.uk/news/worldnews/africaandindianocean/rwanda/9848588/UNs-special-genocide-tribunal-for-Rwanda-a-waste-of-time.html.

121 Translated from French: "*C'était très politique. Des e-mails entre [nom x] et [nom y] ont été découverts par IBUKA, révélant la corruption et il [nom x] a été suspendu pendant deux ans. Ils ont fait des enquêtes. L'ONU. [...] J'ai souvent été exclu des listes de sélection. Mon supérieur [nom] m'a proposé pour certains postes. C'est grâce à lui que j'ai eu du travail. J'étais l'un des rares à pouvoir parler à la fois le français et l'anglais. Cela signifiait que je travaillais plus d'heures et les pires heures. Les week-ends et les nuits. La plupart des autres ne pouvaient parler qu'une seule langue, bien que ce soit une exigence [parler anglais et français]*." (T2).

122 Interviewee T16.

123 International Crisis Group, *International Criminal Tribunal For Rwanda: Delayed Justice*, 7 June 2001. Retrieved from: https://www.crisisgroup.org/africa/central-africa/rwanda/international-criminal-tribunal-rwanda-delayed-justice.

124 Translated from French: "*La gestion au TPIR était le problème.*" (CS19).

125 Interviewee CS21.

> check. The whole system was bureaucratic but there was no system. [...] The people in charge didn't try to adapt. The UN system was very slow but methodical. It was applied to the letter. But there was very little oversight and mistakes were covered."[126]

The lack of management and oversight at the ICTR was particularly troubling in the early years of the Tribunal's existence, namely from 1995 to 1997. Despite being housed in the AICC, an established conference centre, the new employees of the ICTR spent their first months setting up the office space and organising the administration of the Tribunal.[127] The operational establishment of the Tribunal was further complicated given that the most basic office supplies (paper, pens, desks, computers, etc.) failed to arrive due to lengthy bureaucratic red tape and a lack of funding.[128]

Reports of mismanagement, nepotism, racism and sexual harassment from within the ICTR initially emerged in late 1995, in and around the start-up confusion:[129] *"The environment at the Tribunal was, there was incompetence. It was anti-Rwandan, toxic, very political. There were many jealousies and different camps."*[130] In response to these reports, the UN General Assembly adopted Resolution 213 during their 50th session in June 1996 requesting the Office for Internal Oversight Services (OIOS) to review the functioning of the ICTR.[131] The auditors – led by General Karl Paschke, Under-Secretary-General for OIOS – were asked to identify problems and recommend measures to enhance the efficient use of resources.[132] The OIOS's subsequent report, published in February 1997, found that:

> "In the Tribunal's Registry not a single administrative area functioned effectively: Finance had no accounting system and could not produce allotment reports, so that neither the Registry nor United Nations Headquarters had budget expenditure information; lines of authority were not clearly defined; internal controls were weak in all sections; personnel in key positions did not have the required qualifications; there was no property management system; procurement actions largely deviated from United Nations procedures; United

126 Interviewee M2.

127 Eric Husketh, *Pole Pole: Hastening Justice at UNICTR*, Northwestern University Journal of International Human Rights, 2005, 3(1), 8, pp. 9-10; Møse, 2005, p. 2.

128 *ibid.*

129 Husketh, 2005, pp. 9-10; Dawn Rothe, James Meernik and Thordis Ingadóttir (eds.), *The Realities of International Criminal Justice*, Martinus Nijhoff Publishers, 2013, pp. 94-95.

130 Interviewee T5.

131 United Nations General Assembly, *Resolution 50/213C*, A/RES/50/213C, 15 July 1996.

132 Yves Beigbeder, *International Criminal Tribunals: Justice and Politics*, Springer, 2011, p. 91; Paul J. Magnarella, *Justice in Africa: Rwanda's Genocide, Its Courts and the UN Criminal Tribunal: Rwanda's Genocide, Its Courts and the UN Criminal Tribunal*, Routledge, 2018, pp. 60-63.

Nations regulations and rules were widely disregarded; the Kigali office did not get the administrative support needed, and construction work for the second courtroom had not even started."[133]

As a UN-run institution, funded by UN member states, this report regarding the operational shortfall of the Tribunal was damning, and the impact was long lasting. In an interview conducted in 2019, the representative of a Rwandan civil society organisation stated that: *"The judges at the ICTR were corrupt. The system in Arusha was corrupt. For me this was a loss of legitimacy. My preference was to have everyone tried here [Rwanda], through the gacaca system."*[134] Indeed, the mismanagement experienced at the Tribunal played a role in the resignation of two ICTR Judges: Judge Lennart Aspegren from Sweden, who cited incompetence and lack of commitment in the administration of the Tribunal as partly responsible for his decision not to stand for re-election;[135] and Judge Yakov Ostrovsky of Russia, who also referred to incompetence and corruption within the Registry as a reason for his resignation.[136]

This challenge clearly impacted the legitimacy of the Tribunal not only in the eyes of the international community, including those living in the Great Lakes region, but also for ICTR staff:[137] *"[Name] was most corrupt. He pulled the strings. It was full of nepotism. He gave jobs to his mistresses, his friends. He also gave jobs in exchange for houses, for money. The environment was not pleasant".*[138]

Yet internal disappointment with the operational state of affairs – as demonstrated, in part, by the resignations of both Judge Aspegren and Judge Ostrovsky, and recounted by interviewees[139] – was not the only issue at stake. The mismanagement of an organisation has a huge impact on its legitimacy as it reflects the organisation's ability to exercise its

133 United Nations General Assembly, *Audit and investigation of the International Criminal Tribunal for Rwanda*, Fifty-first Session, A/51/789, 6 February 1997, Summary para. 2.

134 Interviewee CS3.

135 Magnarella, 2018, p. 65-67, 87, 97; Laïty Kama, *Statement by Judge Laïty Kama, President of the International Criminal Tribunal for Rwanda*,28 July 1998. Retrieved from: https://search.archives.un.org/uploads/r/united-nations-archives/e/3/a/e3a14a3f584cf3a7d732933d576164d2d02b248ec61be2eb02d400166421bb97/S-1094-0025-04-00013.pdf.

136 Former Russian newspaper *Vremya Novostei* conducted the interview, published on 10 April 2002. Boston Review, *Healing Rwanda: Can an international court deliver justice?* 1 December 2003. Retrieved from: http://bostonreview.net/world/helena-cobban-healing-rwanda; InterNews, *Rwanda: Judge Ostrovsky Criticizes Kigali Tribunal*, 13 May 2002. Retrieved from: https://allafrica.com/stories/200205130370.html.

137 Interviewees T1 & T2; The Telegraph, *UNs special genocide tribunal for Rwanda a waste of time*, 4 February 2013. Retrieved from: https://www.telegraph.co.uk/news/worldnews/africaandindianocean/rwanda/9848588/UNs-special-genocide-tribunal-for-Rwanda-a-waste-of-time.html.

138 Translated from French: *"[Nom] était le plus corrompu. Il a tiré les ficelles. C'était plein de népotisme. Il a donné des emplois à ses maîtresses, ses amis. Il a également donné des emplois en échange de maisons, pour de l'argent. L'environnement n'était pas agréable."* (T1).

139 Interviewees T1, T2, T5 & T24.

authority and operate effectively:[140] *"The ICTR played a role. Just the establishment of the court was important. But the implementation was poor. Especially with such an enormous budget"*.[141] An organisation that is perceived as legitimate is more likely to obtain resources, gain support and independence to make its own decisions, and secure compliance. The opposite occurs when an organisation is deemed illegitimate and incapable of running smoothly: external stakeholders, or regulators, will often take a more active role in monitoring organisational activities, and investors may withhold, or be more cautious with, their funding.[142] In a court established by the international community to prosecute those most responsible for atrocious crimes committed in Rwanda, the Tribunal's legitimacy was in jeopardy during those early years.

5.2.1 Repairing Legitimacy

The challenge was present in the first years of the ICTR's existence, which would point to a need for the Tribunal to *gain* legitimacy. If this was the case, the challenges identified would be categorised as needing to gain support or emphasise its difference in relation to other, comparable organisations working in the same environment; however, these challenges do not relate to the management and staffing challenges experienced by the ICTR between 1995 and 1997. The challenge was rather an internal issue and not linked to finding its place within a competitive – or even desolate – environment of international criminal law.

Former ICTR staff members spoke of irregularities regarding human resources throughout the Tribunal's existence, which could therefore place importance on the ICTR *maintaining* legitimacy.[143] Yet issues of leadership and management do not reflect a change in stakeholders' needs (*"stakeholder heterogeneity"*) or a lack of organisational flexibility (*"organisational homogeneity"*); and the ICTR was not facing reputational damage due to the actions of another, similar organisation (linked to *"institutionalisation"*).[144]

The issue at stake during the internal crisis of 1995 to 1997 – which appears to have continued on during the early 2000s – was therefore a legitimacy challenge linked to performance and value. *Performance* challenges relate to *pragmatic* (exchange) legitimacy

---

140 Derick W. Brinkerhoff, *Organizational Legitimacy, Capacity, and Capacity Development*, University of Kansas. Public Management Research Association (PMRA), 2005.

141 Interviewee CS17.

142 Andrew D. Brown, *Narrative, Politics and Legitimacy in an IT Implementation*, Journal of Management Studies, 1998, 35(1), p. 35; Ralph C. Hybels, On Legitimacy, Legitimation, and Organizations: A Critical Review and Integrative Theoretical Model, Academy of Management Proceedings, Briarcliff Manor, NY 10510: Academy of Management, 1995, p. 243.

143 Interviewees T1, T2, T5 & T24; Suchman, 1995, pp. 593-594.

144 Suchman, 1995, p. 594.

as they are connected to an organisation's capacity to achieve specific outputs;*value* challenges relate to *moral* (ethics) legitimacy as they link to the integrity of an organisation and its staff.[145] The Tribunal needed to act quickly to repair the damage to its legitimacy as this legitimacy challenge also risked threatening its*cognitive* legitimacy, whereby the very existence of the ICTR could be called into question.[146]

5.2.2 Symbolic and Substantive Action

In response to the first-hand accounts being provided by both ICTR employees and representatives from certain UN member states regarding the state of affairs both in Arusha and at the ICTR's office in Kigali,[147] it was the UN that took action.[148] The UN General Assembly requested immediate action to mitigate the risks associated with this challenge that threatened the legitimacy of the ICTR in its early years, and an audit was organised through the OIOS, which reported directly to the UN Secretary-General. This legitimisation activity was therefore organised and implemented by the UN General Assembly, which also happened to be the founder of the ICTR, as well as its sole funder. The action taken in commissioning an audit was substantive and could be classified as *role performance*. As it is linked to the performance of the organisation, this legitimacy challenge, and the legitimisation activity, exemplifies Suchman's *pragmatic* legitimacy type: the stakeholders provide their support in exchange for certain organisational behaviour.[149] In this case, however, the UN acted both as a key stakeholder and on behalf of the ICTR itself.

A similar exchange is demonstrated by the actions taken by the UN Secretary-General, who accepted the resignation of both Adede, the ICTR's registrar from Kenya, and Rakotomanana, the ICTR's deputy prosecutor from Madagascar, shortly after the publication of the OIOS's audit report in February 1997. As registrar of the Tribunal, Adede was responsible for the administration of the ICTR, including the hiring of personnel and management of funds. In his role as deputy prosecutor, it was up to Rakotomanana to set up and oversee the running of the office in Kigali, which had also been heavily criticised in the OIOS report.[150] This legitimisation action may also be categorised as *role*

145 Paul M. Hirsch and John Andrews, *Administrators' Response to Performance and Value Challenges - Or, Stance, Symbols and Behavior in a World of Changing Frames*, in: *Leadership and Organizational Culture: New Perspectives on Administrative Theory and Practice*, 1984, pp. 173-174; Suchman, 1995, pp. 597-598.

146 Ashforth & Gibbs, 1990, p. 180; Suchman, 1995, pp. 597-598.

147 United Nations General Assembly, *Audit and investigation of the International Criminal Tribunal for Rwanda*, Fifty-first Session, A/51/789, 6 February 1997, para. 2.

148 United Nations General Assembly, *Resolution 50/213C*, A/RES/50/213C, 15 July 1996.

149 Ashforth & Gibbs, 1990, p. 178; Suchman, 1995, pp. 578-579.

150 United Nations General Assembly, *Audit and investigation of the International Criminal Tribunal for Rwanda*, Fifty-first Session, A/51/789, 6 February 1997, para. 9-79 & 91; Beigbeder, 2011, p. 91; Magnarella, 2018, pp. 61-63.

performance, and is directly linked to the performance of the Tribunal, relating (again) to the exchange theory characterised by pragmatic legitimacy. The message is clear: the old management is being replaced due to poor management (poor performance) in order to ensure that the Tribunal can achieve its mandate.

The legitimisation action implemented by the ICTR itself was quite different in that there was no action. The ICTR's 1996 annual report – presented in September 1996 – does not mention UN Resolution 50/213C (adopted in July 1996), which related to the need for the OIOS to monitor activities at the ICTR, nor does it mention the presence of OIOS auditors in Arusha and Kigali.[151] Nothing was directly reported to the press, on behalf of the ICTR, at any point.

The second ICTR annual report – presented on 13 November 1997 – does, however, mention the audit and the subsequent resignation of Adede and Rakomanana:

> "In response to a request by the General Assembly and following complaints from Member states and staff members, auditors of the Office of Internal Oversight Investigation undertook an extensive investigation into affairs of the International Criminal Tribunal for Rwanda. As detailed in its report (A/51/789, annex), the Office uncovered serious operational deficiencies and mismanagement in the Tribunal's administration. The Office further found a lack of cooperation between the Registry and the Office of the Prosecutor and stated that the effectiveness of the Tribunal had been affected by the short term funding and lack of proper infrastructure in the offices at both Arusha and Kigali. In its report (ibid., chap. VI), some of which have been implemented or are in the process of being implemented.
> In the wake of the findings of the report, the Secretary-General, on 26 February 1997, appointed Mr. Agwu U. Okali as the new Registrar in the place of Mr. Adronico Adede, and on 20 March 1997 Mr. Bernard Muna as Deputy Prosecutor in place of Judge Honoré Rokotomanana. Further measures of reorganization of the Tribunal's administrative structure and replacement of staff members were taken by the new Registrar in implementation of the report of the Office of Internal Oversight Services."[152]

This section of the ICTR annual report effectively updates the UN General Assembly on the actions taken since their last meeting held in July 1996, in which Resolution 50/213C was adopted calling for an audit of the Tribunal.[153] The resignation of Adede and

151 ICTR, *1st Annual Report*, A/51/399-S/1996/778, 24 September 1996.
152 ICTR, *2nd Annual Report*, A/52/582-S/1997/868, 13 November 1997, Summary para. 3-4.
153 United Nations General Assembly, *Resolution 50/213C*, A/RES/50/213C, 15 July 1996.

Rokotomanana was otherwise not communicated by the ICTR: there was no press release issued, and internal documents relating to the two resignations and/or the OIOS audit were not found during the archival research at the IR-MCT in 2019. However, the UN did issue a press release on the matter in February 1997.[154]

This complex relationship between the ICTR and the UN is highlighted when identifying the targeted stakeholder of these legitimisation activities. Because the ICTR was established and funded by the UN and, as such, was accountable to both the UN Security Council and the UN General Assembly, it needed to promote its legitimacy to UN member states: the ICTR president provided an update on the activities of the Tribunal and its financial status on an annual basis. At the same time, it was in the UN's interest that both the ICTR and the ICTY were a success: these two tribunals symbolised the revival of international criminal law following the military tribunals based in Nuremburg (1945-1946) and Tokyo (1946-1948). Furthermore, the UN and its member states also felt a responsibility to support the work of the Tribunal given the lack of a response to the crimes committed in Rwanda in 1994.[155] The UN therefore played the role of facilitator and supporter of the ICTR, while also assuming the position of regulator and investor.[156]

In the case of the mismanagement at the ICTR, the UN took responsibility for resolving the legitimacy challenges faced by the Tribunal. As the founder and sole funder of the ICTR, it is understandable that the UN stepped in to resolve matters linked to the poor administration of this new criminal tribunal; especially given that the crisis occurred in the first years of the Tribunal's existence, when governance and operating standards were still in their infancy.

However, it is not clear why the ICTR's leadership, namely the president and the prosecutor, made no mention of these developments, and that the resolution of this management crisis – particularly at the Kigali Office, where Rwandans bore witness to the administrative chaos – was not addressed in the Rwandan press. No official statements were released – related either to the mismanagement or to the resignation of the two senior staff members – by the leadership of the Tribunal at the time.[157] Given that no internal memos were found relating to this legitimacy challenge, it is not clear whether the Tribunal

Further information regarding the OIOS audit at the ICTR may have been communicated through other UN channels.

154 UN Press Release, *Secretary-General accepts resignation of Deputy Prosecutor and Registrar of International Criminal Tribunal for Rwanda*, 26 February 1997. Retrieved from: https://www.un.org/press/en/1997/19970226.sgsm6172.html.

155 Peskin, 2008, pp. 159-161; Scheffer, 2013, p. 70.

156 United Nations Security Council, *Statute of the International Criminal Tribunal for Rwanda* (as amended on 31 December 2010), 8 November 1994, Articles 12*bis* & 15; United Nations General Assembly, *Resolution 50/213C*, A/RES/50/213C, 15 July 1996; United Nations Security Council, *Resolution 955*, S/RES/955, 8 November 1994.

157 President Judge Laïty Kama (May 1995 to June 1999); Prosecutor Goldstone (late 1994 to September 1996); Prosecutor Arbour (September 1996 to September 1999).

was exercising a symbolic action known as *concealment*,[158] where the organisation simply suppresses information likely to undermine organisational legitimacy.

As demonstrated above, it appears that the task of legitimisation was taken up by the UN itself. Documents show that the ICTR's management challenges were reported directly to the UN Secretary-General and the UN General Assembly by both ICTR staff members and UN member states.[159] These fundamental structural and operational matters – which occurred in the early years, at the start of the Tribunal's existence – were, therefore, addressed by the UN.

The only time the ICTR president publicly mentioned the mismanagement crisis was in response to comments made by Judge Lennart Aspegren during an interview with a Swedish journalist, in relation to his resignation from the Tribunal.[160] The page and a half statement by the Tribunal's president, Judge Kama, demonstrates *symbolic* legitimisation actions aimed at repairing the legitimacy of the ICTR.[161] Several types of symbolic action can be found in this short statement by Judge Kama.[162] First and foremost, Kama points out that there was a problem with individuals from the previous management team – distancing the legitimacy challenge from the Tribunal itself:

> "The fact that the former administration did not carry out its task properly and efficiently is well-known and is what led to the nomination of a new Registrar in March 1997. Since his arrival, a spirit of cooperation has prevailed, which has led to appreciable changes in the Judges' working conditions."[163]

Emphasising that the problem resided with the "*former administration*" provides an *excuse*for the setback.[164] Despite Judge Kama's role as president at the time, all responsibility was levelled towards those in charge of the Tribunal's administration: the former registrar and former deputy prosecutor.[165] The following section of Kama's statement provides some transparency regarding the current situation at the ICTR by accepting that the turmoil created by the mismanagement does remain; however, the paragraph ends by stating that the toxic culture that previously surrounded the Tribunal was now gone:

158 Ashforth & Gibbs, 1990, p. 180.

159 United Nations General Assembly, *Audit and investigation of the International Criminal Tribunal for Rwanda*, Fifty-first Session, A/51/789, 6 February 1997, Summary, para. 2.

160 Laïty Kama, *Statement by Judge Laïty Kama, President of the International Criminal Tribunal for Rwanda*, 28 July 1998. Retrieved from: https://search.archives.un.org/uploads/r/united-nations-archives/e/3/a/e3a14a3f584cf3a7d732933d576164d2d02b248ec61be2eb02d400166421bb97/S-1094-0025-04-00013.pdf.

161 Ashforth & Gibbs, 1990, p. 180.

162 Kama, 28 July 1998.

163 *idem.*, p. 1.

164 Ashforth & Gibbs, 1990, p. 180.

165 An *excuse* differs from the symbolic action *justification*; the latter describes situations in which an organisation will take responsibility for the situation or event in question (Ashforth & Gibbs, 1990, p. 180).

> "That being said, the situation is not perfect – far from it. Much remains to be done [...] However, in the quest to solve these problems, we feel it more appropriate to favour the path of cooperation over the kind of fruitless confrontation which has so poisoned the atmosphere at the ICTR in the past."[166]

Although recognising that *"Much remains to be done"*, the second sentence emphasises that the problems were related to former working relations and implicitly sends the message that there are no more challenges regarding the administration at the ICTR, which now *"favour[s] the path of cooperation"*. Depending on the state of affairs, this could reveal the use of the symbolic legitimisation action of *denial*, or possibly *concealment*,[167] by removing the impression that there may still be issues related to management within the ICTR.

The statement given by the ICTR president demonstrates symbolic legitimisation actions taken to*repair* legitimacy, following the damaging press interview given by a sitting ICTR Judge. Regardless of whether the comments made by Judge Aspegren are correct or not, the Tribunal was faced with a difficult situation, given that it was one of their own highly regarded judges that had issued negative statements about the ICTR, and Sweden (Judge Aspegren's home state) was one of the key supporters of the Tribunal.[168] Yet the legitimacy challenge was great enough for the ICTR president to respond.

The statement by Kama ends by reaffirming the goals of the ICTR. This symbolic legitimisation action confirms the importance of the ICTR and the need for support in order for it to complete its mandate by promoting its *socially acceptable goals*.[169] This symbolic action is generally used by organisations to underline and advertise their commendable mission – in this case, mandated by the Rwandan people and the international community:

> "In conclusion, mention should be made of the historical importance of the mission entrusted to the International Criminal Tribunal for Rwanda. Only faith in our mandate and cooperation among all will enable us to fulfill this mission and to work together to render justice to the people of Rwanda and the international community."[170]

166 Kama, 28 July 1998, p. 1.

167 Ashforth & Gibbs, 1990, p. 180.

168 For example: the Permanent Representative of Sweden to the UN Security Council negotiated the adoption of Resolution 1165 (United Nations Security Council, *Resolution 1165*, S/RES/1165, 30 April 1998) on behalf of the Tribunal, establishing a third Trial Chamber of three additional judges for the ICTR (ICTR Press release, *Security Council established third Trial Chamber for ICTR*, 1 May 1998. Retrieved from: https://unictr.irmct.org/en/news/security-council-establishes-third-trial-chamber-ictr).

169 Ashforth & Gibbs, 1990, p. 180.

170 Kama, 28 July 1998, p. 2.

In this case, there is no mention of any substantive actions being taken to repair legitimacy,[171] for example implementing procedures in order to monitor internal affairs or to regulate interviews given to the press – Aspegren's interview also revealed his intentions to leave the Tribunal, a snub towards the ICTR that is referred to in Kama's statement: "*we were sorry to learn through this interview, along with the rest of the world, that our colleague, Judge Aspegren, is contemplating leaving the ICTR at the end of this year.*"[172] The statement instead ends on a positive note, emphasising the importance of working together in order to achieve the ICTR's significant mission.[173]

A couple of years later (April 2000), these legitimacy challenges were addressed again during a speech given by Kingsley Moghalu – ICTR spokesperson – at an international conference in Germany.[174] The speech also made use of several symbolic legitimisation actions (namely *excuses* and *justifications*)[175] to address the past challenges faced by the ICTR. In a similar vein to Kama's statement,[176] the speech first refers to the problems of the former administration by emphasising the work of the new registrar, which Moghalu explains has improved the operations at the Tribunal considerably:

> "The ICTR faced significant operational problems in its start-up phase (1995-1996). Since the appointment of a new Registrar for the Tribunal on 26 February 1997, there has been a marked turnaround in the Tribunal's management and judicial support operations."[177]

The symbolic legitimisation action demonstrated in this section is the*excuse*, as Moghalu minimises the ICTR's involvement in these initial teething problems and implies that the root cause was linked to former staff members.[178] Unlike Kama's statement, Moghalu's

171 *idem.*, p. 178.

172 *ibid.*

173 The response to Judge Ostrovsky's resignation in 2002 was less public. The interview had been translated from Russian to English by Moscow News; it was in response to this article that the ICTR spokesperson, Kingsley Moghalu, wrote a letter on to the editor stating that the purpose of the interview had been seriously distorted (Boston Review, *Healing Rwanda: Can an international court deliver justice?* 1 December 2003; Internews, *Rwanda: Judge Ostrovsky Criticizes Kigali Tribunal*, 13 May 2002).

174 Conference on *Replacing the law of force with the force of law – African conflicts and the International Criminal Court* organised by the Committee for an Effective International Criminal Law in Konstanz, Germany, 5 April 2000.

175 Ashforth & Gibbs, 1990, p. 180.

176 Kama, 28 July 1998, p. 1.

177 Kingsley Chiedu Moghalu, *The International Criminal Tribunal for Rwanda and the development of an effective international criminal law – legal, political and policy dimensions*. An address at the International Conference on Replacing the law of force with the force of law – African conflicts and the International Criminal Court organised by the Committee for an Effective International Criminal Law in Konstanz, Germany, 5 April 2000, p. 9.

178 Ashforth & Gibbs, 1990, p. 180.

speech – given almost two years later – paints a more positive picture of the current situation at the Tribunal:

> "Virtually all recommendations of a critical United Nations audit report issued in early February 1997 have been implemented, and additional initiatives undertaken by the management. The Tribunal has thus left its difficult start-up phase behind it, although the process of improvement continues [...] Recent independent evaluations and audits of the ICTR have concluded that substantial improvements have been observed in all areas of the Tribunal's operations."[179]

Moghalu continues by emphasising that the challenges faced by the ICTR were, in part, due to its affiliation with the UN, which operates with specific rules and procedures that may not correspond to the operational needs of a (new) international criminal tribunal. This section of the speech demonstrates the symbolic action labelled as *redefining objectives and goals* through which the organisation frames its past (illegitimate) action in line with the current, acceptable social values.[180] A viable explanation is provided for the initial operational challenges faced by the Tribunal, which also aligns with accepted norms and values of the international audience to whom Moghalu is speaking:

> "Indeed, a frequent challenge encountered by the management of the International Tribunal is that of reconciling the unique operational necessities of the Tribunal with the fact that it is a United Nations body, to be administered in accordance with UN financial and personnel rules – which certainly did not contemplate the operational complexities of an international criminal tribunal [...] It is to the credit of the Tribunal's management that it has progressively improved the servicing of the Tribunal over the past three years in the context of UN administrative rules."[181]

Rather than shying away from the management challenges faced by the ICTR in its early years, the speech by Moghalu emphasises the challenges in running an international criminal tribunal, while adhering to the UN's strict financial regulations and human resources procedures, and operating in a region with limited infrastructure. The paragraph also demonstrates the symbolic legitimisation action of an *excuse*;[182] however, in this case

179 Moghalu, 5 April 2000, p. 9. In February 1998, OIOS provided a follow-up report on the situation at the ICTR (United Nations General Assembly, *Follow-up on audit and investigation of the ICTR*, Fifty-second Session, A/52/784, 6 February 1998).

180 Ashforth & Gibbs, 1990, p. 180.

181 Moghalu, 5 April 2000, p. 10.

182 Ashforth & Gibbs, 1990, p. 180.

Moghalu emphasises the constraints due to UN regulations and the limited resources and infrastructure in Arusha, rather than placing the blame on the actions of former colleagues. Furthermore, the final message provided to the international audience is that of recalibration, focusing on the efforts and achievements of the ICTR's management in running a ground-breaking organisation under such harsh conditions:

> "In assessing the management and judicial support operations of the ICTR, it is sometimes easy to forget a central perspective that should be borne in mind: The Tribunal is a pioneering international institution with a complex task, located in a small town in a developing country – with the attendant infrastructure limitations that made it understandably difficult to achieve an automatic efficiency in its start-up phase."[183]

These short paragraphs – within a speech related to a broader topic of international criminal justice in Africa, and the imminent opening of the ICC – demonstrates the very essence of the symbolic legitimisation action that "*transforms the meaning of acts*".[184] Furthermore, the international audience (comprised of UN member states) is reminded of the importance of the ICTR, which has managed to overcome substantial challenges in order to achieve its mandate.

The statement by Kama and the speech by Moghalu were the only two instances found in which the ICTR itself addressed the mismanagement issues of 1995 to 1997. On other, similar occasions, the topic was not raised; for example during a speech entitled "*The Rwandan Tribunal and accountability in Africa*" presented by the newly appointed deputy prosecutor on behalf of the newly appointed registrar on 1 November 1999, the focus was on the need for justice in Africa, and the important role that the ICTR plays in the region; no mention was made of the accountability challenges recently faced by the Tribunal itself.[185]

5.2.3 Stakeholders

The response to this legitimacy challenge appears to have been directed to the international community, namely the UN General Assembly. All communication is provided by the UN to the UN member states: UN Resolution 50/213C adopted by the UN General Assembly in July 1996 provides the first insight into the management crisis faced by the

183 *ibid.*
184 *ibid.*
185 Agwu Ukiwe Okali, *The Rwandan Tribunal and accountability in Africa*, 26th Ordinary Session of the African Commission on Human and Peoples' Rights, Kigali, Rwanda, 1 November 1999.

ICTR;[186] this is followed by an audit by OIOS, which reports directly back to the UN General Assembly in February 1997.[187] Following the report, the resignation and replacement of the registrar and the deputy prosecutor was coordinated by the UN Secretary-General and communicated to the UN General Assembly through a press release published in February 1997 and later in the ICTR's 2nd annual report, presented in November 1997.[188]

The statement and speech by two ICTR staff members – the president, Judge Kama, in 1998 and ICTR spokesperson, Moghalu, in 2000 – are also directed towards an international audience. No other official statement was found to be made by the ICTR with regard to the management and human resources challenges, or to the resignation of the two prominent staff members: Adede and Rokotomanana.

This legitimacy challenge again highlights the interesting dynamic between the UN and the ICTR: it is the UN that takes action, rather than the Tribunal itself. This is probably due to the nature of the legitimacy challenge, which relates to a lack of managerial leadership at the ICTR, poor oversight and possibly an error in the human resources recruitment process. As such, an external approach – with the UN Secretary-General and UN General Assembly taking the lead – was an understandable course of action. Furthermore, despite interviewees detailing mismanagement and nepotism throughout the Tribunal's existence (from 1995 to 2015), the legitimisation activities associated with the challenges associated with poor management, nepotism and corruption were only evident in 1996 and 1997.

However, another legitimacy challenge that falls within the category of human resources was addressed. It related to the discovery of individuals alleged to be*génocidaires* working within the Tribunal.

5.3 Génocidaires[189]

Legitimacy challenges related to human resources at the ICTR emerged again in May 2001 – just a year after Moghalu's speech in Germany – when an investigator recruited to work for a defence team was recognised as a possible perpetrator of genocidal acts. As news

186 United Nations General Assembly, *Resolution 50/213C*, A/RES/50/213C, 15 July 1996, para. 7 & 9.

187 United Nations General Assembly, *Audit and investigation of the International Criminal Tribunal for Rwanda*, Fifty-first Session, A/51/789, 6 February 1997.

188 UN Press Release, *Secretary-General accepts resignations of Deputy Prosecutor and Registrar of International Tribunal for Rwanda*,26 September 1997. Retrieved from: https://www.un.org/press/en/1997/19970226.sgsm6172.html; ICTR, *2nd Annual Report*, A/52/582-S/1997/868, 13 November 1997, Summary and para. 53-61.

189 *Génocidaire* is the Rwandan term used to refer to a perpetrator of genocide (in French this term would be referred to as *génocideurs)*. In the context of the Rwandan genocide, the term is used to describe both those that have been convicted of committing an act of genocide and those alleged to have committed an act of genocide (Thierry Cruvellier, *Court of Remorse Inside the International Criminal Tribunal for Rwanda*, University of Wisconsin Press, 2010, pp. 4-5).

spread of this discovery, the ICTR was soon accused by the Rwandan government of employing *génocidaires*.[190]

The events started in early May 2001, when Siméon Nshamihigo was recognised by a witness in the hallway of the ICTR:[191] "*We had an interesting development, when a member of a defence team was found to be a génocidaire. The witness was recognised by his voice. I think he had changed his appearance.*"[192] At the time, Nshamihigo was working as an investigator under the name of Sammy Bahati Weza, and was claiming to be a Congolese citizen. 'Sammy' had been working as part of the defence team for a former Rwandan military commander, Samuel Imanishimwe, since 1998. Imanishimwe was posted in the southern Cyangugu region at the time of the genocide and it later emerged that Nshamihigo himself had served as deputy prosecutor in the Cyangugu Prefecture during the 1994 genocide. The claim was that Nshamihigo had been involved in planning and participating in the massacres that occurred in the region.[193]

Following Nshamihigo's arrest, it was revealed that approximately 90% of the 50 defence investigators at the ICTR were Hutu from Rwanda, and that the screening procedure organised by the Registry to assess all employees was not geared to thoroughly checking and validating everyone's identity.[194] As explained by a former ICTR staff member: "*The issue of génocidaires was simply bad screening by the ICTR. It is quite normal as those standing accused wanted to give their family and their friends jobs. It was difficult for them to trust people at the ICTR. Their own people worked as investigators*".[195]

Although this development did not surprise some people working at the Tribunal, the discovery of individuals that may have been involved in committing crimes of genocide in Rwanda came as a blow to the ICTR: the idea that *génocidaires* were working within a criminal tribunal established to prosecute *génocidaires* was a difficult pill for many people to swallow, including the international community.[196] Simply put by one Rwandan interviewee: "*A big [legitimacy] problem was the génocidaires who worked as members of*

190 Peskin, 2008, pp. 195-198.

191 *idem.*, p. 196.

192 Interviewee T21.

193 ICTR, *Prosecutor v. Siméon Nchamihigo*, Judgment and Sentence, ICTR-01-63, 12 November 2008, para. 6-7; ICTR Press Release, *Defence investigator arrested*, 21 May 2001. Retrieved from: https://unictr.irmct.org/en/news/defence-investigator-arrested.

194 Peskin, 2008, p. 197.

195 Translated from French: *"La question des génocidaires était simplement un mauvais dépistage par le TPIR. Il est tout à fait normal que les accusés permanents voulaient donner du travail à leur famille et à leurs amis. Il leur était difficile de faire confiance aux gens du TPIR. Leurs propres travaillaient comme enquêteurs."* (T23).

196 IOL News, *UN Court contains genocide suspects*, 4 December 2001. Retrieved from: https://www.iol.co.za/news/africa/un-court-contains-genocide-suspects-77955; Peskin, 2008, p. 196.

staff at the ICTR".[197] However, it appeared that within the Tribunal this issue was widely known, according to another former ICTR staff member:[198]

> "Many génocidaires worked for the ICTR. Internally this was known. People just knew to call them by their other name. Of course they knew who they were. The best was for these people to work for ICTR. They were on the inside to know what was going on. It was the best place to hide."[199]

In a statement issued on 13 June 2001, the ICTR vowed to set aside sufficient resources to submit all current and prospective employees to a thorough background check;[200] and a month later, on 16 July 2001, the employment contracts of four Rwandan investigators were not renewed due to internal investigations showing that they may have been involved in the 1994 genocide.[201] At the end of the same year, a former ICTR investigator, Joseph Nzabirinda, was recognised in Belgium and subsequently arrested and transferred to the ICTR on 20 March 2002.[202] Nzabirinda was later convicted of having participated in mass executions and rapes in the Sahera region, where he originally came from.[203] In June 2006 it was reported that investigations had started regarding an additional 12 Rwandan employees suspected of having been involved in the genocide.[204]

197 Translated from French: "*Un gros problème était les génocidaires qui travaillaient comme membres du personnel du TPIR.*" (CS6).

198 This was refuted by other former ICTR staff members (T3, T7, T18, T25).

199 Translated from French: "*De nombreux génocidaires travaillaient pour le TPIR. Entre le personnel, cela était connu. Les gens savaient juste qu'il fallait les appeler par leur autre nom. Bien sûr, ils savaient qui ils étaient. Il valait mieux que ces personnes travaillent pour le TPIR. Ils étaient à l'intérieur pour savoir ce qui se passait. C'était le meilleur endroit pour se cacher.*" (T2).

200 ICTR Press Release, *Statement by the Registrar, Mr. Adama Dieng, on some issues relating to the defence of accused persons*,13 June 2001. Retrieved from: https://unictr.irmct.org/en/news/statement-registrar-mr-adama-dieng-some-issues-relating-defence-accused-persons.

201 ICTR Press Release, *Statement by the Registrar, Mr. Adama Dieng on the non-renewal of the employment contracts of certain defence investigators*,16 July 2001. Retrieved from: https://unictr.irmct.org/en/news/statement-registrar-mr-adama-dieng-non-renewal-employment-contracts-certain-defence; Peskin, 2008, p. 198.
One of the four, Aloys Ngendahimana, was wrongly accused given that he shared the same name as a suspect on Rwandan government's wanted list; his employment contract was promptly reinstated (Peskin, 2008, p. 198 – footnote 36).

202 ICTR Press Release, *Nzabirinda arrested in Belgium*, 21 December 2001. Retrieved from: https://unictr.irmct.org/en/news/nzabirinda-arrested-belgium.

203 ICTR, *Prosecutor v. Joseph Nzabirinda*. Sentence. ICTR-2001-77-T, 23 February 2007; ICTR Press Release, *Tribunal Sentences Nzabirinda to Seven Years Imprisonment,* 23 February 2007. Retrieved from: https://unictr.irmct.org/en/news/tribunal-sentences-nzabirinda-seven-years-imprisonment.

204 Global Policy Forum, *UN Tribunal Investigating 12 on Its Payroll*, 29 June 2006. Retrieved from: https://archive.globalpolicy.org/intljustice/tribunals/rwanda/2006/0629payroll.htm.

Yet, as mentioned by previous interviewees, the involvement of ICTR investigators in the 1994 genocide did not come as a surprise, as explained by another former ICTR staff member:

> "The discovery of the génocidaires working here was a huge scandal. But it made sense. These investigators knew who to go to, to find witnesses for the defence. It was another Rwandan who recognised him and asked what he was doing there. I wasn't working there at that time, but I have been in the public gallery with people who have been acquitted. Also with other people who took part in the genocide. As a staff member I had to remain neutral."[205]

In prosecuting one side of a divisive conflict between two ethnic groups - the Hutu and the Tutsi - it was incredibly difficult to find investigators in Rwanda who were willing to assist defence teams in conducting investigations for their Hutu clients:[206] *"Sometimes they employed people who were close to those who did it".*[207] Indeed, most of the accused insisted on compiling a team of trusted individuals, and would often employ relatives and/or friends:[208] *"There was a preselection. Sometimes it was not easy to know whether there were connections. If there was connection, this was unintentional. It could be that someone put a friend or their family member forward. We had an office here in Rwanda to do the interviews."*[209] Furthermore, defence teams needed investigators who spoke Kinyarwanda and who had local knowledge that would assist them in building a credible defence for their clients.[210] As a result, several Rwandans were hired as investigators for the defence teams,[211] some of whom were later accused of participating in the genocide themselves.[212]

To those watching events from outside the Tribunal's walls, the discovery of *génocidaires* working within the ICTR had serious implications on the Tribunal's legitimacy:

---

205 Interviewee T12.

206 Karel De Meester, *The Investigation Phase in International Criminal Procedure. Search of Common Rules*, DPhil thesis, University of Amsterdam, 2014, pp. 505-507.

207 Translated from French: "*Parfois Ils employaient des gens proches de ceux qui le faisaient.*" (T9)

208 Paige Arthur (ed.), *Identities in Transition: Challenges for Transitional Justice in Divided Societies*, Cambridge University Press, 2010, p. 164; ICTR Press Release, *Statement by the Registrar, Mr. Adama Dieng, on some issues relating to the defence of accused persons*, 13 June 2001; Peskin, 2008, p. 197.

209 Translated from French: "*Il y a eu une présélection. Parfois, il n'était pas facile de savoir s'il y avait des connexions. S'il y avait une connexion, ce n'était pas intentionnel. Il se peut que quelqu'un fasse avancer un ami ou un membre de sa famille. Nous avions un bureau ici au Rwanda pour faire les entretiens.*" (T23)

210 De Meester, 2014, pp. 502-503.

211 Sigall Horovitz, *How International Courts Shape Domestic Justice: Lessons from Rwanda and Sierra Leone*, Israel Law Review, 2013, 46, p. 354.

212 ICTR Press Release, *Statement by the Registrar, Mr. Adama Dieng on the non-renewal of the employment contracts of certain defence investigators*, 16 July 2001; Peskin, 2008, pp. 197-198.

> "The court was porous. The porosity was too high. There were influencers. I suspect certain forces were behind this. Maybe the French? Defence lawyers became génocidaires themselves. The ICTR became the source of fake news. Denialism stems from 1959. It is not new. What we see are the rehashing of genocidal thoughts. The ICTR was used as a vehicle for genocidal ideology."[213]

Several interviewees mentioned that during the trials in Arusha, there was a fear in Rwanda that the ICTR might be used as a platform for genocide deniers, especially given that *génocidaires* appeared to be working freely at the Tribunal: *"Those involved in the genocide were staff at the ICTR. The whole institution was incredibly political. They even had genocide deniers flown in as expert witnesses".*[214] The establishment of the Tribunal by the international community served as a recognition of the genocide that took place in 1994 and was created to prosecute those accused of committing acts of genocide, yet the lack of adequate screening of personnel working within the institution seemed to be undermining these efforts and was turning into a significant threat to the Tribunal's legitimacy: *"The negative of the ICTR was the corruption. There were génocidaires used as investigators. There was a good mandate, but not good will. There was interest in arresting some but not others. Why was this?".*[215]

The lack of information and explanations from the ICTR gave room for a variety of interpretations. It was therefore not surprising that the presence of *génocidaires* working within the Tribunal was raised by several interviewees when discussing the legitimacy of the ICTR.[216] Over 18 years after the discovery of Sammy's double identity, the legitimacy challenge linked to *génocidaires* working in Arusha continues to plague the (now closed) ICTR. For one interviewee, the conclusion to this legitimacy challenge was simple: *"This would not have happened if the ICTR had been located in Rwanda".*[217] From 1994 onwards any individual suspected of involvement in the genocide was arrested in Rwanda, and with the arrival of the gacaca courts in 2002, several thousand more were put on trial through this local justice system.[218] It would therefore have been difficult for an alleged *génocidaire* to have been involved in the activities of the ICTR if the trials had taken place in Kigali.

---

213 Interviewee A10.

214 Interviewee J3.

215 Interviewee CS7.

216 Interviewees A6, A9, A10, CS4, CS6, CS7, CS16, CS17, CS21, J1, J2, J3, J4, M2, M3, T1, T2, T5, T6, T9, T12, T21, T22 & T23.

217 Interviewee CS21.

218 Phuong N. Pham, Harvey M. Weinstein and Timothy Longman, *Trauma and PTSD Symptoms in Rwanda Implications for Attitudes Toward Justice and Reconciliation*, Jama, 2004, 292(5), pp. 610-612; Susan Thomson, *The Long Shadow of Genocide in Rwanda*, Current History, 2017, 116(790), pp. 84-86; Lars Waldorf, *Mass Justice for Mass Atrocity: Rethinking Local Justice as Transitional Justice*, Temple Law Review, 2006, 79, pp. 40-55.

5.3.1 *Repairing Legitimacy*

Similar to the administrative challenges that occurred at the ICTR in the late 1990s, the presence of *génocidaires* in Arusha was not related to any start-up challenges faced by the Tribunal – associated with *gaining*legitimacy – nor did this challenge correspond with promoting the ongoing work of the ICTR, which would involve legitimisation activities linked to *maintaining* legitimacy.[219] The reports claiming that *génocidaires* were working within the Tribunal were received as *"an unforeseen crisis"*, which ties the challenge to legitimisation activities designed to *repair* legitimacy.[220]

This legitimacy challenge also touched the core of the ICTR's mission: as a Tribunal established to prosecute those responsible for the gravest crimes committed in 1994, reports that those involved in brutal killings and rapes were working within the ICTR touched on all three challenges linked to *repairing* legitimacy: *performance*, *value* and *meaning*.[221] The presence of alleged génocidaires working freely at the Tribunal in Arusha was a legitimacy challenge connected to the ICTR's *value* (*moral*legitimacy), which relates to norms and societal beliefs of the organisation's environment – in this case involving both Rwanda and the international community.[222] Additionally, the *meaning* and purpose of the ICTR were also questioned – reflecting *cognitive* legitimacy – given that the existence of the organisation was in doubt.[223] It was difficult to imagine that a court of law, established to prosecute those suspected of committing international crimes, would allow the very same individuals to work at the ICTR. As expressed by the special representative for the Rwandan government at the time, Martin Ngoga: *"we are not ready to tolerate this"*.[224]

When examining both the external and internal reports linked to the hiring of the *génocidaires*, it appears, however, that the Tribunal was most focused on protecting its *pragmatic legitimacy*, linked to the performance of the Tribunal. *Performance challenges* are directly related to the actions and behaviour of an organisation.[225] The ICTR had experienced challenges related to recruitment throughout its existence[226] and it appeared that the UN's bureaucratic human resources procedures, used to recruit staff and perform background checks, failed to prevent suspected *génocidaires* from receiving security passes and gaining access to the corridors of the Tribunal.[227]

219 Suchman, 1995, p. 594.
220 *idem.*, p. 597.
221 Deephouse et al., 2017, p. 23; Suchman, 1995, pp. 597-598.
222 Ashforth & Gibbs, 1990, p. 184.
223 *ibid.*
224 IOL News, *UN Court contains genocide suspects*, 4 December 2001.
225 Hirsch & Andrews, 1984, pp. 173-174; Peskin, 2008, p. 196.
226 Kilemi, 2016, p. 2.
227 Peskin, 2008, p. 196.

Ngoga – the Rwandan government's special representative based at the Tribunal – was adamant that such a fiasco would not have happened had the Tribunal been located in Kigali.[228] The Rwandan government's response was therefore focused on *performance* issues (*pragmatic* legitimacy), namely poor employment oversight, rather than casting doubt over the very existence of the Tribunal (*cognitive* legitimacy) or questioning its mission and values (*moral* legitimacy).[229] Furthermore, given that the Registry was responsible for recruiting, hiring and conducting security checks on all staff, the legitimacy challenge and subsequent legitimisation activities centred around the workings of this particular organ of the Tribunal, as opposed to the ICTR as a whole.[230]

5.3.2 *Pragmatic Legitimacy*

The arrest of Siméon Nshamihigo (aka Sammy Bahati Weza) on Saturday 19 May 2001 was the first clear legitimisation action taken by the ICTR. As a court of law, the Tribunal responded to the report that a suspected*génocidaire* was working in its buildings in a manner that would be expected of such an establishment. There is no information regarding the events leading up to the arrest, nor the time it took for the Tribunal to take action. The suspect was recognised in early May (date unknown) and the arrest took place on 19 May. This substantive legitimisation action – the act of arresting a defence investigator that was working at the ICTR – relates to Suchman's *pragmatic* legitimacy type: the ICTR responds in a way that is deemed appropriate, otherwise known as *"role performance"*.[231]

The second legitimisation action taken by the ICTR comes in the form of a statement, made by the registrar on Monday 21 May, two days after Nshamihigo's arrest. The following paragraph clearly places the responsibility for hiring a suspected *génocidaire* with the defence teams:

> "Defence investigators are not staff members of the ICTR. They are independent contractors recruited by defence counsel as part of the defence teams and their fees are part of the legal aid package for indigent accused persons funded by the ICTR. Defence teams are independent in the manner in which they prepare their defence."[232]

---

228 IOL News, *UN Court contains genocide suspects*, 4 December 2001.
229 *ibid.*
230 Peskin, 2008, p. 196.
231 Ashforth & Gibbs, 1990, p. 178; Suchman, 1995, pp. 578-579.
232 ICTR Press Release, *Defence investigator arrested*,21 May 2001.

This statement – identified as a form of *symbolic* legitimisation action[233] – removes the connection between Sammy, a defence investigator, and the Tribunal: "*Defence investigators are not staff members of the ICTR*". This category of symbolic actions relates to the *excuse* as it removes the ICTR from the situation; the focus is pointed towards the defence teams rather than the Tribunal's administrative procedures, namely the staff security checks. *Excuses* are used by an organisation in an attempt to minimise their responsibility or connection for a given situation or event; this legitimisation activity often deflects causality to another party or event and the statement given by the Registry clearly directs responsibility elsewhere: *"They [defence investigators] are independent contractors recruited by defence counsel"*. This line provides an explanation as to how the investigator in question was recruited: the connection is made between the defence teams and the investigators. Furthermore, the investigators are *"independent contractors"*, which further removes the ICTR from any responsibility.

However, the ICTR did not manage to distance itself far enough. The following day, Ngoga, the special representative for the Rwandan government, gave a press conference during which he stated that he: *"disagreed with a claim made in a press release issued on Tuesday by the ICTR stating that defence investigators were not staff of the UN court. 'The ICTR is claiming to be screening these defence investigators. How can they do this if they are not in their payroll?' he asked"*. [234] In response to Ngoga's comments, the ICTR took another approach, providing a second press statement to explain that:

> "[The ICTR] does screen defence investigators, who are hired under contract by defence lawyers with the approval of the tribunal. [The ICTR] says security screening considers, but does not depend on the Rwandan government's list of suspects. Although Nshamihigo's name appears on Rwanda's primary list of top genocide suspects, he had been working under the alias of Sammy Bahati Weza, with a forged passport from the DRC."[235]

The use of the legitimisation activity in the form of an *excuse* remains: defence investigators "*are hired under contract by defence lawyers*"; however, in this second statement the Tribunal takes responsibility for screening the defence investigators. The symbolic legitimisation activity used here related to the *justification*:[236] the ICTR's Registry does perform security screening, however, the fact that the investigator was operating under a false name and provided forged documents made it impossible to find him on the Rwandan government's

233 Ashforth & Gibbs, 1990, p. 180.

234 InterNews, *Government welcomes arrest of investigator*,22 May 2001. Retrieved from: https://www.thenewhumanitarian.org/report/21514/rwanda-government-welcomes-arrest-investigator.

235 *ibid.*

236 Ashforth & Gibbs, 1990, p. 180.

list of suspects. There is no apology for the fact that Nshamihigo was indeed hired following approval from the ICTR and, most importantly, no responsibility is taken for this security breach.

A few weeks later, the Registry released a third statement related to this matter, which announced additional screening measures for those working on the defence teams:

> "Personal history forms to be filled by individuals who are hired by defence counsel as defence investigators, requiring more detailed information about the backgrounds of such individuals to ensure, among others, that they are not related to accused persons detained by the Tribunal. The information requested of such potential investigators is not as detailed as that required of staff members directly employed by the United Nations, which demonstrates that this is part of a normal process and is not discriminatory; Enhanced screening of potential and serving defence investigators to ensure that no members of defence teams obtain positions by false pretences as to identity or have engaged in activity incompatible with the purposes of the Tribunal."[237]

Through this statement, the ICTR maintained its distance from the defence investigators: "*The information requested [...]is not as detailed as that required of staff members directly employed by the United Nations.*"[238] The Tribunal again uses the symbolic legitimisation action of an*excuse*; however, the statement also implies that substantive action is taking place, in the form of *role performance.*[239] Although no evidence was found during this research that confirmed a change in the screening practices, if the statement is to be believed, the ICTR responded to the expectations (and/or possibly the requests) of its stakeholders. This same message was given to the UN General Assembly:

> "While members of defence teams, such as defence investigators, are not staff members of the Tribunal, but independent contractors hired by defence counsel, the Tribunal has taken measures to ensure more effective administrative control over their recruitment before approving such appointments. All prospective defence investigators are now required to provide an undertaking that they are not relatives of any detainee of the Tribunal. Security screening of potential investigators has been markedly increased by the Registry with the assistance of relevant national authorities."[240]

237 ICTR Press Release, *Statement by the Registrar, Mr. Adama Dieng, on some issues relating to the defence of accused persons*, 13 June 2001.

238 *ibid.*

239 Ashforth & Gibbs, 1990, p. 178.

240 ICTR, *6th Annual Report*, A/56/351–S/2001/863, 14 September 2001, p. 25.

Aside from the UN General Assembly, the main stakeholder involved was the Rwandan government, and on 22 May, Internews reported that:

> "The special representative of the Rwandan government to the International Criminal Tribunal for Rwanda (ICTR) in Arusha, Tanzania, Martin Ngoga, has praised the arrest on 19 May of Simeon Nshamihigo, a defence team investigator suspected of involvement in the 1994 genocide. "It's a good beginning. Although it's come late, the tribunal has started some 'house cleaning'," Ngoga told Internews. "It's a courageous move. It's not embarrassing for the ICTR to arrest one of its people. It's more embarrassing to allow these suspects around." Ngoga urged that the ICTR "be cleaned up", noting that some genocide suspects were still among ICTR staff. "The ICTR is Rwanda's partner. Rwanda believes the tribunal can act when alerted."[241]

The legitimisation action performed by the ICTR in this case mirrors the legitimacy challenge related to *performance* and the *pragmatic* legitimacy type. Action is taken to restore confidence in the organisation, which relates to the exchange theory, where stakeholders provide their support in exchange for a certain organisational behaviour.[242] Furthermore, in a second press conference related to this matter, the registrar stated that the actions taken by the Registry were in fact made to "*protect the integrity of the Tribunal's judicial process*".[243] In line with this, an additional legitimisation action was implemented the following month and detailed during a press conference:

> "[...] the Registrar has decided that the employment contracts of certain defence investigators employed by defence counsel in cases before the Tribunal, which have recently expired, will not be renewed. The contract of one defence investigator, which is still valid, has been suspended."[244]

The actions taken by the Registry, as stated here, further reinforce the substantive action in the shape of *role performance*.[245] At this point the Tribunal had still not provided a public apology regarding the presence of a suspected *génocidaire* working on their premises. Legitimisation activities under the form of *excuses* and*justifications* were provided, and the ICTR took action as expected – demonstrating *role performance* – by arresting the

241 *ibid.*
242 Ashforth & Gibbs, 1990, p. 178.
243 ICTR Press Release, *Statement by the Registrar, Mr. Adama Dieng on the non-renewal of the employment contracts of certain defence investigators*, 16 July 2001.
244 *ibid.*
245 Ashforth & Gibbs, 1990, p. 178.

accused, enforcing a stricter screening protocol for defence investigators and by removing four defence investigators suspected of being involved in the 1994 genocide. The final paragraph of the press release further provides the ICTR with an opportunity to emphasise its independence, as an impartial court:

> "It is of utmost importance to stress that, in making these decisions, the Registry of the International Tribunal makes no presumption of the guilt of these individuals for the crimes of which they are suspected or accused. Thus, the Tribunal stands ready to reconsider them for clearance for employment by any defence counsel in the Tribunal should they be cleared of the charges and suspicions against them in the Rwandan judicial system or in the International Tribunal. Official communications of these decisions, including the reasons for them, and the fact that they are made without prejudice to the findings of the relevant legal/judicial processes, have been transmitted to the Defence Counsel on whose teams these Defence Investigators are employed."[246]

This statement highlights the fact that the accused are not to be presumed guilty, which aligns with the substantive legitimisation activity related to *role performance*: the ICTR is an independent court of law and will continue to act as such.[247]

These legitimisation activities did not, however, appear to satisfy the Rwandan government. On 30 November 2001, three news outlets – JusticeInfo, the Daily News and The New Times[248] – reported that the Rwandan government was conducting its own investigation into each of the Rwandan investigators working for defence teams in Arusha: *"Ngoga said Rwanda had submitted a report to the ICTR Registry and was asking the Tribunal to conduct its own investigation. The ICTR has played down the issue, with Registrar Adama Dieng saying that he was "not aware" of Rwanda's report."*[249]

An article in the Daily News published the ICTR registrar's response to Rwanda's investigation: "*We'll not accept any names from the Rwandan government. We have an independent way of conducting our investigations for any doubtful character.*"[250] Regardless of these assurances from the Tribunal's registrar, there was unease within the defence

246 ICTR Press Release, *Statement by the Registrar, Mr. Adama Dieng on the non-renewal of the employment contracts of certain defence investigators*, 16 July 2001.

247 Ashforth & Gibbs, 1990, p. 178.

248 JusticeInfo is an independent media outlet (headquartered in Switzerland) affiliated with the Hirondelle New Agency, which was based at the ICTR; The Daily News and The New Times are national, English language newspapers in Rwanda.

249 JusticeInfo, *ICTR Prosecutor to indict another defence investigator*, 30 November 2001. Retrieved from: https://www.justiceinfo.net/en/hirondelle-news/16499-en-en-ictr-prosecutor-to-indict-another-defence-investigator72657265.html.

250 Daily News, *Rwanda claims genocide suspects work at ICTR*, 5 December 2001.

teams that the Rwandan government might take the opportunity to place any Rwandan working as an investigator in Arusha on their list of suspects, thereby obstructing the work of the defence teams.[251]

A few weeks after this statement, the ICTR was thrown into the spotlight yet again following the arrest of Nzabirinda (a former investigator) in Belgium. A press release was issued regarding the arrest, although just a couple of lines connect the suspect to the ICTR:

> "He was formerly an investigator working for the defence team of Sylvain Nsabimana, former prefect of Butare, another of the accused in the "Butare" case. Nzabirinda's contract was rescinded earlier this month when Registry officials established that he had presented false identity documents to the Tribunal."[252]

The rest of the 306-word statement gives information on the charges against Nzabirinda and provides an overview of the other arrests that had taken place since 1995, highlighting the countries involved in assisting the Tribunal. The fact that this latest suspect used to work at the ICTR is engulfed by the information related to Nzabirinda indictment and the multiple other arrests made in the name of the Tribunal. The statement could be considered as demonstrating the symbolic action related to *promotion of socially acceptable goals,*[253] as it emphasises the achievement of the Tribunal in arresting 56 individuals (including a record of 12 in 2001).

When Nzabirinda's former position at the Tribunal is mentioned, the statement explains that his contract has been rescinded: *"Nzabirinda's contract was rescinded earlier this month when Registry officials established that he had presented false identity documents to the Tribunal".*[254] Revoking Nzabirinda's contract provides an opportunity for the ICTR to demonstrate that its new security checks were working, which relates to *role performance*: the organisation is demonstrating that measures are in place to prevent or to terminate the employment of *génocidaires.*[255]

---

251 Peskin, 2008, p. 198. This dilemma was demonstrated again with the arrest and release of Callixte Gakwaya – lead defence counsel of Yusuf Munyakazi (ICTR Press Release, *Arrest of Counsel Callixte Gakwaya,* 5 September 2006. Retrieved from: https://unictr.irmct.org/en/news/arrest-counsel-callixte-gakwaya; ICTR Press Release, *Counsel Callixte Gakwaya Released,* 5 September 2006. Retrieved from: https://unictr.irmct.org/en/news/counsel-callixte-gakwaya-released; Global Policy Forum, *Rwanda: Government could cut links,* 12 September 2006. Retrieved from: https://archive.globalpolicy.org/intljustice/tribunals/rwanda/2006/0912cutlinks.htm).

252 ICTR Press Release, *Nzabirinda arrested in Belgium*, 21 December 2001.

253 Ashforth & Gibbs, 1990, p. 180.

254 ICTR Press Release, *Nzabirinda arrested in Belgium*, 21 December 2001.

255 Ashforth & Gibbs, 1990, p. 178.

Following this statement, released in December 2001, there is no information regarding the employment of *génocidaires* at the ICTR for almost five years. On 29 June 2006, Everard O'Donnell, the acting deputy registrar, informed reporters that the ICTR was investigating 12 individuals on the Tribunal's payroll with possible links to crimes committed in 1994 – the names were provided by the Rwandan government in March.[256] Aside from this oral statement, no other information was found that mentioned the hiring of *génocidaires*:[257] the interviews, literature review and archival research do not provide any additional information, nor are there any other public statements (known) on this matter. It therefore appears that the Tribunal simply had nothing else to report on this matter. Likewise, there were no additional statements issued by the Rwandan government's special representative.

There was, however, an incident of a slightly different nature that took place on 1 September 2006, involving Callixte Gakwaya – the lead defence counsel for Yusuf Munyakazi's case. Gakwaya apparently featured on the Rwandan government's list of suspected *génocidaires* and as a result was arrested by Tanzanian police on 5 September 2006.[258] However, Gakwaya was released on the same day,[259] and circumstances surrounding both the arrest and the conditions of Gakwaya's release from police custody remain unknown: "*The Registrar of the ICTR observes that he has no warrant of arrest to execute from any Government*".[260]

The Rwandan government claimed that Gakwaya was a genocide suspect and urged the ICTR to terminate his contract.[261] As stated in the two ICTR press releases related to this event,[262] the ICTR was made aware of the arrest and immediately took action: "*As soon as the Tribunal was informed, appropriate measures were taken to secure the welfare of Mr. Gakwaya in police custody. Security officers have visited the Central Police Station in Arusha on several occasions and have spoken to Mr. Gakwaya*".[263]

Although quick to act on this matter, it remains unclear whether additional defence investigators or ICTR staff members were suspended or asked to resign as a result of the

256 Global Policy Forum, *UN Tribunal Investigating 12 on Its Payroll*, 29 June 2006.
257 No press release can be found on this topic, nor is there any mention during speeches or in the annual reports.
258 ICTR Press Release, *Arrest of Counsel Callixte Gakwaya*, 5 September 2006; Global Policy Forum, *UN Tribunal Investigating 12 on Its Payroll*, 29 June 2006.
259 ICTR Press Release, *Counsel Callixte Gakwaya Released*, 5 September 2006.
260 ICTR Press Release, *Arrest of Counsel Callixte Gakwaya*,5 September 2006.
261 Global Policy Forum, *Rwanda: Government could cut links*, 12 September 2006.
262 ICTR Press Release, *Arrest of Counsel Callixte Gakwaya*,5 September 2006; ICTR Press Release, *Counsel Callixte Gakwaya Released*, 5 September 2006.
263 ICTR Press Release, *Arrest of Counsel Callixte Gakwaya*,5 September 2006.

internal investigations described in June 2006. In the case of Gakwaya, the defence lawyer subsequently resigned and was taken off the ICTR's list of possible lawyers.[264]

5.3.3 Stakeholders

Unlike the legitimacy challenges caused by mismanagement in the late 1990s, the legitimacy challenge faced by the Tribunal regarding individuals suspected of committing genocidal acts working within the confines of the ICTR in Arusha was addressed by the Tribunal and not by the UN. Information was provided via the website in the form of press releases, and the separate incidents were reported to the UN General Assembly through the ICTR's annual report. Yet, the dialogue regarding this topic appears to have primarily taken place with the special representative of the government of Rwanda (Martin Ngoga at the time). Indeed, the Rwandan government was closely involved throughout the duration of this challenge and even offered additional resources, namely by providing lists of suspected *génocidaires* and offering to conduct investigations.

This legitimacy challenge demonstrates that the ICTR was walking a fine line, which is best demonstrated by the arrest and detention of Callixte Gakwaya, a member of a defence team working at the Tribunal in Arusha. The Tribunal could not be seen to be harbouring suspected criminals while conducting high-profile trials against those most responsible for crimes committed in Rwanda, and receiving assistance from Rwanda and resources from the international community. However, the Tribunal also needed to demonstrate integrity and protect the process of international criminal law; this included the protection of the defence counsel and their teams, ensuring that there was no intimidation from external parties. Taking the role of impartial adjudicator of international criminal law in a politically sensitive environment was, therefore, not always easy or straightforward. Rwanda was a key stakeholder, with the power to put a stop to all ICTR activity taking place on its territory, yet the Tribunal needed to demonstrate impartiality in order to remain legitimate as a court of law, especially in the eyes of the international community.

264 All Africa News, Rwanda: Gakwaya Fired; Rwanda Demands Details, 18 September 2006. Retrieved from: https://allafrica.com/stories/200609190051.html; BBC, Rwanda singer on genocide charges, 18 September 2006. Retrieved from: http://news.bbc.co.uk/2/hi/africa/5357062.stm.

5.4 Context: Culture, Language and People

At the time of establishment, the ICTR did not have a body of case law to draw on for either the definition or the application of crimes against humanity or genocide.[265] The absence of any legislative process at an international level meant that the work of the OTP at the ICTR was grounded solely on the OTP's own strategy, and the only authority governing and guiding the actions of the chief prosecutor was the UN Security Council.[266] The newness of international criminal law in the early 1990s raised questions not only with regard to the legality of the courts, namely the ICTY and the ICTR, but also the legitimacy of these tribunals, which were questioned, especially given the authority of the OTP and the UN Security Council in deciding the course of proceedings at the ICTR.[267] As one interviewee, a former ICTR staff member, explained: "*If it is legality versus legitimacy, what is needed for legitimacy is agreeing on the facts and understanding the context*".[268]

Understanding the divisiveness of the Rwandan conflict, the environment and the landscape in which the conflict took place, and the context of the genocide, was therefore of great importance, especially given the location of the Tribunal in Tanzania and the fact that the events of 1994 were so difficult to comprehend, even for those who had lived through it: "*During a genocide people become animals. This is very hard to explain. We can't talk about genocide without taking into account its strength, the animality. All humanity was gone. On both sides*".[269] Furthermore, Rwanda's history was key to understanding the importance of the Tribunal's work, and, to some extent, the actions that led to the atrocious crimes committed in 1994: "*Justice was most important. There was no justice for the crimes committed prior to 1994. Despite many other genocides against Tutsi. The survivors didn't expect justice after 1994 as they didn't receive it before.*"[270]

In understanding Rwanda's history, a few interviewees compared the African and the European context with regard to the narrative used by the Tribunal when referring to Rwanda's genocide.[271] This is demonstrated in the following quote from a Rwandan lawyer:

> "Why is it known as the genocide against the Tutsi and moderate Hutu? Why bring up the Hutu? What do they mean by moderate? They didn't do this for

---

265 Robert Cryer, Darryl Robinson and Sergey Vasiliev, *An Introduction to International Criminal Law and Procedure*, Cambridge University Press, 2019, pp. 207-209 & 228-229.

266 Cryer et al., 2019, p. 137; Elies van Sliedregt and Sergey Vasiliev, 2014, *Pluralism in International Criminal Law*, Oxford University Press, pp. 60-69.

267 Section 4.1.

268 Translated from French: "*Si c'est la légalité contre la légitimité, ce qu'il faut pour la légitimité c'est de s'entendre sur les faits et de comprendre le contexte.*" (T23).

269 Interviewee CS5.

270 Interviewee CS7.

271 Interviewees J3, J4 & CS6.

> the Holocaust. There is no mention of moderate Germans. Do they mention the gypsies and other minority groups targeted? The genocide here was conducted against the Tutsi. Hutu were recognised here for their bravery. They were given medals. There is a special graveyard here for politicians. Both Hutu and Tutsi politicians gave their lives. Why should we mention them as part of the genocide? It was not aimed at these moderate Hutu but at eradicating Tutsi."[272]

Aside from the physical distance of the Tribunal from Rwanda, due to its location in Arusha, it was also important for the ICTR to take cultural and historical distance of the courtroom and those who worked at the ICTR into consideration.[273] This was especially important when it came to the languages and the words used in the courtroom: "*Genocide in Africa is very different than the Holocaust in Europe, where everything was documented. In Africa it was very well organised but everything was oral. Witnesses were vital. However this leaves room for misunderstandings.*"[274]

During the course of the ICTR's existence, over 3,400 individuals were called to testify for both the defence and the prosecution.[275] The precision of ICTR judgments and the legitimacy of the Tribunal depended on the accuracy of these testimonies. This in itself presented several challenges, namely the misunderstandings of first-hand witness statements.[276] Early on, during the trial of Jean-Paul Akayesu, the judges were informed that the majority of Rwandans transmit information as if they had witnessed the event first-hand, even if they received the information from another source.[277] Dr. Ruzindana, an expert witness on linguistics,[278] explained that "*most Rwandans live in an oral tradition in which facts are reported as they are perceived by the witness, often irrespective of whether the facts were personally witnessed or recounted by someone else*".[279]

In addition to the cultural misunderstandings, there were fears of corruption and bias with regard to the choice of witnesses that testified in court. Suspicions regarding the provenance and motivations of witnesses who testified at the ICTR were relayed during

272 Interviewee J3.

273 ICTR, *Prosecutor v. Jean-Paul Akayesu*, Judgment, ICTR-96-4-T, 2 September 1998, para. 145-156; Paige Arthur (ed.), *Identities in Transition: Challenges for Transitional Justice in Divided Societies*, Cambridge University Press, 2010, pp. 165-167.

274 Interviewee T24.

275 Klaus Bachmann and Aleksandar Fatić, *The UN International Criminal Tribunals: Transition Without Justice?* Routledge, 2015, p. 77

276 Jose E. Alvarez, *Crimes of States/Crimes of Hate: Lessons from Rwanda*, Yale Journal of International Law, 1999, 24, p. 404.

277 *ibid.*

278 Dr. Mathias Ruzindana was Professor of Linguistics at the University of Rwanda at the time of the trial (ICTR, *Prosecutor v. Jean-Paul Akayesu*, Judgment, ICTR-96-4-T, 2 September 1998, para. 340).

279 ICTR, *Prosecutor v. Jean-Paul Akayesu*, Judgment, ICTR-96-4-T, 2 September 1998, para. 155.

the interviews conducted for this research. In one case, the head of a civil society organisation that represents survivors of the 1994 genocide asked: "*How were they [the witnesses] selected? Were they corrupted? I know of victims that applied to testify but were refused*".[280] A former ICTR employee explained that certain witnesses were often used for multiple trials: "*Witnesses were paid ten dollars a day or a hundred if they stayed in a hotel rather than in the ICTR lodgings. This is a lot of money. Lots of witnesses came several times. They became professional witnesses*".[281] A journalist who reported on the trials in Arusha questioned the ability of an eye witness to recount atrocious events:

> "It was not clear how witnesses were chosen, there was no information. What could we expect? Also, who is the eye witness? If they did see something and did not get killed, how can they remember all the facts under such traumatic circumstances? Also several years after the events?"[282]

Questioning the credibility of the witnesses, and the testimony provided during trials at the ICTR, was a threat to the legitimacy of the Tribunal and the validity of the judgments issued by its Chambers.[283] In 2007, a witness for the prosecution – referred to as GAA – was sentenced to nine months imprisonment for admitting to having provided a false testimony;[284] and in 2016 Augustin Ngirabatware filed a request for the review of the Appeal Chamber's judgment regarding his case, based on letters of retraction provided by four prosecution witnesses whose previous testimony had weighed heavily on the former minister's initial conviction.[285] Witness tampering was also reported in relation to the case of the Rwandan singer, Simon Bikindi, in 2007: "*the Registrar's attention was drawn to an allegation [...] that Maitre Momo had attempted to influence a protected prosecution witness in the Bikindi trial*";[286] and during a staff meeting in 2005, the registrar raised concerns regarding the involvement of ICTR staff in witness tampering:

> "I have received reports that are currently under investigation which indicate that some of the Registry staff who have been entrusted with the delicate

280 Interviewee CS3.

281 Translated from French: "*Les témoins étaient payés dix dollars par jour ou cent s'ils restaient à l'hôtel plutôt que dans les locaux du TPIR. C'est beaucoup d'argent. De nombreux témoins sont venus plusieurs fois. Ils sont devenus des témoins professionnels.*" (T2).

282 Interviewee M2.

283 Nancy A. Combs, *Fact-Finding without Facts: The Uncertain Evidentiary Foundations of International Criminal Convictions*,Cambridge University Press, 2010, pp. 121-122.

284 ICTR, *Prosecutor v. GAA*,Judgment and Sentence, ICTR-07-90-R77, 4 December 2007.

285 IR-MCT, *Prosecutor v. Augustin Ngirabatware*, Review Judgment, MICT-12-29-R, 27 September 2019, para. 5-7 & 63.

286 ICTR Press Release, *Allegations against Bikindi Co-Counsel not well founded*,20 March 2007. Retrieved from: https://unictr.irmct.org/en/news/allegations-against-bikindi-co-counsel-not-well-founded.

> assignment of caring for witnesses, may have been involved in conduct that might prejudice and pervert the course of justice. It is alleged that attempts were made to corrupt and induce some witnesses in order to have them change their statements before the Tribunal."[287]

Aside from challenges related to the witnesses that testified at the Tribunal, the ICTR also needed to take the language barrier into consideration given that Kinyarwanda was the language used by most of the witnesses and by some of the accused.[288] At the time of the Tribunal's establishment, there were no Kinyarwanda translators within the UN system. Most documents submitted to the Tribunal were in Kinyarwanda and needed to be translated first from Kinyarwanda into French, and then from French into English (French and English being the two official languages of the Tribunal).[289] The Registry needed to train a large number of interpreters to manage both the live interpretations and the translation of documents:[290] "*We eventually worked with a template that was very straightforward. Every word or phrase corresponded to the equivalent word in the language we were translating to*".[291]

Yet even with training and an adapted template, there are some Kinyarwanda phrases and words that cannot be translated directly into English and French and *vice versa*:[292] "*You cannot translate directly to Kinyarwanda. The language has a very different structure*".[293] This was especially significant in the courtroom, as translators needed to hear the entire answer to a question, when spoken in Kinyarwanda, before interpreting it into French or English;[294] and, in some cases, the translations did not make sense:[295] "*it was very frustrating to listen to the translations and realise that they were not correct*".[296] Given that there were no Rwandans sitting as judges and few Rwandans working for the OTP the risk was high that any possible mistakes in the translations would be missed.[297] As explained by a Rwandan lawyer:

> "It had its challenges. There was a bias of procedure and misrepresentation. There were not enough Rwandans involved in the process. Counsel was not

287 Adama Dieng, *Registrar's special address to staff members on their ethical duties and obligations*, Simba Hall, Arusha, 20 May 2005, p. 9.
288 Arthur, 2010, p. 166.
289 *idem.*, footnote 44.
290 Combs, 2010, p. 72.
291 Interviewee T8.
292 Arthur, 2010, pp. 166-167; Combs, 2010, p. 87.
293 Interviewee T8.
294 Arthur, 2010, p. 166 – footnote 44; interviewee T8.
295 Combs, 2010, pp. 73-74.
296 Interviewee M2.
297 Combs, 2010, pp. 73-74; Kamatali, 2005, pp. 93-94.

> representing the victims. There was a lack of understanding of Rwanda, of Rwandans."[298]

The use of euphemisms is a good example of this, as they are often used to discuss subjects that are taboo or sensitive within a local culture: the interpreters therefore had to convey the cultural meaning behind certain expressions used by witnesses.[299] The word *rape*, for example, cannot be directly translated into Kinyarwanda but is rather described through five different expressions, all of which have a different connotation.[300] This was also raised by a former ICTR staff member:

> "Judges should take time to understand the context. [...] This was evident in the case of Bikindi, the famous Rwandan singer. His songs could be interpreted as neutral, but at the time they gave people a strong message. It was the same for the Prime Minister who told people to 'go to work'."[301]

A Rwandan lawyer demonstrated the importance of context when examining the language used in Rwanda, by explaining that songs taught and sung by school children in the early 1980s contained divisive, derogatory language that would be interpreted differently by the Rwandan youth of today.[302] Addressing these important linguistic and cultural nuances was of paramount importance for the Tribunal not only to ensure that Rwandan witnesses could give their testimony and be understood during court proceedings, but also to provide an environment in which both witnesses and the accused could share their version of events in a manner that could transcend both cultural and language barriers.

Yet the barriers in the courtroom also extended to the physical differences between the location of the courtroom in Arusha, which was surrounded by vast flat plains, and the crime scenes located in Rwanda, which consisted of endless hills and valleys. As a former ICTR staff member explained:

> "I was able to follow and understand the narrative during the trials as I had been to all these places. I have lived and worked there [Rwanda]. But the judges and lawyers did not visit the country. It was the investigators that went to collect

298 Interviewee J1.
299 Arthur, 2010, pp. 166-167; Combs, 2010, p. 87; interviewees J1, J3, T8, G1 & CS5.
300 Arthur, 2010, p. 167.
301 Interviewee T21.
302 Interviewee J3.

information and speak to people. I had been there and could see the places they were talking about."[303]

It was in November 1999 that a group of ICTR judges – including the president and vice president of the Tribunal, Judges Pillay and Møse – first visited Rwanda. These actions were not lost on Rwandans at the time,[304] as mentioned by one of the interviewees: *"Judge Pillay was the best. When she was president. She mended the reputation. She instructed all the judges to visit Rwanda, to visit and understand the country".*[305]

Despite the efforts made to reduce the cultural, physical and linguistic distances, the courtroom remained a space filled with harrowing testimonies, recounted in an unfamiliar language, with witnesses having to provide testimony in a foreign court, recounting traumatic events while following strange procedures:[306] *"it is difficult to tell your story on a stand in a foreign court".*[307] Bridging the gap between these different worlds, particularly during the first ICTR trials, remained challenging.[308]

In addition, there was an issue of security for the witnesses who agreed to fly to Arusha to give their testimony.[309] In 2001, two civil society organisations working with victims in Rwanda – IBUKA and AVEGA – accused the ICTR of neglecting the security of prosecution witnesses and not taking the plight of victims seriously.[310] From January 2002 onwards, they actively dissuaded victims from both testifying at the Tribunal and working with ICTR personnel in Rwanda, and urged the Rwandan government to follow suit.[311] In a letter to the UN Security Council, dated 17 September 2002, IBUKA explained its grievances, stating that witnesses were receiving serious threats following *"the quasi-systematic*

303 Translated from French: *"J'ai pu suivre et comprendre le récit pendant les procès parce que j'avais été dans tous ces endroits. Mais les juges et les avocats ne se sont pas rendus dans le pays. Ce sont les enquêteurs qui sont allés recueillir des informations et parler aux gens. J'avais été là-bas et pouvais voir les endroits dont ils parlaient."* (T22).

304 JusticeInfo, *ICTR says Rwanda satisfied with judges visit*, 5 November 1999. Retrieved from: https://www.justiceinfo.net/en/15629-en-en-ictr-says-rwanda-satisfied-with-judges-visit63956395.html; Cruvellier, 2010, pp. 134-135.

305 Interviewee M2.

306 Arthur, 2010, pp. 166-167; Leo C. Nwoye, *Partners or Rivals in Reconciliation: The ICTR and Rwanda's Gacaca Courts*, San Diego International Law Journal, 2014, 16, p. 181; Martien Schotsmans and François-Xavier Nsanzuwera, *Victims in the Balance: Challenges Ahead for the International Criminal Tribunal for Rwanda*. International Federation for Human Rights, 2002, pp. 8-9; Göran Sluiter, *The ICTR and the Protection of Witnesses*, Journal of International Criminal Justice, 2005, 3(4), p. 965.

307 Interviewee T21.

308 Arthur, 2010, p. 168.

309 Sluiter, 2005, p. 965.

310 Peskin, 2008, pp. 198-199; Schotsmans & Nsanzuwera, 2002, pp. 5-6.

311 Heidy Rombouts, *Victim Organisations and the Politics of Reparation: A Case-study on Rwanda*, Intersentia, 2004, p. 467; Schotsmans & Nsanzuwera, 2002, pp. 5-6; The New Humanitarian, *ICTR to investigate allegations of witness abuse*, 15 March 2002. Retrieved from: https://www.thenewhumanitarian.org/report/30753/rwanda-ictr-investigate-allegations-witness-abuse.

publicising of testimony given behind closed doors by witnesses who were supposedly protected".[312]

The concern regarding the lack of witness protection was echoed by others: *"The protection of witnesses was not available outside Arusha. Everyone knew when a villager left the village, especially to get on a plane in Kigali. There was no personal touch. The Rwandan context was not present"*.[313] Yet from the Tribunal's perspective, hearing witnesses give their testimony was crucial in order to collect information and evidence regarding the events that took place in 1994. The former director of a civil society organisation in Rwanda gave his view on the situation:

> "The mandate excluded the survivors. The future international criminal courts must include the survivors, those who escaped. They have to include the perspectives of the survivors. Even if just one person is affected, their point of view must be considered. No one can understand the survivor. What they have lived."[314]

The distance through language, cultural differences, and the location of witnesses and crime scenes remained an issue for all parties involved throughout the duration of the Tribunal's existence.[315] However, the inclusion of witnesses at the ICTR was of paramount importance, especially since the Tribunal could not rely on the ballistics experts or military strategists used by the ICTY to understand the evidence presented during a trial, given the manner in which the crimes had been committed in Rwanda – largely using machetes.[316] With proceedings taking place in Tanzania, far from the crime scenes, the witnesses not only made their statements about the crimes committed in Rwanda, they also provided information with regard to the context in which these crimes took place.

---

312 United Nations Security Council, *Letter from Rwanda to the UN President of the Security Council*, S/2002/1043, 19 September 2002. Retrieved from: https://reliefweb.int/report/rwanda/letter-rwanda-un-president-security-council-s20021043.

313 Interviewee M2.

314 Translated from French: *"Le mandat á exclue les survivants. Les futures juridictions pénales internationales doivent inclure les survivants, ceux qui se sont échappés. Ils doivent inclure les points de vue des survivants. Même si une seule personne est touchée, son point de vue doit être pris en compte. Personne ne peut comprendre le survivant. Ce qu'ils ont vécu."* (CS6).

315 Schotsmans & Nsanzuwera, 2002, pp. 5-6 & 13-18.

316 Combs, 2010, p. 13; Ziggy MacDonald, *Official Crime Statistics: Their Use and Interpretation*, The Economic Journal, 2002, 112(477), pp. 89-90; Alette Smeulers and Fred Grünfeld, *International Crimes and Other Gross Human Rights Violations: A Multi- and Interdisciplinary Textbook*, Brill, 2011, pp. 25-27; Patricia M. Wald, *International Criminal Tribunal for the Former Yugolsavia Comes of Age: Some Observations on Day-to-Day Dilemmas of an International Court*, Washington University Journal of Law and Policy, 2001a, 5, p. 101.

5.4.1 *Repairing Legitimacy*

The distance from the realities of Rwanda, and the unfamiliar courtroom setting, certainly did not simplify court proceedings.[317] The cultural distance in the courtroom led to one particularly damaging legitimacy challenge on 31 October 2001. A video clip of the event was subsequently shared among media outlets. It showed judges laughing at a witness, who was being cross-examined about an alleged rape. The video clip was met with outrage, causing deep concern and criticism regarding the operations and ethical standards of the Tribunal.[318] The impact of the event continued to be felt a year later in September 2002 when the UN Security Council received a letter from IBUKA, the Rwandan civil society organisation that works with survivors of the genocide:

> "[...] instead of benefiting from protection, owing to their special condition, vulnerable and sensitive witnesses, particularly female victims of sexual violence, are systematically mistreated, intimidated and humiliated by both investigators and defence lawyers, sometimes in the presence of judges who are clearly not interested in reminding defence attorneys of the most basic ethical rules in this regard."[319]

The Tribunal needed to *repair* its legitimacy following this event.[320] The challenges related to *repairing* legitimacy with regard to this particular incident touched on all three legitimacy types: challenging the *performance* of the ICTR with regard to the actions and behaviour of the judges (pragmatic legitimacy); its *values* related to the ethical conduct of the judges and the Tribunal's organisational culture (moral legitimacy); and the *meaning* of the ICTR, especially concerning the existential benefits of the Tribunal (cognitive legitimacy).

5.4.2 *Symbolic Actions*

The Tribunal's response to the 'laughing judges' incident came a month after the event itself, mainly due to the international media's slow reaction to an article (published in

---

317 Sluiter, 2005, p. 964.

318 Global Policy Forum, *UN Judges Laugh at Rape Victim*, 3 December 2001. Retrieved from: https://archive.globalpolicy.org/intljustice/tribunals/2001/0512rwa.htm; The New Humanitarian, *ICTR denies judges laughed at rape witness*, 17 December 2001. Retrieved from: https://www.thenewhumanitarian.org/fr/node/198108; News24, *Judges 'laughed' at rape victim*, 3 December 2001. Retrieved from: https://www.news24.com/News24/Judges-laughed-at-rape-victim-20011202

319 United Nations Security Council, *Letter from Rwanda to the UN President of the Security Council*, S/2002/1043, 19 September 2002.

320 Suchman, 1995, p. 597.

November 2001) concerning the event.[321] It is the president of the Tribunal, Judge Pillay, who responds:

> "[...] It is important to note that the article does not allege that the judges were laughing at the witness or at any part of the testimony. It is also important to note that an examination of the audio-visual record of the hearing on 31 October 2001 shows that the article amounted to a mischaracterization of the scene in the Trial Chamber [...]."[322]

Regardless of what actually took place in the courtroom on 31 October 2001, this response from the Tribunal demonstrates a legitimisation activity described as *denial*, or the re-framing of the events that took place in October 2001, by bringing the focus back to the content of both the news article and the video clip of the event.[323] Furthermore, the statement removes any suggestion that the judges were laughing at the witness or during the witness's testimony: "*It is also clear [...] that the reactions from the bench described as inappropriate in the article were responses to defence counsel's questions and arose in the course of dialogue with defence counsel*".[324] In short, events did not take place as the media reports were suggesting, and the video clip had been taken out of context. The statement also clearly addresses the *pragmatic, moral* and *cognitive* legitimacy of the ICTR. The behaviour and *performance* of the judges is addressed as follows:

> "Those who sit as judges know that they perform their task under the gaze of many observers. If and when they are criticized in the press and in public, they do not have the luxury of reply and refutation. They may not enter the arena of public debate about their conduct of an ongoing trial."[325]

The last sentence of this paragraph refers to *moral* legitimacy when discussing the conduct of the ICTR's judges; and is referred to again, later in the statement, this time with regard to the conduct of the Tribunal itself:

> "There may be many aspects of the conduct of a trial that call forth criticism from those who do not have the delicate task of balancing the rights of an

321 The New Humanitarian, *ICTR denies judges laughed at rape witness*, 17 December 2001. Retrieved from: https://www.thenewhumanitarian.org/fr/node/198108.
322 ICTR Press Release, *Statement of Judge Pillay, President of the Tribunal*, 14 December 2001. Retrieved from: https://unictr.irmct.org/en/news/statement-judge-pillay-president-tribunal.
323 Ashforth & Gibbs, 1990, p. 180.
324 ICTR Press Release, *Statement of Judge Pillay, President of the Tribunal*, 14 December 2001.
325 *ibid.*

> accused to a fair trial with the need to protect victims and ensure the integrity of judicial proceedings. [...] It would not be appropriate for one judge, including the President of the Tribunal, to discuss the conduct of other judges in their handling of an ongoing trial."[326]

The *cognitive* legitimacy of the Tribunal is addressed in the last paragraph of the statement by emphasising the wider society goals of the Tribunal, which are shared by all those involved in the ICTR's work:

> "I welcome the concern shown by commentators to ensure that our witnesses are protected from mistreatment: it is a concern we all have in common. When an accurate appreciation of the facts is allied to that concern, we can rest assured that we are all working for the same cause: to ensure that the integrity of the judicial process remains the way of reaching an understanding of the truth."[327]

This paragraph connects the ICTR's *raison d'être* – *"reaching an understanding of the truth"*[328] – to the daily workings of the Tribunal, which relates to a definition of legitimacy provided by an interviewee in Chapter 4: *"its purpose was to establish the truth"*.[329] The statement as a whole also denotes the symbolic activity of *"promoting of socially acceptable goals"*, which targets the stakeholders that are seeking recognition for the crimes that occurred in Rwanda in 1994.[330]

Aside from the message itself, the messenger of this legitimisation activity is also important: by issuing a statement through the ICTR president, the message is endorsed by the entire organisation.[331] Furthermore, this demonstrates that the leadership of the ICTR was aware of the activities taking place at the Tribunal and investigated accusations regarding the conduct of its staff, while also confirming the overall objectives of the ICTR. Furthermore, the statement was viewed as an opportunity to demonstrate the efficient working practices and professionalism of the Tribunal:

> "The judges of the ICTR are concerned on a daily basis to make the experience of those who give evidence before the Trial Chambers as painless as circumstances allow. The judges were integral to the planning process that has

326 *ibid.*
327 *ibid.*
328 *ibid.*
329 Interviewee G4.
330 Ashforth & Gibbs, 1990, p. 180.
331 Myriam Merad and Benjamin D. Trump, *The legitimacy principle within French risk public policy: A reflective contribution to policy analytics*, Science of the Total Environment, 2018, 645, p. 1317.

> led to ICTR developing a witness protection regime that is sometimes criticized as being too widely protective. When each witness comes to give evidence, he or she is accompanied by a witness protection officer whose responsibility is to ensure the witness is well looked after. Witnesses who come to Arusha to give evidence are assisted at all stages by Tribunal staff."[332]

Yet, despite these assurances that witness protection was provided by the Tribunal, as stated under Articles 19 and 20 of the ICTR Statute,[333] there remained no protection available when individuals left Arusha.[334]

5.4.3 *Substantive Action*

The substantive response to the challenge of witness protection came in 2009, when the Tribunal provided training for Rwandan witness protection officers as part of the *Cooperation and Capacity Building Programme* established *"to assist Rwanda develop a system which would enable its witness protection programmes to adapt to local dynamics and realities on the ground"*.[335] The programme is a demonstration of a substantive legitimisation activity in the shape of *role performance*, where the organisation responds to the requests (or expectations) of its stakeholders (*pragmatic* legitimacy), particularly the stakeholders that provide the organisation with critical resources.[336] In this case the Rwandan Government had asked for assistance in establishing a witness protection programme, not only for witnesses returning from Arusha, but also for strengthening Rwanda's justice sector, which also aligned with the ICTR's own mandate.[337]

---

332 ICTR Press Release, *Allegations against Bikindi Co-Counsel not well founded*, 14 December 2001.

333 United Nations Security Council, *Statute of the International Criminal Tribunal for Rwanda* (as amended on 31 December 2010), 8 November 1994, Articles 19 (Commencement and Conduct of Trial Proceedings) and 21 (Protection of Victims and Witnesses).

334 Interviewee M2; Mohamed Othman, *The 'Protection' of Refugee Witnesses by the International Criminal Tribunal for Rwanda*, International Journal of Refugee Law, 2002, 14(4), pp. 507-508; Sluiter, 2005, p. 965.

335 ICTR Press Release, *Prosecutors of International Criminal Tribunals Call for Full Cooperation*, 16 November 2009. Retrieved from: https://unictr.irmct.org/en/news/prosecutors-international-criminal-tribunals-call-full-cooperation; Kilemi, 2016, p. 11.

336 Ashforth & Gibbs, 1990, p. 178.

337 United Nations Security Council, *Resolution 955*, S/RES/955, 8 November 1994, p. 2; ICTR, *Completion Strategy Report*, S/2003/946, 6 October 2003, para. 23. Retrieved from: https://unictr.irmct.org/sites/unictr.org/files/legal-library/031006-completion-strategy-en.pdf.

5.4.4 Stakeholders

Those most impacted by the work of the Tribunal were the survivors of the 1994 Rwandan genocide, including those accused of crimes, their families, and the witnesses who testified in court: *"It was traumatic for people to listen and be a witness"*.[338] Yet, witnesses were also an important element in the functioning of the trials, which relied largely on witness testimony, and in order to assist the ICTR in identifying possible witnesses, providing emotional support, and organising logistical arrangements,[339] the Tribunal relied on two civil society organisations: IBUKA and AVEGA.[340] These two organisations were therefore at the forefront of campaigns against the ICTR in the early 2000s when reports that witnesses were mistreated by the Tribunal came to light. Together with the Rwandan government, they were able to shut down the Tribunal's operations in 2002 by refusing to allow witnesses to travel to Arusha.[341]

The Tribunal's legitimisation activities were targeted therefore towards the Rwandan government and these two civil society organisations. It must, however, be mentioned that all communications from the Tribunal to Rwanda were transmitted via the Rwandan government. Although both IBUKA and AVEGA were involved in protesting against the Tribunal's activities, IBUKA was the only civil society organisation from Rwanda to write to the Tribunal on this matter; no letters or communications were received by these organisations directly from the ICTR, communication was always directed via the Rwandan government.[342]

However, the international press had widely reported the 'laughing judges' incident, and the international community was also taking notice of the ICTR's response to the affair. Not only did this reflect badly on the ICTR, the incident also influenced the UN General Assembly, made up of individual member states, who were accountable for creating and funding the Tribunal. The statement presented by the president of the Tribunal, written in English and published on the Tribunal website, appears to have been designed for the international community rather than the future witnesses to the ICTR. In fact, during the interviews conducted for this research, it appeared that the treatment of witnesses on this occasion had still not been properly addressed, according to certain interviewees that had worked closely with witnesses in Rwanda.[343]

338 Interviewee CS22.

339 Arthur, 2010, p. 164; interviewees CS3, CS6, CS7, CS8, CS9, CS13, T2, T11, T15.

340 IBUKA: www.ibuka.rw; and AVEGA: https://avega-agahozo.org/.

341 Kingsley Moghalu, *Rwanda's genocide: the politics of global justice*. Palgrave Macmillan, 2005, pp. 136-143; Valerie Oosterveld and John McManus, *The Cooperation of States with the International Criminal Court*, Fordham International Law Journal, 2002, 25(3), p. 822.
See also Section 7. The Politics of Justice.

342 Interviewees G5, CS6, CS7, CS9 & CS13; archival research Rwanda 2019.

343 Interviewees CS8, CS9, CS13 & CS22; Sluiter, 2005, p. 964.

5.5 THE TWA COMMUNITY

Aside from the witnesses who flew from Kigali to Arusha to provide their testimony, there was another key stakeholder group that appears to have been neglected by the legitimisation activities implemented by the ICTR: the Twa community living in Rwanda. Only two interviewees made the connection between the Tribunal's legitimacy and this (former) ethnic group in Rwanda.[344] Historians have described the pre-colonial distinction between Hutu, Tutsi and Twa groups as a mixture between a class and caste system. Like the caste system, the groups were determined to a certain extent by their occupation: the Hutu were traditionally engaged in cultivation, the Tutsi in raising livestock, and the Twa – the "*forest dwellers*" – in hunting. Yet these occupational lines were not strict.[345] Indeed, many Hutu also owned cattle and goats, and most Tutsi also used their land for agriculture. Aside from the occupation of each group, the labels also provided a class distinction, with the Tutsi at the top of the social hierarchy and the Twa at the bottom:[346] "*Before, during and after the genocide the existence of the Batwa has been incredibly difficult. We are the tools of the country. Even in genocide our community was used by both sides*".[347] The same interviewee explained that life has been particularly difficult for the Twa since the conflict in the early 1990s.[348]

The recognition of a genocide in 1994, which emphasises the division between two ethnic groups – the Hutu and the Tutsi – led to a lack of recognition or acknowledgement of Rwanda's third ethnic group – the Twa. It is still unclear how many members of the Twa community perished during the conflict in 1994, and there has been no monetary or psychosocial support offered to the Twa survivors.[349] Furthermore, since 2001 identifying individuals with the ethnic labels – Hutu, Tutsi or Twa – is considered as "*divisionist*" in Rwanda:[350] "*There's no ethnicity here, we are all Rwandan.*"[351] As a result, there is no longer an opportunity to raise the issue regarding the plight of the Twa community.[352]

---

344 Interviewees G2 & CS10.

345 Magnarella, 2018, pp. 4, 7-9; Taraku & Karlsen, 2002, p. 6.

346 *ibid.*

347 The interview with interviewee G2 was conducted in Kinyarwanda and in English with simultaneous translation provided.

348 Interviewee G2.

349 Meghan Laws, Richard Ntakirutimana and Bennett Collins, '*One Rwanda For All Rwandans': (Un)covering the Twa in Post-Genocide Rwanda*, in: Hannah Grayson and Nicki Hitchcott (eds.), *Rwanda Since 1994: Stories of Change*, Liverpool University Press, 2019, 10, pp. 128-133; Interviewees G2 & CS10; Susan M. Thomson, *Ethnic Twa and Rwandan National Unity and Reconciliation Policy*, Peace Review, 2009, 21(3), p. 317.

350 Rwanda: *Law N° 47/2001 of 2001 on Prevention, Suppression and Punishment of the Crime of Discrimination and Sectarianism [Rwanda]*, 18 December 2001.

351 Translated from French: "*Il n'y a pas d'ethnie ici, nous sommes tous Rwandais.*" (CS6).

352 Scott Straus and Lars Waldorf (eds.), *Remaking Rwanda: State Building and Human Rights After Mass Violence*, University of Wisconsin Press, 2011, p. 308.

Yet as another interviewee explains: "*Who abolishes the groups? The government does not have that power. Just because the government says that groups do not exist, they still do*".[353] It appears that the Twa have twice been forgotten, or overlooked: firstly, in the recognition of a genocide against the Tutsi, perpetrated by the Hutu – the Twa are not recognised as victims or as perpetrators;[354] and secondly, the group remains concealed due to the new laws that prohibit any reference to the three (former) ethnic groups.[355] The Twa are now known as "*historically marginalised people*" in Rwanda, which encompasses all groups that have experienced historical marginalisation including women, the disabled community and the Muslim population.[356] Locally in Rwanda, the community is referred to as "*the potters*".[357]

Yet two years after the adoption of Rwandan *Law N° 47/2001* prohibiting any mention of the three ethnic groups in Rwanda,[358] the ICTR's Trial Chamber III included an annex taking judicial notice of the fact that: "*Between 6 April 1994 and 17 July 1994, citizens native to Rwanda were severally identified according to the following ethnic classifications: Tutsi, Hutu and Twa*";[359] and in 2012, the second indictment issued against Ladislas Ntaganzwa references the Twa alongside Hutu civilians, as being involved – as both victims and perpetrators – in crimes against the Tutsi.[360] However, when discussing the Twa with one interviewee, their place in Rwanda's history appears to be brushed aside: "*They were victims of ignorance. They were illiterate. Now they live better lives. It's strange to see them with a cow. But this is not relevant for your project, for the ICTR. Some were perpetrators, some were victims but not of genocide*".[361]

This perspective is reflected in the three justice mechanisms established to address Rwanda's 1994 genocide: the Twa were not represented during proceedings held at the ICTR, Rwanda's national courts nor at the community-based gacaca courts.[362] Two interviewees explained that initially the community was not interested in getting involved in the trials taking place at the ICTR, given that the group is poor and attentions were focused on getting their basic needs; however, later they contacted the local ICTR

353 Interviewee A9.

354 Nwoye, 2014, p. 180.

355 Interviewees G2, CS5 & CS10.

356 IWGIA website, 'Indigenous peoples in Rwanda': https://www.iwgia.org/en/rwanda/3502-iw2019-rwanda

357 "*We are often referred to as 'potters' because ninety-five percent of those who work make pottery. The government officially labels us as 'historically marginalised people'.*" (CS10).

358 Rwanda: *Law N° 47/2001 of 2001 on Prevention, Suppression and Punishment of the Crime of Discrimination and Sectarianism [Rwanda]*, 18 December 2001.

359 ICTR, *Prosecutor v. Laurent Semanza*, Judgment and Sentence, ICTR-97-20-T, 15 May 2003, Annex II, Part A, para. 1.

360 ICTR, *Prosecutor v. Ladislas Ntaganzwa*, Second Amended Indictment, ICTR 96-9-I, 30 March 2012, para. 45 & 47.

361 Interviewee CS3.

362 Interviewees G2 & CS10.

representatives in Kigali to ask for the Twa to be recognised in the Tribunal's work and nothing materialised from this.[363]

5.5.1 *Maintaining Legitimacy*

The legitimacy challenges faced by the Tribunal in this instance relate to *maintaining* legitimacy, given that the lack of representation and recognition of the Twa falls under both: "*stakeholder heterogeneity*",given that the community is completely disengaged from the Tribunal and its work, which does not appear to recognise them as one of their stakeholders;[364] and "*institutionalisation*," as the Twa are indifferent to the Tribunal's activities, effectively considering the Tribunal to be redundant and unable to meet their needs.[365] Yet, it could be argued that the Tribunal's lack of recognition of one group - which officially does not exist anymore - did not fall under the ICTR's mandate as they did not represent those most responsible for the crimes committed in 1994, and thousands of victims and crimes could not be addressed by the Tribunal. As explained by an interviewee: "*There are different categories of victims. You can't compare this [the Twa]*".[366]

Yet the lack of recognition of the Twa from the ICTR, as well as the during the trials taking place at the gacaca and national courts in Rwanda, has had huge consequences for the community as there is no support – internationally or locally – for the Twa.[367] Despite the abolishment of ethnic labels, there remains a division in Rwandan society, that of the victims – known locally as the survivors – and the perpetrators. When discussing the plight of the Twa, one interviewee laughed and explained that it was not worth discussing.[368]

Since 2003 the government reserves one Senate seat for a representative of the Indigenous People of Rwanda – at the time of writing this was held by Zephyrin Kalimba. This does not, however, change the challenges faced by the Indigenous People (the Twa community) in Rwanda, which these two interviewees believe would have benefitted from an acknowledgement at the Tribunal, symbolising some form of recognition from the international community.[369] Especially given that the ICTR was founded through Resolution 955, which: "*[...] in the particular circumstances of Rwanda, the prosecution of persons responsible for serious violations of international humanitarian law would [...] contribute to the process of national reconciliation*".[370]

363 Interviewee G2.
364 Suchman, 1995, p. 594.
365 *ibid.*
366 Interviewee CS3.
367 Interviewee G2; Thomson, 2009, p. 317.
368 Interviewee CS4.
369 Interviewees G2 & CS3.
370 United Nations Security Council, *Resolution 955*, S/RES/955, 8 November 1994, p. 1.

The Twa community were only recognised by the Tribunal in relation to the judicial notice that documents the three ethnic groups in Rwanda at the time of the genocide; and the former ICTR president, Judge Vagn Joensen, made reference to the Twa in a speech, recognising them as victims alongside the moderate Hutu:

> "Today we commemorate all of the victims of the atrocities that took place throughout Rwanda in 1994 – overwhelmingly these victims were Tutsi, against whom the ICTR has stated as a fact of common knowledge beyond dispute that genocide was committed; but they were also Twa, moderate Hutu and others who stood in opposition to the genocidal campaign."[371]

Yet, including the Twa and the moderate Hutu as victims of the genocide – which was officially recognised by the UN as "*the genocide against the Tutsi*" in 2014[372] – is viewed by some as a means to diminish the 1994 genocide.[373] Indeed, this may be the very reason why the Twa did not participate in the trials at the ICTR: it is not clear how and where the Twa community fit with regard to the arguments describing and defining crimes of genocide.[374] An interviewee explained that when the Twa approached the UN and the African Union for support, they were advised to stay away from the genocide discussions. Involving the Twa as victims and/or perpetrators of the genocide would water down the narrative of a genocide occurring between two ethnic groups: the Hutu as perpetrators and the Tutsi as the victims.[375]

5.6 An Academic Exercise?

In addition to the indifference felt by the Twa community in Rwanda, several other interviewees explained that the legitimisation activities implemented by the ICTR had failed to meet their expectations. One issue raised was the lack of Rwandan representation at the Tribunal,[376] as a Rwandan lawyer explained:

371 ICTR Press Release, 10 April 2014. *Remarks by Judge Vagn Joensen, ICTR President at the ICTR/MICT 20th Commemoration of the 1994 Genocide in Rwanda.* Retrieved from: https://unictr.irmct.org/en/news/remarks-judge-vagn-joensen-ictr-president-ictrmict-20th-commemoration-1994-genocide-rwanda.

372 UN Resolution 2136, 30 January 2014.

373 Interviewee J3.

374 United Nations Security Council, *Statute of the International Criminal Tribunal for Rwanda* (as amended on 31 December 2010), 8 November 1994, Article 2(2).

375 Interviewee G2.

376 Kamatali, 2005, pp. 93-95.

> "The ICTR was doomed from the start. It addressed cases that the court did not understand. People who understand the law but did not understand Rwanda. Rwandans should have been involved. There was no cultural awareness. Rwandans should have been at the ICTR to see the testimony, to be involved in some way."[377]

A Rwandan judge criticised the location of the Tribunal and the very nature of international criminal law, especially when related to transitional justice efforts in Rwanda: *"By definition criminal law is territorial, so how does it work internationally? The injury must be addressed where it happened and Arusha is far. This is symbolic justice. A society can't be rebuilt on symbols"*.[378] In addition to its location in the neighbouring state of Tanzania, the Tribunal's first chief prosecutor, Richard Goldstone, was fully engaged in cases related to the conflict in the former Yugoslavia at the time of the ICTR's creation, which resulted in the decision to keep his main office in The Hague.[379] The two subsequent prosecutors (Louise Arbour and Carla Del Ponte) affirmed their intention to allocate more time to the work of the Rwandan Tribunal; however, they too were based principally at the ICTY in The Hague. This gave the impression that the ICTY remained the primary focus of their attention, while the ICTR needed to make more of an effort to be noticed, over 9,000 kilometres away in Arusha.[380]

Aside from housing the OTP's main offices, the ICTY located in The Hague had another advantage over its sister Tribunal: the proximity to journalists. Given that the closest media hub to Arusha was Nairobi, five hours away by road, and Dar es Salem was just over two hours by plane, the Tribunal was responsible for organising its own media coverage: *"We had to pay transport for journalists to come to see trials, but the finance department in The Hague didn't understand this. In the Hague journalists have easy access and just go"*.[381] Yet locating the Tribunal in The Hague would not have been a popular option:

> "The ICTR was here for several reasons: It was mainly political. We would have had issues if it was all in The Hague. The African states wouldn't be happy. We would not have had support. There was also access and proximity to witnesses [...] it was easier for them to fly out of Kigali to Arusha rather than to The Hague."[382]

377 Interviewee J3.
378 Interviewee J4.
379 Moghalu, 2005, pp. 127-130.
380 *ibid.*
381 Interviewees T18.
382 Interviewee T15.

Despite the relative proximity of witnesses coming from Rwanda, they still needed to be flown in from Kigali or other countries in Africa, and some witnesses – especially those providing testimony for the accused – came from as far away as Europe and America:[383] "*Witnesses came from far. They had to be flown in from all sorts of countries, far away*".[384] As such, the Tribunal also had to foot the bill to ensure that all witnesses could be flown in to give their testimony in person, regardless of their location:[385]

> "The distance was a problem. Witnesses had to travel. Actually, the majority of defence witnesses came from even further away. It cost money and time to move people from South Africa, from France. But it was good that the court was in Africa, in Arusha and not in The Hague."[386]

The distance of the ICTR from Rwanda became especially significant in 2002 when the Rwandan government rolled out its first pilot community-based gacaca courts, a revised system of traditional local justice, which operated within Rwanda and involved Rwandans.[387] The arrival of the gacaca courts had an enormous impact on the legitimacy of the Tribunal, demonstrating how a nimble, local system of justice could prosecute large numbers of *génocidaires* in a fraction of the time, and at a fraction of the cost, of the large, bureaucratic ICTR operating in a foreign land.

Originally, gacaca gatherings were meant to restore order within the community or '*cell*' by addressing any issues that could not be resolved privately, and ensuring that justice was restored to the victims.[388] Yet with the arrival of the Belgian civil law system, Rwandans started bringing their disputes to the local courts and the mediating role of the *Mwami* and the wise men of the village soon lost its prominence; as a result, the use of the gacaca system eventually subsided.[389]

However, following the end of Rwanda's civil war in 1994, a forum was held by the new government in order to discuss what should be done with regard to security and

383 Cryer et al. 2019, pp. 487-488; Othman, 2002, pp. 504-505.

384 Interviewee T21.

385 William A. Schabas, *Genocide Trials and Gacaca Courts*, Journal of International Criminal Justice, 2005, 3(4), pp. 891-893; Sluiter, 2005, p. 963.

386 Interviewee T24.

387 Hollie Nyseyh Brehm, Christopher Uggen and Jean-Damascène Gasanabo, *Genocide, Justice, and Rwanda's Gacaca Courts*, Journal of Contemporary Criminal Justice, 2014, 30(3), p. 336; Pham et al., 2004, pp. 610-612.

388 A *cell* is an administrative entity in Rwanda administration. The country is divided into five provinces (including the City of Kigali), which are further divided into 30 districts. The districts are made up of 416 sectors; and the sectors consist of 2,148 cells, comprising 14,837 villages. Every layer of administration has a specific mandate and is led by elected officials. Retrieved from: https://www.gov.rw/government/administrative-structure#c4493; Taraku & Karlsen, 2002, p. 18.

389 Interviewee J4; Taraku & Karlsen, 2002, p. 18.

justice. Government officials were invited, as well as leaders from civil society organisations.[390] The participants concluded that given the large number of people involved in the genocide, 'classical justice' alone – making use of special chambers in the national courts – would not be possible. They therefore explored the options provided by the former, local justice system – the gacaca – to see if the format could be modified or transformed to address the large number of crimes that had taken place throughout the country:[391] "*There were so many cases. The prisons were full. The gacaca was needed. The government knew that if we do this the international community way it will take thousands of years. We needed to start and process cases. But we had no lawyers*".[392]

There was, however, a lot of push-back from those in the legal field, who expressed concern that this traditional form of justice was designed to resolve neighbourhood disputes rather than the atrocious crimes witnessed during the civil war, and later the genocide: "*There are different standards for each mechanism: the gacaca, ordinary courts and the ICTR. First you try to solve the problem in the family, if this doesn't work you ask a family friend, if the issue is between family members you ask the community. This is the idea behind gacaca*".[393] Indeed, the re-introduction of this community-based system of justice came at a risk:

> "It was very informal and subjective. People could be influenced through their family ties or their experiences. Maybe people were not getting fair justice. The training was of two to three months and then they were judging. Someone had to, for example, judge their brother-in-law. It was very sensitive, very delicate."[394]

Despite the clear shortcomings of the traditional system, the government decided to go ahead with plans for a new form of gacaca. Two pilot phases were organised in selected cells and the first phase was rolled out in June 2002.[395]

> "The cultural resolution in Rwanda came in the form of the gacaca courts. This was the basis for transitional justice in Rwanda. People had to tell the truth. The genocide had occurred openly, during the day, so this was a way for the truth to come out. Homemade justice. This also served as a relief for the community, as an opportunity for them to discover where their family members were buried. Rwanda had the biggest number of prisoners after the conflict.

390 Including interviewees CS6, CS7, CS12, G2 & G4; Schabas, 2005, p. 884.
391 Interviewees A3, CS12 & J4; Schabas, 2005, pp. 880-881.
392 Interviewee A3.
393 Interviewee CS23.
394 Interviewee A3.
395 Interviewee CS12; Schabas, 2005, pp. 891-893; Nyseyh Brehm et al., 2014, p. 336.

> People who had been caught in action. The civilised world told Rwanda to either release or quickly try all these people. It wasn't that easy, and release was not an option. The civilised world also told Rwanda that the gacaca courts were not professional enough. But justice in any form is vital. We must remove impunity."[396]

Following the pilot phase, the gacaca was formerly introduced in 2005 and attendance at the trials was mandatory, which did not please everyone. As a Rwandan university professor explains: "*Kumvira means just obey. At the end of every month there is community service. On a Saturday. This was the same as gacaca. Everyone had to attend. People obey. I did not like to go. It was the same as watching a hyena putting a dog on trial. I didn't want this*".[397]

Despite some reservations regarding the gacaca system, this community event was a far cry from the distant trials of Rwanda's former military and political leaders taking place in Arusha. The gacaca court system in Rwanda epitomised "*justice [...] seen to be done*",[398] which was lacking at the foreign international criminal tribunal based in Tanzania: "*The ICTR was put in place in Arusha. Representatives from the government were there for a certain period of time. But the gacaca was easy to follow as it was happening in the cells, at local level and everyone was expected to be involved*".[399] Indeed, for those who had experienced the genocide first-hand, this was a more accessible way of experiencing justice:[400]

> "The gacaca was very good as everyone was involved. Even the children could talk about what they had seen and heard. Everyone contributed. It was direct justice. The ICTR was so remote. There was so much procedure. Everything was communicated through the voice of another, which made it unattainable. It was remote."[401]

The sense of 'owning' justice for crimes that had been committed through this grassroots system was mentioned in several interviews. As a Rwandan judge explained: "*The gacaca was owned by the people. The ICTR was not. Rwandans thought that it would be like*

396 Interviewee G4.
397 Interviewee A8.
398 Interviewee CS7.
399 Interviewee CS12.
400 Pham et al., 2004, pp. 610-612.
401 Translated from French: "*La gacaca était très bonne car tout le monde était impliqué. Même les enfants pouvaient parler de ce qu'ils avaient vu et entendu. Tout le monde a contribué. C'était la justice en direct. Le TPIR était si éloigné. Il y avait tellement de procédure. Tout était communiqué par la voix d'un autre, ce qui le rendait inaccessible. C'était éloigné*" (CS13).

Nuremberg. That trials would happen here in Rwanda, including Rwandan judges. That was not the case."[402]

This sentiment of social cohesion was often raised in contrast to the perception of the ICTR: "*Gacaca means transitional justice. It helped with rebuilding society. The ICTR was a textbook court, an academic exercise*".[403] Those working for civil society organisations also explained that the proximity of the gacaca not only provided a tangible sense of justice, it also assisted in reconciling communities: "*The preference was to have everyone tried through the gacaca system. It provided a time to discuss, bring Hutu and Tutsi together. It gave a time for healing. It was a therapy for the community*".[404] Bringing together the two sides of the divisive conflict was a key objective of the gacaca, as explained by an interviewee involved in the early discussions regarding the post-conflict situation in Rwanda:

> "One plan was to start the gacaca courts as they were cost effective and a way to heal communities. It is seen as being hugely successful. National courts were too expensive and too slow, so gacaca was the answer. Additionally, it was a system that the locals could learn and they understood. It also demonstrated that not all Hutu were bad and it became a way to find more bodies."[405]

Yet, some interviewees shared another perspective: "*There were negatives and positives for all mechanisms including the gacaca. [...] There were judges who wanted revenge in some cases*".[406] Furthermore, the proximity of the community-based gacaca system did not necessarily result in promoting reconciliation:

> "Genocide occurs with proximity. It is very hard to ensure security as everyone was involved. Everyone is affected. The sister of my friend was killed in 1994. My friend's husband was part of a group that killed many people. He had been part of the genocide and didn't want his wife, my friend, to testify, to talk about her sister. Violence as a consequence of genocide is still high. After the gacaca closed this lessened. Now the violence in more material. People are trying to get their property back. But usually people are arrested if there is any violence. There is now a research into interfamily violence, which is linked to the genocide. People are used to violence and have not processed this. They have not processed the violence of the genocide. Still today."[407]

402 Interviewee J4.
403 Interviewee M2.
404 Interviewee CS3.
405 Interviewee CS7.
406 Interviewee CS11.
407 Interviewee CS22.

The gacaca trials ended in 2012, with reports of a total of 1,958,634 cases, from which 1,681,648 individuals were found guilty of a crime connected to genocide.[408] The numbers far exceed the 80 individuals prosecuted before the ICTR.[409] However, the ICTR was established to prosecute those most responsible for crimes committed in 1994 and, as one interviewee stated: *"It is hard to compare the gacaca and the ICTR. They had different roles. The role of the ICTR was to denounce these horrific crimes".*[410] The crimes prosecuted by Rwanda's national courts and the gacaca were, for their part, organised into four categories[411] (later reduced to three): *"The ICTR tried the leaders and the planners of genocide. Arresting these leaders was very difficult. We needed the international community. Their lawyers were very good. The gacaca was different. The gacaca was for everyone".*[412]

However, two key issues were highlighted following the arrival of the gacaca courts: the enormous cost of the ICTR,[413] and its distance from Rwanda – both physically and symbolically, with regard to the lack of Rwandan representation at the Tribunal and its foreign rules and procedures. Indeed, the reports of the ICTR's high running costs, together with its location in Arusha, resulted in a variety of challenges that questioned the legitimacy of the Tribunal, and the people working there:

> "The management of the court was motivated by money. The resources allocated by the UN were given for the outcomes. There was a gap. The leadership should have been Rwandan. There was a lack of commitment. The gacaca courts, they

---

408 Nyseyh Brehm et al., 2014, p. 340.

409 ICTR website, 'Key figures'. Retrieved from: https://unictr.irmct.org/en/cases/key-figures-cases

410 Translated from French: "*C'est difficile de comparer le gacaca et le TPIR. Ils avaient des rôles différents. Le rôle du TPIR était de dénoncer ces terribles crimes.*" (T23).

411 Category 1 included those responsible for leading and instigating the genocide, well-known killers, and rapists; Category 2 included those responsible for killings and serious assaults; and Category 3 covered those responsible for stealing, destroying or damaging property (Nyseyh Brehm et al., 2014, p. 336; Taraku & Karlsen, 2002, p. 19).

412 Translated from French: "*Le TPIR a jugé les dirigeants et les planificateurs du génocide. Arrêter ces dirigeants a été très difficile. Nous avions besoin de la communauté internationale. Leurs avocats étaient très bons. Le gacaca était différent. Le gacaca était pour tout le monde.*" (T9); Until June 2008, Category 1 suspects continued to be tried by the conventional courts, not by gacaca courts. From June 2008, most of these cases too were transferred to the gacaca system.

413 The costs of running the ICTR did, however, remain lower than the ICTY. For example, the ICTR's budget for 2018 and 2019 was approximately US$ 270 million compared to US$ 342 million for the ICTY (United Nations General Assembly, *Financing of the International Criminal Tribunal for Rwanda (ICTR) and the International Tribunal for the Former Yugoslavia (ITY) for the biennium 2008-2009*, Sixty-third session, A/63/595, 10 December 2008, para. 12 & 20. Retrieved from: https://www.un.org/ga/search/view_doc.asp?symbol=A/63/595; Daniel McLaughlin, *International Criminal Tribunals: a visual overview*, Leitner Center for International Law and Justice, 2013, pp. 13 & 27. Retrieved from: http://www.leitnercenter.org/files/News/International%20Criminal%20Tribunals.pdf.

> operated without incentives. The location of the ICTR, this was not an issue of location, it was an issue of willingness."[414]

Although exact figures were not mentioned during the interviews, several interviewees mentioned the high costs of running the ICTR as an issue, as explained by one interviewee: *"One challenge to the legitimacy of ICTR was that lots of money was spent. Locally it isn't clear where the money went. People did not see justice being done"*.[415] With an estimated USD 2 billion spent over the course of its 20-year lifespan,[416] another interviewee asked: *"Where did all the money from the ICTR go?"*[417] A total of 93 people were indicted by the Tribunal: 80 were eventually prosecuted, with 62 people convicted and 14 individuals acquitted; and an additional four individuals referred to national jurisdictions, including three to Rwanda.[418] Even a former staff member who was involved in putting together the ICTR budgets agreed that the costs of running the Tribunal in Arusha were high:

> "You cannot imagine the cost. Incredible costs involved in flying judges in. Their daily allowance, their hotel costs, transport. Also, the defence, who are not staff. They get the same wage as staff, plus extra to cover health, their health insurance. Organising a trial or a hearing was expensive. We also had to pay for journalists to come."[419]

In terms of gaining legitimacy, the use of an international criminal justice system to address crimes committed within one country – especially with the arrival of the gacaca court system – raised questions with regard to the necessity of such an expensive international tribunal.[420] Indeed, as early as 1998, the then Secretary-General of the Ministry of Justice, Gerald Gahima, declared that if Rwanda had received one twentieth of the *"$50 million budget"* given to the Tribunal, it *"would have gone a long way towards solving our problems"*.[421]

The criticism related to the costs of running the ICTR was not only felt by external stakeholders, those working within the Tribunal also expressed their disbelief at the amount

414 Interviewee CS21.

415 Interviewee A6.

416 See ICTR financial reports and audited financial statements (ACABQ reports to the UN General Assembly, 1999 to 2016). Retrieved from: https://www.un.org/ga/acabq/documents/all.

417 Translated from French: *"Où c'est passé tout l'argent du TPIR?"* (CS6).

418 ICTR website, 'Key figures'. Retrieved from: https://unictr.irmct.org/en/cases/key-figures-cases.

419 Interviewee T4.

420 Barbara Oomen, *Justice Mechanisms and the Question of Legitimacy. The Example of Rwanda's Multi-layered Justice Mechanisms*, in: Kai Ambos, Judith Large, and Marieke Wierda (eds.), *Building a Future on Peace and Justice*, Springer Berlin Heidelberg, 2009, pp. 188-189.

421 The Christian Science Monitor, *For Rwandans, Justice Done Only for Others*,11 September 1998. Retrieved from: https://www.csmonitor.com/1998/0911/091198.intl.intl.4.html.

of money spent: *"Rwandans always said, give us the money and we will do this. For just 62 people, it was too long, too expensive"*;[422] and another former ICTR staff member explained that *"the ICTR never worried about budget. Every time they would say that the ICTR would only exist another few years, but it continued. Even today, jobs are coming up again. The machine continues to function in Arusha"*.[423] A former spokesperson and information officer for the ICTR, Tim Gallimore, spoke out during an interview with the BBC stating: *"I don't think there's any jurisdiction anywhere in the world that if you did a comparable assessment of the price and the number of people involved that would say the investment was a good return"*.[424]

Linked to the cost of the ICTR is the issue of time: *"The ICTR lasted for years and cost a lot of money"*.[425] The effective management of trials not only requires control of the courtroom, but confidence in systems of justice also depend on the perception that the court is independent, impartial and fair, where efficiency also plays an important role.[426] When trials are time-consuming, this may be perceived as inefficient, or the judges and lawyers incompetent.[427] Yet an international trial is different from domestic proceedings, and as such, the ICTR judges were faced with challenges that are not easily comparable to those encountered by national courts.[428] International criminal law is a specialised and technical area of the law, given that it has multiple sources and refers to the judicial decisions of other courts.[429] Additionally, the same act (for example killing someone) could be a crime against humanity or a war crime depending on the contextual elements, rather than any physical differences related to the act itself.[430]

---

422 Translated from French: "*Les Rwandais ont toujours dit: donnez-nous l'argent et nous le ferons. Pour seulement 63 personnes, c'était trop long, trop cher.*" (T1).

423 Translated from French: "*Le TPIR ne s'est jamais inquiété du budget. Chaque fois, ils disaient que le TPIR n'existerait que quelques années, mais il a continué. Aujourd'hui encore, les emplois reprennent. La machine continue de fonctionner à Arusha.*" (T2).

424 BBC, *Rwanda genocide: International Criminal Tribunal closes*, 14 December 2015. Retrieved from: https://www.bbc.com/news/world-africa-35070220.

425 Interviewee M2.

426 Tom R. Tyler, *A Psychological Perspective on the Legitimacy of Institutions and Authorities*,in: John T. Jost and Brenda Major (eds.), *The Psychology of Legitimacy: Emerging Perspectives on Ideology*, Justice, and Intergroup Relations, Cambridge: Cambridge University Press, 2001, p. 416.

427 *ibid.*

428 Alvarez, 1999, p. 404; Mohamed Elewa Badar, *Drawing the Boundaries of Mens Rea in the Jurisprudence of the International Criminal Tribunal for the former Yugoslavia*, International Criminal Law Review, 2006, 6(3), pp. 346-348; Cryer et al., 2019, p. 44.

429 van Sliedregt & Vasiliev, 2014, p. 68.

430 Antonio Cassese, *The Nexus Requirement for War Crimes*, Journal of International Criminal Justice, 2012, 10(5), p. 1395; John R. Cencich, *International Criminal Investigations of Genocide and Crimes Against Humanity: A War Crimes Investigator's Perspective*, International Criminal Justice Review, 2009, 19(2), p. 5; William A. Schabas, *State Policy as an Element of International Crimes*, The Journal of Criminal Law and Criminology, 2008a, pp. 960-964.

Furthermore, international criminal trials tend to be factually complex compared to most domestic criminal cases: the crimes are often undertaken by hierarchical groups working together, rather than one individual, and take place across multiple locations over different periods of time. An international criminal trial therefore consists of *"documenting an episode or even an era of national or ethnic conflicts"*,[431] rather than merely prosecuting an individual for a particular crime. Since some of the facts are highly technical, particularly those relating to mass grave exhumations, the use of particular weapons or military tactics, they require expert witnesses to help translate their meaning.[432]

Over the years, it was important for the ICTR judges to do their utmost to reduce delays in trial proceedings, while ensuring that there would be no doubt about the fairness of the activities taking place in the courtroom. However, the trials conducted before the Tribunal involved a large number of witnesses, the use of three languages (English, French and Kinyarwanda), and in some cases consisted of several defendants.[433] Furthermore, the ICTR operated at a slow pace in part because of administrative problems, such as assuring the attendance of witnesses and counsel for the defence; poor coordination between investigators and prosecutors; and the failure to fill certain positions.[434] Yet the delay can also be traced back to extended time-off taken by certain judges: according to one study, the Tribunal was in recess for four months during one 12-month period.[435] Indeed, as one Rwandan government official stated:

> "My biggest regret is the time it took. Especially in the cases where the accused died before a judgment was given. This is just as bad for the accused as it is for the victims. Why did it have to take so long? The ICTR had all the means at its disposal. This is also a human right, to be tried without undue delay."[436]

The longest trial at the ICTR took ten years and ten days. This long stretch of time required the court to revisit or summarise past evidence, to ensure that everyone was kept up to date and also meant that the composition of defence and OTP teams changed.[437]

---

431 Patricia M. Wald, *To Establish Incredible Events by Credible Evidence: The Use of Affidavit Testimony in Yugoslavia War Crimes Tribunal Proceedings*, Harvard International Law Journal, 2001b, 42, pp. 536-537.

432 MacDonald, 2002, pp. 89-90; Smeulers & Grünfeld, 2011, pp. 25-27.

433 *"the Tribunal was to hear seven multi-accused cases, each including high-ranking persons accused of being leaders during the 1994 events: Butare (six accused); Cyangugu (three); Military I (four); Military II (four); Media (three); Government I (four); and Government II (four)"* (Møse, 2005, p. 924).

434 Kilemi, 2016, pp. 7-10; Møse, 2005, pp. 921-924.

435 Karin N. Calvo-Goller, *The Trial Proceedings of the International Criminal Court: ICTY and ICTR Precedents*, Brill Nijhoff, 2006, p. 59.

436 Interviewee G3.

437 Relief Web, *ICTR record breaking case comes to a close*,24 June 2011. Retrieved from: https://reliefweb.int/report/rwanda/ictr-record-breaking-case-comes-close; ICTR, *Prosecutor v. Pauline Nyiramasuhuko, Arsène*

5.6.1 *Maintaining Legitimacy*

As mentioned in Chapter 2, activities linked to legitimisation involve the continuous testing and redefinition of organisational legitimacy, which is achieved through an ongoing interaction with its environment.[438] Communication is particularly important in order to demonstrate that an organisation shares the same values (moral legitimacy) and understands the needs and interests (pragmatic legitimacy) of their stakeholders.[439] The challenge was therefore to continue to convey information about the proceedings in Arusha to the Rwandan population, of whom a large number lived in rural areas and where the illiteracy rate was high:[440] *"It was so far away. It was hard to connect to it. The only information about the ICTR was through the television, radio and newspapers, and of course those who came back from trials. The court was located in a foreign country. We had no contact at all. Especially those living in villages."*[441] Several interviewees explained that *"justice must be seen to be done. Especially by survivors"*.[442] The distance and lack of communication led many to wonder what was happening in Arusha:

> "Rwandans did not know what was going on and they should have known as it was dealing with issues and crimes that had occurred in their country. The ICTR owed it to them to show what was happening. Due to the lack of communication many people got the wrong idea. They thought it was a five-star hotel, that the accused were living a great life there. They got the wrong impression."[443]

This highlights a fear raised by Bocar Sy, the ICTR's Head of Press and Information, who explained that *"misinformation emerges from lack of information"*.[444] The impact of this

---

Shalom Ntahobali, Sylvain Nsabimana, Alphonse Nteziryayo, Joseph Kanyabashi and Élie Ndayambaje,Judgment and Sentence, ICTR-98-42T, 24 June 2011.

438 The organisational environment is composed of stakeholders or institutions that affect the operations, resources and performance of an organisation (Bryson, 2018, pp. 45-46).

439 Margaret Levi, Audrey Sacks and Tom R. Tyler, *Conceptualizing Legitimacy, Measuring Legitimating Beliefs*, American Behavioral Scientist, 2009, 53(3), pp. 356-359; Henri Tajfel (ed.), *Social Identity and Intergroup Relations*, Cambridge University Press, 2010, p. 255.

440 Alison L. Des Forges, *Leave None to Tell the Story: Genocide in Rwanda*, New York: Human Rights Watch, 3169(189), 1999, p. 58.

441 Translated from French: *"C'était si loin. Il était difficile de s'y connecter. Les seules informations sur le TPIR provenaient de la télévision, de la radio et des journaux, et bien sûr de ceux qui revenaient des procès. Le tribunal était situé dans un pays étranger. Nous n'avons eu aucun contact. Surtout ceux qui vivent dans les villages"* (CS11).

442 Interviewee CS7.

443 Interviewee G3.

444 Bocar Sy,Interview conducted by Tribunal Voices (video 652), 30 October 2008. Retrieved from: http://www.tribunalvoices.org/voices/video/652.

lack of visibility, or lack of information, can be damaging, as demonstrated by one interviewee's view of the Tribunal:

> "My impression of the ICTR is that it was corrupt. Why should the trials take place in Arusha and not Rwanda? I do not know anything about the ICTR apart from what was spoken about among Rwandans who had been to Arusha. The witnesses, when they came back. Sometimes I saw something in the newspaper."[445]

The gacaca system introduced in Rwanda therefore stood in stark contrast with the ICTR based in Arusha: trials took place locally in Rwandan villages, they took relatively little time and were inexpensive, while involving all Rwandans in the process.[446] The challenge in *maintaining* legitimacy during this period is linked to *"organisational homogeneity"*, when an organisation experiences competition from smaller, more versatile organisations offering similar services.[447]

Additionally, the challenge in maintaining legitimacy could be linked to *"stakeholder heterogeneity"*, given that satisfying, or even recognising, all of an organisation's stakeholders is virtually impossible for any organisation.[448] As explained by an interviewee: *"The educated people see the value, despite the challenges. The non-educated people see the loss of resources. We should look at the outcomes, there have been big achievements. Was it the responsibility of the court to educate people?"*[449] This comment raises two questions: who was the Tribunal for? and did it achieve what it set out to do? The answer to these questions varies considerably depending on the stakeholder(s) involved: survivors and perpetrators of the genocide, the Rwandan government, former ICTR staff members, representatives of civil society organisations, UN member states, or the academic community.

Several interviewees[450] suggested that the Tribunal catered mainly to the academic community, which links to another challenge in maintaining legitimacy: *"institutionalisation"* – when an organisation is targeted on ideological grounds, if it is perceived as redundant or because it symbolises an unsolicited or unwanted societal constraint.[451] The cost, the distance and length of trials at the ICTR, gave some the impression that the ICTR had developed into an academic exercise rather than a court to assist in reconciling Rwanda: *"The gacaca was transitional justice, it helped rebuilding*

445 Interviewee CS4.
446 Pham et al., 2004, pp. 610-612.
447 Suchman, 1995, p. 594.
448 *idem.*, p. 594.
449 Interviewee CS21.
450 Interviewees CS6, CS7, CS11, CS14, G3, M2 & T24.
451 Suchman, 1995, p. 594.

society. The ICTR was a textbook court, an academic exercise".[452] This opinion was shared by several other interviewees: *"The ICTR was for academics. The gacaca was for the people"*,[453] and *"The ICTR was for intellectuals. It was not domesticated"*.[454]

Following the Tokyo and Nuremberg Trials held in the 1940s after World War II, the ICTY and the ICTR were reviving the practice of international criminal law: *"Besides its success in holding accountable the so-called 'big fish' among the genocide perpetrators, the Tribunal has made substantial contributions to international criminal jurisprudence and to the developing human rights legal regime"*.[455] Indeed, it was an exciting time for those working at the Tribunal: *"Can you imagine. It was like going to class. Every day in the courtroom was completely new. Like debate class at school. Everyone was looking to find boundaries, to test ideas"*.[456] However, this academic practice led others to feel disconnected with the Tribunal, including former staff members: *"The ICTR was too academic, you don't see the deliverables. Look at the Nyiramasuhuko case. The trials were too long"*.[457] It appears that some interviewees disengaged from the tribunal's activities at a certain point: *"The ICTR was a stepping stone for international criminal law. The issue was a lack of understanding of the local context. A hybrid court, at the very least, would have had a higher impact"*.[458]

In order to address these challenges, the ICTR implemented the two legitimisation activities related to maintaining legitimacy: *perceiving a future crisis* and *protecting past accomplishments.*

5.6.2 Perceiving Future Crises

Legitimisation activities focused on *perceiving a future crisis* are commonly referred to as risk mitigation strategies. In the case the *pragmatic* legitimacy type, an organisation will focus its efforts on monitoring any emerging stakeholder demands. Through annual meetings and regular reports, the UN General Assembly and UN Security Council were involved in the ICTR's decision-making process. Additionally, the ICTR remained engaged with the Rwandan government with the establishment of a special representative of the Rwandan government, who had a physical office at the Tribunal from 1999 to 2009 and

---

452 Interviewee M2.

453 Translated from French: "*Le TPIR était destiné aux academique. La gacaca était pour le people.*" (CS6)

454 Interviewee CS7.

455 Interviewee T3.

456 Translated from French: "*Vous vous imaginez. C'était comme aller en classe. Chaque jour dans la salle d'audience était complètement nouveau. Comme une classe de débat à l'école. Tout le monde cherchait à trouver des limites, à tester des idées.*" (T23).

457 Interviewee T24.

458 Interviewee CS14.

held regular meetings with the registrar and president of the Tribunal.[459] During one of his first meetings with the ICTR registrar, Martin Ngoga explained that *"he had been appointed in order to fill a "gap" between the Rwandan Government and the Tribunal which had sometimes resulted in "actions and reactions" by Rwandan authorities regarding the work of the Tribunal which were later found not to have had the benefit of full and accurate information on the situation at the Tribunal"*.[460]

The presence of the special representative, and indeed the frequent contact with the UN Secretary-General, the UN Security Council and the UN General Assembly also provided the Tribunal with regular feedback on their operations in Arusha and Rwanda.[461] This activity also reflects the Tribunal's efforts to maintain their *moral* legitimacy,[462] which assesses any changing values systems in the environment. Legitimisation activities aimed at maintaining moral legitimacy often relate to the organisational culture and the manner in which it interacts with both internal and external stakeholders. This is most commonly achieved through the establishment of an oversight team, which was reflected in the work of the *External Relations and Strategic Planning Section* (ERSPS) at the ICTR. One interviewee explained the essence of their work within the ERSPS:

> "My main role was to advise the president and the registrar on policy issues and to listen to the UN and member states. We would often be invited to meetings with the Friends of the Tribunal[463] in Dar es Salaam or Nairobi. [...] Also the visibility of the Tribunal. It was important to highlight the work being done. We had a clear mandate. We had to inform the public and UN member states. I was also the point of entry for all visitors, all inquiries. And finally, I was the spokesperson for Arusha."[464]

The activities of the ERSPS also demonstrate an organisation seeking to maintain *cognitive* legitimacy, where the organisation must keep track of any cultural or societal developments that are linked to the meaning of the organisation, its activities and/or to the environment

459 From 1999 to 2004, Martin Ngoga served in this role; his successor was Alloys Mutabingwa, who served from 2004 to 2009.

460 ICTR Press Release, *Special representative of Rwandan government visits Tribunal*,13 October 1999. Retrieved from: https://unictr.irmct.org/en/news/special-representative-rwandan-government-visits-tribunal

461 Interviewee T25.

462 Suchman, 1995, p. 595.

463 *"The Friends of ICTR is a Focus Group established towards the end of 2004 in Dar es Salaam by some of the donor states. It is chaired by the British High Commissioner for Tanzania and the members are: the Canadian High Commissioner, the Ambassador of the Netherlands, the Ambassador of Norway, the Ambassador of Belgium, the Ambassador of Germany the Ambassador of France and the US Chargé d'Affaires."* (ICTR Newsletter, January 2005, p. 4. Retrieved from: https://unictr.irmct.org/sites/unictr.org/files/news/newsletters/jan05.pdf).

464 Interviewee T25.

in which the organisation finds itself.[465] The objective behind this legitimisation activity is to directly address those who are questioning the organisation's existence or who are sceptical of the organisation's activities.

This activity was apparent during the archival research at the IR-MCT, as the majority of the documents consulted (linked to the Tribunal's administrative work) related to media reports: a large collection of press clippings had been organised by year and by theme.[466] Most of the clippings included instructions regarding what sort of action should be taken in response to the content of the news article. These findings are consistent with information provided by another former ICTR staff member working within the ERSPS: *"I looked at news reports coming from Rwanda and other places. Any news mentioning the Tribunal was sent to [name], who would forward it to the appropriate department".*[467] The notes found in the ICTR archive indicated that at least two people were tasked with overseeing the media reports in Arusha and passing on information to the relevant individual or organ within the Tribunal.[468] Former public information officer, Charles Kamuru, explains that one of his main tasks was to collect newspaper clippings and to look, and listen out, for television and radio broadcasts that referred to the Tribunal:

> "[...] number one, I'm supposed to make a brief news summary about all the news that are circulated by the local and even foreign media about the activities of the tribunal. In other words, I'm supposed to make a weekly news summary of all news circulated by the local and foreign media, related to the ICTR."[469]

The ICTR therefore put considerable effort and resources into monitoring its environment and addressing any negative stories found in the press, while keeping communication channels with the special representative for Rwanda and UN representatives open, in order to address any new developments or potential challenges to its work or completing its mandate.

Furthermore, additional measures were taken to address specific challenges related to the Tribunal's daily operations, illustrating that the ICTR was acutely aware of the slow pace of trials and was examining ways to deal with this:

> "This will be the first trial in which measures to speed up cases, adopted on 8 June 1998 by the 5th Plenary Session of Judges, will be applied. The measures

---

465 Suchman, 1995, p. 595.
466 For example, coverage of visits made by – or visits to – the Tribunal or the response to ICTR judgments.
467 Interviewee T3.
468 Interviewee T3.
469 Charles Kamuru, Interview conducted by Tribunal Voices (video 362), 28 October 2008. Retrieved from: http://www.tribunalvoices.org/voices/video/362.

> include the decision that judgement and sentencing will be dealt with as one and not two separate procedures. They also included the decision to have conferences before either of the parties present their evidence, during which parties may be ordered to outline contested and non-contested issues in order to allow judges to shorten examination of some witnesses, or to reduce the number of witnesses to be called to prove the same facts."[470]

These new measures relate to the substantive legitimisation activity described as *"role performance"* (associated with repairing legitimacy), which occurs when an organisation responds to stakeholder expectations and/or demands.[471] The Tribunal also decided to conduct *"multi-accused cases"* in order to speed up the process;[472] however, according to Gallimore, former spokesperson and public information officer for the ICTR, these efforts did not work out in the long-term:

> "It has been acknowledged that the early prosecution strategy of conducting joint [multiple-accused] trials slowed down the process and added to the overall cost of operating the Tribunal. That practice has been discontinued but the joint trials, some of which are still in progress more than a decade later [see the Butare trial ICTR -98-42], have consumed more resources than they would have consumed had they been tried as single-accused cases."[473]

This last quote demonstrates the balancing act that takes place during legitimisation. There is a risk that a legitimisation activity aimed at mitigating one legitimacy challenge could create a new challenge. In this case, more needed to be done to salvage the Tribunal's legitimacy.

5.6.3 *Protecting Past Accomplishments*

According to Suchman, an organisation will attempt to *protect its past accomplishments* by converting short-term legitimacy to long-term recognition and acceptance.[474] An organisation striving to maintain *pragmatic* legitimacy will ensure that all exchanges with

470 ICTR Press Release, *Trial of Alfred Musema to begin on 25 January 1999*, 20 January 1999. Retrieved from: https://unictr.irmct.org/en/news/trial-alfred-musema-begin-25-january-1999.
471 Ashforth & Gibbs, 1990, p. 178.
472 Møse, 2005, p. 924.
473 Foreign Policy Blog, *My interview with Tim Gallimore, Former Spokesman for the ICTR Prosecutor*,27 May 2011. Retrieved from: https://foreignpolicyblogs.com/2011/05/27/my-interview-with-tim-gallimore-former-spokesman-for-the-ictr-prosecutor/.
474 Suchman, 1995, p. 595.

its stakeholders are consistent and predictable. It will also *"stockpile"* legitimacy by demonstrating a constant ability to deliver the goods and services that stakeholders need or expect, therefore building a relationship of trust with its stakeholders.[475]

In line with this, a former ICTR staff member explains that the Tribunal had two key objectives: the first was to prosecute those most responsible for crimes committed in 1994; the second to provide outreach programmes that would explain the work of the ICTR:

> "We had two important objectives. The awareness raising with populations, especially secondary school children, and capacity building. For this we targeted government officials, lawyers, expats in different domains. The government gave the premises for the office in Kigali, and ten regional offices. We had direct access to the ICTR. We mainly received students. We had approximately a hundred people a day. The library was mainly accessed by students, lawyers, academics, also people from abroad. We also visited prisons."[476]

Indeed, the success of the outreach programme, including the library, was reiterated by another former ICTR staff member:

> "There is nothing like this in the region. We have the most comprehensive library and online access. We collaborate with regional universities in Kampala, Nairobi, Butare and Dar es Salaam and with the East African Community and the African Court for Human Rights. Many students came, and they still come. We also get lawyers and legal practitioners, and foreign researchers like you. We are also part of the UN library and work with a network of Tribunals, the ICJ, the ICTY and the ICC. The EU funded the outreach work. Your country [NL] funded a lot of the work. Also the EU Commission and Sweden and Denmark. This comprised of seminars, and sending information through the radio and television. They had seminars also with prisoners and secondary school children."[477]

475 *ibid.*

476 Translated from French: *"Nous avions deux objectifs importants. La sensibilisation des populations, en particulier les lycéens, et le renforcement des capacités. Pour cela, nous avons ciblé les fonctionnaires, les avocats, les expatriés travaillant dans différents domaines. Le gouvernement a donné les bâtiments pour les bureaux ici à Kigali, ainsi que dix bureaux régionaux. On avait un accès direct au TPIR. Nous avons principalement reçu des étudiants. Nous avions accueilli une centaine de personnes par jour. La bibliothèque était principalement consultée par des étudiants, des avocats, des universitaires, ainsi que des étrangers. Les centres de sensibilisation ont fermé en 2014."* (T9).

477 Interviewee T20.

A third former ICTR staff member explained that: "*The outreach programmes were not only used to explain the work of the ICTR, but also the aims of international criminal law.*"[478] In relation to providing information regarding international criminal law, the focus of the Tribunal's legitimisation activities was also directed towards the Rwanda judiciary, [479] which illustrates activities designed to maintain *moral* legitimacy. As Suchman's research explains, these activities demonstrate the authority of the organisation, while building a relationship based on *mutual respect.*[480]

In order to prosecute certain individuals in Rwanda itself, the ICTR required proof of radical reform in Rwanda regarding the independence of the judiciary, witness protection, fair trial rights, detention facilities and sentencing practices; notably, the death sentence was to be abolished.[481] These requirements demonstrated the Tribunal's authority and its power to prevent accused persons from being tried in Rwanda. Yet, the ICTR also built a relationship of collaboration with Rwandan officials, in order to assist them in making the required reforms, as explained by one interviewee involved in the process:

> "The ICTR worked. There was strong collaboration between the national prosecutor here and the OTP in Arusha. The 11 bis law was very important in referring cases. This is what I worked on with the OTP in Arusha. Once this was approved with the ICTR national jurisdictions started sending the accused to Rwanda for trial."[482]

In maintaining *cognitive* legitimacy, an organisation will stockpile legitimacy by creating casual connections with its social environment.[483] In this regard, the Tribunal had to demonstrate its worth to the wider social context. This opportunity arrived in 2003, in the form of the Friedrich-Ebert-Stiftung Human Rights Award:

> "The International Criminal Tribunal for Rwanda (ICTR) has become the first organization of its kind to receive the Friedrich-Ebert-Stiftung Human Rights Award. The award, which recognizes a significant contribution to human rights, was conferred in acknowledgement of the ICTR's unwavering support for the due process of law, and its contribution to the goal of national reconciliation following the Rwandan genocide. The award – the first to be conferred on an International Tribunal - also commends the ICTR's strong commitment to law

478 Interviewee T3.
479 Interviewees G3, J1, J2, T3, T21, T24 & T25.
480 Suchman, 1995, p. 596.
481 Interviewees G3 & J4. ICTR, Completion Strategy Report, S/2003/946, 6 October 2003, para. 23.
482 Interviewee G3.
483 Suchman, 1995, p. 596.

> and justice in Rwanda, and the building-up of confidence as the basis for peace and democracy, not only in Rwanda but throughout the international community as a whole. [...] During the award's presentation, the German Federal Minister of Justice, Mrs. Brigitte Zypries, paid tribute to the ICTR, its objectives and its accomplishments. Mrs. Zypries also acknowledged the exceptional contribution of the ICTR to international criminal jurisprudence."[484]

This was the first time that an international tribunal received this internationally recognised award, which is presented to individuals or organisations that have made outstanding contributions in the field of human rights:

> "Besides arresting and punishing those who committed heinous crimes in Rwanda, the Tribunal has established jurisprudence that has received significant endorsement from academics, representatives of member states and organs of civil society, and constitutes a reliable body of presidents for the international criminal court. [...]
> Today, one cannot deny that the ICTR has made remarkable achievements and that misconceptions of the past by the media are on the decline. In recognition of its achievements, the Tribunal received the Friedrich-Ebert-Stiftung Human Rights Award in May this year. They would recognize the ICTR's unwavering support for due process of law and its contribution towards national reconciliation and post-genocide Rwanda."[485]

In this case, the legitimacy of the Tribunal was promoted by a third-party organisation, yet the communication of this award illustrates the cognitive nature of this legitimisation activity: the press release informs stakeholders of the ICTR's award by emphasising activities that aligned with its broader societal objectives in a lowkey, casual, matter-of-fact manner.

5.6.4 Stakeholders

Yet, it appears that the presence of a special representative based at the Tribunal in Arusha, the collaboration with the Rwanda judiciary, the frequent meetings with UN representatives

---

484 ICTR Press Release, *ICTR Becomes First International Tribunal to Receive Prestigious Human Rights Award*,26 May 2003. Retrieved from: https://unictr.irmct.org/en/news/ictr-becomes-first-international-tribunal-receive-prestigious-human-rights-award.

485 Roland Kouassi G. Amoussouga, The Challenges and Achievements of the International Criminal Tribunal for Rwanda, Annual Conference of the Law Society of Kenya, Whitesands Hotel, Mombasa-Kenya, 30 August 2003, pp. 13-14.

and individual UN member states, the establishment of the ERSPS, and even the Friedrich-Ebert-Stiftung award, did not address the legitimacy challenges linked to the complexity of international trials – involving huge costs, and lengthy investigation and trial times.

The arrival of the gacaca in Rwanda continues to be used as a means to highlight the slow process and high costs of international criminal law. However, this section demonstrates how legitimisation activities are targeted at, and received by, specific stakeholders. The disparity between interviewee perceptions in this section demonstrates that those who either worked directly with, or were receptive to, the activities of the Tribunal had a higher chance of perceiving the ICTR as a legitimate institution. This was mainly due to the fact that the activities implemented to maintain the Tribunal's legitimacy by "*perceiving future crises*" and "protecting past accomplishments" were largely conducted through links with the Rwanda government and UN member states: *"The link with Rwanda was through the Ministry of Justice and with States was through the Ministry of Foreign Affairs."*[486]

Furthermore, although the information centres based in Rwanda were staffed by Rwandan citizens, all communication on the ICTR's website was presented in English, followed by the French language. Only three press releases were issued in Kinyarwanda. The reason given for this, provided by one former ICTR staff member, was due to a lack of resources and also the fact that *"most people in Rwanda speak French or English"*.[487] This demonstrates the cultural and contextual distance between the Tribunal based in Arusha and the survivors located in Rwanda, as well as providing an indication regarding the target audience of the ICTR's legitimisation activities. It appears that, although some ICTR staff members were physically present in Rwanda, the Tribunal's was more focused on its foreign audience.

5.7 The Politics of Justice

With regard to the judicial workings of the Tribunal, trials remained long and complex, and external relations efforts and media outlets were principally focused on the final decisions made by the ICTR judges.[488] The conviction and sentencing of those accused of being involved in the 1994 genocide was often celebrated, especially in Rwanda, while the

486 Interviewee T18.
487 Interviewee T25.
488 Interviewee T18.

acquittals and – later on – the early release of those convicted for crimes of genocide were met with disbelief and outrage:[489]

> "The ICTR also helped the country but it was very slow. The Rwandan population thought it would solve all their problems but it didn't. Public opinion was particularly low in the case of the acquittals or when the prisoners were released early."[490]

The early release of individuals convicted by the ICTR were in line with the practices of the ICTY, where offenders were eligible for early release once they had served two-thirds of their sentence.[491] Yet as Choi demonstrates in his research, it is unclear where this provision for early release comes from,[492] and as the current prosecutor for the IR-MCT, Serge Brammertz, stated: *"I think that at least someone who is released before completing their sentence should be given specific conditions such as not to be a Genocide denier or someone who glorifies the crimes committed".*[493] The practice remains difficult for many to understand, with one former ICTR employee suggesting that the decision was a political one: *"They always go together justice and politics. The early release of genocidaires was a big mistake. It is hard to comprehend this".*[494]

One particular ICTR judge was singled out by several interviewees for controversially overturning a series of rulings, resulting in the release or reduction in the sentences of several individuals that had been in power at the time of the genocide:

> "The early release of genocidaires is a very serious matter. Judge [name] had no remorse. I met him in Arusha and asked him why he allowed this. He replied that the files are empty. Those convicted, the génocidaires, never showed any remorse, they gave no apology. I have a theory on this. Judge [name] is Jewish. Maybe he doesn't want to recognise that there was another genocide. He does

---

489 Taraku & Karlsen, 2002, p. 30; The New Times, Pardoning of Genocide convicts sparks debate, 15 May 2012; The New Times, ICTR acquittals shocking but expected, 11 February 2013. Retrieved from: https://www.newtimes.co.rw/section/read/62785.

490 Translated from French: *"Le TPIR a également aidé le pays, mais cela a été très lent. La population rwandaise pensait que cela résoudrait tous leurs problèmes, mais ce n'est pas le cas. L'opinion publique était particulièrement faible dans le cas des acquittements ou lorsque les prisonniers étaient libérés prématurément."* (CS11).

491 Jonathan H. Choi, *Early Release in International Criminal Law*, Yale Law Journal, 2013, 123, p. 1788; Jessica M. Kelder, Barbora Holá and Joris van Wijk, *Rehabilitation and Early Release of Perpetrators of International Crimes: A Case Study of the ICTY and ICTR*, International Criminal Law Review, 2014, 14(6), p. 1202.

492 Choi, 2014, pp. 1791-1804.

493 The New Times, *MICT prosecutor admits to slow progress in hunt for key fugitives*,14 February 2018. Retrieved from: https://www.newtimes.co.rw/section/read/230088.

494 Translated from French: *"Ils vont toujours ensemble, la justice et la politique. La sortie anticipée des génocidaires était une grosse erreur. Cela est difficile de comprendre."* (T9).

> not want the African genocide that happened here to overshadow the Holocaust."[495]

In 2011, the ICTR's Appeals Chamber reduced the sentences of Theoneste Bagosora and Anatole Nsengiyumva from life to 35 years and 15 years respectively;[496] and in February 2014, the Appeals Chamber acquitted Augustin Ndindiliyimana and Francois Xavier Nzuwonemeye, while Innocent Sagahutu had his sentence reduced from 20 to 15 years.[497] Several interviewees, including an academic who teaches international criminal law at the University of Rwanda, found these actions difficult to comprehend: "*The legacy of the ICTR is both positive and negative. If you talk of Judge [name], he was highly insensitive. It is hard to understand. The acquittal of Bagasora. The interpretation was poor. Also in the military case. How did this happen?*"[498]

In Rwanda, these decisions were met with outrage; notably in February 2013, when hundreds of Rwandans took to the streets to protest the acquittals of Justin Mugenzi and Prosper Mugiraneza.[499]

> "Judge [name] was an impossible guy. Why did he have an issue with Rwanda? How was he allowed to act in such a way? People were freed who had not

495 Translated from French: "*La libération anticipée des génocidaires est une question très sérieuse. Le juge [nom] n'avait aucun remords. Je l'ai rencontré à Arusha et je lui ai demandé pourquoi il avait permis cela. Il a répondu que les fichiers sont vides. Les condamnés, les génocidaires, n'ont jamais montré de remords, ils n'ont présenté aucune excuse. J'ai une théorie à ce sujet. Le juge [nom] est juif. Peut-être qu'il ne veut pas reconnaître qu'il y a eu un autre génocide. Il ne veut pas que le génocide africain qui s'est produit ici éclipse l'Holocauste.*" (CS6).

496 Theoneste Bagosora served as cabinet director to the minister of defence during the 1994 genocide; Anatole Nsengiyumva served as head of the Intelligence Bureau of the Army General Staff and commander of the Gisenyi Operational Sector from June 1993 to July 1994.
ICTR, *Prosecutor v. Theoneste Bagasora and Anatole Nsengiyumva*, Judgment, ICTR-98-41-A, 14 December 2011, pp. 258-260.

497 Augustin Ndindiliyimana was chief of staff of the National Gendarmerie from September 1992 to July 1994; Francois Xavier Nzuwonemeye was the commander of the Reconnaissance Battalion within the Rwandan army during the 1994 genocide; Innocent Sagahutu held the rank of captain and was second-in-command of the Reconnaissance Battalion of the Rwandan army.
ICTR, *Prosecutor v. Augustin Ndindiliyimana, Francois Xavier Nzuwonemeye and Innocent Sagahutu*, Judgment, ICTR-00-56-A, 11 February 2014, para. 418 & 448.

498 Interviewee A10.

499 Justin Mugenzi was minister of trade and industry; Prosper Mugiraneza was minister of the civil service from March 1993 to July 1994.
CTV News, *Hundreds in Rwanda march in protest over acquittals at genocide tribunal*,11 February 2013. Retrieved from: https://www.ctvnews.ca/world/hundreds-in-rwanda-march-in-protest-over-acquittals-at-genocide-tribunal-1.1152276; News of Rwanda, *Massive Protest Against ICTR Acquittals*,13 February 2013. Retrieved from: http://www.newsofrwanda.com/featured1/17083/massive-protest-against-ictr-acquittals/; The New Times, *Rwanda protest against ICTR acquittals*,11 February 2013. Retrieved from: http://www.newtimes.co.rw/section/read/62747.

> repented. It's hard to understand. Also there was no involvement of Rwandans. It is the same indifference as in 1994. The damage has been done."[500]

The political undertone regarding the very possibility of an early release, or a reduction in the sentence of convicted *génocidaires,* was expressed during several of the interviews conducted for this research. According to one interviewee, the judicial arguments of the judges involved in these decisions were not unanimous: "*Have you met Judge [name]? He told me that he would not do the same as Judge [name], [...]. He was much despised by many Rwandans due to the early releases*".[501] For some interviewees, the actions of certain judges were clearly politically motivated:

> "It was more a political tribunal than really justice giving. The behaviour of Judge [name] is too strange. In a country that is healing from genocide, you cannot release the planners of the genocide. What message does this send? He released people who planned this."[502]

The news of acquittals also challenged the legitimacy of the Tribunal: the ICTR and its staff were reported as being: "*incompetent, a mockery of justice, an insult to the memory of the victims of genocide, the very epitome of insensitivity, an obscenely expensive operation*".[503] Indeed, each of the 14 acquittals were reported by media outlets with the same expression of shock.[504] One former ICTR staff member provided a practical explanation for the number of acquittals, explaining that the exoneration of certain indictees had more to do with the quality of the defence teams than political positioning of the ICTR judges:

> "There was a general impression that the ICTR could judge and that others, certainly in Rwanda, couldn't. Yet there were so many incompetent people at the ICTR. Particularly in the prosecution teams. Most of the time there were acquittals or low sentences because the defence was far better than the prosecutors hired by the UN. Some defence teams were very strong. Not all defence teams of course, but some were very good. This meant that the accused

500 Interviewee J3.

501 Translated from French: "*Avez-vous rencontré le juge [nom]? Il m'a dit qu'il ne ferait pas la même chose que le juge [nom]. Il était très méprisé par de nombreux Rwandais en raison des libérations anticipées.*" (CS9)

502 Interviewee CS17.

503 New Times, ICTR acquittals shocking but expected, 11 February 2013. Retrieved from: https://www.newtimes.co.rw/section/read/62785.

504 New Times, *How the ICTR has let down Rwanda,* 12 February 2014. Retrieved from: https://www.newtimes.co.rw/section/read/73046.

were not judged for the crime but on the competence of the defence versus the prosecution teams."[505]

From the perspective of a defence lawyer, however, the negative response to the acquittals was due to the general lack of education and understanding about the procedure of criminal trials: *"People did not understand what an acquittal meant. We were being scrutinised. How could we even defend such people? People didn't understand that it was the role of lawyers. We had to explain this"*.[506] However, the work of international criminal courts and tribunals has often been associated with providing a historical record of events.[507] Some would even go as far as to say that the ICTR's responsibility was to set the record straight: *"[...] its purpose was to establish the truth"*.[508] Arresting and prosecuting former government officials for their role in planning and instigating the genocide was therefore considered as proof enough for a conviction.

In line with this, a seemingly unforeseen consequence of acquitting those accused of genocidal acts – and in some cases those released early or who had served their full sentence – was that the individuals in question were unable, or unwilling, to return to Rwanda:

> "The biggest failure of the court has been towards those acquitted or those released who can't go back to Rwanda for fear of their lives. Maybe not fear of the government, but someone would kill them. They can't apply for a Rwandan passport without going to Rwanda, so they are currently stateless, living in a safehouse in Arusha. I believe over ten of them currently living there. Those who are released from prison also get sent back there if there are no other options. Many Western countries do not want to be associated with them. They do not take them in. Their lives are therefore lost. The first acquittal was for Ignace Bagilishema, former bourgmestre of Mabanza by the Appeals Chamber in 2002. He is still in Arusha. His son died two years ago, but he was not allowed

505 Translated from French: *"Les personnes acquittées se trouvent toujours en Tanzanie. [...] Il y avait une impression générale que le TPIR pouvait juger et que d'autres, certainement au Rwanda, ne le pouvaient pas. Pourtant, il y avait tellement de personnes incompétentes au TPIR. En particulier dans les équipes de poursuite. La plupart du temps, il y a eu des acquittements ou des peines légères car la défense était bien meilleure que les procureurs engagés par l'ONU. Certaines équipes de défense étaient très fortes. Pas toutes les équipes de défense bien sûr, mais certaines étaient très bonnes. Cela signifiait que les accusés n'étaient pas jugés pour le crime mais sur la compétence de la défense par rapport aux équipes de poursuite."* (T1).

506 Translated from French: *"Les gens ne comprenaient pas ce que signifiait l'acquittement. Les gens nous étudiaient minutieusement. Comment est-ce-qu'on peut même défendre de telles personnes ? Les gens ne comprenaient pas que c'était le rôle des avocats. Nous avons dû expliquer cela. C'était le rôle pédagogique de la loi."* (T23).

507 William A. Schabas, *The UN International Criminal Tribunals: The Former Yugoslavia, Rwanda and Sierra Leone*, Cambridge University Press, 2006, p. 489.

508 Interviewee G4.

to go to France for the funeral. Many of them are in ill health. Initially the UN paid for everything, now they provide each person with an allowance."[509]

In September 2019, there were 11 individuals living in the UN's safe house in Arusha; two had recently left for Ghana, where they had been granted residency.[510] This predicament was raised by several interviewees, who viewed the plight of those stranded in the Arusha safe house as a critical failure of the ICTR: *"I am a lawyer but also believe in social justice. The fact that the acquitted can't go back to Rwanda is a huge issue. They are welcome by Rwanda and Rwandans, but they clearly feel shame in their hearts. There are other countries that do not want them".*[511]

Regardless of the reason given for their stateless status in Arusha, the situation represented an important legitimacy challenge for the Tribunal on several levels. *"We have done everything we can, but we are stuck with this problem. These men are suffering, but there is not much we can do. [...] It also costs a lot of money to keep them here".*[512]

5.7.1 The Barayagwiza Case

The controversies following the early releases and acquittals at the ICTR were particularly heightened in the case of Jean-Bosco Barayagwiza. Barayagwiza had been a senior official in the Foreign Ministry and chair for the Gisenyi prefecture of the *Coalition pour la Défense de la République* (CDR), a far-right political party that boycotted the 1993 Arusha Peace Agreement; he was also one of the founders and a senior director of *Radio Télévision Libre des Mille Collines* (RTML), which played a significant role during the 1994 genocide.[513] Following the genocide, Barayagwiza fled Rwanda and settled in the Cameroon. In March

---

509 Translated from French: "*Le plus grand échec de la Cour a été à l'encontre des personnes acquittées ou libérées qui ne peuvent pas retourner au Rwanda par crainte pour leur vie. Peut-être pas peur du gouvernement, mais quelqu'un les tuerait. Ils ne peuvent pas demander un passeport rwandais sans se rendre au Rwanda, ils sont donc actuellement apatrides et vivent dans un refuge à Arusha. Je crois que plus de 10 d'entre eux y vivent actuellement. Ceux qui sortent de prison sont également renvoyés là-bas s'il n'y a pas d'autres options. De nombreux pays occidentaux ne souhaitent pas y être associés. Ils ne les accueillent pas. Leurs vies sont donc perdues. Le premier acquittement concernait Ignace Bagilishema, ancien bourgmestre de Mabanza par la Chambre d'appel en 2002. Il se trouve toujours à Arusha. Son fils est décédé il y a deux ans, mais il n'a pas été autorisé à se rendre en France pour les funérailles. Beaucoup d'entre eux sont en mauvaise santé. Au départ, l'ONU a tout payé, maintenant elle verse à chaque personne une allocation.*" (T22).

510 The eleven residents in the UN 's safe house (Arusha, Tanzania) in September 2019 included: Prosper Mugiraneza, Justin Mugenzi, Protais Zigiranyirazo, François-Xavier Nzuwonemeye, André Ntagerura, Casimir Bizimingu, Gratien Kabiligi, Jérôme Bicamumpaka, Augustin Ndindiliyimana, Anatole Nsengiyumva and Tharcisse Muvunyi.

511 Interviewee T21.

512 Interviewee T11.

513 Moghalu, 2005, p. 102; ICTR, *Prosecutor v. Ferdinand Nahimana, Jean-Bosco Barayagwiza and Hassan Ngeze (Media Case)*, Judgment and Sentence, ICTR-99-52-T, 3 December 2003, para. 6.

1996, Rwanda's general prosecutor issued an international arrest warrant for Barayagwiza, followed by a request for extradition, and by mid-April Barayagwiza was arrested in the Cameroon. The hearings on Rwanda's extradition application began a few days later. At the same time, the ICTR's prosecutor requested provisional measures with regard to Barayagwiza, pursuant to Rule 40 of the Rules of Procedure and Evidence (RPE), which resulted in the Yaounde Court of Appeal suspending the extradition hearing on 31 May 1996, explaining that they were acting pursuant to Article 8(2) of the ICTR Statute, which asserts the ICTR's primacy over all cases linked to the Rwandan genocide and requires states to relinquish jurisdiction in its favour.[514]

However, in a letter dated 15 October 1996, the new ICTR prosecutor, Louise Arbour, informed the authorities in the Cameroon that the ICTR was not interested in prosecuting Barayagwiza. The Yaounde Court of Appeal therefore resumed the extradition hearing, which eventually denied Rwanda's extradition request, and ordered the release of Barayagwiza.[515] Barayagwiza was due to be released from detention on 21 February 1997; however, on the same day the ICTR prosecutor reversed her position and issued an urgent request for the provisional detention of Barayagwiza, pursuant to Rule 40 (RPE). A few days later the OTP requested an order for the transfer of the accused to the ICTR in accordance with Rule 40bis (RPE), which was signed by Judge Lennert Aspegren on 3 March 1997 and issued the following day.[516]

In September 1997, after months of detention in the Cameroon, Barayagwiza filed a *writ for habeas corpus*, which was never met with a response from the ICTR – it does not appear to have come before any of the ICTR's judges.[517] The president of the Cameroon finally authorised Barayagwiza's transfer on 21 October 1997, and a month later, on 19 November 1997, Barayagwiza was transferred from the Cameroon to the UN Detention Facility in Arusha.[518] On 23 February 1998, Barayagwiza appeared before the ICTR judges for the first time and pleaded not guilty to all counts in the indictment. The next day he filed an *Extremely Urgent Motion* seeking to nullify his arrest. The motion was dismissed on 17 November by Trial Chamber II.[519]

On 27 November Barayagwiza appealed the decision pursuant to Rule 72(D), and in its decision of 3 November 1999, the Appeals Chamber ordered Barayagwiza to be returned to the authorities in the Cameroon, dismissing the OTP's indictment *"with prejudice to*

514 ICTR, *Prosecutor v. Jean-Bosco Barayagwiza,* Decision, ICTR-97-19-AR72, 3 November 1999, para. 5.

515 *idem.*, para. 7.

516 ICTR, *Prosecutor v. Jean-Bosco Barayagwiza*, Order, ICTR-97-19-DP, 3 March 1997; ICTR, *Prosecutor v. Jean-Bosco Barayagwiza,* Decision, ICTR-97-19-AR72, 3 November 1999, para. 7.

517 ICTR, *Prosecutor v. Jean-Bosco Barayagwiza,* Decision, ICTR-97-19-AR72, 3 November 1999, para. 8.

518 *idem.*, para. 9.

519 ICTR, *Prosecutor v. Jean-Bosco Barayagwiza*, Decision on the Extremely Urgent Motion by the Defence for Orders to Review and/or Nullify the Arrest and Provisional Detention of the Suspect, ICTR-97-19-I, 17 November 1998.

the Prosecutor".[520] The decision made by the Appeals Chamber was made in accordance with the judicial process and with the ICTR judges demonstrating the impartial nature of proceedings: "*As troubling as this disposition may be to some, the Appeals Chamber believes that to proceed with the Appellant's trial when such violations have been committed, would cause irreparable damage to the integrity of the judicial process"*.[521]

The response to the Appeals Chamber decision was indeed "*troubling*" to many. One interviewee described the disbelief at hearing of Barayagwiza's acquittal: *"It is unacceptable that they allowed acquittals purely for technical reasons"*.[522] The Rwandan government responded by suspending its cooperation with the Tribunal: investigators were prevented from accessing crime scenes and speaking to witnesses, and demonstrations took place outside the ICTR's Kigali office.[523] The pressure of this boycott on the ICTR was immense, as explained by Roland Amoussouga, who was working as a legal officer at the ICTR at the time:

> "[...] we have had decisions that have tested the will of all parties concerned. Barayagwiza. When the court decided that ok, Barayagwiza, the Prosecutor violated his rights therefore he should be set free. Immediately there was a big fight with Rwanda government. [...] They put pressure on witnesses not to come and there was a threat from the Tribunal to report Rwanda to the Security Council until the time appeals chamber come and reverse and then we got – the relationship got normalized."[524]

Following the backlash related to the Chamber's dismissal of the OTP's indictment against Barayagwiza, the same Appeals Chamber suspended their decision a few weeks later, on 25 November 1999. In response to requests from both the OTP and the Rwandan government, the Chamber agreed to a new hearing in order to consider new facts brought forward by the new prosecutor, Carla Del Ponte.[525]

5.7.1.1 Repairing Legitimacy

At this point, the ICTR was experiencing an important legitimacy challenge. Given the sensitive context in which the Tribunal's was working, the fluctuation of legitimacy related

520 ICTR, *Prosecutor v. Jean-Bosco Barayagwiza*, Decision, ICTR-97-19-AR72, 3 November 1999, para. 108.
521 *ibid.*
522 Interviewee M2.
523 Moghalu, 2005, p. 108; Peskin, 2008, pp. 181-182; The New Humanitarian, *Hundreds protest against Barayagwiza release*,16 November 1999. Retrieved from: https://www.thenewhumanitarian.org/fr/node/179881.
524 Roland Kouassi G. Amoussouga, Interview conducted by Tribunal Voices (video 89), 29-30 October 2008. Retrieved from: http://www.tribunalvoices.org/voices/video/89.
525 ICTR, *Prosecutor v. Jean-Bosco Barayagwiza*, Order, ICTR-97-19-AR72, 25 November.

to acquittals was, in most cases, beyond its control. However, the acquittal of Barayagwiza due to technical reasons provided the ICTR with an existential problem. During the new hearing, the ICTR prosecutor, Carla Del Ponte, and the Attorney General for Rwanda, Gerald Gahima, presented arguments as to why the Appeals Chamber should reverse its decision.[526] A key argument from Del Ponte was that the Tribunal had been established to promote national reconciliation in Rwanda, and that the prosecution of Barayagwiza was in the interest of justice of both the victims of the 1994 genocide and the international community.[527] This relates to the Tribunal's mission and vision, and therefore implicates the *moral* legitimacy of the ICTR; whilst also threatening the Tribunal's *cognitive* legitimacy, given that its very existence was in question.[528]

However, it appears that the decision to suspend the Appeals Chamber decision of 3 November – despite the ruling that "*to proceed [...] would cause irreparable damage to the integrity of the judicial process*"[529] – was directed towards the Rwandan government. The Tribunal was responding to the public outcry and pressure to resume operations following the suspension of all Tribunal activities in Rwanda. This demonstrates a substantive legitimisation activity labelled as *coercive isomorphism*, whereby an organisation is forced to act in line with the expectations of its stakeholders.[530]

The Tribunal managed this legitimisation activity, while emphasising its moral legitimacy by conforming to their own norms and procedure: "*The Prosecutor of the ICTR, Ms Carla Del Ponte, had asked the Chamber [...] to review its judgment of 3 November 1999, a procedure provided for by the Statute and the Rules of Procedure of the Tribunal*".[531] This statement demonstrates a *justification* – a symbolic legitimisation action that explains the actions and behaviour of the Tribunal, which not only highlights the pragmatic and moral legitimacy of the Tribunal – demonstrating that it has procedures in place that allow a case to be reviewed – but also validates the substantive legitimisation action taken, which relates to the core values of the organisation (*cognitive* legitimacy)– why it exists and how it should function: "*the remedy ordered by the Appeal Chamber in its judgement of 3 November 1999, [...] now appeared disproportionate in relation to the circumstances and had to be revised*".[532]

Furthermore, the suspension of the Appeals Chamber decision on 3 November represents a legitimisation action consistent with *role performance*, demonstrated by

526 ICTR, *Prosecutor v. Jean-Bosco Barayagwiza*, Decision, ICTR-97-19-AR72, 31 March 2000, para. 34.
527 *idem.*, para. 22.
528 Suchman, 1995, pp. 579-583.
529 ICTR, *Prosecutor v. Jean-Bosco Barayagwiza*, Decision, ICTR-97-19-AR72, 3 November 1999, para. 108
530 Ashford & Gibbs, 1990, p. 178.
531 ICTR Press Release, *Barayagwiza to be tried by ICTR*, 31 March 2000. Retrieved from: https://unictr.irmct.org/en/news/barayagwiza-be-tried-ictr.
532 *idem.*

organisations seeking to repair their *pragmatic* legitimacy;[533] while the subsequent hearing was moved to a courtroom Arusha, rather than being held in The Hague where the ICTR's Appeals Chamber was located, which shows significant steps taken by the ICTR to demonstrate the transparency and fairness of its proceedings, thereby promoting its *moral* legitimacy.[534]

On 31 March 2000, the Appeals Chamber confirmed that Barayagwiza's rights had been violated, yet not as severely as originally found; and on 3 December 2003, Barayagwiza was found guilty of committing crimes of genocide and crimes against humanity.[535] The new approach put forward by the Appeals Chamber suggests that the decision to go ahead with a trial, and eventually convict Barayagwiza, was understood to be due to the crippling effect of the Rwandan government's suspension of all Tribunal activities in Rwanda.[536] Both the prosecutor and the Rwandan government had succeeded in what they had set out to achieve. However, Judge Nieto-Navia argued otherwise on 31 March 2000, emphasising the independence of the Tribunal as an international judicial body:

> "I refute most strenuously the suggestion that in reaching decisions, political considerations should play a persuasive or governing role, in order to assuage States and ensure cooperation to achieve the long-term goals of the Tribunal. On the contrary, in no circumstances would such considerations cause the Tribunal to compromise its judicial independence and integrity. This is a Tribunal whose decisions must be taken, solely with the intention of both implementing the law and guaranteeing justice to the case before it, not as a result of political pressure and threats by an angry government."[537]

Despite Nieto-Navia's statement to the contrary, the legitimisation activities implemented in this situation appear to have damaged the legitimacy of the Tribunal for other stakeholders: *"For the RPF, the Arusha tribunal's judicial process is a means to seal its military victory over the forces of genocide."*[538] As a result, the impression that the ICTR

533 Ashford & Gibbs, 1990, pp. 178 & 183.

534 Peskin, 2008, p. 182.

535 ICTR, *Prosecutor v. Ferdinand Nahimana, Jean-Bosco Barayagwiza and Hassan Ngeze (Media Case)*, Judgment and Sentence, ICTR-99-52-T, 3 December 2003, pp. 28-29.

536 ICTR, *Prosecutor v. Jean-Bosco Barayagwiza*, Decision, ICTR-97-19-AR72, 31 March 2000, Separate Declaration, para. 2; Moghalu, 2005, p. 111-113; Peskin, 2008, p. 183.

537 ICTR, *Prosecutor v. Jean-Bosco Barayagwiza*, Decision, ICTR-97-19-AR72, 31 March 2000, Separate Declaration, para. 7.

538 Moghalu, 2005, p. 137.

was being used as a political tool, rather than a mechanism to promote reconciliation in Rwanda, was starting to take shape.[539]

5.7.2 *The Removal of the ICTR Prosecutor*

This was not the last time that the ICTR's prosecutor, Carla Del Ponte, would be embroiled in a controversy related to the ICTR. During the Barayagwiza case, Del Ponte had placed the ICTR judges in a difficult position after having stated at a hearing, on 22 February 2000, that:

> "Whether we want it or not, we must come to terms with the fact that our ability to continue with our prosecution and investigations depend on the government of Rwanda. That is the reality that we face. What is the reality? Either Barayagwiza can be tried by this Tribunal, in the alternative; or the only other solution that you have is for Barayagwiza to he handed over to the state of Rwanda to his natural judge, judex naturalis. Otherwise I am afraid, as we say in Italian, possiamo chiudere la baracca. In other words we can as well put the key to that door, close the door and then open that of the prison. And in that case the Rwandan government will not be involved in any manner."[540]

The suggestion of political influence on the reasoning of the Appeal Chamber's judges in the Barayagwiza case had been vigorously denied, notably by Judge Nieto-Navia. Nevertheless, the prosecutor's statement implied that the Tribunal should comply with the Rwandan government's request if it were to have a chance to continue its operations. The tables turned, however, when Del Ponte came under fire from the Rwandan government for starting investigations into the actions of the RPF in 1994.[541]

Shortly after her appointment in 1999, Del Ponte had announced that she would tackle not only the crimes committed by the Hutu in 1994, but also the international crimes that witnesses claimed had been committed by RPF soldiers.[542] The ICTR's first prosecutor, Richard Goldstone, had avoided the issue of investigating the RPF, working instead on

539 Kasaija Phillip Apuuli, *Procedural due process and the prosecution of genocide suspects in Rwanda*, Journal of Genocide Research, 2009, 11(1), pp. 21-24; Yolande Bouka, *(Oral) History of Violence: Conflicting Narratives in Post-Genocide Rwanda*, in: *Oral History Forum d'histoire orale*, 2013b, pp. 23-26.

540 ICTR, *Prosecutor v. Jean-Bosco Barayagwiza*, Decision, ICTR-97-19-AR72, 31 March 2000, Separate Declaration, para. 2.

541 Moghalu, 2005, p. 134.

542 ICTR Press Release, *Prosecutor outlines future plans*, 13 December 2000. Retrieved from: https://unictr.irmct.org/en/news/prosecutor-outlines-future-plans; Moghalu, 2005, p. 133; Peskin, 2008, pp. 188-189.

building a relationship of cooperation between the ICTR and the Rwandan government. At the time, an agreement had been made to allow the Rwandan government to prosecute any crimes committed by its own soldiers.[543] Louise Arbour, who was the ICTR's second prosecutor – from 1996 to 1999 – explored the possibility of investigating the RPF's actions, but these investigations were soon abandoned for security reasons. Arbour later stated that *"[Kagame's government] could turn on and off the co-operative tap at will, depending whether they were pleased or not with the work that was being done"*.[544] It was therefore Carla Del Ponte, the third prosecutor – from 1999 to 2003 – who finally established a *Special Investigations* team dedicated to looking into the possibility that the RPF may have committed international crimes in 1994.[545]

Yet, as soon as they started, the *Special Investigations* team were confronted with serious operational obstacles. As in the case of Barayagwiza, the message from the Rwandan government was clear: cooperation with the Tribunal would be suspended if investigations into the actions of RPF soldiers continued.[546] The popular opinion in Rwanda agreed: pursuing crimes allegedly committed by those who had put a stop to the genocide in 1994 was out of the question, as explained by the representative of a civil society organisation working in Rwanda at the time: *"The RPF stopped the genocide, the Unity government came to power. It was they who decided to fight impunity. The genocide convention of '48 had been signed but never put into place due to the government's genocidal plan at the time. [...] Del Ponte was looking the wrong way"*.[547] The prosecutor's actions also drew criticism from within the Tribunal, as described by a former ICTR staff member:

> "She was most interested in her image. Not the victims. They didn't have enough information about other crimes. If she had this, she would have brought the case to court. She didn't. How could she go to the government to say she wanted to prosecute them? It was destined to fail. She should have found another way. We have a poor image of Carla Del Ponte. She was a strong prosecutor from Italy. She was used to the mafia. She wanted to show her skills. But bringing this justice to destroy peace and the government? This was not right."[548]

543 Susan Thomson, *The Long Shadow of Genocide in Rwanda*, Current History, 2017, 116(790), p. 185.

544 The Globe and Mail, *Kagame government blocked criminal probe, former chief prosecutor says*, 26 October 2016. Retrieved from: https://www.theglobeandmail.com/news/world/kagame-government-supporters-complicated-un-efforts-to-investigate-crimes/article32524359/

545 Moghalu, 2005, p. 133; Peskin, 2008, pp. 188-191.

546 The reason given for the suspension of all cooperation with the Tribunal was the poor treatment of witnesses (Peskin, 2008, pp. 187 & 212-213).

547 Interviewee CS7.

548 Translated from French: *"Elle était surtout intéressée par son image. Pas les victimes. Ils n'avaient pas suffisamment d'informations sur ces autres crimes. Si elle avait eu cela, elle aurait porté l'affaire devant les tribunaux. Elle ne l'a pas fait. Comment a-t-elle pu s'adresser au gouvernement pour dire qu'elle voulait les poursuivre. C'était voué à l'échec. Elle aurait dû trouver un autre moyen. Nous avons une mauvaise image*

As in the Barayagwiza case, the actions of the OTP resulted in the Rwandan government boycotting all activities related to the Tribunal. This time the government went a step further than in 1999, causing the ICTR to temporarily shut down its operations: visa applications for ICTR staff were rejected or withdrawn, preventing investigators from working in Rwanda; and airport landing permits were denied, stopping all flights between Arusha and Kigali that were carrying investigators and witnesses to and from the ICTR. The sudden lack of witnesses arriving in Arusha brought the work of the Tribunal to a complete standstill.[549] The government's actions provoked a series of tense exchanges between the UN Secretary-General and the ICTR, with Del Ponte demanding that the UN exert pressure on Rwanda to *"cooperate fully"* with the Tribunal, as required by UN Resolution 955.[550]

5.7.2.1 Repairing Legitimacy

Following several weeks of discussions – involving the Rwandan government, the UN Secretary-General, UN member states (in particular the USA and the UK) and the ICTR's prosecutor herself – a decision was made by the UN Security Council to remove Del Ponte from the ICTR.[551] With completion strategies for both the ICTY and the ICTR in place, it was reported that the UN Security Council agreed that two separate prosecutors were needed – one for each Tribunal – in order to ensure that both the ICTR and the ICTY could meet their deadlines and close on time.[552] And in August 2003, the UN Security Council adopted UN Resolution 1503, which *"requests the Secretary-General to nominate a person to be the Prosecutor of the ICTR"*.[553] This effectively removed Carla Del Ponte (at the time prosecutor for both the ICTR and the ICTY) from her post as prosecutor for the ICTR.[554] Following the adoption of this resolution, the UN Security Council amended article 15 of the ICTR Statute removing the following sentence from the original Statute:

---

de Carla Del Ponte. Elle était une forte procureure italienne. Elle était habituée à la mafia. Elle voulait montrer ses compétences. Mais amener cette justice pour détruire la paix et le gouvernement? Ce n'était pas juste." (T9).

549 Moghalu, 2005, p. 134; Peskin, 2008, pp. 187 & 213.

550 Peskin, 2008, pp. 218-219; United Nations Security Council, *Resolution 955*, S/RES/955, 8 November 1994, para. 2.

551 Cryer et al. 2019, p. 140; Peskin, 2008, pp. 220-222; Sudetic & Del Ponte, 2011, Chapter 9.

552 Peskin, 2008, p. 220; New York Times, *Rwanda Is Said to Seek New Prosecutor for War Crimes Court*, 28 July 2003. Retrieved from: https://www.nytimes.com/2003/07/28/world/rwanda-is-said-to-seek-new-prosecutor-for-war-crimes-court.html.

553 United Nations Security Council, *Resolution 1503*, S/RES/1503, 28 August 2003, para. 8

554 ICTR Press Release, *The Security Council Appoints Separate Prosecutors for the two ad hoc UN Tribunals*,4 September 2003. Retrieved from: https://unictr.irmct.org/en/news/security-council-appoints-separate-prosecutors-two-ad-hoc-un-tribunals; UN Press Release (28 August 2003). *Security Council splits prosecutorial duties for Rwanda, Yugoslavia Tribunals, unanimously adopting Resolution 1503 (2003).* Retrieved from: https://www.un.org/press/en/2003/sc7858.doc.htm.

"The Prosecutor of the International Tribunal for the Former Yugoslavia shall also serve as the Prosecutor of the International Tribunal for Rwanda".[555]

The removal of Del Ponte exposed the UN Security Council to claims that it had sacrificed the ICTR's prosecutor in order to prevent the Tribunal from issuing RPF indictments, therefore yielding to the Rwandan government's demands.[556] These allegations were strengthened by Del Ponte's own accusations against both the UN and the Rwandan government: *"[I was] expelled from Rwanda because I wanted to do justice [...] if I had conceded [to their demands] I would still be in my place".*[557] However, others interpreted the actions of the Tribunal differently:

> "With the RPF, the prosecutors made a choice. They needed to make a distinction between the crimes. Carla Del Ponte mixed things up. The crimes are so different. They are different levels. The ICTR wanted to show they were doing something. They didn't prosecute everyone involved in the genocide. The Priest and the Bishop were killed by RPF. These people were tried in Rwanda with monitoring by the ICTR. The ICTR had to start with most important criminals. The most important crimes."[558]

Despite launching the *Special Investigations* in 2000, no indictments had yet been made and the team of investigators allocated to the investigation (located first in Rwanda and then in Arusha) was officially withdrawn in May 2003.[559] The sensitivity surrounding the removal of Carla Del Ponte as the prosecutor for the ICTR is highlighted in an interview with one of the Tribunal's former presidents, Judge Vagn Joensen, in 2016:

> "Our mandate covers all atrocities that happened in Rwanda in 1994 including those that were committed by the RPF in retaliation of the genocide. I know that was especially a dispute between prosecutor Carla Del Ponte and the

---

555 ICTR Statute, 2010, art. 15(3).

556 Peskin, 2008, pp. 220-221.

557 Translated from Italian: *"cacciata dal Ruanda perché volevo fare giustizia. [...] Se mi fossi piegata sarei ancora al mio posto"* (La Repubblica, Del Ponte: cacciata dal Ruanda perché volevo fare giustizia, 4 January 2010. Retrieved from: http://www.repubblica.it/2003/i/sezioni/esteri/delponte/delponte/delponte.html?refresh_ce).

558 Translated from French: *"Avec le FPR, les procureurs ont fait un choix. Ils devaient faire une distinction entre les crimes. Carla Del Ponte a mélangé les choses. Les crimes sont tellement différents. Ce sont des niveaux différents. Le TPIR voulait montrer qu'il faisait quelque chose. Ils n'ont pas poursuivi toutes les personnes impliquées dans le génocide. Le prêtre et l'évêque ont été tués par le FPR. Ces personnes ont été jugées au Rwanda sous la surveillance du TPIR. Le TPIR devait commencer par les criminels les plus importants. Les crimes les plus importants."* (T9).

559 Peskin, 2008, pp. 220-221; William A. Schabas, *International Criminal Tribunals: A Review of 2007*, Northwestern Journal of International Human Rights, 2008b, 6, p. 389.

> Rwandan government which ended with the Security Council deciding that we should have our own prosecutor because, initially, we had a joint prosecutor with the ICTY. This hybridization of prosecution into one for both ICTY and ICTR happened in connection with the complete strategy that was adopted. Part of that complete strategy was that we could not issue new indictments after 2004. So the new prosecutor, Hassan Bubacar Jallow, was actually barred from issuing new indictments, whereas Del Ponte could have done it but was unable to because she didn't get the collaboration from Rwanda that she asked for."[560]

In removing Del Ponte from her position as prosecutor, the UN Security Council made it clear that any crimes committed by RPF soldiers would not fall within the Tribunal's jurisdiction.[561] As in the Barayagwiza case, this action relates to *coercive isomorphism*, where an organisation is pressured into responding to the expectations of its stakeholders. However, the difference here is that the decision to remove Carla Del Ponte as prosecutor for the ICTR was effectively taken out of the hands of the Tribunal. It was the UN Security Council that took the decision to reduce the role of the prosecutor to focus on the work of one Tribunal, rather than two.

5.7.3 *Stakeholders*

While the removal of Del Ponte from the ICTR is a clear example of a*coercive* measure, it also demonstrates the dual role of the UN in relation to the ICTR. Although the Tribunal was created as an independent court of law, it was established and fully funded by the UN, which also had the authority to alter provisions in the ICTR's Statute, as demonstrated in this case. The UN provides a*justification* for their actions in this situation through UN Resolution 1503[562] and the completion strategy.[563] Although the reason given for this structural change was to improve the efficiency of both tribunals, the timing of UN Resolution 1503 – following weeks of heated discussions between the Rwandan government, Del Ponte and the UN Secretary-General regarding the *Special Investigations* – gave many observers the impression that the removal of Del Ponte was not necessarily designed to

560 Jambonews, *Closing interview with the President of the International Criminal Tribunal for Rwanda (ICTR) – Part I,* 18 January 2016. Retrieved from: https://www.jambonews.net/en/actualites/20160118-closing-interview-with-the-president-of-the-international-criminal-tribunal-for-rwanda-ictr-part-i/.

561 *ibid.*; Peskin, 2008, pp. 224-226.

562 United Nations Security Council, *Resolution 1503*, S/RES/1503, 28 August 2003, p. 2.

563 ICTR, Completion Strategy Report, S/2003/946, 6 October 2003, para. 2.

improve the productivity of the ICTR, but rather was due to the pressure exerted by the Rwandan government, a key stakeholder.[564]

Given the ICTR's dependence on the UN for funding and operational support, the option of *altering resource dependencies* as a substantive legitimisation activity used to repair organisational legitimacy – which would have provided the Tribunal with more freedom in its actions – was not possible.[565] The UN clearly played an important role with regard to the autonomy of the ICTR. Likewise, the Tribunal's dependence on the Rwandan government, as demonstrated by its ability to paralyse the Tribunal's daily operations both in this situation and in the Barayagwiza case, also prevented the ICTR from behaving as an autonomous organisation.

The legitimisation activities implemented in response to these two situations appear to have been effective in the short-term: by ensuring the continued operations of the Tribunal, and enforcing the notion that the Tribunal was legitimate as an organisation established to *"prosecute persons responsible for serious violations of international humanitarian law committed in the territory of Rwanda [...] between 1 January 1994 and 31 December 1994"*.[566] However, the long-term consequences of these legitimisation activities, especially related to the ICTR's legitimacy to other stakeholders, may have played an important role in defining Rwanda's future and possibly also influenced the practice of international criminal law.

5.8 Fugitives

The task of tracking down the last fugitives has now been passed on to the IR-MCT, which works alongside Interpol and the Rwanda's own *Genocide* Fugitive Tracking Unit (GFTU).[567] Tracking fugitives involved in a conflict that took place over 25 years ago is challenging: the strategies used by fugitives to evade justice include not only changing their identity but also ensuring their ability to constantly move across east, central and southern Africa, and inaccessible areas of the DRC.[568] Unlike national systems, the ICTR did not have a police force, or the authority to arrest a suspect; it was reliant on the cooperation of national governments to track and detain fugitives: *"International criminal tribunals [...] have neither territories of their own, nor any real coercive power outside their seats that would*

564 Apuuli, 2009, pp. 21-24; Bouka, 2013b, pp. 23-26; Peskin, 2008, pp. 219-222; Schabas, 2008b, p. 389.

565 Ashford & Gibbs, 1990, p. 178.

566 United Nations Security Council, *Resolution 955*, S/RES/955, 8 November 1994, Article 1.

567 The GFTU was founded by the Rwandan government in November 2007. IR-MCT website, 'Searching for the fugitives'. Retrieved from: https://www.irmct.org/en/cases/searching-fugitives; France24, *Seeking justice: the long hunt for Rwanda's killers*, 2 April 2009. Retrieved from: https://www.france24.com/en/20190402-seeking-justice-long-hunt-rwandas-killers.

568 Interviewee G3.

enable them to be self-sufficient".[569] The commitment of UN member states in assisting the ICTR was therefore crucial, especially in the countries where the fugitives were suspected of having taken refuge.

> "Going forward, the ICTR should have willingness to judge all fugitives. They must now be arrested. There are still so many cases of genocide perpetrators. There needs to be more activity in bringing these perpetrators to account. Countries should make an effort to find the fugitives and send them to Rwanda. Some countries are really playing their part in this, others are not. Justice must be seen to be done, especially by survivors."[570]

Furthermore, UN Resolution 955 was binding on all UN member states: they were under the obligation to engage with the ICTR at all stages of the process regarding the investigation and prosecution of an accused individual.[571] Such obligations included compliance "*without undue delay*" with requests for assistance in: gathering evidence; recording the testimony of witnesses, suspects and experts; identifying and locating the accused; and serving documents.[572] States were also obliged to carry out the requests issued by the ICTR trial chambers, such as summonses, subpoenas, arrest warrants, and transfer orders.[573]

Additionally, UN member states were required to contribute to the ICTR's budget, to make personnel available, and to adopt concrete judicial and legislative measures into domestic laws so as to be able to implement the provisions stated in the ICTR Statute and UN resolution 955.[574] The engagement of states was therefore a crucial element in ensuring that the Tribunal functioned smoothly. This was particularly important given that the ICTR had no concrete provisions to punish a state that failed to cooperate or did not amend its national legislation to incorporate the obligations derived from the ICTR Statute.[575] As such, enforcing the various obligations was a delicate matter: UN member states were crucial in both apprehending fugitives and in providing the ICTR with essential resources. The Tribunal had very little leverage to hold states to account:

---

569 Adama Dieng, *Supplementary agreements, arrangements and other forms of cooperation and assistance, experiences in relation to the Court and other international judicial bodies, a consideration of challenges and how these might be overcome*, International Criminal Court Review Conference, 8th Plenary Stocktaking of International Criminal Justice Cooperation, Kampala, Uganda, 3 June 2010, p. 1.

570 Interviewee CS7.

571 United Nations Security Council, *Statute of the International Criminal Tribunal for Rwanda* (as amended on 31 December 2010), 8 November 1994, Article 28; United Nations, *Charter of the United Nations*, 24 October 1945, Article 103.

572 ICTR Statute, 2010, Article 28.

573 *ibid.*

574 United Nations Security Council, *Resolution 955*, S/RES/955, 8 November 1994, para. 2 & 4.

575 ICTR Statute, 2010, Article 28.

> "The fugitives need to be arrested. Something in the tracking unit needs to change. Maybe they need more resources? More action is needed. One fugitive was seen by my colleague in Hong Kong with his family. He informed INTERPOL. They called him for more information two years later. This is useless."[576]

An example of a state's failure to engage with the work of the ICTR can be given in the case of Reverend Atanasio Sumba Bura. Following the 1994 genocide Bura fled Rwanda, arriving in Italy a few years later, where he was allocated to a local parish in Florence. In 1999, Bura was recognised to be Athanase Seromba, who had participated in the Nyange massacre during the 1994 genocide;[577] yet, it was not until July 2001 that the ICTR's OTP charged Seromba with crimes of genocide, conspiracy to commit genocide and crimes against humanity.[578] Despite the indictment, there was no legal basis for the Italians to proceed with an arrest as Italy had not yet ratified a law regulating judicial assistance and cooperation with the Tribunal. This was eventually implemented a year later, in August 2002;[579] however, by this time Serombo had already surrendered to the Tribunal.[580]

Another fugitive who evaded international criminal justice for over 25 years was Félicien Kabuga, a wealthy businessman who is believed to have provided weapons to the Interahamwe during the genocide. As Benoit Kaboyi, Executive Secretary of IBUKA, explained: "*Kabuga is our Osama bin Laden*".[581] Following the establishment of the ICTR, Kabuga became one of the main suspects under investigation by the OTP and was eventually indicted by the Tribunal in 1997. However, despite two attempted arrests in Kenya, and sightings of him in South-East Asia and Belgium, Kabuga managed to evade the authorities.[582] In December 2002, Pierre-Richard Prosper – US ambassador-at-large for war crimes – formally accused the Kenyan government of protecting Kabuga by making

576 Translated from French: "*Les fugitifs doivent être arrêtés. Quelque chose dans l'unité de suivi doit changer. Peut-être ont-ils besoin de plus de ressources? Il faut plus d'action. Un fugitif a été vu par mon collègue à Hong Kong avec sa famille. Il a informé INTERPOL. Ils l'ont appelé pour plus d'informations deux ans plus tard. Cela ne sert à rien.*" (T2).

577 Julien Seroussi, *The devils from The Thousand Hills*, 4 April 2016. Retrieved from: https://booksandideas.net/The-devils-from-the-Thousand-Hills.html; ICTR, *Prosecutor v. Athanase Seromba*, Judgment, ICTR-2001-66-I, 13 December 2006, para. 13.

578 ICTR, *Prosecutor v. Athanase Seromba*, Indictment, ICTR-2001-66-I, 5 July December 2001.

579 Italy: *Legge 2 agosto 2002, n. 181, di cooperazione con il Tribunale internazionale competente per gravi violazioni del diritto umanitario commesse nel territorio del Ruanda* (Law No. 181 of 2 August 2002 on Cooperation with the International Tribunal responsible for Serious Violations of Human Rights Committed in the Territory of Rwanda and Adjacent States).

580 ICTR, *Prosecutor v. Athanase Seromba*, Judgment, ICTR-2001-66-I, 13 December 2006, para. 13 & 398.

581 Moghalu, 2005, p. 153.

582 Interviewees T2 & G3; The Conversation, *What Kabuga's Arrest Means for International Criminal Justice – and Rwanda*, 1 June 2020. Retrieved from: https://theconversation.com/what-kabugas-arrest-means-for-international-criminal-justice-and-rwanda-139393.

use of governmental resources to prevent his arrest.[583] The sentiment was echoed by interviewees for this research,[584] one of whom explained: "*Why are some fugitives still free? Kabuga? This is simply corruption. These people have huge amounts of money, they are businessmen. They are protected by the country they are in. They pay off people*".[585]

Kabuga was finally arrested in Asnières-sur-Seine, a suburb of Paris, in May 2020.[586] Media outlets reported that prior to his arrest, Kabuga had spent time in several UN member states including Switzerland, Belgium, Burundi, the DRC, Kenya, and Germany. It appears that Kabuga's movements were facilitated by his enormous wealth and the assistance of his five children, as well as the uncoordinated response of UN member states.[587] Some reports speculated that the COVID-19 lockdown experienced in Europe from mid-March 2020 onwards played a role in leading to the arrest of Rwanda's most wanted fugitive: facilitating the tracking of Kabuga's children in Paris, which eventually led to his arrest in May 2020.[588]

Although a major breakthrough for international criminal justice, the arrest of Kabuga – following his 26 years on the run – did raise questions as to how the Rwandan businessman could have evaded capture for so long. For others the answer was simple: "*The ICTR had a lot of money. So do the fugitives*".[589] IBUKA France considered legal action to uncover why French authorities were so slow in finding and arresting Kabuga; for many it was inconceivable that Kabuga was able to live in Paris undetected for the previous four years: "*He was our Klaus Barbie, our Eichmann*".[590] The IR-MCT prosecutor chose instead to thank the various states involved in the tracking and arrest:

---

583 Guardian, *Bloody end as trap for man behind massacres backfires*,22 January 2003. Retrieved from: https://www.theguardian.com/world/2003/jan/22/jamesastill; The New Humanitarian, *ICTR investigators to meet new Kenyan government*,2 January 2003. Retrieved from: https://www.thenewhumanitarian.org/fr/node/208974; The Times, *Rwandan terror paymaster under protection of Moi aide*,22 December 2002. Retrieved from: https://www.thetimes.co.uk/article/rwandan-terror-paymaster-under-protection-of-moi-aide-ktfnrg3ftr9.

584 Interviewees G3, T1, T2 & CS6.

585 Translated from French: "*Pourquoi certains fugitifs sont-ils encore libres? C'est simplement de la corruption. Ces gens ont d'énormes sommes d'argent, ce sont des hommes d'affaires. Ils sont protégés par le pays dans lequel ils se trouvent. Ils paient les gens.*" (CS6).

586 Reuters, *Rwanda genocide suspect Kabuga arrested in France after decades on the run*,16 May 2020. Retrieved from: https://www.reuters.com/news/picture/rwanda-genocide-suspect-kabuga-arrested-idUSKBN22S0G5.

587 BBC, *Rwanda genocide: How Félicien Kabuga evaded capture for 26 years*,24 May 2020. Retrieved from: https://www.bbc.com/news/world-africa-52758693; Adama Dieng, *The Interpol's Fugitive Investigative Assistance: One of the Most Critical Requirements for the ICTR's Successful Completion Strategy*, 19th African Regional Conference for INTERPOL, Arusha, Tanzania, 11 July 2007, p. 2.

588 BBC, 24 May 2020; Carlson, 2020; Bruce Zagaris and Michael Plachta, Genocide, Crimes Against Humanity, and International Tribunals, *International Enforcement Law Reporter*, 2020, 36(191), p. 191.

589 Translated from French: "*Le TPIR avait beaucoup d'argent. Et les fugitifs aussi.*" (T1).

590 Zagaris & Plachta, 2020, p. 191; Al Jazeera, *Rwandan genocide fugitive Felicien Kabuga due before Paris court*,19 May 2020. Retrieved from: https://www.aljazeera.com/news/2020/05/rwandan-genocide-fugitive-felicien-kabuga-due-paris-court-200519105137803.html.
IBUKA France is the French-based genocide victim support group: www.ibuka.rw.

> "I would like to extend our appreciation to France and its law enforcement authorities, particularly the Central Office for Combatting Crimes Against Humanity, Genocide and War Crimes and the Office of the Procureur Général of the Paris Cour d'Appel. This arrest could not have been made without their exceptional cooperation and skill. It is important to also recognize the many other partners whose contributions were essential, including law enforcement agencies and prosecution services from Rwanda, Belgium, the United Kingdom, Germany, the Netherlands, Austria, Luxembourg, Switzerland, the United States, EUROPOL and INTERPOL. This arrest demonstrates the impressive results that can be achieved through international law enforcement and judicial cooperation."[591]

The arrest of Kabuga was indeed a great feat for international justice. However, the fact remained that when the ICTR closed its doors in December 2015, eight fugitives were at large: *"There were many challenges. Many people criticise the court for not doing enough. Lots of money was spent and there are fugitives still out there"*.[592] The Tribunal indicted 93 individuals for serious violations of international humanitarian law committed in 1994. In total, proceedings for 80 individuals were concluded and four cases were referred to national jurisdictions. Yet for one interviewee this was not enough: *"The work is not done. Trials have not been completed. Fugitives are still free"*.[593]

5.8.1 *Maintaining Legitimacy*

The task of tracking and arresting fugitives was present throughout the Tribunal's existence, and demonstrates another perspective to managing, and indeed maintaining, legitimacy. To operate, and be perceived, as a legitimate criminal court, the ICTR needed individuals to prosecute, and without the assistance of UN member states the Tribunal could not arrest and transfer individuals to its detention house in Arusha. Finding, arresting and prosecuting fugitives therefore had an influence on the Tribunal's legitimacy and placed it in a particularly difficult position: on the one hand, organisational legitimacy was needed to ensure that UN member states engaged with the Tribunal and continued to support its efforts through funding; on the other, the ICTR could only operate if UN member states tracked, arrested and transferred fugitives to Arusha, in order for trials to take place. A key stakeholder group – the UN member states – was therefore crucial in assisting the

591 IR-MCT Press Release, *Mechanism fugitive Félicien Kabuga arrested today*, 16 May 2020. Retrieved from: https://www.irmct.org/en/news/20-06-09-mechanism-fugitive-felicien-kabuga-arrested-today.

592 Interviewee CS21.

593 Interviewee J4.

ICTR in maintaining its legitimacy, while the Tribunal also needed to demonstrate its legitimacy to the same group in order to receive assistance.

Furthermore, the ICTR was operating alongside the ICTY, which also required support and resources from the UN and its member states. There was, therefore, competition for funding and recognition from the UN member states. The Tribunal needed to continue to demonstrate its legitimacy in order to remain relevant in the eyes of the UN, while also asking them for vital support and resources.

Apprehending fugitives by the ICTY was just as painstaking as for the ICTR. However, after a slow start in finding and arresting the 161 individuals indicted, by July 2011 the ICTY's last remaining fugitive – Goran Hadžić – had been arrested. This was largely due to efforts made by the international community, not least by the USA and UK:

> "In May 1997 everything changed and the fortunes of the Hague tribunal were revived by a single, apparently unrelated, event, which was the election in Britain of the Labour government. The Labour party of Blair arrived in office promising an 'ethical foreign policy'. The new foreign secretary, Robin Cook, was aware of Arbour's bold stance [...] now he won cabinet approval to use the SAS to go after war crimes suspects. With Cook backing the idea, Albright pushed America to give its support."[594]

The same 'push' could not be said for the ICTR's eight remaining fugitives. Indeed, as one researcher observed: *"It is quite remarkable how little attention these 'forgotten fugitives' – Augustin Bizimana, Félicien Kabuga, Fulgence Kayishema, Protais Mpiranya, Phénéas Munyarugarama, Aloys Ndimbati, Charles Ryandikayo and Charles Sikubwabo – have received in the media"*.[595] The ICTR needed to regain the momentum felt in the early days of the Tribunal: "*We had considerable success working with national authorities of African countries. As a result we had many high-ranking accused in custody from an early stage*".[596] Yet, over the years the number of arrests reduced in number and the need for resources and engagement from the international community became urgent.

In May 2003, the ICTR registrar asked for support in tracking and arresting fugitives when addressing delegates at a conference in Kigali,[597] and the prosecutor made a similar

---

594 Chris Stephen, *Judgement Day: The Trial of Slobodan Milošević*, London: Atlantic Books, 2005, p. 128.

595 Christophe Paulussen, *Arrest and Transfer*, in: Anne-Marie De Brouwer and Alette Smeulers (eds.), *The Elgar Companion to the International Criminal Tribunal for Rwanda*, Edward Elgar Publishing, 2016, p. 287.

596 Gavin F. Ruxton, *The View of the Public Prosecutor of ICTY*, in: W. A. M. Van Dijk and J. L. Hovens (eds.), *Arresting War Criminals*, Wolf Legal Productions, 2001, p. 20.
Gavin F. Ruxton was a Legal Advisor at the Office of the Prosecutor, based in The Hague.

597 ICTR Press Release, *ICTR Registrar Seeks Support of African Community*, 9 May 2003. Retrieved from: https://unictr.irmct.org/en/news/ictr-registrar-seeks-support-african-community.

appeal during the Irish prime minister's visit to Arusha in June 2006: *"The Prosecutor, Mr. Jallow appealed to the Irish Government to assist in apprehending fugitives at large as well as providing material support to states which will be willing to prosecute cases transferred from the Tribunal before the end of its mandate in 2008".*[598]

Although the challenge faced by the ICTR in apprehending fugitives occurred over the course of the Tribunal's existence, it does not appear to directly equate to the three distinct challenges in *maintaining* legitimacy: "*stakeholder heterogeneity*", reflecting unanticipated demands, or a change in needs, from a diverse set of stakeholders; "*organisational homogeneity*", which prohibits the organisation from responding to fluctuating conditions; and "*institutionalisation*", when the organisation comes under attack for the actions of a comparable organisation.[599] However, the ICTR did need to adapt due to a change in its *environment.* With the arrival of the ICC in The Hague,[600] as well as several hybrid international criminal courts,[601] the field of international criminal law was growing fast, and with it the demands on UN member states and state parties to the Rome Statute also increased.

The challenge in maintaining the Tribunal's legitimacy, when faced with competition from other international courts for vital resources, therefore appears to have been a combination of addressing: "*stakeholder heterogeneity*" due to the change in focus of the UN member states rather than the diversity of stakeholder needs from the organisation; and "*organisational homogeneity*", in connection to the arrival of similar international criminal courts with different mandates, rather than linked to an inability to compete with more versatile organisations offering similar services.

5.8.2 Pragmatic Legitimacy

The legitimisation activities implemented with regard to the ICTR's ability to track, arrest and prosecute fugitives – with the help of UN member states – demonstrates a *pragmatic* approach to *protecting past accomplishments.* The Tribunal demonstrates actions that are consistent and predictable, and its ability to deliver the services that its stakeholders expect. The following press release demonstrates the US Secretary of State's recognition of this:

---

598 ICTR Press Release, *Irish President Visits Tribunal*, 21 June 2006. Retrieved from: https://unictr.irmct.org/en/news/irish-president-visits-tribunal.

599 Suchman, 1995, p. 594.

600 United Nations General Assembly, *Rome Statute of the International Criminal Court* (last amended 2010), 17 July 1998.

601 Tribunals that are often mentioned in this category are: Special Panels and Serious Crimes Unit in East-Timor (2000); Regulation 64 Panels in the Courts of Kosovo (2000); Special Court for Sierra Leone (2002); Extraordinary Chambers in the Courts of Cambodia (2003); Special Tribunal for Lebanon (2009); Extraordinary African Chambers (2013); and Kosovo Specialist Chambers and Specialist Prosecutor's Office (2015).

> "The ICTR representatives reported on the high number of trials currently in progress in Arusha and emphasized the need for sufficient resources to implement the ICTR's Completion Strategy. They also requested American cooperation on several matters where the Tribunal needs the assistance of national governments to accomplish its mission."[602]

The *"ICTR representatives"* emphasise the high number of trials taking place, while asking UN member states for assistance, which is a demonstration of pragmatic legitimacy: an organisation receives support if it fulfils the stakeholder's needs and expectations.[603] The message is clear: there are still fugitives, there is still work to be done, and the ICTR is capable of doing it if it receives support from the international community. The same approach is demonstrated in a speech by the registrar, Adama Dieng, during the African regional conference for INTERPOL in Arusha in 2007:

> "Although the ICTR can be proud of itself because of its honourable track records, it goes without saying that in order to successfully complete its work within the timeframe that has been prescribed by the security council as part of its completion strategy, the ICTR has intensified its tracking and diplomatic efforts to secure the arrest and transfer of ICTR fugitives for trial. Kenya, the Democratic Republic of Congo, as well as other countries neighbouring Rwanda are the focus of tracking and diplomatic activities in search of fugitives."[604]

The message is reiterated in a press release published a couple of days later.[605] Furthermore, the registrar emphasises the time pressure that is being felt by the ICTR due to the completion strategy. In an apparent signal to the new, emerging international criminal courts, the ICTR's OTP issued a manual in 2013 detailing the lessons learnt in apprehending fugitives: *"The document released today documents those lessons and makes practical recommendations for those tasked with apprehending international fugitives from justice"*.[606] The manual gives an insight into the legal and political landscape regarding the

602 ICTR Press Release, *ICTR President and Prosecutor Meet U.S. Secretary of State*, 17 June 2005. Retrieved from: https://unictr.irmct.org/en/news/ictr-president-and-prosecutor-meet-us-secretary-state.

603 Suchman, 1995, pp. 578-579.

604 Adama Dieng, *The Interpol's Fugitive Investigative Assistance: One of the Most Critical Requirements for the ICTR's Successful Completion Strategy*, 19th African Regional Conference for INTERPOL, Arusha, Tanzania, 11 July 2007, p. 2.

605 ICTR Press Release, *Press Statement: Interpol Conference Calls for Action on Rwandan War Crimes Fugitives*, 13 July 2007. Retrieved from: https://unictr.irmct.org/en/news/press-statement-interpol-conference-calls-action-rwandan-war-crimes-fugitives.

606 ICTR Press Release, *Prosecutor Releases Lessons Learnt Manual for the Tracking and Arrest of Fugitives from International Justice*, 16 August 2013. Retrieved from: https://unictr.irmct.org/en/news/prosecutor-releases-lessons-learnt-manual-tracking-and-arrest-fugitives-international-justice.

apprehension of international fugitives, and it provides an overview of the resources available and the legal frameworks that both help and hinder the work of investigators working with national authorities. With this manual, the Tribunal demonstrates a professional and competent operation that successfully arrested 83 fugitives. Furthermore, it cements the relationship of trust, both with the international community and its peers.

5.8.3 Stakeholders

The ICTR needed UN member states to engage with its work and to assist the Tribunal in apprehending suspects: without their assistance there could be no ICTR. Yet the bar was set high, with 93 indictees and a completion strategy announced in October 2003. The IR-MCT was established to take over from the ICTR in December 2010 and the pressure to find and arrest the final fugitives grew. At the review conference for the Rome Statute of the ICC,[607] the ICTR registrar stressed the importance of state involvement in international criminal justice, illustrating the unnecessary technical obstacles that delayed the process of extradition:

> "Several international tribunal's indictees remain at large. States have sometimes sought clarification regarding the relevance of national extradition practice, whether conditions can be placed on the transfers, or whether there was a need for a special agreement prior to transfer. ICTY and ICTR have consistently maintained that transfers should not be subjected to any conditions, and that security council's resolutions, the statute and rules constitute as a sufficient legal basis for transfers. Because the international tribunal's requests are mistakenly treated more or less as requests for extradition, they often give rise to an unwarranted extensive domestic judicial review. This causes unnecessary delays."[608]

This statement demonstrates that after 15 years of existence, there is still a need for the ICTR to emphasise *"that transfers should not be subjected to any conditions, and that security council's resolutions, the statute and rules constitute as a sufficient legal basis for*

607 Following the adoption of the Rome Statute implemented in 1998, a review conference of the Statute was held in Kampala, Uganda, from 31 May to 11 June 2010. The conference involved ICC states parties, observer states, international organisations, NGOs, and included representatives from the ICTR and ICTY.

608 Adama Dieng, *Supplementary agreements, arrangements and other forms of cooperation and assistance, experiences in relation to the Court and other international judicial bodies, a consideration of challenges and how these might be overcome*, International Criminal Court Review Conference, 8th Plenary Stocktaking of International Criminal Justice Cooperation, Kampala, Uganda, 3 June 2010, pp. 1-2.

transfer".[609] Yet, unlike the ICTR's struggle to apprehend its last remaining fugitives, the ICTY's final fugitive was arrested and in custody the following year.

In their efforts to receive assistance in apprehending the final fugitives, the ICTR's legitimisation activities were directed at the UN member states. The Tribunal needed to ensure that funding was directed towards their operations – especially working alongside other international criminal courts and tribunals – while also urging states to provide resources to find, arrest and transfer the fugitives. The Tribunal in Arusha also positioned itself as equal to the ICTY, with regard to its mission, the management of its operations and the structure of the working environment.[610]

5.9 Conclusion

Examining the legitimacy challenges faced by the Tribunal and the legitimisation activities implemented in order to mitigate or resolve these challenges highlights the complexities and multifaceted nature of legitimacy. First and foremost there are a multitude of stakeholders involved, not only in perceiving legitimacy challenges, but also in implementing legitimisation activities. The relationship between the UN and the ICTR is the clearest demonstration of this, as the UN sought to promote the legitimacy of the Tribunal, while also requiring the ICTR to demonstrate its legitimacy and show that it was worthy of further support: during the mismanagement crisis in the early years of the Tribunal's existence, it is the UN that takes the reins in implementing legitimisation activities to bring order and restore the ICTR's legitimacy. Yet, when it came to garnering support to track and arrest fugitives of the Tribunal, it was up to the ICTR to engage UN member states in providing assistance.

Furthermore, the Tribunal itself occasionally held opposing roles (between the organs) when it came to managing its legitimacy. This was most apparent during the Barayagwiza trial, which involved the OTP negotiating with the Appeals Chamber to reconsider their position on Barayagwiza's acquittal; and again when the prosecutor, Carla Del Ponte, sought to investigate and prosecute members of the RPF, which was met with resistance by both internal and external stakeholders. These two examples demonstrate the chameleon-like nature of legitimacy, and also highlight the delicate balance in appeasing all stakeholders. The review of Barayagwiza's case was a victory for the OTP and the Rwandan government, although the reversal of the Appeal Chamber's judgment also raised questions regarding the Tribunal's legitimacy for other stakeholders, who viewed the judges' change of direction as an indication of political interference in the workings of the

609 *idem.*, p. 2.
610 Section 5.1.1; Moghalu, 5 April 2000, pp. 9-10.

Tribunal. The same can be said for the removal of Carla Del Ponte by the UN Secretary-General in 2003, and the failure to investigate crimes committed by the RPF: the Tribunal may have salvaged its relationship with the Rwandan government, but it took a risk with regard to its legitimacy as an impartial, independent court of law.

Also of interest is how the theoretical framework described in Chapter 2 works in practice. The difficulties experienced by the ICTR in tracking, arresting and prosecuting fugitives appears to encapsulate a legitimacy challenge in maintaining legitimacy. Yet, when categorising the challenge, Suchman's findings do not correspond to the situation at the ICTR.[611] The challenge of "*stakeholder heterogeneity*" was linked to the change in UN member states' focus (towards the ICC and emerging hybrid courts) rather than the diversity of needs that a stakeholder demands from an organisation; and "*organisational homogeneity*" was not caused by the arrival of more versatile organisations, but rather due to the emergence of a new wave of international criminal courts: the ICC and hybrid courts.

Similarly, the challenge of mismanagement – which occurred throughout the Tribunal's existence, but was most apparent in the early years of the ICTR – did not correspond to efforts in gaining legitimacy, but rather the need for the Tribunal to repair its legitimacy. Although the ICTR was brand new when these teething issues emerged, the challenges did not correspond to its external environment, but rather to the inner workings of the ICTR. Repairing legitimacy may therefore occur at any phase of an organisation's life, regardless of how new an organisation is, or how much legitimacy it has already acquired. Alternatively, repairing the ICTR's legitimacy may connect, again, to its affiliation to the UN.

Indeed, the relationship with the UN, the founder and sponsor of the ICTR, is particularly noteworthy. Although the Tribunal was established as a new international criminal tribunal, in a region (and on a continent) that had never experienced such a court, the UN is a longstanding organisation, widely known and perceived as a legitimate. This is evident in the perception of the Tribunal's legitimacy, which many interviewees associated with its link to the UN, and the resources that this afforded the Tribunal in achieving its mandate.

Indeed, the fact that the ICTR was established as an independent court of law, not a branch of the UN, was not always apparent during the interviews. The confusion is, however, understandable when examining the legitimisation activities of the ICTR, especially when the UN stepped in to address legitimacy challenges facing the Tribunal. During the mismanagement crisis in the late 1990s, the actions of the UN Secretary-General and General Assembly were understandable, given that it was in the UN's interest that the ICTR and the ICTY were successful: the two tribunals symbolised the revival of international criminal law. In the case of the ICTR, the establishment of the Tribunal also reflected the

611 Suchman, 1995, p. 594.

international community's delayed response to the crimes committed in Rwanda in 1994. The UN therefore played the role of facilitator and supporter of the ICTR, while also assuming the position of regulator and investor. The Tribunal was also tasked with keeping the UN, and its member states, on board, especially while working in parallel with the ICTY and with the emergence of new international criminal courts.

Another key stakeholder regarding the ICTR's legitimacy – particularly apparent during the trial of Barayagwiza and later with the removal of Carla Del Ponte as chief prosecutor for the ICTR – was the Rwandan government. In establishing the ICTR across the border in Tanzania, investigators and ICTR staff required permission from the Rwandan government to operate in Rwandan territory. Witnesses living in Rwanda could only attend hearings in Arusha by being flown in from Kigali, with flight permissions granted by the Rwandan government. The access to crime scenes and witnesses, and the need for witnesses to provide evidence during trials, became a tool that the Rwandan government appeared to use to negotiate the direction of the OTP's prosecutorial strategy, and even impacted a decision taken by the ICTR's Appeals Chamber.[612]

The challenges related to the Tribunal's location in Arusha were also apparent through cultural and linguistic misunderstandings in the courtroom, which emphasised a contextual distance between the ICTR and Rwanda. With the rebuilding of Rwanda's broken infrastructure and an increase in qualified lawyers, some interviewees could not understand why ICTR trials continued to be held in Arusha, rather than in Rwanda itself. The arrival of the gacaca courts in 2002 only strengthened this argument, and highlighted the high costs and the duration of trials taking place at the ICTR in Arusha: *"The gacaca was very good as everyone was involved. [...] Everyone contributed. It was direct justice. The ICTR was so remote. There was so much procedure".*[613] Additionally, one stakeholder group – the Twa community – remained excluded from the Tribunal's legitimisation activities, which has had a lasting effect on the community.

The legitimacy challenges and legitimisation activities presented in this chapter demonstrate the fluidity of the notion of legitimacy, which comes in all shapes and forms, is interpreted in various ways, and is difficult to capture in theoretical models or frameworks. The framework presented in Chapter 2 presents a linear response to managing legitimacy, explaining the management of legitimacy from the perspective of an organisation responding to its environment. However, in reacting to one legitimacy challenge several other challenges may transpire; or legitimisation activities that appease some stakeholders may raise concern in others. Likewise, the challenges themselves may arise from the external environment or internally, and at different, specific moments, or over several years – even spanning the duration of the Tribunal's 20-year existence.

---

612 ICTR, *Prosecutor v. Jean-Bosco Barayagwiza*, Decision, ICTR-97-19-AR72, 31 March 2000.
613 Interviewee CS13.

This chapter does not address all the legitimisation activities implemented by the Tribunal, nor does it describe all the legitimacy challenges faced by the ICTR from its conception in 1994 to its closure in 2015. However, the 8 sections presented in this chapter provide an overview of the variety of challenges faced by the ICTR that were found in the literature and raised by the interviewees over the course of this research. Time also plays a role in the perceptions of interviewees looking back, providing examples of legitimacy challenges and making assessments regarding the legitimacy of the ICTR; the needs and expectations of the Tribunal also changed over the years.[614] Yet, the legitimacy challenges presented in this chapter also derive from accounts found in literature and news articles dating back to 1994, and with documents found during the archival research.

Aside from addressing specific legitimacy challenges, the following chapter takes a step back from examining specific legitimacy challenges faced by the Tribunal in order to examine how the ICTR maintained its legitimacy over the years. In doing so, the chapter examines how the Tribunal managed its legitimacy in relation to its mandate, making use of its legitimacy to garner support from its stakeholders and to ensure continued support in achieving the ICTR's key objectives, namely prosecuting those responsible for committing international crimes in Rwanda and fostering peace and reconciliation in Rwanda and the Great Lakes region.

614 Section 3.2.2.4.

6 DISCONNECTED LEGITIMISATION

The concept of organisational legitimacy is influenced by a multitude of internal and external factors which justify an organisation's position in society and assist it in attracting resources and support from a variety of stakeholders.[1] The previous chapter described legitimacy challenges faced by the ICTR, and examined how the actions taken by the Tribunal can be made sense of in terms of legitimisation. Yet, aside from managing legitimacy challenges, legitimisation activities were also implemented to maintain legitimacy in order to garner support for the Tribunal's ongoing work in Arusha.

The aim of this chapter is, therefore, to examine whether – and how – the Tribunal maintained its legitimacy in relation to its mandate, making use of its existing legitimacy to ensure access to the resources needed to achieve its key objectives. In doing so, this chapter revisits the first sub-question for this research – *Why was legitimacy important for the ICTR?* – by identifying the Tribunal's short- and long-term objectives in relation to the legitimisation activities implemented to maintain the Tribunal's legitimacy over its 20-year lifespan. Furthermore, the chapter seeks to identify whether the legitimisation activities used to maintain its pragmatic, moral and cognitive legitimacy – by *"perceiving a future crisis"* or *"protecting past accomplishments"*[2] – created unforeseen legitimacy challenges.

The chapter has been divided into three sections. The first section identifies the ICTR's key objectives through documents and speeches given by representatives of the UN and the ICTR. These objectives are categorised as being either short-term in nature, which consist of measurable annual targets found, for example, in the Tribunal's annual reports; or long-term objectives, which are more difficult to measure and refer to the ICTR's broader societal goals. Given the *ad hoc* nature of the Tribunal and its limited lifespan, the long-term objectives were more difficult to quantify and measure during the Tribunal's 20-year existence. However, there appears to have been a clear drive, by both the UN and the ICTR, to achieve these long-term goals. This may be due, in part, to the role that the Tribunal's long-term objectives had in promoting the ICTR's moral and cognitive legitimacy, by emphasising the relevance of its work in restoring peace in Rwanda and the Great Lakes region.

It is through this lens that the second section of this chapter examines the relationship between the legitimisation activities implemented by the ICTR, and the Tribunal's short-

1 Alex Bitektine, *Toward a Theory of Social Judgments of Organizations: The Case of Legitimacy, Reputation, and Status*, Academy of Management Review, 2011, 36(1), pp. 151-179.

2 Suchman, 1995, pp. 594-597.

and long-term objectives. As noted in Chapter 5, the Tribunal was dependent on specific stakeholders: primarily the Rwandan government, for access to crime scenes and witnesses, and the UN, for operational support and funding. There was therefore a certain pressure to ensure that the ICTR's short-term objectives were met (to ensure *pragmatic* legitimacy), while also promoting its long-term objectives (*moral* and *cognitive* legitimacy), which also aligned with the mission and societal values of the UN (the Tribunal's founder).

The working dynamics between the ICTR and these two key stakeholders are further explored in third section of this chapter, which examines the effect that the Tribunal's completion strategy had on its staff and their approach to achieving the Tribunal's short-term objectives. This section also describes the work that civil society organisations were undertaking in Rwanda while the ICTR was operating in Arusha, and highlights the benefits that collaboration may have brought to the Tribunal, not only in facilitating and disseminating the ICTR's work in Rwanda, but also in promoting its legitimacy. The chapter concludes with a discussion regarding the final destination of the ICTR's archive, a decision made before the closure of the Tribunal in 2015. It remains unclear why the archive is housed in Arusha, and whether the new, bespoke facility serves to maintain the legitimacy of the ICTR, or whether the decision was purely practical in nature. To explore these points further, the following section starts by identifying the objectives of the ICTR.

6.1 The Objectives of the ICTR

For the first time in its history, the UN Security Council established two international criminal tribunals in the early 1990s – the ICTY (1993) and the ICTR (1994) – through Chapter 7 of the UN Charter. In keeping with the UN's core mission, the two *ad hoc* tribunals were created to contribute to peace and reconciliation in two war-torn regions: the former Yugoslavia and Rwanda.[3] As such, the founding principles of the UN were fundamental to the establishment of both tribunals, especially with regard to the first principle under Article 1 of the UN Charter:

> "To maintain international peace and security, and to that end: to take effective collective measures for the prevention and removal of threats to the peace, and for the suppression of acts of aggression or other breaches of the peace, and to bring about by peaceful means, and in conformity with the principles of justice

3 William A. Schabas, *The UN International Criminal Tribunals: The Former Yugoslavia, Rwanda and Sierra Leone*, Cambridge University Press, 2006, p. 8.

> and international law, adjustment or settlement of international disputes or situations which might lead to a breach of the peace."[4]

In line with the UN Charter, the ICTR was established for retributive, deterrent and restorative purposes. During the sentencing of Jean Kambanda, the Trial Chamber states that: "*The penalties imposed on accused persons found guilty by the Tribunal must be directed, on the one hand, at the retribution of the said accused who must see their crimes punished and, [...] on the other hand, at deterrence*";[5] while the Tribunal's *Best Practices Manual for the Prosecution of Sexual Violence* states that: "*By holding perpetrators responsible and imposing substantial penalties against them for their criminal conduct, others who would perpetrate similar crimes are deterred from doing so and victims are provided with a sense of justice that facilitates lasting reconciliation.*"[6]

In accordance with the UN's mandate to "*maintain international peace and security*",[7] the adoption of UN Resolution 955 – which led to the creation of the ICTR – specifies an objective not only to restore peace in Rwanda, but also to contribute to national reconciliation: "*Convinced that in the particular circumstances of Rwanda, the prosecution of persons responsible for serious violations of international humanitarian law would enable this aim to be achieved and would contribute to the process of national reconciliation and to the restoration and maintenance of peace.*"[8]

In addition to the short-term objectives of prosecuting and punishing those who violate international laws, these two international criminal tribunals were therefore also expected to contribute to long-term objectives, including post-conflict reconciliation efforts, as stated by the ICTR registrar in 2004:

> "Having reviewed the challenges of international criminal justice, we have concluded that the ideal behind the establishment of each of our institutions is the same: to end impunity for the most serious crimes that plague humankind, and to contribute to peace and the prevention of future crimes."[9]

---

4 United Nations, *Charter of the United Nations*, 24 October 1945, Article 1.

5 ICTR, *Prosecutor v. Jean Kambanda*, Judgment and Sentence, ICTR-97-23-S, 4 September 1998, para. 28.

6 ICTR, *Best Practices Manual for the Investigation and Prosecution of Sexual Violence Crimes in Post-Conflict Regions: Lessons Learned from the Office of the Prosecutor for the International Criminal Tribunal for Rwanda*, 2014, p. 2. Retrieved from: https://unictr.irmct.org/sites/unictr.org/files/legal-library/140130_prosecution_of_sexual_violence.pdf.

7 United Nations, *Charter of the United Nations*, 24 October 1945, Article 1.

8 United Nations Security Council, *Resolution 955*, S/RES/955, 8 November 1994, preamble. The same statement can be found in the preamble of the ICTR Statute (United Nations Security Council, *Statute of the International Criminal Tribunal for Rwanda* (as amended on 31 December 2010), 8 November 1994).

9 Adama Dieng, *The Challenges of Administration of International Criminal Tribunals with Specific Reference to ICTR*, Prosecutor's Colloquium on the Challenges of International Criminal Justice, Arusha, Tanzania, 25 November 2004, p. 7.

The ICTR's *Best Practices Manual* further explains the link between the short-term objective of prosecution and the long-term objective of reconciliation:

> "While no sentence can erase the loss and pain inflicted by those who have been convicted, sentencing remains critically important to all victims, [...]. Sentencing delivers a sense of justice to survivors by providing official recognition from the international or national community that a grave violation of their rights was committed. This official recognition helps restore a sense of power and personal dignity to those who have been victimized. Further, a sentence that reflects the gravity of the crimes can promote reconciliation by enabling survivors to move forward with their lives."[10]

Indeed, the international community's recognition of the 1994 genocide in Rwanda, through the establishment of the ICTR and the subsequent judicial notice regarding the genocide as *"a fact as certain as any other"*,[11] was mentioned by several interviewees as a particularly important step in putting a stop to the cycle of ethnic violence in Rwanda and ending impunity for its military and political leaders,[12] while also playing a significant role in solidifying the ICTR's legitimacy.[13]

However, despite references to reconciliation and the restoration of peace,[14] the impression that emerges from the ICTR's annual reports is that, as a criminal tribunal, the ICTR had one main objective: to prosecute those most responsible for the 1994 genocide in Rwanda. In every annual report, from 1996 to 2015,[15] the number of individuals indicted, arrested, transferred to Arusha and prosecuted appears to be the main indicator through which the ICTR's activities and achievements were measured; whilst also solidifying the Tribunal's stance as a legitimate court of law.[16]

The lack of reporting on reconciliation efforts in Rwanda gives a sense that the promotion of peace and reconciliation in Rwanda may have been a secondary plan. Indeed, during negotiations regarding Resolution 955, a UN delegate from the Czech Republic,

10 ICTR, *Best Practices Manual for the Prosecution of Sexual Violence*, 2014, p. 69.

11 ICTR, *Prosecutor v. Édouard Karemera, Matthieu Ngirumpatse and Joseph Nzirorera*, Decision on Prosecutor's Interlocutory Appeal of Decision on Judicial Notice, ICTR-98-44-AR73(C), 16 June 2006, para. 35.

12 Section 4.2.1.

13 *ibid.*

14 The message was particularly important given that the ICTR was established by the UN Security Council with the aim of maintaining international peace and security (UN Resolution 955, 1994, preamble; Schabas, 2006, p. 8).

15 ICTR, Annual Reports, 1996 – 2015. Retrieved from: https://unictr.irmct.org/en/documents/annual-reports

16 See, for example, ICTR, *Financial statements for the biennium ended 31 December 2003*, A/59/5/Add.11, pp. 7-8. Retrieved from: https://undocs.org/en/A/59/5/ADD.11(SUPP).

Karel Kovanda, expressed doubts regarding a criminal tribunal's capacity to promote reconciliation:

> "Justice is one thing; reconciliation however is another. The Tribunal might become a vehicle of justice, but it is hardly designed as a vehicle of reconciliation. Justice treats criminals whether or not they see the error of their ways; but reconciliation is much more complicated, and it is certainly impossible until and unless the criminals repent and show remorse. Only then can they even beg their victims for forgiveness, and only then can reconciliation possibly be attained."[17]

Yet, a few years after the establishment of the ICTR, then UN Secretary-General Kofi Annan clearly reconfirmed and connected the Tribunal's work to the UN's primary mandate: *"This measure [establishing the ICTR] was also intended to contribute to the process of national reconciliation in Rwanda and to the maintenance of peace in the region"*.[18] During a conference in April 2000, an ICTR spokesperson, Kingsley Moghalu, informed UN member states of the Tribunal's three main objectives: accountability, deterrence and contribution to reconciliation in Rwanda, which he believed should serve to evaluate the Tribunal's work:

> "In order to properly assess the achievements and remaining challenges for the Tribunal, it is necessary to remind ourselves of exactly why the ICTR was established. The Tribunal's raison d'être is elegantly and evocatively articulated in Security Council Resolution 955 of 8 November 1994. [...] the main objectives of the ICTR appeared to be threefold - accountability for the genocide and related crimes, deterrence, and to contribute to national reconciliation on the maintenance of peace."[19]

---

17 United Nations Security Council, *The Situation Concerning Rwanda*, Provisional Report of the 3453rd Meeting, S/PV.3453, 8 November 1994, p. 7. Retrieved from: https://digitallibrary.un.org/record/167764/files/S_PV.3453-EN.pdf.

18 Translated from French: "*Cette mesure visait aussi à contribuer au processus de réconciliation nationale au Rwanda et au maintien de la paix dans la région.*" (Kofi Annan, Speech given by the UN Secretary-General, Kofi Annan, at the appointment of Judge Asoka de Zoysa Gunawardena to the ICTR, 23 April 1999).

19 Kingsley Chiedu Moghalu, *The International Criminal Tribunal for Rwanda and the development of an effective international criminal law - legal, political and policy dimensions*, International Conference on Replacing the Law of Force with the Force of Law - African Conflicts and the International Criminal Court, organised by the Committee for an Effective International Criminal Law in Konstanz, Germany, 5 April 2000, pp. 4-5.

Four years later, during the visit of the prime minister of Norway to Arusha, the ICTR registrar, Adama Dieng, reiterated these objectives and assigned them to the specific organs within the Tribunal:

> "The ICTR mandate encompasses two important components. The first component is being handled very effectively by the Prosecutor and the Judges who are establishing the fundamental role of the rule of law, under which persons found guilty, or held accountable for their offenses. The second component is being vigorously pursued by myself as Registrar by ensuring a wide dissemination of the work of the Tribunal through its Outreach Programme. This programme is aimed at promoting unity and national reconciliation in Rwanda as well as strengthening peace in the Great Lakes region of Africa."[20]

These quotes demonstrate that, along with the short-term objective of prosecuting those responsible for the crimes committed in Rwanda, the long-term objectives of reconciliation in Rwanda and peace in the Great Lakes region were also part of the ICTR's mandate. The short- and long-term nature of these objectives is emphasised by Moghalu:

> "Justice and accountability are important elements in resolving conflict because the punishment of the perpetrators of mass atrocities builds the foundation for genuine reconciliation. When justice is done – and seen as having been done – it provides a catharsis for those physically or psychologically scarred by war crimes. Deep-seated resentment are removed, and people on various sides of the divide can feel that a clean slate has been provided for co-existence. This is the foundation the ICTR hopes to help the Rwandan society to build. Healing in Rwanda, however, will undoubtedly be a long-term process."[21]

The link between these short-term (justice and accountability) and long-term objectives (reconciliation and peace) is also made clear in UN Security Council Resolution 1820: "*The consistent and rigorous prosecution of sexual violence in conflict is essential to the fight against impunity and securing long lasting peace, justice, truth and national reconciliation*".[22]

However, the ICTR's lifespan was limited, and in March 2004 the UN Security Council adopted Resolution 1534 requesting the ICTR to complete its investigations by the end of

20 Adama Dieng, *Address by the Registrar on the occasion of the visit of the Prime Minister of Norway to the International Criminal Tribunal for Rwanda*, Arusha, Tanzania, 11 October 2004, p. 2.

21 Moghalu, 5 April 2000, p. 12.

22 United Nations Security Council, *Resolution 1820*, S/RES/1820, 19 June 2008, para. 1.

2004; to finalise all trial activities in first instance by 2008; and to complete all activities within the Tribunal's mandate by 2010, in accordance with its completion strategy.[23] Achieving the ICTR's short-term objectives, let alone its long-term vision for peace and reconciliation, was a tall order within this short timeframe, especially given the apparent constraints on the Tribunal's budget and the annual process of requesting funds from the UN.[24]

The ICTR's wide-ranging mandate and long-term objectives were highlighted by Judge Pillay in the first years of the Tribunal's existence: "*We have a long way to go in establishing the rule of international law, to effectively safeguard the principles of peace and justice which are so fundamental and yet seem so elusive at times*".[25] However, since the UN had established the ICTR – together with the ICTY in The Hague – it was expected that both *ad hoc* tribunals could count on UN support, as Judge Pillay expressed in her address to the UN General Assembly later that same year:

> "Through the establishment of two ad hoc tribunals, the international community has given expression to a truly global desire for justice and respect for the rule of law and has made international criminal justice a reality that we hope will effectively deter future atrocities. [...] in establishing the ICTR, as well as the ICTY, the Security Council has created an historic initiative for peace and human rights. To realize the potential of this initiative we need your continued support."[26]

Indeed, both the ICTR and the ICTY received support from the UN. A financial budget was provided yearly, following the presentation of an annual report on the activities and achievements of the two tribunals.[27] These reports understandably focused on short-term, tangible objectives and results: detailing activities accomplished by each organ of the

23 United Nations Security Council, *Resolution 1534*, S/RES/1534, 26 March 2004, p. 1.

24 The allocation of resources was challenging given the unpredictable judicial calendar: fugitives could be arrested, initiating trial proceedings; the absence or illness of witnesses or the accused could delay a trial; as could the change in Defence Counsel, or even a part of a defence strategy (Sarah M. Kilema, *ICTR Legacy: Administrative Achievements and Challenges*, ICTR Legacy Symposium 6-7 November 2014, p. 4).

25 Navanethem Pillay, *The Future of the International Criminal Tribunals: Exploring the strengths and the weaknesses of the International Criminal Tribunals*, Speech given at The Hague Appeal for Peace Conference, The Hague, The Netherlands, 11 May 1999.

26 Navanethem Pillay, *Judge Pillay's address to UN General Assembly as President of ICTR*, 8 November 1999.

27 Starting in 2002 budgets were provided for two years (ACABQ, *Financing of the International Criminal Tribunal for the Prosecution of Persons Responsible for Genocide and Other Serious Violations of International Humanitarian Law Committed in the Territory of Rwanda and Rwandan Citizens Responsible for Genocide and Other Such Violations Committed in the Territory of Neighbouring States between 1 January and 31 December 1994 (ICTR)*, A/56/666, 29 November 2001, p. 2). Retrieved from: https://www.un.org/ga/search/view_doc.asp?symbol=A/56/666.

Tribunal, for example the number of ongoing trials and judgments rendered (Chambers); the arrest of fugitives and preparation of cases (OTP); and the number of visitors to the ICTR and updates on communications with the Rwandan government (Registry).[28]

As a newly created entity, the ICTR needed to demonstrate its added value to UN member states by showing what it could offer. As such, the ICTR's approach of focusing on its short-term objectives was logical – and in line with gaining and maintaining pragmatic legitimacy, which relates to the immediate needs and interests of the organisation's key stakeholders.[29] It was also clear that an *ad hoc* tribunal with a limited lifespan should focus on short-term objectives rather than working on, and attempting to validate, its long-term objectives.

6.2 The Legitimising Role of the ICTR Mandate

Despite the need to demonstrate clear, tangible, short-term outputs, the ICTR did not lose sight of the long-term objectives that inspired its creation. Promoting reconciliation in Rwanda and peace in the Great Lakes region relates to Suchman's description of moral legitimacy (demonstrating ethical conduct and doing *"the right thing"*) and cognitive legitimacy (producing meaningful results for society);[30] connecting the ICTR's long-term objectives with its moral standing and the very essence of its existence, while also aligning with the UN's societal values and norms.

The ICTR's long-term objectives therefore played a key role in validating its legitimacy, resulting in access to vital resources such as funding, personnel, the use of UN systems and processes, as well as the admission, through visas and permits, to witnesses and crime scenes in Rwanda. These objectives also relate to pragmatic legitimacy, addressing the immediate needs and interests of the Tribunal's key stakeholders – the UN member states, including the Rwandan government. In addition to the exchange of resources, legitimacy is also necessary to ensure effective communication between an organisation and its environment,[31] which was also key for the ICTR operating from Arusha; gaining and maintaining organisational legitimacy was therefore imperative from the outset.

The long-term objectives of the ICTR are echoed in speeches given by ICTR staff members, which underline the Tribunal's moral duty and emphasise the existential necessity of the organisation. All three types of legitimacy are illustrated in the ICTR registrar's

28 ICTR, Annual Reports, 1996-2015. Retrieved from: https://unictr.irmct.org/en/documents/annual-reports.

29 Mark C. Suchman, *Managing Legitimacy: Strategic and Institutional Approaches,* Academy of Management Review, 1995, 20(3), p. 578.

30 Suchman, 1995, pp. 579-582.

31 Ralph C. Hybels, On Legitimacy, Legitimation, and Organizations: A Critical Review and Integrative Theoretical Model, Academy of Management Proceedings, Briarcliff Manor, NY 10510: Academy of Management, 1995, p. 243.

presentation to the Rwandan Parliament in 2003, in which the Tribunal's important progress in achieving these long-term goals is highlighted:

> "The work of the Tribunal has contributed directly to the search for peace in the Central African region in recent months through the arrest and transfer to the Tribunal of a number of key suspects and indictees who have played important roles in the conflicts in the region. [...] Further, the work of the ICTR has impacted directly on the social and political evolution of the African continent. By spearheading a shift from a culture of impunity to a culture of accountability, the ICTR has made it possible to now visualize a day when African political and military leaders will no longer contemplate with impunity, of depriving groups of their citizens of the right to life, of freedom from physical harm, sexual abuse and political or religious persecution. The success of the ICTR in bringing erstwhile ruthless leaders to judicial accountability has impacted on the acceptability of international criminal law with the prospect of bringing peace closer to the region."[32]

Indeed, the registrar links the arrests and transfers of suspects – responding to its stakeholders' immediate needs and expectations (pragmatic legitimacy)[33] – with a shift in values and culture, from impunity to accountability, thereby emphasising the moral character of the ICTR (in doing *"the right thing"*)[34] as well as the essential nature of its existence (cognitive legitimacy) – without the Tribunal "*ruthless leaders*" would still be free.[35]

In 2000, the ICTR spokesperson refers specifically to the Tribunal's moral and cognitive legitimacy (aligned with the UN's own mission) during his speech to representatives of UN member states: *"[There is a] need to foster the Security Council's objective of national reconciliation in Rwanda and the moral and practical necessity of making the work of the Tribunal relevant to the principal group it is meant to address, the victims and survivors of the genocide"*.[36] The ICTR registrar reiterates this message to a Senegalese delegation during a roundtable discussion organised in Arusha: "*In our daily work we are confronted with the question of our rooting in Rwanda to influence the process of national reconciliation,*

32 Adama Dieng, *Statement to the Rwandan Parliament on the progress of the International Criminal Tribunal for Rwanda (the ICTR)*, Kigali, Rwanda, Thursday 6 March 2003, p. 2.
33 Suchman, 1995, p. 587.
34 *idem.*, p. 579.
35 *idem.*, p. 582.
36 Moghalu, 5 April 2000, p. 8.

another important part of the mandate of the Tribunal".[37] The ethical nature of the ICTR's operations, and its role in facilitating reconciliation in Rwanda, is emphasised by both the ICTR registrar and spokesperson to ensure that it maintains its moral and cognitive legitimacy.[38]

However, given the short timeframe allotted to the ICTR, with its periodic allocation of funds, there was a clear gap in the Tribunal's capacity and its potential to meet these high expectations: "*With such a heavy caseload, the ICTR needs therefore additional resources that would enable it to discharge its mandate effectively and conclude it work in the next few years.*"[39] Outreach efforts were recognised as a way to link the long- and short-term objectives of the ICTR, as well as providing a means to promote its legitimacy:

> "For Tribunals like ours that have a limited duration and no permanent staff, it may not always be possible for Tribunal staff to conduct face-to-face meetings. Protocols, therefore, should be established for the regular distribution of written summaries of trial and appeal judgements in a language or languages that will be easily understood by the community where the crimes occurred. These summaries should be broadly distributed to national authorities, NGOs, victim groups, local media outlets, and posted on public websites and other social media. Outreach efforts like these help promote community awareness and understanding of prosecutions, and may ultimately contribute to the process of reconciliation."[40]

The outreach programme, including press briefings, newsletters and information sessions, was of particular importance given that the Tribunal was located in Arusha and – in line with the ICTR's pragmatic legitimisation activities (*performance*)[41] – was implemented to demonstrate the Tribunal's activities.[42] The press briefings provided ICTR staff members with an opportunity to send a direct message to external stakeholders and were considered

37 Translated from French: "*Dans notre labeur quotidien nous sommes confrontés à la question de notre enracinement au Rwanda pour influer sur le processus de la réconciliation nationale, un autre volet important du mandate du Tribunal.*" (Adama Dieng, Presentation given during a roundtable meeting with COSEWA (Construire le Sénégal avec le Président Wadz) in Arusha, Tanzania, 7 April 2004).

38 Suchman, 1995, pp. 579-582.

39 Roland Kouassi G. Amoussouga, *The Challenges and Achievements of the International Criminal Tribunal for Rwanda*, Annual Conference of the Law Society of Kenya, Whitesands Hotel, Mombasa-Kenya, 30 August 2003, p. 15.

40 ICTR, *Best Practices Manual for the Prosecution of Sexual Violence*, 30 January 2014, pp. 75-76.

41 Ashforth & Gibbs, 1990, p. 178; Suchman, 1995, p. 578.

42 Victor Peskin, *Courting Rwanda: The Promises and Pitfalls of the ICTR Outreach Programme*, Journal of International Criminal Justice, 2005a, 3(4), pp. 954-955.

the main mouthpiece of the Tribunal, with press releases uploaded to the ICTR website and distributed to news agencies around the globe.[43]

> "The Registry is a neutral organ and is not prepared to abdicate this essential aspect of its role. While carrying out its fundamental function of disseminating information relevant to the Tribunal's business to the outside world, it will always observe the required neutrality between the different theses put forward by the parties before the judges. Settled points of facts and law may in the process be referred to. The Registry may also expose in an even manner the different points of view expressed by the parties on a contentious issue - even one yet to be decided - in so far as the issue is not of a confidential nature. By so doing, the Registry does not express its own view."[44]

Indeed, as explained by one journalist based in Arusha at the time: "*[Name] was a real politician. He answered all questions without really answering them. His main aim was to protect his institution*";[45] this was echoed by a former ICTR staff member: "*[Name] emphasised our role to sell the work of the Tribunal.*"[46] The press briefings therefore provided another means of promoting the Tribunal's pragmatic (*performance*), moral (*values*) and cognitive (*meaning*) legitimacy by presenting a professional image of the Tribunal and giving regular updates regarding its activities.[47]

Aside from the press briefings, both scholars and policy-makers, and indeed those working within international criminal tribunals and courts, agree that for international criminal justice to contribute to national reconciliation processes it is important for the population affected to be provided with a comprehensive understanding of the court or tribunal's work:[48] "*The Outreach Programme is central to accomplishing the Tribunal's mandate of establishing the rule of law, promoting national reconciliation in Rwanda, and restoring peace in the Great Lakes Region of Africa.*"[49] In the case of the ICTR, introducing an outreach programme to inform and educate its stakeholders of the activities and

43 Interviewees T9, T10 & T15.

44 ICTR Press Release, *Press Statement*, 30 November 2006. Retrieved from: https://unictr.irmct.org/en/news/press-statement.

45 Translated from French: "*[Nom], il était un vrai politicien. Il a répondu à toutes les questions sans vraiment y répondre. Son objectif principal était de protéger son institution.*" (M3).

46 Translated from French: "*[Nom] a souligné notre rôle de vendre le travail du Tribunal.*" (T9)

47 Ashforth & Gibbs, 1990, p. 180; David Deephouse, Jonathan Bundy, Leigh Plunkett Tost and Mark Suchman, *Organizational Legitimacy: Six Key Questions*, The SAGE Handbook of Organizational Institutionalism, 2017, p. 28.

48 Section 1.3.

49 Adama Dieng, *The Registrar's presentation on the UNICTR's Public Information & Outreach Programme*, Meeting of the Registrars of the International Criminal Tribunals, Arusha, Tanzania, 8 February 2005, p. 4.

workings of the Tribunal based in Arusha was essential. The initial idea for such a programme was introduced in 1998:

> "A fundamental barometer of the success or otherwise of the ICTR is the impact of the Tribunal's work in Rwanda. To that end the ICTR commenced an outreach program to Rwanda in 1998 with the purpose of increasing awareness and appreciation in the country of the Tribunal's work and achievements. This will undoubtedly increase support for the ICTR and Rwanda. So far, the main component of the program has been twofold. The first aspect was the arrangement whereby the ICTR provided office space and other logistical support for the establishment of permanent Bureau of Radio Rwanda at Arusha. [...] A second aspect of the program has been that of visits to the Tribunal by members of the Rwandan national assembly, senior judicial officials and other members of the nascent legal profession, several members of which were victims of the genocide."[50]

Given the popularity of radio at the time, daily broadcasts of the trials taking place in Arusha were also considered, but these plans never materialised. Instead, the ICTR arranged to broadcast the final judgment of each case on Rwandan airwaves via a satellite link.[51] Yet, with little understanding of the process taking place in Arusha, those listening in would only tune it to hear the words 'guilty' or 'not guilty'.[52]

A key resource in reaching thousands of people living in Rwanda was therefore neglected, and the opportunity to form a connection between the trials taking place in Arusha and the reconciliation of a nation appears to have been overlooked. Survivors did not hear the testimony of those that had planned and instigated the genocide, or the evidence of those that had responded to their call for action; they did not listen to the process of justice taking place in Arusha. In this instance, the opportunity to promote the Tribunal's legitimacy to a wider group of stakeholders was lost.

6.2.1 Funding Challenges (and Opportunities)

The reason given for the failure to broadcast the trials taking place in Arusha was the allocation of funds: "*We used radio to broadcast certain parts of the trials live, but it was*

50 Moghalu, 5 April 2000, p. 16.
51 Interviewees T3, T4 & T25.
52 Interviewees CS1, CS18, CS21, J3, T25.

not enough. The UN could have done more with the resources they had."[53] The frustration was also apparent during an interview with Roland Amoussouga in 2008, the former chief of the ERSPS:

> "[…] to the third registrar when he took over in March 2001. I said, "Sir, there is a need for you to request New York to give you access to the bandwidth utilized by the broadcasting station of radio UNAMIR in Rwanda. So that the equipment that they use there we can use it and have to throw directly all what we have to Rwanda, to DRC, to Burundi, to Uganda, to Kenya as the Security Council Resolution said that our judicial output could contribute to this." Because I was in Rwanda and I know how effective was the UN radio. And it was powerful because I was very often on the radio training people, having debates with the people."[54]

Aside from the radio project, the ICTR also had trouble finding funds for the rest of its outreach work. Despite providing the linchpin between the short-term (prosecution) and long-term (reconciliation) objectives of the Tribunal, the outreach programme was not funded through the ICTR's regular budget but rather through voluntary donations from UN member states to the ICTR's Voluntary Trust Fund:[55]

> "The Trust Fund is utilized to fund work programmes of the Tribunal deemed essential for the effective discharge of its mandate but which are not provided for in the organization's regular budget of assessed contributions from Member States. […] The programme is designed to enable the work of the Tribunal to impact on Rwandan society and facilitate reconciliation by making our efforts known both to the public and reaching out to the grass roots population."[56]

The Tribunal's outreach work was kept separate from the functions of the Tribunal's external relations – focusing on state cooperation, including host country matters – which came under the responsibility of the Registry for which UN funds were allocated.[57] In 2000, the ICTR established an information centre in Kigali with financial support from the Trust

---

53 Translated from French: "*Nous avons utilisé la radio pour diffuser certaines parties des procès en direct, mais ce n'était pas suffisant. L'ONU aurait pu faire plus avec les ressources dont elle disposait.*" (T9).

54 Roland Kouassi G. Amoussouga, Interview conducted by Tribunal Voices (video 89), 29-30 October 2008. Retrieved from: http://www.tribunalvoices.org/voices/video/89.

55 ICTR, 5th *Annual Report*, A/55/435–S/2000/927, 2 October 2000, para. 106-107. Retrieved from: https://unictr.irmct.org/sites/unictr.org/files/legal-library/001002-annual-report-en.pdf.

56 Dieng, 6 March 2003, p. 8.

57 ICTR, *Financial Reports*, 1997-2016. Retrieved from: https://documents.un.org/prod/ods.nsf/home.xsp

Fund:[58] "*Arusha supported the work being done in Rwanda, but our outreach work was not funded from the regular budget of the ICTR. We were funded by the Trust Fund. It was not part of the ICTR budget*".[59] In the following years, ten additional regional centres were launched through funding from the European Union.[60] However fundraising for the Trust Fund was a continuous concern for ICTR staff:

> "The Outreach Programme is financed through the Tribunal's Voluntary Contribution Trust Fund. The Fund is now being depleted. Despite good efforts and will, there is a danger that the current level of available resources under the Trust Fund, by the end of 2004, will not permit the Tribunal to continue implementing flagship projects, and other envisaged activities and programs that significantly support or supplement the substantive work programmes and activities of the Tribunal. It is therefore extremely important for the ICTR to seek renewed support and fresh contributions from member states to replenish the ICTR Trust Fund, without which, the ICTR cannot reach out to the grassroots population in Rwanda and target audiences in Africa and throughout the world."[61]

Given the continuous need for funds, in addition to the annual budget received from the UN, the outreach programme served several functions according to this internal memorandum:

> "The mission of the ERSPS Public Information and Outreach Program is:
> - Increasing public awareness of the work of the Tribunal in Rwanda, in the Great Lakes region of Africa and throughout the world;
> - To increase knowledge of the work and relevance of ICTR among Rwandans and engage key target groups to take action on the issues such as human rights;

58 ICTR, *6th Annual Report*, A/56/351–S/2001/863, 14 September 2001, para. 145. Retrieved from: https://unictr.irmct.org/sites/unictr.org/files/legal-library/010914-annual-report-en.pdf.

59 Translated from French: "*Arusha a appuyé le travail qui se faisait au Rwanda, mais notre travail de sensibilisation n'était pas financé par le budget ordinaire du TPIR. Nous avons été financés par le fonds de contributions volontaires, le 'Trust Fund'. Cela ne faisait pas partie du budget du TPIR.*" (T9).

60 ICTR, *14th Annual Report*, A/64/206–S/2009/396, 31 July 2009, para. 62; ICTR, *15th Annual Report*, A/65/188–S/2010/408, 30 July 2010, para. 61; ICTR Press Release, *ICTR Opens Two More Information Centres in Rwanda*, 23 February 2009. Retrieved from: https://unictr.irmct.org/en/news/ictr-opens-two-more-information-centres-rwanda. Funding was received from the European Instrument for Democracy and Human Rights (EIDHR) through the country-based support scheme.

61 Dieng, 11 October 2004, p. 2.

- To strengthen the capacity of Rwandan judicial officials as part of the contribution to the rule of law in general and to implement the ICTR completion strategy;
- Building a positive image of the Tribunal;
- Mobilizing financial resources through advocacy and fundraising campaigns."[62]

In addition to the outreach work, the ERSPS was also tasked with promoting the Tribunal's legitimacy in order to raise funds. As explained by a former ICTR staff member: "*The outreach programme was part of the External Relations Strategic Planning Unit. [Name] was my direct boss. He knew the importance of external relations and emphasized our role to sell the work of the Tribunal*".[63] The ERSPS's fundraising role is also demonstrated in a speech given by head of the Section at a conference in Mombasa, during which African states were asked to assist in the ICTR's outreach work, especially through funding:

> "It is important that member states of the African Union extend significant political and material support to the International Criminal Tribunal for Rwanda, [...] in particular through the following specific actions:
> - Financial and other material contributions to the Voluntary Contributions Trust Fund of the ICTR;
> - Public statements on the work of the Tribunal, it's contributions to Africa's development in particular and respect for human rights and the rule of law at the global level;
> - Active promotion of the Tribunal through publicity of its work in the media of African states; [...]
> - Encouraging active involvement of African legal scholars, students, researchers and legal practitioners in the work of the Tribunal so as to ensure a wider dissemination of the work of the tribunal in the African academic institutions and other relevant institutions to enable a positive development of African doctrine on international humanitarian and human rights laws;
> - Sustained and coordinated pressure on the international community for the establishment of an International Trust Fund for preparation, compensation, social and medical rehabilitation of victims and survivors of the genocide, crimes against humanity and war crimes committed in

62 Dieng, 8 February 2005, p. 1.

63 Translated from French: *"Le programme de sensibilisation faisait partie du ERSPS. [nom] était mon chef. Il savait l'importance des relations extérieures et a souligné notre rôle de vendre le travail du Tribunal."* (T9).

> Rwanda in 1994. This fund would be independent of the ICTR, as the mandate of the Tribunal does not provide for such restitutive justice by the ICTR, and could be administered by an international special victims rehabilitation and compensation commission."[64]

Although the Trust Fund existed at the time of this speech, the donations were voluntary and irregular; and states that had donated were often asked to donate again: *"In this regard, the Tribunal wishes in the very near future to count on the support of Sweden to strengthen the impact of its program of dissemination and promotion of its action on the ongoing national reconciliation process in Rwanda"*.[65] Here too, the ICTR's long-term objectives of fostering reconciliation efforts in Rwanda, related to both *moral* and *cognitive* legitimacy, are brought to the fore in order to raise funds. A similar message was transmitted to the Rwandan government during a meeting with the ICTR's registrar in 2003: *"I solicit the support of the members of parliament as natural partners in our common objective of bringing peace and reconciliation to the Rwandan people through justice"*.[66]

Raising funds was a key priority for the Registry, and in order to do so the greater goal of the Tribunal was brought to the fore, promoting the ICTR's moral and cognitive legitimacy.[67] An internal memorandum, circulated in preparation for the visit of a delegation from the European Commission, demonstrates these actions:

> "- Words of appreciation for the European Union's continued assistance to the ICTR's work which has contributed to ongoing achievements of the Tribunal.
> - Importance of the visit which comes at a very crucial time when the Tribunal is preparing for the last phase of its completion strategy.
> - It is important that everyone is aware of what specific contribution the EU is committed to make to the Tribunal.
> - As this is an umbrella project the EU funding will strengthen the managerial and operational capacity of the ICTR.

---

64 Amoussouga, 30 August 2003, p. 19.

65 Translated from French: "*A cet égard, le Tribunal souhaite dans un très proche avenir compter sur l'appui de la Suède pour renforcer l'impact de son programme de dissémination et de promotion de son action sur le processus de réconciliation nationale en cours au Rwanda.*" (Adama Dieng, Speech given when Sweden signed the agreement on the enforcement of ICTR sentences, Arusha, Tanzania, 27 April 2004).

66 Dieng, 6 March 2003, p. 5.

67 Suchman, 1995, p. 579-583.

- The three clusters which are part of the umbrella project will first and foremost address the protection and assistance of witness and victims, which in many ways is the backbone of ending the culture of impunity."[68]

In this case, the talking points had a positive result: "*The European Commission to Fund Tribunal Projects*".[69] The positive outcome of the visit was celebrated by Tribunal staff, who confirmed that the funding would be put to good use by increasing the speed of operations in Arusha: "*We strongly believe that the EU funding will secure the foundation of international law to combat impunity and human rights abuses that has been laid out by the Tribunal while increasing the qualitative and quantitative value of its operations and speeding up the pace of its work*".[70]

The fundraising efforts taken by the Registry correspond to the substantive legitimisation activity "*altering resource dependencies*"[71] (linked to repairing legitimacy), which provides an organisation with a certain degree of freedom by tapping into different resources and networks, rather than being dependent on a particular stakeholder. In this case, the UN operated as one entity in funding the ICTR through its annual budget. By targeting individual UN member states and different international bodies (such as the European Commission and INTERPOL), the Tribunal was widening its pool of resources. However, in this case, the need for funding to continue the work of the Tribunal was of paramount importance.

In order to raise these funds the ICTR's long-term objectives were promoted, emphasising the Tribunal's cognitive legitimacy – through its capacity of fostering peace and reconciliation through its work – and its moral legitimacy – by emphasising the Tribunal's role in addressing "*impunity and human rights abuses*". The funds received were then used to "*strengthen the managerial and operational capacity of the ICTR*",[72] which relates to the pragmatic nature of legitimacy: the organisation was doing its job.[73]

In publicising the donation of funds to the ICTR also serves as a means to maintain legitimacy: demonstrating the confidence that key stakeholders had in the Tribunal's work and promoting "*the legitimacy they have already acquired*".[74] The Tribunal's stakeholders – principally UN member states and the Rwandan government – were kept

68 Adama Dieng, *A few talking points for the Registrar's briefing*, Monday 10 May 2004, 17:00hrs, Arusha, Tanzania, 10 May 2004, p. 1.

69 ICTR Press Release, *The European Commission to Fund Tribunal Projects*, 10 May 2004. Retrieved from: https://unictr.irmct.org/en/news/european-commission-fund-tribunal-projects.

70 Dieng, 10 May 2004, p. 2.

71 Ashford & Gibbs, 1990, p. 178.

72 Dieng, 10 May 2004, p. 1.

73 Suchman, 1995, p. 578.

74 *idem.*, p. 595.

abreast of activities taking place in Arusha through conferences, speeches, newsletters and the website.

6.3 Key Stakeholders

Despite the outputs provided through the Tribunal's operational activities (conducting investigations and delivering verdicts), thereby strengthening its pragmatic legitimacy, the Tribunal continued to broadcast the Tribunal's far-reaching, long-term goals – maintaining its moral and cognitive legitimacy. This is demonstrated in a speech to INTERPOL, an institution made up of 194 member states and a key partner in tracking and arresting the ICTR's remaining fugitives:

> "Your presence here is a value added to the significance of the global fight against impunity that the ICTR is spearheading in the area of adjudication of cases involving genocide, crimes against humanity and war crimes." [...] As you know, the UNICTR[75] has been entrusted with a common quest for the eradication of impunity and the triumph of the rule of law and respect for law and order throughout the world. [...] it will leave a legacy of international jurisprudence that can guide future courts, deter potential perpetrators, and prevent impunity for these grave crimes."[76]

Yet, the director of a civil society organisation in Rwanda explained that the outreach programmes focused on a specific target population: *"The outreach, the communication was not designed for the general public. Even the information centre based here in Kigali was only accessible to academics, students, and lawyers"*.[77] The audience identified by the ICTR for its outreach work is reflected in an internal memo regarding the newsletter produced by the Tribunal, which was *"targeted at a relatively specialized audience including lawyers, academics, diplomats, NGOs and specialised journalists"*.[78] The ICTR newsletter

---

75 In this speech and in many others given by Adama Dieng (ICTR registrar from 2001 to 2012), the ICTR is referred to as the UN-ICTR and Dieng himself holds the title of United Nations Assistant Secretary-General. Although the ICTR was an independent organ from the UN, Dieng often highlighted their affiliation, which indicates a shared mission and promotes the Tribunal's cognitive legitimacy (Suchman, 1995, p. 592). Aside from emphasising the ICTR's greater, long-term goal – *"the global fight against impunity that the ICTR is spearheading"* – Dieng is also painting the ICTR with the same brush as the legitimately perceived and recognised UN.

76 Adama Dieng, *Welcoming address and opening remarks*, INTERPOL Second International Training Course for Investigators of Genocide, War Crimes and Crimes Against Humanity held in room S355, Arusha, Tanzania, 20 October 2010, p. 2.

77 Interviewee CS14.

78 Tom Kennedy, *ICTR Newsletter*, Interoffice Memorandum, ICTR/INFO-9-1-128, 16 July 2001, para. 2.

was relaunched in 2001 given that previous editions – circulated between June 1997 and February 1999, provided in French, English and Kinyarwanda – had been discontinued due to translation and printing issues. It was decided that the new newsletter (the *ICTR Bulletin*)[79] would be published in the two UN languages (English and French) and not in Kinyarwanda, in order to avoid any delays due to the translation of articles.[80]

The ICTR's push to reach academics and lawyers coincided with the establishment of the ICC. The ICTY and ICTR had played a pivotal role in reviving international criminal law, and the success of these two *ad hoc* tribunals was of paramount importance for those lobbying for the establishment of a permanent international criminal court. Thanks to the early successes of both tribunals, the Rome Statute was adopted by 120 states in 1998, which paved the way for the creation of the ICC in 2002.[81] This may explain why the ICTR's outreach work, focused on free access to 10 information centres in Rwanda, appears to have appealed mainly to those interested in international law:

> "All the judgments. Any information request from the ICTR here in Rwanda was met. I was able to get in touch with the court in Arusha easily. We had a library specialised in international humanitarian law, which students could access. We had 100 students per day on average. Other visitors included lawyers, and people interested in international law."[82]

The ICTR's outreach team in Rwanda also provided information sessions to secondary school children and prisoners: "*We looked at how to connect with people. People could use the internet to follow cases. Our target group consisted mainly of young people in secondary schools. They are the future of our country. [...] The ICTR also did outreach work in prisons.*"[83] Yet, an internal document regarding the ERSPS's key target group and activities did not appear to focus on the general population living in Rwanda:

79 The title *bulletin* was used as it worked well in both English and French (Tom Kennedy, *Note for file, Preparation of Tribunal Bulletin*, Meeting of the working group, Thursday 16 August 2001, para. 1).

80 *ibid.*

81 United Nations General Assembly, Fiftieth Session, 52nd plenary meeting, A/50/PV.52, 7 November 1995, New York, p. 7.

82 Translated from French: "*Tous les jugements. Toute demande d'information du TPIR ici au Rwanda a été satisfaite. J'ai pu facilement entrer en contact avec le tribunal d'Arusha. Nous avions une bibliothèque spécialisée en droit international humanitaire, à laquelle les étudiants pouvaient accéder. Nous avions en moyenne 100 étudiants par jour. Parmi les autres visiteurs figuraient des avocats et des personnes intéressées par le droit international.*" (T9).

83 Translated from French: "*Nous avons examiné comment établir des liens avec les gens. Les gens pourraient utiliser Internet pour suivre les cas. Notre groupe cible était principalement constitué de jeunes du secondaire. Ils sont l'avenir de notre pays. [...] Le TPIR a également effectué un travail de sensibilisation dans les prisons.*" (T9).

> "The External Relations and Strategic Planning Section regularly sends information to journalists throughout the world, and provides them with all facilities when they come to the seat of the Tribunal. Information is also provided to a variety of people enrolled in the Tribunal's mailing list which is constantly enriched. It also manages a website providing to the public information regarding the different facets of the Tribunal.
> Under the leadership of the Registrar, the External Relations and Strategic Planning Section contributes to the building of a positive image of the Tribunal, while harnessing political and financial support of the Tribunal. It assists in increasing awareness and interest in the Tribunal's work from all interested stakeholders and partners, as well as seeking the corporation of states, institutional and governmental and non-governmental organizations for the work of the Tribunal."[84]

The memorandum provides an insight into the internal understanding of the ERSPS's function, which is described as *"building of a positive image of the Tribunal, while harnessing political and financial support of the Tribunal"*.[85] This indicates that while the Registry continued to promote the ICTR's long-term objective of fostering reconciliation in Rwanda (emphasising its moral and cognitive legitimacy), the ERSPS's key objective was to harness *"political and financial support"* to ensure the trials could continue in Arusha – maintaining the ICTR's pragmatic legitimacy.

The lack of funding and distance from Rwanda left the ERSPS in a difficult position. As explained by one former ICTR staff member: *"Outreach work was a struggle to do. [...] it remained difficult to get support"*.[86] The Tribunal's messaging, its capacity (with limited resources, a limited timeframe and based in Arusha) and the outreach activities it was pursuing, appeared, therefore, to be disconnected.

The ICTR was focused on maintaining all three legitimacy types to ensure the continued support of its stakeholders. Yet, in conducting trials in Arusha and communicating its activities to a specific group of stakeholders, the only clear deliverable related to pragmatic legitimacy: trials were taking place in Arusha. The dissemination of these activities to a wider audience, in order to fulfil the retributive, deterrent and restorative objectives of the ICTR,[87] reflecting the moral and cognitive legitimacy of the Tribunal, was less evident.

84 Dieng, 25 November 2004, para. 24.

85 *ibid.*

86 Interviewee T5.

87 ICTR, *Prosecutor v. Jean Kambanda*, Judgment and Sentence, ICTR-97-23-S, 4 September 1998, para. 28; ICTR, *Best Practices Manual for the Prosecution of Sexual Violence*, 2014, p. 69.

Yet, the promise to assist Rwanda and the Great Lakes region in finding peace and fostering reconciliation not only came from the Registry, or specifically the ERSPS. In 1999, Judge Møse[88] provided the same message:

> "It is a court that is there to do justice. The goal of the ICTR is not only to combat impunity but also to work for reconciliation. This decision clearly signifies, as others have said before me, that one could be a Hutu during the genocide, hold a position of responsibility, and not be a genocidaire. This is not a decision against victims, but a decision that gives us hope in justice."[89]

This message from 1999 was shared by others working in Arusha: "*Reconciliation is not just reconciliation between Hutus and Tutsis, but reconciliation for individuals.*"[90] Yet, the rationale behind this thinking was not widely shared or explained beyond the UN member states, and academic and media circles on the ICTR's distribution list.[91]

Demonstrating to the UN member states (including the Rwandan government) and the academic community that the Tribunal was a legitimate organisation, pursuing the goals and activities that fit with the broad social understandings of what was "*desirable, proper, or appropriate*",[92] appeared to take priority, even for the Tribunal's outreach activities. However, in order for international courts and tribunals to achieve these greater goals, and be effective in assisting with reconciliation, their work needs to reach the populations living in a post-conflict state or region, who are the ultimate "*peace-builders*".[93]

During a UN workshop held in 2012, centred on reconciliation and the role of the international community, Henk-Jan Brinkman[94] expressed the need for the international community to be realistic about its potential to contribute to post-conflict reconciliation: "*If society is not ready for reconciliation, the international community cannot force the*

88 ICTR president from 2003 to 2007.

89 Erik Møse, *Internal memorandum*, 8 December 1999, in: Thierry Cruvellier, *Court of Remorse Inside the International Criminal Tribunal for Rwanda*, University of Wisconsin Press, 2010, pp. 129-130.

90 M.-L. Lambert, Interview conducted by Tribunal Voices (video 551), 23 October 2008. Retrieved from: http://www.tribunalvoices.org/voices/video/551.

91 Hand-written note found in the ICTR archive with a list the international news agencies [official agency name and country of origin added]: Knight Ridder Newspaper [USA]; AP [Associated Press, USA]; VOA [Voice of America, USA]; Picasso Productions [Broadcasting & media production company, USA]; Reuters [UK]; BBC [British Broadcasting Corporation, UK]; Kyodo [Japan]; Asahi Shimbun [Japan]; DPA [Deutsche Presse-Agentur, Germany]; ZDF [Zweites Deutsches Fernsehen, Germany]; IPS [Inter Press Service, Italy]; Ecumenical International News Agency [Switzerland]; Central African News Agency [South Africa].

92 Suchman, 1995, p. 574.

93 Franca Baroni, *The International Criminal Tribunal for the Former Yugoslavia and Its Mission to Restore Peace*, Pace International Law Review, 2000, 12, p. 243.

94 Chief of Peacebuilding Strategy and Partnerships at United Nations Peacebuilding Support Office.

process".[95] The efforts to bring about peace and reconciliation must come from within the country or region in question. This sentiment was echoed during an interview with a Rwandan judge: *"To rebuild society you can't just rely on the law; you also need to address the heart. This is needed to stop, to prevent the cycle of genocide. There is a need to go deeper into the fabric of society. [...] There is a need to understand the crimes, to understand what happened in 1994"*.[96] This does not mean that efforts made by external parties are redundant, but rather that there must be collaboration with local partners.[97]

An understanding of the Tribunal's work and collaboration with local partners was especially important in the case of the ICTR. International criminal law was a re-emerging field of law, unfamiliar to many, including those living in Rwanda, who had just experienced a four-year-long conflict:

> "Generally, the judicial system is not accessible. They believe that if the door is open, there is public access. That is their idea of outreach. There is no need for anything more. With mass crimes, this is a different story. The justice system has to do more. It needs to be accessible. It needs to be understood."[98]

The UN itself was aware of the capacity and potential of transitional justice mechanisms in contributing to peace and reconciliation within a post-conflict state, when working together with other institutions, including civil society organisations[99] and victims:

> "Justice, peace and democracy are not mutually exclusive objectives, but rather mutually reinforcing imperatives. Advancing all three in fragile post-conflict settings requires strategic planning, careful integration and sensible sequencing

---

95 UN, Building Just Societies: Reconciliation in Transitional Justice Settings. Workshop Report, Accra, Ghana, 5-6 June 2012, p. 23. Retrieved from: https://www.un.org/peacebuilding/sites/www.un.org.peacebuilding/files/documents/12-58492_feb13.pdf.

96 Interviewee J4.

97 Baroni, 2000, p. 243; UN report, 5-6 June 2012, p. 23; Barbara Oomen, *Justice Mechanisms and the Question of Legitimacy. The Example of Rwanda's Multi-layered Justice Mechanisms*, in: Kai Ambos, Judith Large, and Marieke Wierda (eds.),rest *Building a Future on Peace and Justice*, Springer Berlin Heidelberg 2009, p. 184.

98 Translated from French: *"En général, le système judiciaire n'est pas accessible. Ils croient que si la porte est ouverte, il y a un accès public. C'est leur idée de la sensibilisation. Ils n'ont plus besoin de plus. Avec les crimes de masse, c'est une autre histoire. Le système judiciaire doit faire plus. Ça doit être accessible. Ça doit être compris."* (CS18).

99 *Civil society organisations* should not be interpreted as only referring to non-governmental organisations (NGOs), as the term also includes community-based organisations, churches, business associations, traditional leaders, women's and youth associations, research centres, diasporas, etc. This wider understanding of the term allows for a better appreciation of the capacity that these organisations might bring to the work on reconciliation – particularly when they are embedded in social constituencies that are essential to inclusive reconciliation processes.

of activities. Approaches focusing only on one or another institution, or ignoring civil society or victims, will not be effective."[100]

Yet, the focus of the ERSPS appeared to be different, as demonstrated by the following quote from an interview given by the head of the Section in 2008, when discussing the Tribunal's outreach programmes:

> "We identify different target groups starting from the judges and the court system, the media, the coverage of any proceedings because we understand that one of the key issues there, is the communication of the information coming from the judicial sector to the public and also all the other periphery-core elements such as universities for the training, student, the civil society like human right groups et cetera, et cetera.
> So basically although the UN did not give us money to put in those programs, we managed to use the scarce resources that we have as well as some resources that were given to us by the European Commission. And we were able to set our training module for the people of Rwanda. One of the training modules targeted the legal information management, the legal reporting, the media case jurisprudence for legal reporting journalists."[101]

Providing training on legal reporting was aimed at enabling communication*"from the judicial sector to the public"*[102] and even though there was a dedicated press room within the ICTR in Arusha,[103] most Rwandans remained ill-informed of the Tribunal's work.[104] The outreach activities in Rwanda appeared to focus predominantly on those interested in international criminal law, and on the lawyers and judges working within the criminal justice system.[105]

On the one hand, the re-emergence of international criminal law and the momentum created by the ICTY and ICTR appears to have been encouraged through the conferences organised by the Tribunal and speeches given by ICTR staff members, promoting the

100 United Nations Security Council, *Rule of law and transitional justice in conflict and post-conflict societies.* Report of the Secretary-General, 23 August 2004, S/2004/616, Summary, para. 2. Retrieved from: https://www.securitycouncilreport.org/atf/cf/%7B65BFCF9B-6D27-4E9C-8CD3-CF6E4FF96FF9%7D/PCS%20S%202004%20616.pdf.

101 Amoussouga, 29-30 October 2008, video 89.

102 *ibid.*

103 Interviewee T9; Cruvellier, 2010, p. 175.

104 Jean-Marie Kamatali, *From the ICTR to ICC: Learning from the ICTR Experience in Bringing Justice to Rwandans,* New England Journal of International and Comparative Law, 2005, 12, p. 90; Peskin, 2005a, p. 954.

105 Tim Gallimore, *The ICTR Outreach Programme: Integrating Justice and Reconciliation,* Conference on Challenging Impunity, Kigali Novotel, Rwanda, 8 November 2006, p. 4; Interviewees CS14, CS18 & T9.

legitimacy of this new branch of international law. These activities also stimulated debate and interest in international criminal law and the new ICC, which would become a key player in other conflicts taking place on the African continent.[106]

On the other hand, the activities (such as legal training) organised by the ICTR were also aligned with the Rwandan government's objective to start prosecuting cases in Rwanda, and the Tribunal's own mandate to strengthen Rwanda's justice sector.[107] In line with pragmatic legitimacy,[108] the Tribunal worked together with Rwandan government officials to foster Rwanda's substantive and procedural laws, which would eventually allow the transfer of ICTR cases to the Rwandan courts: *"The 11 bis law was very important in referring cases. [...] Once this was approved with the ICTR national jurisdictions started sending the accused to Rwanda for trial"*.[109] The collaboration and training sessions resulted not only in national jurisdictions transferring cases to Rwanda, but also in the Tribunal referring a total of eight cases to Rwanda.[110] In fact, as explained by one interviewee: *"the Rwandan government was part of the completion strategy"*[111] as the substantial changes to Rwanda's legislation formed an important part of the ICTR's completion strategy.[112] As a result, Rule 11 *bis* left a lasting mark on the rule of law in Rwanda, while also cementing the Tribunal's position as a legitimate court in the eyes of legal practitioners and scholars observing the potential of international criminal law.[113]

Yet, in failing to reach out to more stakeholders, the full capacity and potential of the ICTR – established through Chapter 7 of the UN Charter, with its key objectives for

106 Human Rights Watch, *Rwanda: Justice After Genocide – 20 Years On*, 28 March 2008. Retrieved from: https://www.hrw.org/news/2014/03/28/rwanda-justice-after-genocide-20-years; Kamatali, 2005, p. 102; Victor Peskin, *International Justice in Rwanda and the Balkans: Virtual Trials and the Struggle for State Cooperation*, Cambridge University Press, 2008, pp. 254-256; Schabas, 2006, p. 7; United Nations General Assembly, Fiftieth Session, 52nd plenary meeting, A/50/PV.52, 7 November 1995, New York, p. 7.

107 United Nations Security Council, *Resolution 955*, S/RES/955, 8 November 1994, p. 2.

108 Suchman, 1995, pp. 578-579.

109 Interviewee G3.

110 United Nations Security Council, Letter dated 17 November 2015 from the President of the International Criminal Tribunal for Rwanda addressed to the President of the Security Council, S/2015/884, 17 November 2015, para. 19. Retrieved from: https://www.securitycouncilreport.org/atf/cf/%7B65BFCF9B-6D27-4E9C-8CD3-CF6E4FF96FF9%7D/s_2015_884.pdf.

111 Translated from French: "*le gouvernement rwandais faisait partie de la stratégie d'achèvement.*" (T23)

112 ICTR, *Completion Strategy Report*, S/2003/946, 6 October 2003, para. 23. Retrieved from: https://unictr.irmct.org/sites/unictr.org/files/legal-library/031006-completion-strategy-en.pdf.

113 Interviewee G3; Nicola Palmer, *Transfer or Transformation?: A Review of the Rule 11 bis Decisions of the International Criminal Tribunal for Rwanda*, African Journal of International and Comparative Law, 2012, 20(1), pp. 1-21; United Nations Security Council, *ICTR Rules of Procedure and Evidence* (as amended on 13 May 2015), 29 June 1995, rule 11*bis*. Retrieved from: https://unictr.irmct.org/sites/unictr.org/files/legal-library/150513-rpe-en-fr.pdf.

retribution, deterrence and reconciliation[114] – was not achieved, with the possibility of threatening its moral and cognitive legitimacy.

6.3.1 *Long- versus Short-Term Objectives*

Connecting an organisation's long- and short-term objectives has been demonstrated to help instil a positive organisational culture by infusing the underlying goals of the organisation in the daily tasks of all staff members.[115] The awareness of an organisation's long-term objectives not only motivates and inspires staff members, it also ensured that policies and strategies are implemented that aim to achieve both the long- and short-term objectives of an organisation, which provides the organisation with a clear direction and transparent decision making.[116] This transparency also promotes the organisation's legitimacy and enhances support from its stakeholders if (or when) it is faced with legitimacy challenges.[117]

From 2003 onwards, the completion strategy provided clear, short-term outputs for the Tribunal and its staff in order to prepare for the imminent closure of the *ad hoc* Tribunal.[118] As with the ICTR's annual reports, the completion strategy reports mention the Tribunal's long-term objectives,[119] however, the focus of these reports was to communicate the targets achieved (indictees arrested and prosecuted, number of trials completed, etc.) versus the work left to be done, and the need for additional resources to ensure the completion of all trials within the allocated time.[120]

The long-term objectives were not found in documents relating to the daily work of the ICTR, where the attention was focused on tracking and arresting fugitives, completing trials, and finding a place to send those acquitted or convicted by the Tribunal: "*The biggest challenge [for the Registry] was relying on state support. They can sign all sorts of agreements,*

114 ICTR, *Prosecutor v. Jean Kambanda*, Judgment and Sentence, ICTR-97-23-S, 4 September 1998, para. 28; ICTR, *Best Practices Manual for the Prosecution of Sexual Violence*, 2014, p. 69.

115 Michael Harber, *The role of institutional investors in promoting long-term value creation: A South African perspective,* African Review of Economics and Finance, 2017, 9(1), p. 284.

116 *ibid.*

117 Julia Black, *Constructing and contesting legitimacy and accountability in polycentric regulatory regimes,* Regulation & Governance, 2008, 2(2), pp. 141-142 & 154; Vivien A. Schmidt, *Democracy and Legitimacy in the European Union Revisited: Input, Output and 'Throughput',* Political Studies, 2013, 61(1), pp. 2-8.

118 United Nations, *ICTR Financial report and audited financial statements for the biennium ended 31 December 2003 and Report of the Board of Auditors*, General Assembly Official Records, Fifty-ninth Session, Supplement No. 5K, A/59/5/Add.11, pp. 12-14. Retrieved from: https://undocs.org/en/A/59/5/ADD.11(SUPP)

119 Aside from the first completion strategy report in which no mention of long-term objectives is made (ICTR, Completion Strategy Report, S/2003/946, 6 October 2003).

120 ICTR Completion Strategy Reports 2003-2015. Retrieved from: https://unictr.irmct.org/en/documents/completion-strategy-reports.

but these agreements needed to be implemented".[121] Indeed, the long-term objectives of the ICTR appeared far from the mind of one former Rwandan staff member, who explained that "*[working at the ICTR] put food on the table and has given my children a good education*".[122] A sentiment that was shared by two other Rwandan staff members.[123] Working towards peace and national reconciliation for their country was not mentioned as a motivation for applying for a job at the Tribunal.

Although the external communications of the ICTR continued to emphasise the long-term objectives of the Tribunal in fostering reconciliation and peace in Rwanda and the Great Lakes region, promoting the moral and cognitive legitimacy of the Tribunal, the staff in Arusha focused predominantly on achieving pragmatic legitimacy, by reaching the short-term objectives stated in the completion strategy.

Indeed, focusing on short-term objectives without making the connection with the Tribunal's long-term objectives appears to have prevented opportunities for collaboration with civil society organisations based in Rwanda. According to interviews with the representatives of some of these civil society organisations, there was no apparent room for an alliance with the Tribunal: "*We [the ICTR] don't have the mandate, that's the excuse, they did not even discuss it*".[124]

Yet, according to research, civil society organisations play an important role in influencing public opinion, particularly when it comes to establishing (or challenging) organisational legitimacy.[125] Collaboration with civil society organisations based in Rwanda would have facilitated the legitimisation of the Tribunal's work in Rwanda and the promotion of its broader goals,[126] while also enabling the Tribunal to perceive a future crisis by enhancing its "*ability to recognise stakeholder reactions and foresee emerging challenges.*"[127]

Unfortunately, aside from working with Rwandan specific government officials, the ICTR did not collaborate or communicate directly with any civil society organisations working in Rwanda.[128]

121 Interviewee T18.

122 Interviewee T12.

123 Interviewees T1 & T2.

124 Translated from French: "*Nous n'avons pas le mandat, c'est l'excuse, ils n'en ont même pas discuté.*"(CS20).

125 Alex Bitektine and Patrick Haack, *The "Macro" and the "Micro" of Legitimacy: Toward a Multilevel Theory of the Legitimacy Process,* Academy of Management Review, 2015, 40(1), pp. 49-75.

126 Kamatali, 2005, pp. 93-95.

127 Suchman, 1995, p. 595.

128 Interviewees A10, M2, J4, T1, T2, T5, CS3, CS6, CS7, CS8, CS10, CS11, CS13, CS15, CS16, CS17, CS18, CS19, CS20, CS22 & CS24.

6.3.2 *Civil Society in Rwanda*

At the end of the summer of 1994, while the UN Security Council was discussing the creation of the ICTR, civil society organisations were delivering emergency aid in Rwanda; they also provided communication channels between local communities and the new National Unity government – both of which were finding their feet following the end of the brutal conflict. Certain civil society organisations were asked to assist the new government in finding solutions to the wide variety of issues facing post-conflict Rwanda: "*Debates were held at local and national level. A big forum was held by the government after the genocide to discuss what should be done. [...] How to find a way to live together*".[129] A key objective for the new government was rebuilding the country; notably by rehabilitating genocide survivors and prosecuting those who had committed crimes of genocide.

With national trials starting to take place in Rwanda itself, and ongoing deliberations regarding the creation of an international criminal court, a delegation of representatives from four civil society organisations – Amnesty International, Médecins Sans Frontières, Causes Communes, and the Association of Democratic Lawyers – met in Kigali to discuss how each of their organisations could contribute to the rebuilding of Rwanda.[130] In addition to working with local civil society organisations, including victim and perpetrator support, and retaining their own individual operations in Rwanda, the four organisations decided to create a new entity called Réseau Citoyens-Citizens Network (RCN),[131] with a joint understanding that this independent, non-governmental organisation could act as a liaison between the courtrooms and the general population: explaining the legal proceedings taking place both in Rwanda[132] and at the upcoming international court, and helping to promote efforts taking place that would ensure justice for the survivors of the genocide: "*The first priority of our organisation after the genocide was to help the Ministry of Justice to rebuild the justice system*".[133]

In the early days of RCN, the small team consisted of both Rwandans and international staff; over time the team transformed to consist mainly of Rwandan staff.[134] There was little change in the operations of RCN when the ICTR finally opened its doors in 1995,

129 Interviewee CS12.

130 Interviewee CS18.

131 The organisation now operates under the name RCN Justice & Démocratie. For more information, see website: https://rcn-ong.be.

132 Avocats Sans Frontières (ASF) also played an important role in transcribing and translating all the genocide cases that were prosecuted before the national courts in Rwanda: https://www.asf.be/action/field-offices/archives/asf-in-rwanda/.

133 Translated from French: "*La première priorité de notre organisation, après le genocide, était d'aider le ministère de la Justice à reconstruire le système judiciaire.*" (CS18).

134 Interviewee CS18.

and started its work from Arusha. In fact, it appeared that *"[through the ICTR] the international community provided a parallel system"*.[135]

Indeed, all interviews with civil society organisations in Rwanda explained that there had been little to no contact with the ICTR: "*Our work was a collaboration between members of the EU: Belgium, The Netherlands, Switzerland and Sweden. There were no financial resources from the ICTR, only the occasional intellectual exchanges, for example through conferences*".[136] As a result, the work of civil society organisations based in Rwanda focused mainly on supporting survivors and perpetrators of the genocide, and assisting with information sessions related to the justice systems working in Rwanda:

> "We worked alongside the national courts and the gacaca in Rwanda. This was already enough work. The ICTR outreach work, it consisted of information centres, which were geared primarily for researchers, students and some legal practitioners. There was very little outreach to communities, to the people."[137]

Consequently, it appears that the international community was often better informed of the Tribunal's proceedings than people in Rwanda. While journalists and news agencies – such as the Associated Press, the BBC and Reuters – informed the world about the ICTR, "*the majority of the [Rwandan] population knew little of what was happening at Arusha*".[138] Aside from legal practitioners and academics, not many people understood what events were taking place at the Tribunal, what the charges were against those indicted and tried, and why some – publicly recognised as *génocidaires* – were acquitted or accorded an early release.[139]

Despite the information centres dotted across Rwanda and various outreach activities that took place in secondary schools and prisons,[140] there was a lack of information available in Rwanda and little understanding regarding the Tribunal's activities over the course of the Tribunal's 20-year lifespan.[141] Yet, during an interview conducted in 2002, the historian

135 Interviewee CS12.

136 Translated from French: "*Notre travail était une collaboration entre des membres de l'UE: la Belgique, les Pays-Bas, la Suisse et la Suède. Il n'y avait pas de ressources financières du TPIR, seulement des échanges intellectuels occasionnels, par exemple à travers des conférences.*" (CS19).

137 Translated from French: "*On a travaillé aux côtés des tribunaux nationaux et le gacaca au Rwanda. C'était déjà assez de travail. Le travail de sensibilisation du TPIR, c'était des centres d'information, destinés principalement aux chercheurs, aux étudiants et à certains juristes. Il y avait très peu de sensibilisation envers les communautés, les gens.*" (CS18).

138 Alison L. Des Forges, *Leave None to Tell the Story: Genocide in Rwanda*, Human Rights Watch, 1999, p. 742. Retrieved from: https://www.hrw.org/reports/1999/rwanda/.

139 Kamatali, 2005, p. 90; Peskin, 2005a, pp. 955-961.

140 Interviewees T3, T5, T6 & T9.

141 Kamatali, 2005, p. 90; Peskin, 2005a, pp. 955-961. This was also evident during both informal conversations and formal interviews that took place during field research in Rwanda.

and human rights activist, Alison Des Forges explains that the legitimacy of this international criminal tribunal was key in deterring future crimes and contributing to national reconciliation:

> "[...] the question of credibility is of enormous importance. Not just in the short term – how the accused feels about his condemnation or how his supporters accept or reject it – but in the future. We know that there are people who deny the Holocaust and there are people who deny the Rwandan genocide. If the evidence has not been solid, if the trial has not seemed to be fair, a certain number of people will reject that conviction and will use it to prove that these trials represent victors' justice or even worse are part of a larger plot."[142]

Even when the local media outlets did provide reports on the activities of the ICTR, the accounts were not in-depth or substantial enough to provide audiences with a clear understanding of the Tribunal's activities.[143] The ICTR's operations in Arusha remained a mystery to most people living in Rwanda.[144] Functioning alone, in both Rwanda and Tanzania, and charged with the overwhelming mandate of promoting national reconciliation in Rwanda, while prosecuting those most responsible for committing international crimes within a short-time frame, both hindered the ICTR's potential and harmed its legitimacy. As demonstrated through Oomen's research:

> "An international court has the greatest chance of being perceived as legitimate if it involves the people concerned in its set-up, includes values held and procedures respected locally and explicitly communicates its underlying values, justifies the fact that it acts on behalf of a community of belonging, and – in its selection of cases and wider aims – takes people's perceptions into account and communicates its results to them."[145]

Furthermore, aside from the Rwandan government's special representative, who had an office in Arusha from 1999 to 2009, government officials had little contact with the ICTR in the first years of its existence. This was acknowledged by the deputy registrar during his welcome address to a delegation of Rwandan government officials in 2004, nine years after the establishment of the Tribunal, stating that the visit was "*the first of its kind by*

---

142 Alison L. Des Forges, *Interview conducted with Arnaud Grellier for the Justice Tribune*, 6 June 2002 (Cruvellier, 2010 p. 37).

143 Kingsley Chiedu Moghalu, *Rwanda's Genocide: The Politics of Global Justice*. Palgrave Macmillan, 2005, p. 194; interviewee M2.

144 Interviewees CS4, CS15 & CS21.

145 Oomen, 2009, p. 184.

senior government officials of Rwanda to the Tribunal".[146] This is troubling given that a UN report, issued just a few weeks prior to this visit, highlights that a key component of transitional justice is institutional reform in the post-conflict state:

> "Recent years have seen an increased focus by the United Nations on questions of transitional justice and the rule of law in conflict and post-conflict societies, yielding important lessons for our future activities. [...] The United Nations must therefore support domestic reform constituencies, help build the capacity of national justice sector institutions, facilitate national consultations on justice reform and transitional justice and help fill the rule of law vacuum evident in so many post-conflict societies."[147]

The value and potential of international criminal courts and tribunals to contribute to the reconciliation efforts in a post-conflict state or region were understood by the UN, and the messaging coming from the ICTR also highlighted reconciliation and peace as key objectives. In relation to this, the ICTR did collaborate with Rwandan officials regarding the rule of law in Rwanda, specifically related to Article 11 *bis*: "*There was strong collaboration between the national prosecutor here [Rwanda] and the OTP in Arusha*";[148] and the Tribunal staff also offered trainings to promote the necessary judicial reforms Rwanda: "*The Tribunal helped with the capacity building of the legal sector. Lawyers, judges and students of law all had training there [Arusha]*".[149] Indeed, collaboration between the ICTR in Arusha, the Rwandan government and Rwandan universities was a key element in achieving some of the objectives laid out in UN Resolution 1503, in 2003.[150]

However, all the ICTR's communications in Rwanda appear to have been channelled through the Rwandan government – "*The link with Rwanda was through the Ministry of Justice*"[151] – which occasionally led to bottlenecks and a lack of support for certain legitimisation activities. The Tribunal therefore had its hands tied when it came to promoting its legitimacy to a wider audience in Rwanda. This is demonstrated through the failed attempt to set up daily radio broadcasts:

---

146 Lovemore G. Munlo, *Opening Ceremony of the High Level Meeting between Senior Officials of the Government of Rwanda and of the ICTR Registry*, Arusha, Tanzania, 20 September 2004, p. 1.
A delegation of senior Rwandan government officials led by Mr. Martin Ngoga, deputy prosecutor General, and a delegation of senior members of the ICTR Registry led by Mr. Lovemore Munlo, deputy registrar, held discussions on practical modalities which prepared the ground for an agreement between the Rwandan government and the UN regarding enforcement of ICTR sentences in Rwanda.

147 United Nations Security Council, *Rule of law and transitional justice in conflict and post-conflict societies*, Report of the Secretary-General, S/2004/616, 23 August 2004, Summary, para. 1.

148 Interviewee G3.

149 Interviewee J2.

150 United Nations Security Council, *Resolution 1503*, S/RES/1503, 28 August 2003.

151 Interviewee T18.

> "We also design a strategy with the national radio station to broadcast live decisions of the court. Unfortunately, we did not have authorization to link up the Tribunal to the national radio so that they can follow on a day-to-day basis live proceedings from Arusha. Unfortunately, it did not happen. [...] For us our first move was to have the government to authorize the broadcasting of all the proceedings. It could have been magnificent because the Rwandan people are known to listen carefully to radio. [...] TV is something that the most fortunate have. But the radio, my goodness, they can listen. And we know the role that the radio played in the genocide. And it was our philosophy that by using the radio to convey this, it will be very effective. But we did not get support from the government."[152]

As a result, the lack of collaboration with civil society organisations based in Rwanda may have been due to constraints set by the Rwandan government, or possibly due to the allocation of resources, and attempts to consolidate funds in order to achieve certain goals (later stated in the completion strategy), for example by focusing on legal training and the rule of law in Rwanda.

In any event, the need for authorisation from the Rwandan government for the ICTR to work in Rwanda, and the sensitive, post-conflict situation in which the Tribunal was operating, are important factors to take into account when examining the ICTR's legitimisation activities. As a key stakeholder in ensuring that trials could continue in Arusha, the Rwandan government held a certain amount of authority over the activities of the Tribunal. However, when it came to the ICTR archive, the power dynamic shifted once again.

6.4 The ICTR Archive

The post-conflict situation in November 1994 led to the establishment of the ICTR in Arusha, Tanzania, rather than in Kigali. This was a point of contention at the time, with the Rwandan delegation to the UN Security Council arguing that the Tribunal should be located in Rwanda.[153] Additionally, the seat of the Tribunal in Arusha created several legitimacy challenges for the ICTR: investigators needed to travel to Rwanda to gain access to crime scenes and speak to witnesses, and witnesses needed to travel to Arusha to give their testimony – both scenarios needed the approval of the Rwandan government, which

152 Amoussouga, 29-30 October 2008, video 89.
153 United Nations Security Council, S/PV.3453, 8 November 1994, p. 16.

caused additional legitimacy challenges for the Tribunal.[154] Furthermore, the Tribunal was located far from the survivors of the genocide, who were unable to travel to Arusha to attend trials being held; justice was not "*seen to be done*" by the survivors of the genocide,[155] which hindered the ICTR's long-term objectives of retribution, deterrence and reconciliation.[156]

Despite the legitimacy challenges incurred due to the location of the ICTR in Arusha, rather than in Rwanda, almost 20 years later a report published by the UN Secretary-General in 2013 announced the "*Construction of a new facility for the International Residual Mechanism for Criminal Tribunals, Arusha branch*":[157]

> "The [IR-MCT] Arusha branch is currently co-located with the International Criminal Tribunal for Rwanda in the Arusha International Conference Centre compound in Arusha, United Republic of Tanzania. While the Conference Centre has provided adequate support to the activities of the Tribunal, it is unsuitable for the specific programmatic and functional requirements of the much smaller institution of the Mechanism. Because of certain structural features, it does not and cannot effectively meet minimum internationally recognized archival standards or address security risks exacerbated by the progressive reduction of the United Nations presence in the compound."[158]

In 2013 Rwanda was no longer the post-conflict state of 1994. The country boasted a strong economy, excellent infrastructure and social development, earning the nickname of "*the Switzerland of Africa*".[159] Yet when discussing the location for the African branch of the IR-MCT, the UN Security Council decided otherwise: a UN report underlines the need for a new facility to ensure security requirements, which justified "*an initial amount of $3 million for the overall construction of the proposed new premises of the Arusha branch of the Mechanism*".[160] As explained by a former ICTR staff member: "*There was a big push to get the MICT [IR-MCT] to Arusha. The Tanzanian government was also very keen to*

---

154 Section 5.7.

155 Interviewees CS7 & CS11.

156 ICTR, *Prosecutor v. Jean Kambanda*, Judgment and Sentence, ICTR-97-23-S, 4 September 1998, para. 28; ICTR, *Best Practices Manual for the Prosecution of Sexual Violence*, 2014, p. 69.

157 United Nations Security Council, *Construction of a new facility for the International Residual Mechanism for Criminal Tribunals, Arusha branch*. Report of the Secretary-General, A/67/696, 16 January 2013. Retrieved from: https://www.irmct.org/sites/default/files/documents/130116-A.67.696-en.pdf.

158 *idem.*, para. 5.

159 Bloomberg, *Africa's Would-Be Switzerland Shows Economic Clout With WEF*, 10 May 2016. Retrieved from: https://www.bloomberg.com/news/articles/2016-05-09/africa-s-would-be-switzerland-flaunts-economic-prowess-with-wef.

160 UN Report of the Secretary-General, A/67/696, 16 January 2013, para. 6.

keep the focus here in Arusha. They call it the Geneva of Africa".[161] Inevitably, the push by various staff members and the Tanzanian government was successful; discussions regarding the establishment of the IR-MCT had already started in 2010:

> "The Security Council continues its discussions on the structure and functioning of the Residual Mechanism for our Tribunal and our sister Tribunal in the Hague. A resolution on this issue in the near future will help us in preparing in the best possible manner for a timely and smooth transition to this Residual Mechanism. For now, we continue to work intensely so that once our mandate is completed, the Mechanism will be equipped to take over the remaining tasks without greater difficulties. This preparatory work is time and resource intensive, in particular with respect to the archives of the Tribunal. They will document our legacy and will form part of the historical memory for Rwandans, their neighbouring countries in the Great Lakes Region and the entire international community. We have to ensure that they will be easily accessible in the future for all those who are interested, the general public as well as historians and other researchers."[162]

Given the requirement of easy access, several interviewees were confused as to why the ICTR archive was located on the outskirts of Arusha and not in Rwanda; or why copies were not made accessible in the ICTR's information centres, in libraries located in Rwanda, or at a UN facility based in Rwanda.[163] A Rwandan lawyer could not comprehend the need to house the ICTR archive so far from Rwanda: "*The archives are not in Rwanda. Why not? This is hard to understand. They could be housed by the UN in Rwanda. Why are they in Arusha? This is Rwanda's story. Rwandans should have access*";[164] and a government official who had collaborated closely with the ICTR was also frustrated with the message that the newly built archive facility gave:

> "Why are the archives in Arusha, not here [Rwanda]? The evidence was collected in Rwanda. It belongs to Rwanda. The resolution that says that archives must

161 Interviewee T16.

162 Dennis C. M. Byron, *Address to the United Nations General Assembly, 15th Annual Report of the International Criminal Tribunal for Rwanda*, Judge Dennis Byron, President, 65th Session, New York, USA, 8 October 2010.

163 Interviewees T2, T5, T9, CS17, CS18 & CS21.

164 Interviewee J3.

> stay in Arusha until the end of activities there. This needs to be reviewed. We need to ensure the eventual return of the archives to Rwanda."[165]

Even former ICTR staff members questioned the decision to locate the ICTR archive in Arusha: "*The archives, why are they still in Arusha? What is the logic? They are not accessible there [Rwanda]. Such a huge source of information, and now it is even outside Arusha*".[166] Aside from ownership issues – "*The Minister of Justice Johnson, he spoke of the archives as being protected like in a game reserve. He thanked [name] for looking after his archives*"[167] – the reasons for this choice of location included the security of witnesses who testified anonymously.[168] Yet as one Rwandan judge stated: "*The archives should be in Rwanda. At least copies of the archives. If the capacity is not here for the archives, for example, why not help the country build it?*"[169]

Together with the Rwandan government, a former ICTR spokesperson, Tim Gallimore, proposed the establishment of a UN Information Centre in Rwanda, which would oversee the archive and continue the education and outreach work of the ICTR's Information Centre in Kigali, which had closed in 2014.[170] The main argument for rehousing the archive in Rwanda was its contribution to reconciliation in Rwanda, one of the Tribunal's key objectives. As one interview explained: "*The historical documentation, the processes, how it happened. This is very important for future generations. This information should be made available to the public. Why are the videos of the trials not shared with populations? If it is for history. Why not share it?*"[171] The testimonies of witnesses and survivors play an important role in Rwanda's history and can provide a basis on which to build a new collective identity, as another interviewee explained: "*The archives have not been transferred.*

165 Translated from French: "*Pourquoi les archives sont-elles à Arusha et pas ici? Les preuves ont été recueillies au Rwanda. Ils appartiennent au Rwanda. La résolution qui dit que les archives doivent rester à Arusha jusqu'à la fin des activités là-bas. Cela doit être revu. Nous devons garantir le retour éventuel des archives au Rwanda.*" (G5).

166 Translated from French: "*Les archives, pourquoi sont-elles toujours à Arusha? Quelle est la logique? Ils n'y sont pas accessibles. Une telle source d'informations, et maintenant elle est même en dehors d'Arusha.*" (T9)

167 Interviewee T17.

168 *ibid.*; Adama Dieng, *Address to ICA CITRA Annual Conference*, Cape Town, South Africa, 20 October 2003, pp. 1-2.

169 Interviewee J4.

170 The New Times, *Experts on why Rwanda should take custody of ICTR archives*, 10 February 2015. Retrieved from: https://www.newtimes.co.rw/section/read/185831.

171 Translated from French: "*La documentation historique, les processus, comment cela s'est passé. C'est très important pour les générations futures. Ces informations devraient être mises à la disposition du public. Pourquoi les vidéos des procès ne sont-elles pas partagées avec les populations? Si c'est pour l'histoire. Pourquoi ne pas le partager?*" (CS20).

Not even copies of the archives. Why not? This is Rwanda's story. [...] They are a collection of very important documents for the future. They should be here [Rwanda]."[172]

A government official explained that the ICTR archive contained documents that had originated from the Rwandan government's archives, including information from the Ministry of Defence; documents taken from Rwandan institutions, such as banks; and testimonies from Rwandan citizens, including both the witnesses and the accused: "*The UN archives are in Arusha, but they got everything from Rwanda*".[173] The ICTR's archive is a unique resource, invaluable to Rwandans as well as to the UN, UN member states, and the wider international community. It consists not only of a valuable historic record of the ICTR's trials, but also contributes to the collective memory of events that took place in Rwanda in 1994. These form a record of the human rights violations that occurred and hold the testimonies of those who lived through, and witnessed, these atrocious crimes – including the perpetrators.[174] As explained by Gallimore in 2006:

> "The records of the Tribunal will be useful for future generations of Rwandans and all peoples of the world. Researchers and historians may find the records useful for refuting genocide ideology in establishing an authentic public historical record against negationism and revisionism. Policymakers and political leaders may find the ICTR archive and records useful for national reconciliation by creating from them a new history and basis for the re-imaging of Rwanda."[175]

The legitimacy of the ICTR, and the need for its work to continue beyond its closure in 2015 – especially with regard to reconciliation – was reiterated by another former ICTR staff member: "*The work post-ICTR is not finished. It still has an impact here in Rwanda, also in terms of knowledge. We are just missing the files*".[176] Yet prior to the creation of the IR-MCT, the UN had other ideas as to where and how to house the impressive archive that was being amassed over the course of the ICTR's existence:

---

172 Translated from French: "*Les archives n'ont pas été transférées. Même pas des copies des archives. Pourquoi pas? C'est l'histoire du Rwanda. [...] Ce sont une collection de documents très importants pour l'avenir. Ils devraient être ici.*" (CS6).

173 Interviewee G3.

174 ICTR website, 'archives': https://www.irmct.org/en/archives; RCN Justice & Démocratie (2015), *The Issues and Challenges faced by Memory Initiatives on Contemporary International Crimes. Lessons learnt from the practices of the actors involved.* Seminars held in Brussels, Belgium, 12 December 2014, 18-19 June 2015, p. 2. Retrieved from: https://rcn-ong.be/wp-content/uploads/2020/11/The-issues-and-challenges-faced-by-memory-initiatives-on-contemporary-international-crimes.pdf; The New Times,10 February 2015.

175 Gallimore, 8 November 2006, p. 1.

176 Translated from French: "*Le travail post-TPIR n'est pas terminé. Cela a un impact ici au Rwanda, également en termes de connaissances. Il nous manque juste les fichiers.*" (T23).

> "Another project that the ICTR will embark upon next year is to develop close working relations with several national archives in Africa to deposit copies of our jurisprudence. The purpose of this project is to facilitate the access to these records within Africa. The ICTR is an ad-hoc organisation and as such, we have a limited mandate. On expiration of this mandate, we will be depositing our archival collection at the United Nations HQ archives in New York. This of course does not make things easy for researchers in Africa to consult the records, hence our desire to address this issue by depositing complete copies of our records in several archives in Africa."[177]

No records were found to show that Rwanda was ever considered as a location for the ICTR's archive. When asked why this was the case, one former ICTR staff member explained that "*The library and archives belong to the UN. The UN must decide what will happen to them*".[178] The new facilities and location of the archive in Arusha might be perceived as a show of authority on the part of the UN, given that, generally speaking, "*archives and records, in their creation and use by their makers and in their appraisal and management by archivists, will always reflect power relationships*".[179] Although Rwanda had requested the assistance of the international community in establishing an international criminal court, the ICTR was established by the UN and, as a result, its archive remains in UN custody.

Yet housing the archive in Arusha may also be considered as a final legitimisation activity, this time enacted by the UN Security Council on behalf of the ICTR and its work of 20 years. As with all narratives, archives also serve a purpose, and are rarely considered as an objective and neutral collection of materials. The process of archiving documents, audio files and video clips is not a submissive exercise, and the archivist who manages the procedures, and provides access to files, cannot be considered a "*passive guardian of evidence*".[180] In handing over the ICTR's archive to Rwanda, or providing a replica, the UN would not only be providing the names of both prosecution and defence witnesses, it would also be exposing investigative techniques and analyses used for trials. Given the tense relationship between the Rwandan government and the Tribunal, notably regarding the acquittal or early release of some of the accused, it is possible that the conclusion of certain trials may be questioned – claiming flaws in investigations or proving certain facts to be false – which could lead to arguments calling for a retrial, or demonstrating a mis-use of UN funds.

177 Dieng, 20 October 2003, p. 3.

178 Interviewee T16.

179 Terry Cook and Joan M. Schwartz, *Archives, Records, and Power: From (Postmodern) Theory to (Archival) Performance,* Archival Science, 2002, 2(3-4), p. 172.

180 *idem.*, p. 175.

As stated previously by the ICTR spokesperson: "*Policymakers and political leaders may find the ICTR archive and records useful for national reconciliation by creating from them a new history and basis for the re-imaging of Rwanda*".[181] This may have been perceived as an unwanted risk by the Tribunal. By retaining the archives in Arusha, the UN may have been acting to safeguard the legitimacy of the ICTR, peace and reconciliation in Rwanda, and possibly even the survival of international criminal law.

Furthermore, by the time the decision had been taken to keep the ICTR archive in Arusha, the ICC based in The Hague had opened investigations into violations of international criminal law in several African states.[182] This had provoked fierce debate within the African Union (AU), which accused the ICC of acting as a "*neo-colonist instrument*";[183] while the president of Rwanda, Paul Kagame, was also a vocal opponent of the ICC, stating in 2013 that the international court "*has shown open bias against Africans. Instead of promoting justice and peace, it has undermined efforts at reconciliation and served only to humiliate Africans and their leaders, as well as served the political interests of the powerful*" .[184]

These developments relate to the legitimacy challenge of "*institutionalisation*", whereby a particular organisation, or group of similar organisations, comes under attack for the actions of a comparable organisation.[185] The legitimacy of the ICTR was at risk due to its association with the ICC.

Relations between the Tanzanian government and the ICC, however, remained good. Despite the AU's calls to collectively withdraw from the Rome Statute in 2017, Tanzania (along with nine other African states)[186] had decided to remain a member of the court.[187] It may be possible that the legitimacy challenges facing the ICC brought by several African countries (including Rwanda) is the reason why the UN decided the ICTR's archive should remain in Tanzania where relations remained good, ensuring that "*the legitimacy they*

181 Gallimore, 8 November 2006, p. 1.

182 By 2013 the ICC had authorised investigations related to situations in the Central African Republic (CAR), the Côte d'Ivoire, the Democratic Republic of the Congo (DRC), Kenya, Libya, Mali, Sudan, Uganda. Retrieved from: https://www.icc-cpi.int/pages/situation.aspx.

183 Tim Murithi, *The African Union and the International Criminal Court: An Embattled Relationship?*Institute for Justice and Reconciliation, Policy Brief, 2003, (8), p. 5.

184 Paul Kagame, *Address to the 68th UN General Assembly by President Paul Kagame*, New York, 25 September 2013. Retrieved from: https://www.paulkagame.com/address-to-the-68th-un-general-assembly-by-president-paul-kagame-new-york-25th-september-2013; Reuters, *Rwanda's foreign adventures test West's patience*, 5 April 2014. Retrieved from: https://www.reuters.com/article/us-rwanda-politics-idUSBREA3406L20140405.

185 Suchman, 1995, p. 594.

186 A total of ten states decided not to follow the African Union's decision to break away from the ICC. They include: Botswana, Burkina Faso, Cape Verde, Chad, Ivory Coast, Mali, Nigeria, Senegal, Tanzania and Tunisia (Brendon Cannon, Dominic Pkalya and Bosire Maragia, *The International Criminal Court and Africa: Contextualizing the Anti-ICC Narrative*, African Journal of International Criminal Justice (2016), 2017, no. 1-2, pp. 24-25).

187 Cannon et al., 2017, pp. 20 & 24-25.

have already acquired"[188] could be maintained and protected within the archive based in Arusha.

Yet, aside from the political whirlwind surrounding international criminal law, it appeared that the ICTR's long-term objectives of fostering reconciliation in Rwanda and peace in the Great Lakes region were a far cry from the daily operations taking place at the new IR-MCT in Arusha: "*The [IR-MCT] library usually works with foreign researchers, and most of them make contact online, with requests for literature or access to documents in the archives*".[189] In 2013, two years before the official closure of the ICTR, the archive was moved to the custody of the IR-MCT and appeared destined to stay in Tanzania, in a new facility completed in 2015: "*This is the largest, and only, purpose built archives. We have a state-of-the-art cooling system, which is kept between ten and fifteen degrees, and we have humidity control*".[190]

The impressive, new Arusha branch of the IR-MCT, set on a hill just outside Arusha and overlooked by the imposing Mount Meru, not only includes a large building constructed to house the hundreds of thousands of documents, audio files, films, interlocutory decisions and judgments from the ICTR, but also includes a courtroom and continues to conduct trials. The downside is that the new premises are situated 12 kilometres from the town of Arusha, which provides the IR-MCT with additional challenges regarding a lack of access and visibility: "*Our location now is difficult, as people need to make an effort to come. They can't pop in during their lunchtime*".[191] In housing the archive just outside Arusha, another opportunity to bring the ICTR closer to the survivors of the Rwandan genocide – connecting the trials that took place in Arusha with the Tribunal's objectives for retribution, deterrence and reconciliation – has been discounted.

By protecting its past accomplishments in a state-of-the-art facility, ensuring control over its 20-years of work and avoiding any unexpected events that might reawaken scrutiny from its stakeholders, the legitimacy of the Tribunal is maintained. Yet these actions could also create unforeseen legitimacy challenges that threaten not only the ICTR's legitimacy, but also the legitimacy of the historical narrative provided by the Tribunal and the Rwandan government, and, as a result, also threaten the legitimacy of international criminal law.

The ICTR closed its doors on 31 December 2015, after several extensions of its original deadline. Yet the legitimacy challenges faced by the Tribunal's legitimacy remain and disseminating the important work of the Tribunal is now harder than when it was conducting trials. Furthermore, a key link to the ICTR's legitimacy, and an important

188 *ibid.*
189 Interviewee T7.
190 Interviewee T17.
191 Interviewee T11.

connection between the Tribunal's long-term and short-term objectives, remains housed in Arusha.

6.5 Conclusion

While Chapter 5 described the legitimacy challenges faced by the ICTR and the subsequent legitimisation activities implemented to gain, maintain and repair its legitimacy, this chapter focused on the link between the three legitimacy types (pragmatic, moral and cognitive) and the ICTR's short- and long-term objectives, examining how the Tribunal implemented legitimisation activities in line with its mandate in order to maintain the its legitimacy over its 20-year lifespan.

The Tribunal was established to prosecute those responsible for the genocide and other serious violations of international humanitarian law that took place in Rwanda and its neighbouring countries in 1994. It was also mandated to restore peace in the Great Lakes region and to foster reconciliation in Rwanda, in line with Chapter 7 of the UN Charter, through which UN Resolution 955 found its footing. Furthermore, with the arrival of the first completion strategy in 2003, the Tribunal needed to complete all activities within a specific timeframe.

Yet the ICTR operated on an annual budget and the allocation of resources was identified by some interviewees as a challenge. The Tribunal therefore made use of legitimisation activities in order to ensure the continued (and additional) support from key stakeholders. The ICTR's long-term objectives were emphasised in speeches and reports, promoting a legitimate organisation worthy of support, in line with moral and cognitive legitimacy; while annual reports and press releases detailed the daily operations of the Tribunal, demonstrating its pragmatic legitimacy.

With most communication provided through conferences, speeches and reports presented in English or French, and with little information disseminated regarding the trials themselves (aside from the broadcast of the final judgment), the ICTR's legitimisation activities aimed at maintaining its legitimacy were directed towards the UN member states, including the Rwandan government. These stakeholders played a significant role in the ICTR's existence. The UN provided material support including infrastructure, operational procedures and funding, while the Rwandan government provided investigators and prosecutors with access to crime scenes and witnesses.

The ICTR therefore focused on maintaining all three legitimacy types to ensure ongoing support of these key stakeholders. Yet, in conducting trials in Arusha and communicating its activities to a specific set of stakeholders, the only clear deliverables were linked to pragmatic legitimacy: fugitives were being arrested and international trials were taking place in Arusha. Furthermore, the Tribunal was assisting the Rwandan government in training legal practitioners and working towards the transfer of cases to Rwanda, in accordance with its mandate. In the eyes of the UN member states, these activities arguably also relate to moral legitimacy, the Tribunal was acting ethically, and cognitive legitimacy, demonstrating a crucial role in strengthening Rwanda's justice sector; while the arrival of the ICC in 2002 also solidified the ICTR's moral and cognitive legitimacy, through its role (together with the ICTY) in reviving international criminal law.

However, over time, promoting the Tribunal's moral and cognitive legitimacy to the UN member states became a priority for the Registry, notably within the ERSPS. Collecting newspaper clippings and reporting on the content of television and media broadcasts was a key task in the outreach centres located in Rwanda. Furthermore, given that funding for the Tribunal's outreach work was not part of the ICTR's annual UN budget, additional resources were required through voluntary donations, which transformed the ERSPS into a quasi-fundraising department. As a result, aside from the operational focus on achieving its short-term objectives, thereby ensuring the Tribunal's pragmatic legitimacy, the ICTR continued to emphasise the Tribunal's long-term objectives, promoting its moral and cognitive legitimacy in order to raise funds and remain relevant on the international stage.

Achieving the short-term objectives was key; connecting these short-term actions to the bigger picture, the long-term objectives, was not. In any event, the long-term objectives of the Tribunal were ambitious. Aside from the impressive plan to prosecute the 93 individuals regarded as those most responsible for crimes committed during the 1994 genocide, the ICTR was also established with a mandate to contribute to reconciliation efforts in Rwanda and to promote peace within the Great Lakes region. An impressive feat for an international criminal tribunal operating on a limited budget, restricted resources and within a tight time-frame.

However, there were civil society organisations based in Rwanda that could have facilitated the Tribunal's task in both *"perceiving a future crisis"* and *"protecting past accomplishments"*[192] – had there been room for collaboration. Interviews with representatives of various organisations based in Rwanda highlighted the lack of interaction with the Tribunal. This may, in part, be linked to the restriction of communications in Rwanda, enforced by the Rwandan government, or possibly the Tribunal's own focus on achieving its short-term objectives, which was enforced by the UN to ensure that the ICTR stayed on course to close within a certain timeframe (maintaining its pragmatic legitimacy). The lack of collaboration with these civil society organisations may, however, have been counterproductive, given their capacity to endorse the work of the Tribunal, which would have assisted in (gaining and) maintaining its legitimacy and enhanced the ICTR's potential to realise both its long- and short-term objectives.

---

192 Suchman, 1995, pp. 594-597.

The final act of the UN, with regard to the ICTR, concerns the Tribunal's archive. The location of the ICTR in Arusha was a necessity at first, given Rwanda's fragile state in 1994, following four years of conflict. As the years progressed, the situation in Rwanda improved considerably, yet in 2013 the UN adopted a resolution to house the ICTR's archive in Arusha. The strategy behind constructing new premises, just outside the town of Arusha, rather than establishing the IR-MCT, together with the ICTR archive, in Rwanda, is unknown. Retaining the UN-funded facilities in Arusha was said to have been a logistical decision, given the large number of documents to be moved across the border and the presence (in Arusha) of former ICTR staff members with organisational knowledge. It may also be considered as a final legitimisation activity enacted by the UN Security Council on behalf of the Tribunal in order to safeguard the ICTR's 20-year legacy (*"protecting past accomplishments"*)[193] and possibly even to ensure the maintenance of peace in Rwanda. Yet, many others believe that the archive holds important information regarding Rwanda's history, which forms part of the country's future, and, as such, it should be located in Rwanda. Regardless of the motivations behind the UN's decision: the housing of a state-of-the-art archive in Arusha raise questions regarding the ICTR's legitimacy, and neglect yet another opportunity to promote the ICTR's work, by connecting the international trials conducted in Arusha with the Tribunal's long-term objectives for retribution, deterrence and reconciliation.

By the time the ICTR closed its doors in 2015, the international community seemed to have moved on, with its efforts and attention directed towards the permanent ICC based in The Hague, rather than completing the work of the ad hoc Tribunal established to foster reconciliation in Rwanda, following a conflict that ended in 1994. Yet, the ICTR's legitimacy continues to play an important role in defining Rwanda's future and seeking to maintain peace in the Great Lakes region, and – maybe more importantly – in the practice of international criminal law.

193 *idem.*, p. 594.

7 Discussion and Concluding Remarks

The purpose of this research was to examine how the ICTR implemented legitimisation activities to gain, maintain and/or repair its legitimacy. The objective behind this choice of research question was to examine the concept of legitimacy and its importance for international criminal courts by focusing on the legitimisation activities implemented by the ICTR, which faced various legitimacy challenges from its establishment in 1994 until its closure in 2015. In order to answer this main research question, three sub-questions have been addressed:

- Why was legitimacy important for the ICTR?
- What challenges did the ICTR face that threatened its legitimacy?
- How did the ICTR respond to the threats to its legitimacy?

The purpose of this concluding chapter is to present the main findings from this study and make recommendations for existing and future international criminal courts. The chapter is divided into three sections, with Section 1 revisiting the central research question and sub-questions in order to highlight the main conclusions of this study.

Taking into account the research findings, Section 2 of this chapter makes general recommendations related to promoting the legitimacy of existing and future international criminal courts. The recommendations explain the need for international courts to recognise and manage organisational legitimacy given its importance to the success of their work. It has also been shown that engaging with stakeholders is critical to the realisation of an international court's mandate as this enhances a relationship of trust and further increases the perception of legitimacy within the organisation's environment. The importance of the different types of legitimacy (pragmatic, moral and cognitive), as well as the importance for organisations to be aware of them, is also highlighted in this chapter, as is the need to understand the local environment in which an international criminal court operates.

Section 3 closes this chapter and identifies areas for further research.

7.1 Key Findings from This Research

The aim of this study is to look back at the operations of the ICTR in order to inform the work of existing and future international criminal courts. This section summarises the main findings for the three sub-questions of this research (Sections 1.1-1.4) and concludes with a general discussion to answer the main research question (Section 1.5). To begin with, the sub-question of *why legitimacy was important for the ICTR* will be discussed by first taking a closer look at what is meant by the term legitimacy, and examining why legitimacy was important for the Tribunal in Arusha, especially given that the notion of legitimacy can be defined or interpreted in a multitude of ways.

7.1.1 What Is Legitimacy?

This study started by examining the concept of legitimacy through a literature review, and soon delved into organisational legitimacy due to the focus on the ICTR, an international criminal court. The literature related to organisational legitimacy frequently refers to a definition by Mark Suchman from his 1995 article, in which he states that organisational legitimacy is *"a generalized perception or assumption that the actions of an entity are desirable, proper, or appropriate within some socially constructed system of norms, values, beliefs, and definitions"*.[1] This definition has since been revisited,[2] although the core principles behind Suchman's original research remain the same, namely that three types of organisational legitimacy (pragmatic, moral and cognitive) are constructed through a system of socially accepted values and norms.[3]

The empirical part of this research examined how legitimacy is interpreted by those who worked within or alongside the ICTR: the first question in each interview was about how the interviewee understood this concept.[4] Generally speaking, the interviewees answered in accordance with the definition of legitimacy given in the literature, describing the close relationship between legality and legitimacy.[5] Although the term legitimacy was immediately recognisable to all interviewees, as the interview progressed and anecdotes related to the legitimacy of the ICTR were discussed, interviewees described or alluded to other features associated with the concept of legitimacy, namely the different forms of legitimacy described in the literature, such as input versus output legitimacy, and normative versus empirical legitimacy.[6] However, the discussions also revealed areas that had not been addressed in the literature consulted for this research.

---

1 Mark C. Suchman, *Managing Legitimacy: Strategic and Institutional Approaches,* Academy of Management Review, 1995, 20(3), p. 574.

2 Suchman and his colleagues suggested a new definition in 2017: "*Organizational legitimacy is the perceived appropriateness of an organization to a social system in terms of rules, values, norms, and definitions.*" (David Deephouse, Jonathan Bundy, Leigh Plunkett Tost and Mark Suchman, *Organizational Legitimacy: Six Key Questions,* The SAGE Handbook of Organizational Institutionalism, 2017, p. 32).

3 Section 2.1.4.

4 Section 4.1.

5 Section 4.1.

6 Section 4.2.
Input legitimacy assesses an organisation's legitimacy based on the systems or structures through which it was established or selected; while output legitimacy assesses legitimacy based on the output or performance of an organisation. Normative legitimacy refers to a set of standards by which an organisation is judged to be legitimate; while empirical legitimacy refers to the perception or belief that an organisation is legitimate.

First and foremost, contrary to a pre-conceived assumption generated during the literature review, the interviewees did not once question the input and normative legitimacy of the ICTR. The establishment of the Tribunal through UN Resolution 955 – adopted by the UN Security Council and accepted by the UN General Assembly – provided the ICTR with its legitimacy, according to the interviewees.[7] Regardless of the UN's failure to prevent or stop the 1994 genocide from unfolding, the authority of the UN was decidedly key in providing the Tribunal with its legitimacy. Furthermore, despite its request for the establishment of an international tribunal, the Rwandan government had vetoed the establishment of the Tribunal through its capacity as a temporary member of the UN Security Council at the time. In fact, during the first ICTR trial, Kanyabashi's defence team argued against the legality of the Tribunal, questioning why the UN was getting involved in an internal conflict.[8] These two initial legitimacy challenges were not mentioned during any of the interviews conducted for this research. On the contrary, most interviewees stated that the mere establishment of the ICTR meant that the international community recognised the international crimes committed in Rwanda in 1994,[9] and apart from the references found in the ICTR's case law, the legality of the ICTR was not mentioned in any of the interviews.[10]

In line with the above, the second factor that came to light relates to the source of the ICTR's legitimacy, examining where the initial perceptions of organisational legitimacy came from.[11] As mentioned previously, the Tribunal's legitimacy was largely *"taken for granted"* by those interviewed.[12] This appears to be related to the legitimacy of its founder, the UN, which provided the Tribunal with 'input' legitimacy; while the establishment of the Tribunal itself represented the international community's recognition of the Rwandan genocide, demonstrating 'output' legitimacy.[13] The moral and cognitive legitimacy of the ICTR appeared to have been established early on.

Yet, interviewees also stated that the Tribunal was legitimate given its ability to prosecute those most responsible for the crimes committed in 1994.[14] However, it could be argued that the arrest and prosecution of the 'big fish' responsible for crimes committed during the genocide in Rwanda was only possible because of the Tribunal's existing legitimacy at the time. This conundrum of cause and effect played a role when interviewees described

7 Section 4.2.3.
8 Sections 4.1 and 4.2.3.
9 Section 4.2.1.
10 This may also be due to selection bias (Sections 3.2.1 and 3.4).
11 Section 4.2.
12 Suchman, 1995, pp. 582-583.
13 Sections 2.1.3, 4.2.1 and 4.2.3.
14 Section 4.2.2.

their assessments of the ICTR's legitimacy: legitimacy was needed in order to carry out certain actions, but achieving these actions also confirmed the ICTR's legitimacy.

On the other hand, the Tribunal's legitimacy could have been gained and maintained through a domino effect, whereby the initial acceptance of organisational legitimacy allows for another legitimising act to take place. This implies that in order to achieve organisational legitimacy, a seed must first be sown: the key to the legitimacy of the ICTR could arguably be linked solely to the legitimacy of the UN itself: the UN was a reputable organisation in its own right and UN resolutions regarding the ICTR were adopted with the overwhelming support of UN member states. The legitimacy conferred on the ICTR through its affiliation with the UN was further cultivated by the symbolism of the Tribunal's establishment, which represented the international community's recognition of the 1994 genocide.

In addition to examining the source of the ICTR's legitimacy, the third finding of this study relates to the various shades of legitimacy projected by the ICTR. Despite the unanimity shown in accepting the legitimacy of the Tribunal, further discussion with interviewees revealed that some of its actions were considered illegitimate; and the contradiction in this narrative – a legitimate court carrying out illegitimate activities – was never questioned.[15] Although the Tribunal was perceived as legitimate, the legitimacy challenges it encountered – for example, linked to reports of nepotism and corruption, the employment of *génocidaires*, acquittals and early releases, etc. – never detracted from the sum of their parts. As a result, the empirical legitimacy of the Tribunal may have fluctuated over time, but its normative legitimacy remained, regardless of whether certain activities, people or departments were perceived differently.[16]

The fourth finding is a definitional one. This research made use of the term legitimacy, which was recognised and defined during the literature review, the interviews and the archival research. Yet, similar meaning is given to other terms, notably the word image which was often used synonymously with the word legitimacy.[17] This was most evident, and consistent, when reading documents produced by the ICTR: a key task of the ERSPS was to build and maintain a positive image of the Tribunal, a refrain that was found in speeches and internal memos, and repeated during the interviews for this research. The image of the ICTR appeared to be incredibly important to those working within the Tribunal, however, most interviewees did not explicitly equate this to the discussion regarding the ICTR's legitimacy. It is unclear where or why the idea to focus on the Tribunal's image came from; however, it is interesting that although image was clearly

15 This may be due to the words used to describe certain events, which are addressed in the following paragraph.
16 Chapters 4 and 5.
17 Section 4.3.

important for the ICTR, the activities designed to promote the Tribunal's image were not considered legitimisation activities by the former ICTR staff interviewed for this research.[18]

Lastly, during the interviews there was an underlying sense that despite the legitimacy challenges faced by the Tribunal, the ICTR needed to be legitimate. Regardless of the organisation that the interviewees were affiliated with, their academic or social background, and/or how nuanced their opinion was of the Tribunal, the general consensus was that the Tribunal was a legitimate international criminal court. There may be several reasons for this, none more obvious than the possible selection bias of this research: all the interviewees were chosen due to their affiliation or link to the ICTR and this connection may have driven them to conclude that the Tribunal was, generally speaking, a legitimate organisation.[19] Another reason could be linked to the underlying need for the Tribunal to be legitimate: despite the legitimacy challenges that it faced, the Tribunal represented a recognition of the 1994 genocide that took place in Rwanda, and the capacity of the international community to respond to such atrocious crimes committed by political and military leaders.[20] There is no doubt that the presence of both the ICTR and the ICTY, and the role of the UN in creating these two tribunals, were fundamental in the adoption of the Rome Statute in 1998 and the creation of the ICC in 2002,[21] as well as the subsequent emergence of hybrid courts. The legitimacy of the ICTR was therefore important to multiple stakeholders on several levels.

Yet, this research focused specifically on the ICTR's actions and why legitimacy was important for the Tribunal. There were numerous stakeholders interested in the success of the Tribunal (albeit for different reasons and with different interpretations regarding the notion of success), which occasionally resulted in legitimacy challenges; however, in line with the second part of this first research question, the following section will first examine why legitimacy was specifically important for the ICTR.

7.1.2 *Why Was Legitimacy Important for the ICTR?*

The typology offered in Suchman's research regarding different forms of legitimacy (pragmatic, moral and cognitive) provides a way to interpret and understand the interplay between legitimacy and organisational behaviour: highlighting how, when and why organisations respond to legitimacy challenges, and demonstrating that organisational

18 Section 4.3.
19 Section 3.2.
20 Sections 4.2 and 4.2.1.
21 United Nations General Assembly, Fiftieth Session, 52nd plenary meeting, A/50/PV.52, 7 November 1995, New York, p. 7.

legitimacy is important for any organisation.[22] This was confirmed in the literature review, which emphasised the importance of organisational legitimacy in acquiring resources, building networks and obtaining a certain level of operational and managerial freedom, which was reflected in the actions of the ICTR in managing its own legitimacy.[23]

As the second international criminal tribunal established following a 45-year gap in the practice of international criminal law, the ICTR was also the first criminal tribunal of its kind created on the African continent to address international crimes that had been committed in a country that had voted against its very establishment. Furthermore, the Tribunal in Arusha was working alongside the ICTY, a more visible Tribunal operating from its location in The Hague and addressing an ongoing conflict taking place in Europe. Although the conflict in Rwanda also involved UN member states, the conflict had ended in July 1994, before the establishment of the Tribunal. The ICTR therefore had to promote itself as a legitimate international court to a diverse set of stakeholders in order to secure its position as a relevant Tribunal, capable of addressing international crimes committed during the horrific conflict that took place in Rwanda.[24]

Chapters 4, 5, and 6 – and Section 7.1.4 of this chapter – highlight a variety of legitimisation activities implemented by the ICTR in order to manage its legitimacy, and the various objectives behind the need for the Tribunal to gain, maintain and/or repair its legitimacy. The multifaceted nature of legitimacy is exemplified through the numerous ways in which this concept assisted the Tribunal in achieving its long- and short-term objectives, while addressing diverse stakeholders.[25] In particular, this research has shown that promoting the Tribunal's legitimacy was key in gaining and maintaining the support of two specific stakeholders – the UN (including the individual UN member states) and the Rwandan government – which were vital in safeguarding the daily functioning of the ICTR and the achievement of its mandate. Examining the legitimisation activities implemented by the ICTR to manage its legitimacy challenges highlights the power that these two stakeholders held over the Tribunal's legitimacy and, as a result, its very existence: the Rwandan government was crucial in providing the Tribunal with access to crime scenes and witnesses, while the UN provided all the material support including infrastructure, operational systems and funding.[26]

Viewed from this perspective, it may be argued that the actions taken by the Tribunal had nothing to do with legitimacy, but were solely designed to keep the ICTR operational. Yet, research has shown that the operations of an organisation are directly linked to

22 Suchman, 1995.
23 Sections 2.1.2, 2.1.3 and 2.1.4; and Chapter 6.
24 Section 5.1.1.
25 Section 6.3.
26 Sections 5.9 and 6.3.

pragmatic legitimacy, which assesses the performance of an organisation.[27] Furthermore, the relationship between the ICTR and these two stakeholders demonstrates the very essence of legitimacy and its link to power and politics as described in Chapter 2,[28] which was also highlighted by a Rwandan judge who continues to work on genocide cases in Rwanda: *"The Rwandan government clashed with the ICTR. This demonstrated that the ICTR was not as powerful as it thought it was"*.[29] Although the legitimacy challenges described in this research represent only a handful of examples taken from the Tribunal's 20-year existence, they demonstrate the sensitivity of the Tribunal's work and the challenges it faced in balancing its legitimacy and operational needs, illustrating the importance of organisational legitimacy, while also demonstrating how it may be perceived differently through the eyes of a diverse set of stakeholders.

7.1.3 What Challenges Did the ICTR Face That Threatened Its Legitimacy?

In order to identify individual legitimacy challenges, Chapters 4, 5 and 6 untangled the elements that made up the Tribunal's legitimacy, highlighting the essence of its complex nature. Specifically, Chapter 5 describes the operational challenges experienced during the ICTR's first years in Arusha, which were paired with an urgent need to prosecute high profile political and military leaders who had fled Rwanda following the conflict.[30] This presented an additional host of challenges for the ICTR that relied on state engagement to track, arrest and transfer the individuals that had been indicted by the OTP.[31] The Tribunal therefore faced a variety of legitimacy challenges throughout its lifespan, not least due to its location in Arusha, Tanzania, over 900 kilometres from the Rwandan border, far from the crime scenes and survivors of the 1994 genocide.[32]

This distance from Rwanda created numerous legitimacy challenges.[33] The cultural and linguistic misunderstandings in the courtroom emphasised the contextual distance between the ICTR and Rwanda, which was exacerbated by a lack of regular field visits to Rwanda by the foreign ICTR staff based in Tanzania.[34] With the rebuilding of Rwanda's broken infrastructure and an increase in qualified Rwandan judges and lawyers, it remained unclear as to why the ICTR's trials could not involve more Rwandans and/or be moved to the Rwandan capital of Kigali. The arrival of the locally established gacaca court system

27 Section 2.1.4.
28 Section 2.1.1.
29 Interviewee J4.
30 Sections 5.2 and 5.8.
31 Section 5.8.
32 Section 5.1.
33 Sections 5.1, 5.4, 5.6 and 5.7.
34 Section 5.4.

emphasised the distance between Rwanda and the ICTR: the physical proximity and involvement of Rwandans in the gacaca system, as well as the low costs and much shorter trial time, stood in stark contrast with the ICTR operating in Arusha.[35]

The distance further impeded the Tribunal's work when it came to acquittals and the early release of individuals accused of crimes of genocide.[36] The ICTR experienced a tense relationship with the Rwandan government throughout its lifespan, starting before its creation with the Rwandan delegation's veto of UN Resolution 955 in 1994.[37] Yet the relationship reached a fever pitch with the unexpected acquittal of Jean-Bosco Barayagwiza in 1999. The acquittal itself impacted the Tribunal's legitimacy, yet it also provoked additional legitimacy challenges when the Rwandan government responded by curtailing the Tribunal's activities in Rwanda, essentially paralysing the ICTR.[38] A few years later the ICTR's activities were suspended again, this time due to the Rwandan government's reaction to the OTP's *Special Investigations* into crimes allegedly committed by members of the RPF, launched by the then chief prosecutor, Carla Del Ponte.[39] In response to the Rwandan government's blockade of ICTR activities in Rwanda, Del Ponte was removed from her position as chief prosecutor for the ICTR.[40] Although the prosecution of Barayagwiza and the removal of Del Ponte appeased the Rwandan government, allowing the Tribunal to continue its important work in Rwanda, it may have played a role in damaging its legitimacy as an impartial court of law.[41]

Indeed, Chapter 6 provides additional examples as to how the ICTR's legitimisation activities also risked challenging its legitimacy. This was an unexpected finding that did not surface during the literature review. For example, in order to operate its outreach programme – a legitimisation activity that included the dissemination of information related to the trials taking place in Arusha and training programmes for Rwandan students, lawyers and judges – the ICTR needed to establish a Voluntary Trust Fund to raise funds that were not available through the UN budget. However, fundraising for the Trust Fund directed the attention of the Tribunal's staff (namely the ERSPS) away from the outreach programmes and required UN member states to donate additional funds to the Tribunal: two actions that risked damaging the Tribunal's legitimacy.[42]

The chapter also examines how certain pressures to meet the expectations or requirements of stakeholders could also result in creating legitimacy challenges, even if

35 Section 5.6.
36 Section 5.7.
37 Section 4.2.3.
38 Section 5.7.1.
39 Section 5.7.2.
40 Section 5.7.2.1.
41 Section 5.7.3.
42 Section 6.2.1.

these challenges are not immediately apparent.[43] For example, the Tribunal had to provide annual reports to the UN General Assembly, demonstrating the progress of its work, which, along with the arrival of the completion strategy in 2003, was designed to provide clear guidelines that directed the ICTR's resources. However, in order to achieve the annual projections, the focus on these short-term deliverables may have directed the Tribunal's attention and resources away from its longer-term objectives of fostering reconciliation and peace in Rwanda and the Great Lakes region, which may also have harmed the Tribunal's legitimacy in the eyes of certain stakeholders.[44]

The location of the ICTR archive, which is housed in a purpose built facility just outside Arusha, provides another example of how legitimisation activities may provoke legitimacy challenges. Although the establishment and availability of such an impressive, state-of-the-art archive provided another means of maintaining the Tribunal's legitimacy (*"protecting past accomplishments"*),[45] the presence of the archive in Arusha cast a shadow over the legitimacy of the ICTR's work for some of the Tribunal's stakeholders.[46] Building a new facility in Arusha to house documents concerning Rwanda's recent history signifies that the UN intends to keep the archive in Tanzania for the foreseeable future rather than transferring the historical records to Rwanda. The lack of communication and transparency regarding this decision may threaten the Tribunal's long-term objectives regarding peace and reconciliation in Rwanda, given that *"misinformation emerges from lack of information"*,[47] which could run the risk of buffering any underlying denialist discourse regarding the 1994 genocide.[48]

Aside from identifying and highlighting the ICTR's legitimacy challenges, it soon became apparent that not all challenges identified for this research followed the theoretical framework described in Chapter 2.[49] Labelling the ICTR's challenges as concerns related to gaining, maintaining or repairing legitimacy provided a means to better understand the nature of these challenges.[50] However, although certain challenges appeared to fit relatively easily into the theoretical framework, others did not. For example, the challenge of mismanagement occurred when the Tribunal started operating in Arusha, and although the characteristics of this legitimacy challenge were related to repairing legitimacy, rather than gaining legitimacy, it involved the ICTR's internal management rather than obstacles created by its external environment. It appears, therefore, that challenges associated with

43 Section 6.3.
44 Section 6.3.1.
45 Section 2.1.2; Suchman, 1995, p. 594.
46 Section 6.4.
47 Bocar Sy, Interview conducted by Tribunal Voices (video 652), 30 October 2008. Retrieved from: http://www.tribunalvoices.org/voices/video/652.
48 Gallimore, 8 November 2006, p. 1.
49 Section 2.2.
50 *ibid.*

repairing legitimacy may strike at any phase of an organisation's life, regardless of how new it is or how much legitimacy it has acquired.[51]

Likewise, the struggles associated with tracking and arresting fugitives appear to highlight a challenge in maintaining legitimacy. However, the sub-categories of "*organisational homogeneity*" and "*stakeholder heterogeneity*" do not accurately describe the challenge faced by the Tribunal, which was due to the emergence of a new wave of international criminal courts and the change in focus of UN member states, rather than the arrival of more versatile organisations.[52] Including an additional sub-category – for example, "*stakeholder redirection*" – where the attention and resources of the stakeholder(s) are directed towards a new or different place or purpose would represent a legitimacy challenge describing an organisation that loses relevance within its environment through no fault of its own, but rather as a result of transient trends and/or diminished public interest.

Building on the research conducted by Suchman, Deephouse, Bundy and Tost,[53] this study designed a framework[54] to examine organisational legitimacy in the particular context of an international criminal tribunal, reliant on two stakeholders. Identifying and categorising the ICTR's legitimacy challenges provided a way in which to understand the wide-ranging nature of legitimacy, and to examine the potential for challenges to be created in both the internal and external environment of the Tribunal. Indeed, challenges related to legitimacy demonstrate the same fluid characteristics found in the concept of legitimacy itself: defining and identifying the source, and discovering the nuances of a legitimacy challenge reflect the findings related to legitimacy described in Section 1.1 of this chapter. Examining how the ICTR responded to these challenges provides yet another angle from which to better understand the complexities of organisational legitimacy in relation to the activities of the ICTR.

7.1.4 How Did the ICTR Respond to Legitimacy Challenges?

Although the Tribunal did not appear concerned with its legitimacy, there were great efforts made to promote its image. The responsibility for handling all matters related to public information and external relations fell to the Registry, which delegated the task to a specialised section – the ERSPS – from 2003 onwards. The ERSPS ensured a wide

51 Section 5.2. It was not clear from Suchman and Deephouse et al.'s research whether repairing legitimacy can only occur once legitimacy has been gained by an organisation (Suchman, 1995, p. 597; Deephouse et al., 2017, pp. 23-24).

52 Section 5.8.1.

53 Deephouse, et al., 2017; Suchman, 1995.

54 Section 2.3.

dissemination of information regarding the activities of the ICTR through the Tribunal's website, newsletters, press briefings, and attending and organising conferences, as well as making use of the information centres located in Rwanda. The ERSPS also paid close attention to what was being reported on by media outlets by keeping abreast of television and radio shows that mentioned the work of the Tribunal, and collecting news articles written by the press. Aside from addressing communications, the Tribunal also demonstrated full transparency by providing the Rwandan government with an office for their special representative, who attended regular meetings with the ICTR's president and registrar.[55]

By focusing on specific legitimacy challenges, Chapter 5 examines the legitimisation activities implemented to gain, maintain and repair the ICTR's pragmatic, moral and/or cognitive legitimacy. Although all three types of legitimacy were endorsed by the Tribunal in response to the challenges it faced, the Tribunal was established and managed as a temporary institution, which could explain the emphasis it placed on pragmatic legitimacy, as opposed to a longer-term approach that would require a more concerted effort in managing its moral and cognitive legitimacy. The ICTR's lifespan was 20 years, yet from the outset it was not clear how long the Tribunal would remain active and its operational budget was initially provided on a yearly basis. As described in Chapter 6, reporting to the UN Security Council and the UN General Assembly remained a fixed annual event and the ICTR's attention was focused on providing immediate results related to yearly targets: communicating, for example, the number of arrests and trials conducted by the Tribunal. The attention given to the Tribunal's performance (pragmatic legitimacy) also explains why the ICTR's legitimisation activities were largely focused on the UN and the Rwandan government, which were crucial in keeping the Tribunal operational.[56]

The other stakeholders that claimed the attention of the ICTR's legitimisation activities at the time were the media and academic institutions.[57] The 1990s saw the revival of international criminal law (almost 50 years after the two military tribunals established after World War II) with both the ICTY and the ICTR playing a pivotal role in revitalising the international community's responsibility in ensuring accountability for gross human rights violations committed by political and military leaders.[58] Yet, in comparison to the ICTR, the ICTY experienced continuous global media coverage throughout its existence due, in part, to the political interest in the proceedings taking place there, and its seat in The Hague, where it was located in close proximity to the Peace Palace, the ICC (from 2002), and a number of academic institutions and think tanks focusing on international

55 Section 4.3.
56 Sections 6.1 and 6.2.
57 *idem.*, Section 6.3.
58 United Nations General Assembly, Fiftieth Session, 52nd plenary meeting, A/50/PV.52, 7 November 1995, New York, p. 2.

criminal law. Located in Arusha, the ICTR did not experience the same media interest or exposure, in some cases paying journalists' travel costs to guarantee their presence at the Tribunal. Ensuring that the ICTR was considered a legitimate international criminal court was therefore crucial in assuring its global standing and relevance, particularly in the early years of its existence and due to its location in Arusha working in parallel with the ICTY located in The Hague.[59]

While the ICTR often acted as one united organisation when catering to its diverse set of stakeholders, this research also shows that the Tribunal occasionally held opposing views when it came to managing its own legitimacy. This was most apparent during the Barayagwiza trial, which involved the OTP negotiating with the Appeals Chamber to reconsider their position on Barayagwiza's acquittal. The review of Barayagwiza's case was a victory for the OTP and the Rwandan government; however, the reversal of the Appeal Chamber's judgment raised questions regarding the Tribunal's legitimacy for other stakeholders, who viewed the judges' change of direction as an indication of political interference in the workings of the Tribunal. The same can be said for the removal of Del Ponte and the failure to investigate crimes allegedly committed by the RPF. In both of these cases, the Tribunal prioritised its relationship with the Rwandan government to ensure ongoing access to witnesses and crime scenes in Rwanda, but in doing so it took a risk with regard to its legitimacy as an impartial, independent court of law.[60]

Aside from responding directly to legitimacy challenges – presented in Chapter 5 – Chapter 6 demonstrates how the ERSPS also implemented legitimisation activities in order to attract additional resources from key UN member states.[61] There is therefore another angle to managing legitimacy that is less apparent in the literature and the theoretical framework described in Chapter 2, which relates to the possibilities of quantifying the influence of organisational legitimacy. This would provide an indication as to how much legitimacy is desirable and sustainable for an organisation. The possible consequences of exploiting the legitimacy of an organisation have not been researched, particularly in the case of international criminal courts. Chapter 6, though, demonstrates that there are consequences to using legitimisation activities in order to further promote the work of an organisation that may hinder rather than promote organisational legitimacy.

7.1.5 Discussion

In conclusion, and to answer the main research question of *how the ICTR developed and implemented legitimisation activities to gain, maintain and/or repair its legitimacy*, this

59 Section 5.1.
60 Section 5.7.
61 Sections 6.1 and 6.2.

research proposed a theoretical framework that exposes the multifaceted, fluid nature of legitimacy, and the consequences that organisational legitimacy – and the need for legitimacy – has on an international criminal court. Furthermore, this research highlights the importance of two specific stakeholders throughout the ICTR's existence: the UN and the Rwandan government.

In establishing the ICTR across the border in Tanzania, ICTR staff members required a permit from the Rwandan government to operate on Rwandan territory, and witnesses travelling to Arusha from Rwanda could only attend hearings if permission to take a flight had been granted by the government. The access to crime scenes and witnesses in Rwanda and the need for witnesses to give evidence during trials provided the Rwandan government with a means of influencing the Tribunal's activities. As a result, the ICTR sought to promote its legitimacy to this particular stakeholder in order for operations to continue, allowing it to achieve both its short- and long-term objectives. There was, therefore, a fine line between working with the Rwandan government to gain, maintain and repair the ICTR's legitimacy, as an international tribunal able to operate and complete its mandate, while retaining the Tribunal's status as a fair and objective court, the very reason behind the decision to establish the ICTR in Tanzania rather than in Rwanda.

Yet, it is the relationship with the ICTR's other key stakeholder – the UN – that is particularly noteworthy. The situation surrounding the need to establish this international criminal tribunal placed the UN in a complicated position. On the one hand, the creation of the Tribunal reflected the UN's lack of response to the crimes committed in Rwanda in 1994; and it was also in the UN's interest that the ICTR – alongside the ICTY – was a success, as the Tribunal symbolised the revival of international criminal law. On the other hand, the ICTR was dependant on the UN for funding, and, as such, was accountable to the UN Security Council and the UN General Assembly for its annual budget and operational systems. The UN therefore held a dual role as the key advocate and promoter of the ICTR, while also assuming the position of regulator and principal investor.

This particular relationship with the UN was also highlighted in the interviews, during which many interviewees associated the Tribunal's legitimacy with its link to the UN and the resources that this afforded the ICTR in achieving its mandate. Surprisingly, the UN's failure to prevent or stop the genocide in Rwanda in 1994, and the Rwandan delegate's vote against UN Resolution 955, did not diminish the legitimacy awarded to the Tribunal; on the contrary, the creation of an international criminal tribunal provided the survivors of the genocide with the recognition that atrocious crimes had been committed in Rwanda in 1994.[62]

Although the ICTR closed its doors in December 2015, the challenges the Tribunal faced, as well as the legitimisation activities it implemented, continue to affect the practice

62 Section 4.2.3.

of international criminal law. The location of the ICTR archive remains one such legitimacy challenge. This final act executed by the UN is a far cry from the rush to establish a criminal tribunal following the harrowing events of 1994. It is also an act that appears removed from the ICTR itself, given that the archive is now managed by the IR-MCT. Aside from frustrating the survivors of the genocide, who consider the archive as an important chapter in the history of their country, the location of the archive may also play a role in threatening the peace that the UN has been striving to maintain. The lack of clarity, and the apparent unwillingness of the UN to pass on the custodianship of the ICTR files to the Rwandan government, could lead to questions related to the validity of the mainstream narrative regarding the 1994 genocide in Rwanda, fuelling a denialist discourse and possibly even challenging the legitimacy of the Rwandan government. This would undo the international community's recognition of the Rwandan genocide, which was demonstrated through the establishment of the Tribunal in 1994.[63]

In light of this, it may be argued that the legitimacy challenges surrounding the ICTR's closure in December 2015 were just as important as the challenges faced during the creation of the Tribunal in 1994 and throughout its 20-year existence in Arusha. What is not in doubt is the importance of organisational legitimacy, and its potential to influence the long- and short-term objectives of international criminal courts.

In examining the legitimacy and legitimisation activities of the ICTR, this research has sought to highlight the complex environment in which the Tribunal was operating, and the various stakeholders that were involved in its functioning. The ICTR operated at a different moment in time, when the international criminal law project was still in its infancy. A lot has changed since the creation of the Tribunal in 1994, and even since it closed its doors in 2015. Yet despite the changes, there is still much to learn from the successes, mistakes and challenges faced by the ICTR. The following section, and indeed this research as a whole, attempts to highlight a handful of these lessons from the past.

7.2 Recommendations

Although specific to the ICTR in Arusha, this study sheds light on legitimacy challenges that may arise in other international criminal courts operating in complex (post-)conflict environments, and that are created through UN resolutions or international treaties involving a diverse set of stakeholders. With this in mind, this section presents recommendations that aim to increase the potential of existing and future international courts by focusing on the opportunities that organisational legitimacy can provide.

63 Section 4.2.1.

7.2.1 Recognising Organisational Legitimacy

The ICTR was established by the UN Security Council and was perceived as a legitimate international criminal court. As discussed in Chapter 2, legitimacy is often connected to the notion of legality given that normative assessments of legitimacy can make use of the legal standards of the rule of law.[64] In line with this, several interviewees were adamant that the Tribunal was a legitimate court of law, and that its legitimacy was never in question.[65] Yet when examining the activities of the ICTR and the challenges it faced during its 20-year existence, a nuanced notion of legitimacy begins to emerge. Although generally perceived as legitimate, certain actions taken by the ICTR were deemed illegitimate, and various situations arose that challenged the Tribunal's legitimacy.[66] Indeed, certain legitimisation activities implemented by the ICTR were themselves considered as threats to its own legitimacy;[67] and certain legitimacy challenges were not even acknowledged by the Tribunal.[68] This demonstrates the importance of recognising organisational legitimacy, while also monitoring the legitimisation activities implemented by an organisation in order to prevent the creation of any unwanted legitimacy challenges.

This research has shown that the ICTR was aware of its organisational image, and resources were allocated to promoting a positive image of its work.[69] Aside from managing its image, the Tribunal also responded to events that threatened its operational capacity. Yet there was no clear coordinated response to legitimacy challenges, nor was there an evident connection between the various legitimisation activities implemented by the Tribunal with regard to any specific legitimacy challenge.[70] In taking an empirical approach to legitimacy, this research has examined the ICTR's interaction with its environment and demonstrated that promoting a positive image and addressing challenges that threaten the operational capacity of an organisation can be addressed simultaneously through legitimisation activities, which is facilitated by an awareness of the concept and potential of organisational legitimacy.

Furthermore, organisational legitimacy has been shown to be an important organisational resource.[71] Recognising organisational legitimacy and understanding how it works, as well as identifying the stakeholders that play a role in influencing organisational legitimacy, can assist an organisation in capitalising on its resources – particularly if those resources are limited or constrained – and in identifying activities that can best promote

64 Section 2.1.1.
65 Section 4.1.
66 Sections 5.1 to 5.8.
67 Sections 5.7, 6.2.1, 6.3 and 6.4.
68 Section 5.5.
69 Sections 4.3 and 6.2.
70 Sections 5.1 to 5.8; and Chapter 6.
71 Section 2.1.2.

its legitimacy.[72] Even small actions related to staff behaviour or external communications can influence the perceived legitimacy of an organisation. Being aware of the potential of organisational legitimacy is therefore key to the survival of an organisation.[73]

Recognising organisational legitimacy also provides organisations with a tool to identify future legitimacy challenges. Understanding what legitimacy is, and what it means to certain stakeholders, provides an advantageous insight into any possible threats to an organisation's legitimacy. This awareness also provides an opportunity to better understand the environment in which an organisation is positioned.[74]

In a similar vein, and as demonstrated through this research, recognising organisational legitimacy may also be used as a means to understand both organisational and stakeholder behaviour. Although legitimisation activities may be labelled differently, most organisations engage in legitimacy management as the need to promote pragmatic, moral and cognitive legitimacy is vital for their existence.[75] A greater understanding and recognition of organisational legitimacy, particularly in the case of international courts that may assume to possess legitimacy due to their legal status, is imperative to the functioning of organisations and in understanding how they operate in different environments with diverse stakeholders.

7.2.2 Legitimacy Management

Once organisational legitimacy has been recognised, it must also be managed. Chapters 5 and 6 demonstrate how the response to a certain challenge may provoke or create other legitimacy challenges.[76] Legitimisation activities may therefore carry the risk of challenging the legitimacy of an organisation further. International criminal courts are particularly vulnerable in this regard given that they often operate in post-conflict environments that may be tense and politically charged, and that involve a diverse set of internal and external stakeholders.[77]

Regardless of the name or label given to the actions of an organisation's external relations – legitimisation activities or promotion of image – or how they are organised, an organisation has a vested interest in whether or not its stakeholders perceive it as legitimate.[78] The ICTR conducted its external relations through the ERSPS, and yet the president, the registrar and the chief prosecutor – and occasionally the UN Security Council

72 Section 2.2.
73 *ibid.*
74 *ibid.*
75 *ibid.*
76 Sections 5.7, 6.2.1, 6.3 and 6.4.
77 Sections 1.2.2 and 1.2.3 and 2.1.3.
78 Section 2.1.

and/or the UN Secretary-General – also took part in external relations in line with their responsibilities at the ICTR. This resulted in the use of different channels of communication and a variety of legitimisation activities, which sometimes created mixed messaging that risked challenging the Tribunal's legitimacy. This is best demonstrated in the Barayagwiza case and in the fall-out following the *Special Investigations* launched by the ICTR's chief prosecutor, both of which involved various organs of the ICTR and the UN Security Council.[79] The ICTR's approach to promoting its image and responding to challenges also changed over time, with new presidents, prosecutors and registrars taking a different approach from their predecessors.[80] In recognising organisational legitimacy, and the need for it to be managed, an international court can better coordinate its legitimisation activities to avoid sending different messages that may do more harm than good.

Chapters 5 and 6 also highlight the wide range of stakeholders involved in the ICTR, together with their diverse needs, values and cultural backgrounds. This is reflective of the different stakeholder groups involved in all international courts: the nature of a court's creation, its operations and its objectives all involve stakeholders with different needs and expectations, as well as different social and cultural norms.[81] While certain stakeholder groups are now familiar with the operations of international courts – for example, member states, academics, journalists and legal practitioners – other groups – including the survivors, witnesses and perpetrators of a conflict – may not be. Furthermore, this latter group of stakeholders may hold a negative perception of the international community and its involvement in their domestic affairs. The various expectations and possible reactions to the creation of, or the arrival of representatives from, an international criminal court must be taken into account when managing legitimacy.

In the case of the ICC – for example – each situation investigated by the OTP reflects a new set of stakeholders with distinctive needs and expectations related to a conflict situated in a new environment.[82] In order for legitimacy management to be effective, there is a need to understand the culture, values and expectations of each stakeholder group.[83] One way to ensure effective and efficient legitimacy management is to engage with the key stakeholders of an international criminal court, which leads to the following recommendation.

79 Section 5.7.
80 Section 6.2.
81 Sections 1.2.3 and 2.1.3.
82 ICC, 'Situations under investigation': https://www.icc-cpi.int/pages/situation.aspx.
83 Section 2.1.3.

7.2.3 Stakeholder Engagement

Recognising and managing organisational legitimacy provides organisations with an awareness of their environment and forms a bridge between an organisation and its stakeholders. Gaining knowledge of the needs, expectations and values of each stakeholder group provides an organisation with valuable information that may enhance or inform its activities, increasing its legitimacy and potential for success.[84]

International criminal courts are restricted in achieving their mandates given the very nature of their existence: *"the giant who has no arms and no legs"* as Judge Cassesse famously stated.[85] Indeed, without external support an international criminal court is unable to operate. The need for international courts to engage with states in order to receive support is described in Chapter 5, namely with regard to tracking and arresting indicted individuals, and imprisoning those convicted for committing international crimes.[86] Yet aside from requiring assistance with these essential operational needs, there are other ways that an international court can engage with states and organisations (both international and local) in order to enhance their legitimacy and achieve their short- and long-term objectives.[87]

For example, stakeholder engagement is an effective way of communicating with different stakeholder groups, providing an additional channel through which to disseminate information regarding the activities and achievements of an international criminal court, without further burdening its budget. In the case of the ICTR, funds for the outreach programme were not accounted for in its own general budget and led to the creation of the Voluntary Trust Fund, which was dependant on the fundraising efforts of ICTR staff members and additional contributions of UN member states.[88] Yet, engagement with civil society organisations may have presented another means of disseminating information about the Tribunal's work without this additional cost, making use of organisations and networks that were already operational in Rwanda and ready to assist the Tribunal.[89]

Furthermore, stakeholder engagement through a demonstrated openness and interest in stakeholder needs and their culture may also be considered a legitimisation activity. By gaining the trust of its stakeholders, an international criminal court may receive legitimacy that then provides access to new resources, networks or information, as well as assisting in the achievement of its longer-term objectives (such as fostering peace and reconciliation). Being aware of the stakeholders involved in, or affiliated with, the activities of an

---

84 *ibid.*

85 United Nations General Assembly, Fiftieth Session, 52nd plenary meeting, A/50/PV.52, 7 November 1995, New York, p. 2.

86 Section 5.8.

87 Section 6.3.

88 Section 6.2.1.

89 Section 6.3.2.

international criminal court may enable the court to enhance its limited resources, cater to the various needs and expectations of its stakeholders, and find alternative ways to achieve its mandate.

7.2.4 *Understanding the Local Environment*

In line with stakeholder engagement is the need to understand the local environment in which an organisation operates. Suchman's definition of organisational legitimacy explains that legitimacy is achieved when "*the actions of an entity are desirable, proper, or appropriate within some socially constructed system of norms, values, beliefs and definitions*".[90] An organisation must therefore adhere to, and understand, the social norms, values and needs of its environment in order to gain, maintain and repair its legitimacy in order to survive. This need for organisational legitimacy also provides an opportunity to form a better understanding between the organisation and its environment.[91]

In the case of the ICTR, the political networks and the organisation of Rwandan society, with its intricate bureaucratic layers, all needed to be interpreted by the Tribunal's staff in order to ensure a clear understanding of the crimes that took place in Rwanda in 1994. Yet the insights and knowledge of Rwandan norms and values that were key in informing the ICTR's activities were often left aside, which increased the risks of harming the Tribunal's legitimacy. In the early years of the ICTR's existence, efforts were made by President Pillay to reduce the distance between Arusha and Rwanda by organising trips to Rwanda for the Tribunal judges. Yet, this was not common practice, and the initiative did not include other ICTR staff members.[92] Given that organising regular ICTR staff visits to Rwanda may have been logistically challenging, the Tribunal could have found other innovative ways to reduce the physical and cultural distance between the two locations.

The challenge of distance may have been resolved through collaboration with Rwandan partners in order to build networks through which insights relating to the post-conflict environment could be provided, information about the Tribunal's work disseminated, and a greater understanding of both the Rwandan context and the ICTR's activities shared.[93] Additionally, or alternatively, the Tribunal could have explored the possibility of conducting certain trials in Kigali or employing more Rwandans in Arusha. During the initial discussions regarding the Tribunal's location, operating from Kigali was perceived as a legitimacy risk as the ICTR needed to project a neutral, impartial stance. As a result, the Tribunal remained in Arusha. Rwandans were eventually employed as lawyers, translators

90 Suchman, 1995, p. 574.
91 Section 2.2.
92 Section 5.4.
93 Section 6.3.2.

and investigators, or worked for the witness protection unit or the outreach programme; yet, the decision to conduct all trials in Arusha and to refrain from hiring Rwandan judges to work for the ICTR remained,[94] in order to protect the Tribunal's legitimacy. A decision that may have been counter-productive.[95]

This lack of cultural understanding also threatened the legitimacy of the trial process, as translators attempted not only to translate the words of the witnesses and the accused, but also their meaning. As demonstrated through the legitimacy challenges faced by the ICTR, knowledge of the local environment is particularly important for international criminal courts in order to better represent the survivors and perpetrators of a conflict, and to decipher the facts of a case that may only be understood through a deeper knowledge of the culture and context in which the events took place. This local knowledge enhances the legitimacy of both the international criminal court's work and the outcome of its trials, which may be shown to be conducted with a full understanding of the environment in which crimes took place. Furthermore, a demonstrated understanding of the local environment allows an international court to work efficiently and effectively, which in turn increases its legitimacy and provides opportunities to achieve its longer-term objectives.[96]

In this regard, understanding the local environment of every situation under investigation is particularly challenging for the ICC based in The Hague: the international court has not been established for any specific conflict, country or continent, and as such, each situation under investigation presents a new history, a different culture and conflict, and diverse stakeholders for investigators, judges, and prosecutors (sometimes also defence teams) to familiarise themselves with.

These challenges are reduced when an international court is located within the country itself, where it is (at the very least) visible to the local population, as is the case for the Extraordinary Chambers in the Courts of Cambodia located in Phnom Penh and the Special Court for Sierra Leone based in Freetown.[97] These hybrid courts provide a way to incorporate the local with the international, thereby reducing the additional attention needed to understand the local environment. Yet, there are also means through which international courts located in a foreign country could engage with local partners to ensure a thorough understanding of the local environment in order improve the management of its legitimacy.

94 No Rwandan national served as a judge at the ICTR, and no Rwandan nationals appeared on the UN Security Council list of candidates nominated to fill the position of judge (see ICTR Press Releases, for example: ICTR Press Release, *Security Council forwards to General Assembly 18 candidates for judges to ICTR*, 2 October 1998.

95 Section 5.4.

96 Sections 5.4 and 5.5.

97 Legitimacy challenges do, however, remain. See Section 1.3.

7.2.5 The Three Types of Legitimacy

Having discussed the importance of legitimacy, stakeholder engagement, and understanding the local environment, this final section circles back to the concept of legitimacy to take a closer look at the three legitimacy types: pragmatic, moral and cognitive. In line with the need for international courts to recognise and manage legitimacy, it is also important for courts to acknowledge and understand the importance of these three legitimacy types, which ensures that the full potential of international criminal courts is reached.

This research demonstrates the differences between pragmatic, moral and cognitive legitimacy: pragmatic legitimacy responds directly to individual and/or societal needs and interests; moral legitimacy focuses on the appropriateness of actions or behaviour measured against societal values and norms; and cognitive legitimacy concentrates on the meaning of the organisation, and its actions and behaviour, in a broader cultural context. When an organisation is confronted with a legitimacy challenge, all three legitimacy types may be addressed through legitimisation activities. However, research has shown that often one legitimacy type is dominant within an organisation.[98]

Throughout its existence, the legitimacy challenges faced by the ICTR resulted in swift and direct action to protect its pragmatic legitimacy. In general, the Tribunal focused on promoting its pragmatic legitimacy by performing in line with stakeholder expectations. This is most probably due to the short-term, ad hoc nature of the ICTR, and the manner in which it received support from its key stakeholders: the allocation of an annual budget, and access to crime scenes and witnesses located in Rwanda were key to the functioning of the Tribunal, and they were only made possible through its role as a legitimate international criminal court. The focus on achieving moral and cognitive legitimacy was, therefore, less prominent, possibly due to the ICTR's affiliation with the UN.[99]

Chapter 6 demonstrates the consequences of this focused approach in achieving short-term objectives rather than incorporating legitimisation activities that promoted the ICTR's long-term potential.[100] By focusing predominantly on one legitimacy type – in this case pragmatic legitimacy – the benefits of the two other legitimacy types (moral and cognitive legitimacy) may be overlooked, while the capacity for all three legitimacy types to enhance each other is lost. For example, if international criminal courts concentrate primarily on their pragmatic legitimacy (performance), they may fail to promote their long-term mandates and lose the opportunity to integrate international criminal law within the value system and culture of the environment in which they operate. Furthermore,

98 Suchman, 1995, p. 585; Ben Thirkell-White, *Institutional Legitimacy and the International Financial Architecture*, European Consortium for Political Research, Joint Sessions of Workshops, Edinburgh, March 2003, p. 7.

99 Sections 4.2.3 and Section 5.9.

100 Sections 6.2 and 6.3.

acquiring a better understanding of each legitimacy type, how they work together and influence organisational legitimacy, provides a better understanding of an organisation's potential to address a wide variety of stakeholders and societal needs.

7.3 Further Research

From the start of this research it was clear that collecting testimony from all parties affected by the ICTR's legitimisation activities would not be feasible, due to time and research limitations. As a result, this research has focused on one side of the story, by examining the legitimisation activities implemented by the ICTR when faced with certain legitimacy challenges. In doing so, this research identifies two key stakeholders that were critical to the Tribunal's work – the UN (including its member states) and the Rwandan government – while media institutions and academics were also identified as receiving attention from the ERSPS. It would, therefore, be interesting to examine the ICTR's legitimacy across a wider range of demographics in Rwanda, providing information on how different parts of society responded to the legitimisation activities of the Tribunal, for example comparing the opinions of those living in urban versus rural areas, and making use of additional information available regarding the age, gender and/or socio-economic background of respondents. Such research should also take into account those living outside Rwanda, in Africa, Asia, Europe and the Americas, which would give further information on the perception of the ICTR's legitimacy from beyond Rwanda's borders. This would complement this study and provide additional material from which to examine the legitimacy of the ICTR and the effects of the various legitimisation activities implemented.

It would also be interesting to delve deeper into the relationship between the ICTR, the UN, and the Rwandan government. The dynamic between these three organisations played an important role in the period of transition that took place in Rwanda following the 1994 genocide, and the actions of all three entities provide valuable information that highlight the political sensitivities present in the post-conflict environment, particularly related to legitimacy. Although this research focuses on the ICTR, the tensions within and between the Rwandan government and the UN are exposed through the Tribunal's legitimacy challenges and legitimisation activities. Examining the legitimacy challenges described in this research from the angle of the UN and the Rwanda government, and analysing the legitimisation activities implemented by these two stakeholders, would enhance the current research by painting a fuller picture regarding the influence of legitimacy on the actions and decisions made by these three organisations.

There are other international courts currently in operation that could provide additional insights related to legitimacy challenges and the legitimisation actions that they may have implemented. This could provide more nuance to this topic, especially related to the nature of the conflict and cultural aspects of legitimisation that were not addressed in this research. The ICC would be a particularly interesting case study given that this international criminal court prosecutes those responsible for international crimes committed far from its location in The Hague. Furthermore, the permanent nature of the court and its establishment through a treaty as opposed to a UN resolution would provide another angle through which to assess the different types of legitimacy gained and maintained by the ICC. Does the ICC possess the same moral and cognitive legitimacy awarded to the ICTR due to its affiliation with the UN and/or the recognition that it gave to the 1994 genocide in Rwanda? The challenge in gaining, maintaining, and indeed repairing the ICC's legitimacy would also be different given the capacity of member states to withdraw from the Rome Statute if and when they wish, while the obligation to assist the court in arresting indictees has already produced a cascade of legitimacy challenges for the court.[101]

Additionally, while this research highlights an interesting dynamic between the ICTR, the UN, and the Rwandan government, the ICC is involved in multiple conflicts – several of which are ongoing – concerning numerous governments on different continents. Untangling the role of legitimacy by examining the interactions between UN, the Rwandan government and the ICTR would provide the basis from which to conduct broader research focusing on the ICC and its key stakeholders, including its own relationship with the UN Security Council.

As this research has shown, there is no doubt about the importance and power of organisational legitimacy, let alone the legitimacy of an international criminal court established on the assumption that it will make impartial decisions. There is, therefore, a need to better understand the concept of legitimacy in relation to these courts. Furthermore, it is important to move away from the notion that international criminal courts are inherently legitimate merely by virtue of their legal status and their role in upholding the rule of law.

101 ICC, *Prosecutor v. Omar Hassain Ahmad Al-Bashir*, Decision of the Pre-Trial Chamber II on the Prosecutor's request for a finding of non-compliance against the Republic of the Sudan, ICC-02/05-01/09, 9 March 2015; ICC, *Prosecutor v. Omar Hassain Ahmad Al-Bashir*, Decision under Article 87(7) of the Rome Statute on the non-compliance by South Africa with the request by the Court for the arrest and surrender of Omar Al-Bashir, ICC-02/05-01/09-302, 6 July 2017.

Index of Figures and Tables

Figures

Tables

References

Interview Codes

Code	Type	Code	Type	Code	Type
A1	Academic	CS1	Civil Society	T1	ICTR Registry
A2	Academic	CS2	Civil Society	T2	ICTR Regsitry
A3	Academic	CS3	Civil Society	T3	ICTR Registry
A4	Academic	CS4	Civil Society	T4	ICTR Registry
A5	Academic	CS5	Civil Society	T5	ICTR Registry
A6	Academic	CS6	Civil Society	T6	ICTR Registry
A7	Academic	CS7	Civil Society	T7	ICTR Registry
A8	Academic	CS8	Civil Society	T8	ICTR Registry
A9	Academic	CS9	Civil Society	T9	ICTR Registry
A10	Academic	CS10	Civil Society	T10	ICTR Registry
A11	Academic	CS11	Civil Society	T11	ICTR Registry
G1	Government	CS12	Civil Society	T12	ICTR Registry
G2	Government	CS13	Civil Society	T13	ICTR OTP
G3	Government	CS14	Civil Society	T14	ICTR Registry
G4	Government	CS15	Civil Society	T15	ICTR Registry
G5	Government	CS16	Civil Society	T16	ICTR Registry
J1	Judiciary	CS17	Civil Society	T17	ICTR Registry
J2	Judiciary	CS18	Civil Society	T18	ICTR Registry
J3	Judiciary	CS19	Civil Society	T19	Chambers
J4	Judiciary	CS20	Civil Society	T20	ICTR Registry
M1	Media	CS21	Civil Society	T21	ICTR Registry
M2	Media	CS22	Civil Society	T22	ICTR Registry
M3	Media	CS23	Civil Society	T23	Defence
		CS24	Civil Society	T24	ICTR OTP
	Language			T25	ICTR Registry
	English				
	French				
	Kinyarwanda				

Bibliography

Adler, P. A., & Adler, P. (1994). Observational Techniques. In N. K. Denzin & Y. S. Lincoln (Eds.), *Handbook of Qualitative Research* (pp. 377-392). Thousand Oaks, CA, US: Sage Publications, Inc.

Aldrich, H. E., & Ruef, M. (2006). *Organizational Evolution and Entrepreneurship*. Sage Publications.

Alvarez, J. E. (1999). Crimes of States/Crimes of Hate: Lessons from Rwanda. *Yale Journal of International Law*, *24*, 365.

Ambos, K., Large, J., & Wierda, M. (Eds.). (2008). *Building a Future on Peace and Justice: Studies on Transitional Justice, Peace and Development: the Nuremberg Declaration on Peace and Justice*. Springer Science & Business Media.

Andreopoulos, G., Barberet, R., & Levine, J. P. (Eds.). (2010). *International Criminal Justice: Critical Perspectives and New Challenges*. Springer Science & Business Media.

Apuuli, K. P. (2009). Procedural due process and the prosecution of genocide suspects in Rwanda. *Journal of Genocide Research*, *11*(1), 11-30.

Aristotle, Barker, E. & Stalley, R. (1998). *Politics*. Oxford: Oxford University Press.

Arthur, P. (Ed.). (2010). *Identities in Transition: Challenges for Transitional Justice in Divided Societies*. Cambridge University Press.

Arzt, D. E. (2006). Views on the Ground: The Local Perception of International Criminal Tribunals in the former Yugoslavia and Sierra Leone. *The ANNALS of the American Academy of Political and Social Science*, *603*(1), 226-239.

Ashforth, B., & Gibbs, B. (1990). The Double-Edge of Organizational Legitimation. *Organization Science*, *1*(2), 177-194.

Bachmann, K., & Fatić, A. (2015). *The UN International Criminal Tribunals: Transition Without Justice?* Routledge.

Badar, M. E. (2006). Drawing the Boundaries of Mens Rea in the Jurisprudence of the International Criminal Tribunal for the former Yugoslavia. *International Criminal Law Review*, *6*(3), 313-348.

Barker, R. (2001). *Legitimating Identities: The Self-Presentations of Rulers and Subjects*. Cambridge University Press.

Baroni, F. (2000). The International Criminal Tribunal for the Former Yugoslavia and Its Mission to Restore Peace. *Pace International Law Review*, *12*, 233.

Bassiouni, M. C. (1994). Former Yugoslavia: Investigating Violations of International Humanitarian Law and Establishing an International Criminal Tribunal. *Fordham International Law Journal*, *18*, 1191.

Bassiouni, M. C. (2013). *Introduction to International Criminal Law*. Brill Nijhoff.

Bauman, Z. (1991). The Uniqueness and Normality of the Holocaust. In: *Modernity and the Holocaust.* Cambridge: Polity Press.

Beetham, D. (1991). *The Legitimation of Power.* Basingstoke: Macmillan.

Beetham, D. (2001). *Political Legitimacy* (pp. 107-116). Malden and Oxford: Blackwell.

Beetham, D. (2013). Revisiting Legitimacy, Twenty Years On. *Legitimacy and Criminal Justice: An International Exploration*, 19-36.

Beigbeder, Y. (2011). *International Criminal Tribunals: Justice and Politics.* Springer.

Besson, S., & Tasioulas, J. (Eds.). (2010). *The Philosophy of International Law.* Oxford University Press.

Bitektine, A. (2011). Toward a Theory of Social Judgments of Organizations: The Case of Legitimacy, Reputation, and Status. *Academy of Management Review, 36*(1), 151-179.

Bitektine, A., & Haack, P. (2015). The "Macro" and the "Micro" of Legitimacy: Toward a Multilevel Theory of the Legitimacy Process. *Academy of Management Review, 40*(1), 49-75.

Black, J. (2008). Constructing and contesting legitimacy and accountability in polycentric regulatory regimes. *Regulation & Governance, 2*(2), 137-164.

Blau, P. M. (1963). Critical Remarks on Weber's Theory of Authority. *American Political Science Review, 57*(2), 305-316.

Bodansky, D., Dunoff, J. L., & Pollack, M. A. (2013). Legitimacy in International Law and International Relations. *Interdisciplinary Perspectives on International Law and International Relations: The State of the Art*, 321-41.

Bonvent, L. (2011). *Les Gens d'Arusha.* Paris: Cartouche.

Bottoms, A., & Tankebe, J. (2012). Beyond Procedural Justice: A Dialogic Approach to Legitimacy in Criminal Justice. *The Journal of Criminal Law and Criminology*, 119-170.

Bouka, Y. A. (2013a). *In the Shadow of Prison: Power, Identity, and Transitional Justice in Post-Genocide Rwanda.* American University.

Bouka, Y. A. (2013b). (Oral) History of Violence: Conflicting Narratives in Post-Genocide Rwanda. In *Oral History Forum d'histoire orale* (Vol. 33).

Brannigan, A., & Jones, N. A. (2009). Genocide and the Legal Process in Rwanda: From Genocide Amnesty to the New Rule of Law. *International Criminal Justice Review, 19*(2), 192-207.

Breeze, R. (2012). Legitimation in corporate discourse: Oil corporations after Deepwater Horizon. *Discourse & Society, 23*(1), 3-18.

Bresser-Pereira, L. C. (2010). The Global Financial Crisis and a New Capitalism? *Journal of Post Keynesian Economics, 32*(4), 499-534.

Brinkerhoff, D. W., & Crosby, B. (2002). *Managing Policy Reform: Concepts and Tools for Decision-makers in Developing and Transitioning Countries.* Kumarian Press.

Brinkerhoff, D. W. (2005). *Organizational Legitimacy, Capacity, and Capacity Development.* University of Kansas, Public Management Research Association (PMRA).

Brinkman, H. J. (2013). Peace, Justice and Governance in the Post-2015 Development Framework. *Journal of Peacebuilding & Development*, *8*(3), 92-101.

Brown, A. D. (1998). Narrative, Politics and Legitimacy in an IT Implementation. *Journal of Management Studies*, *35*(1), 35-58.

Brown, M. B., Herman, E. S., & Peterson, D. (2004). *The Trial of Slobodan Milosevic* (No. 2). Spokesman Books.

Bryson, J. M. (2018). *Strategic Planning for Public and Nonprofit Organizations: A Guide to Strengthening and Sustaining Organizational Achievement*. John Wiley & Sons.

Buchanan, A. E. (2007). *Justice, Legitimacy, and Self-Determination: Moral Foundations for International Law.*Oxford University Press.

Calvo-Goller, K. N. (2006). *The Trial Proceedings of the International Criminal Court: ICTY and ICTR Precedents*. Brill Nijhoff.

Cannon, B., Pkalya, D., & Maragia, B. (2017). The International Criminal Court and Africa: Contextualizing the Anti-ICC Narrative. *African Journal of International Criminal Justice*, *2*(1-2), 2016.

Carroll, C. M. (2000). An Assessment of the Role and Effectiveness of the International Criminal Tribunal for Rwanda and the Rwandan National Justice System in Dealing with the Mass Atrocities of 1994. *Boston University International Law Journal, 18*, 163.

Cassese, A. (1998). On the Current Trends towards Criminal Prosecution and Punishment of Breaches of International Humanitarian Law. *European Journal of International Law*, *9*(1), 2-17.

Cassese, A. (2012). The Nexus Requirement for War Crimes. *Journal of International Criminal Justice*, *10*(5), 1395-1417.

Cencich, J. R. (2009). International Criminal Investigations of Genocide and Crimes Against Humanity: A War Crimes Investigator's Perspective. *International Criminal Justice Review*, *19*(2), 175-191.

Chaskin, R. J. (2003). Fostering Neighborhood Democracy: Legitimacy and Accountability within Loosely Coupled Systems. *Nonprofit and Voluntary Sector Quarterly*, *32*(2), 161-189.

Child, J. (1972). Organizational Structure, Environment and Performance: The Role of Strategic Choice. *Sociology*, *6*(1), 1-22.

Choi, J. H. (2013). Early Release in International Criminal Law. *Yale Law Journal, 123*, 1784.

Chorazy, E. (2020). *Coke and health*. In Crawford, R., Brennan, L., & Khamis, S. (Eds.). (2020). *Decoding Coca-Cola: A Biography of a Global Brand*. Routledge.

Cisse, C. (1998). The End of a Culture of Impunity in Rwanda? Prosecution of Genocide and War Crimes before Rwandan Courts and the International Criminal Tribunal for Rwanda. *Yearbook of International Humanitarian Law*, *1*, 161-188.

Clark, I. (2005). *Legitimacy in International Society*. Oxford: Oxford University Press.

Clark, I. (2007). *International Legitimacy and World Society*. Oxford: Oxford University Press.

Clark, J. N. (2009). International War Crimes Tribunals and the Challenge of Outreach. *International Criminal Law Review*, *9*(1), 99-116.

Clark, J. N. (2010). National unity and reconciliation in Rwanda: A flawed approach? *Journal of Contemporary African Studies*, *28*(2), 137-154.

Cohen, J. L. (2012). *Globalization and Sovereignty: Rethinking Legality, Legitimacy, and Constitutionalism*. Cambridge University Press.

Cohen, S. (1995). State Crimes of Previous Regimes: Knowledge, Accountability, and the Policing of the Past. *Law and Social Inquiry*, *20*(1), 7-50.

Coicaud, J., & Heiskanen, V. (2001). *The Legitimacy of International Organizations*. Tokyo: United Nations University Press.

Combs, N. A. (2010). *Fact-Finding without Facts: The Uncertain Evidentiary Foundations of International Criminal Convictions*. Cambridge University Press.

Cook, T., & Schwartz, J. M. (2002). Archives, Records, and Power: From (Postmodern) Theory to (Archival) Performance. *Archival Science*, *2*(3-4), 171-185.

Corbin, J. M., & Strauss, A. (1990). Grounded Theory Research: Procedures, Canons, and Evaluative Criteria. *Qualitative Sociology*, *13*(1), 3-21.

Creed, W. D., Scully, M. A., & Austin, J. R. (2002). Clothes Make the Person? The Tailoring of Legitimating Accounts and the Social Construction of Identity. *Organization Science*, *13*(5), 475-496.

Cruvellier, T. (2010). *Court of Remorse Inside the International Criminal Tribunal for Rwanda*. University of Wisconsin Press.

Cryer, R., Robinson, D., & Vasiliev, S. (2019). *An Introduction to International Criminal Law and Procedure*. Cambridge University Press.

Dagher, R. (2018). Legitimacy and post-conflict state-building: the undervalued role of performance legitimacy. *Conflict, Security & Development*, *18*(2), 85-111.

Danner, A. M. (2003). Enhancing the Legitimacy and Accountability of Prosecutorial Discretion at the International Criminal Court. *American Journal of International Law*, 510-552.

Darehshori, S. (2007). Lessons for Outreach from the Ad Hoc Tribunals, the Special Court for Sierra Leone, and the International Criminal Court. *New England Journal of International and Comparative Law*, *14*, 299.

David, M., & Sutton, C. D. (Eds.). (2011). *Social Research: An Introduction*. Sage.

Deephouse, D. L. (1996). Does Isomorphism Legitimate? *Academy of Management Journal*, *39*(4), 1024-1039.

Deephouse, D. L., & Carter, S. M. (2005). An Examination of Differences Between Organizational Legitimacy and Organizational Reputation. *Journal of Management Studies*, *42*(2), 329-360.

Deephouse, D. L., & Suchman, M. (2008). Legitimacy in Organizational Institutionalism. *The Sage Handbook of Organizational Institutionalism*, *49*, 77.

Deephouse, D. L., Bundy, J., Tost, L. P., & Suchman, M. C. (2017). Organizational Legitimacy: Six Key Questions. *The SAGE Handbook of Organizational Institutionalism*, 27-54.

De Meester, K. (2014). *The Investigation Phase in International Criminal Procedure. Search of Common Rules.* DPhil thesis, University of Amsterdam.

Des Forges, A. L. (1999). *Leave None to Tell the Story: Genocide in Rwanda* (Vol. 3169, No. 189). New York: Human Rights Watch.

Dogan, M. (1992). Conceptions of Legitimacy. *Encyclopedia of Government and Politics, 1*, 116-126.

Dowling, J., & Pfeffer, J. (1975). Organizational Legitimacy: Social Values and Organizational Behavior. *Pacific Sociological Review*, *18*(1), 122-136.

Drumbl, M. A. (2007). *Atrocity, Punishment, and International Law*. Cambridge University Press.

Easterby-Smith, M., & Lyles, M. A. (2011). The Evolving Field of Organizational Learning and Knowledge Management. *Handbook of Organizational Learning and Knowledge Management*, *2*, 1-20.

Elsbach, K. D. (2003). Organizational Perception Management. *Research in Organizational Behavior*, 25, 297-332.

Epstein, D. Z. (2014). Rationality, Legitimacy, & the Law. *Washington University Jurisprudence Review*, *7*, 1.

Eyada, B. (2020). Brand Activism, the Relation and Impact on Consumer Perception: A Case Study on Nike Advertising. *International Journal of Marketing Studies, 12*(4).

Fidahić, B. (2018). *Linguistic Justice: Translation and Interpretation at the International Criminal Tribunal for the former Yugoslavia*. Maastricht University.

Flick, U. (2004). Triangulation in Qualitative Research. *A Companion to Qualitative Research*, 178-183.

Flyvbjerg, B. (2006). Five Misunderstandings About Case-study Research. Qualitative Inquiry, 12(2), 219-245.

Føllesdal, A., Schaffer, J. K., & Ulfstein, G. (Eds.). (2013). The Legitimacy of International Human Rights Regimes: Legal, Political and Philosophical Perspectives (Vol. 4). Cambridge University Press.

Ford, S. (2012a). A Social Psychology Model of the Perceived Legitimacy of International Criminal Courts: Implications for the Success of Transitional Justice Mechanisms. *Vanderbilt Journal of Transnational Law*, *45*, 405.

Ford, S. (2012b). How Special is the Special Court's Outreach Section? In: *The Sierra Leone Special Court and Its Legacy: The Impact for Africa and International Criminal Law*. Charles Chernor Jalloh (Ed.), Cambridge University Press, 2014.

Forsythe, D. P. (2009). *Encyclopedia of Human Rights* (Vol. 1). Oxford University Press.
Galaskiewicz, J. (1985). Professional Networks and the Institutionalization of a Single Mind Set. *American Sociological Review*, 639-658.
Gallimore, T. (2007). The Legacy of the International Criminal Tribunal for Rwanda (ICTR) and its Contributions to Reconciliation in Rwanda. *New England Journal of International and Comparative Law, 14,* 239.
Gilley, B. (2006). The Determinants of State Legitimacy: Results for 72 Countries. *International Political Science Review, 27*(1).
Glanville, L. (2009). Is "genocide" still a powerful word? *Journal of Genocide Research, 11*(4), 467-486.
Glasius, M. (2012). Do International Criminal Courts Require Democratic Legitimacy? *European Journal of International Law, 23*(1), 43-66.
Goldstone, R. (2004). A View from the Prosecution. *Journal of International Criminal Justice, 2,* 380.
Gomm, R. (2008). Social Research Methodology: A Critical Introduction. Macmillan International Higher Education.
Greenwood, R., & Hinings, C. R. (1988). Organizational Design Types, Tracks and the Dynamics of Strategic Change. *Organization Studies, 9*(3), 293-316.
Grossman, N., Cohen, H. G., Føllesdal, A., & Ulfstein, G. (Eds.). (2018). *Legitimacy and International Courts.* Cambridge University Press.
Grove Ditlevsen, M. (2012). Revealing corporate identities in annual reports. *Corporate Communications: An International Journal, 17*(3), 379-403.
Gutterman, E. (2015). Banning Bribes Abroad: US Enforcement of the Foreign Corrupt Practices Act. *Osgoode Hall Law Journal, 53,* 31.
Hannan, M. T., & Freeman, J. (1989). *Organizational Ecology.* Harvard University Press.
Harber, M. (2017). The role of institutional investors in promoting long-term value creation: A South African perspective. *African Review of Economics and Finance, 9*(1), 272-291.
Hardin, R. (2007). Compliance, Consent, and Legitimacy. *The Oxford Handbook of Comparative Politics.*
Harff, B. (2003). No Lessons Learned from the Holocaust? Assessing Risks of Genocide and Political Mass Murder since 1955. *American Political Science Review, 97*(01), 57-73.
Hazan, P. (2006). Measuring the impact of punishment and forgiveness: a framework for evaluating transitional justice. *International Review of the Red Cross, 88*(861), 19-47.
Helfer, L. R., & Slaughter, A. M. (1997). Toward a Theory of Effective Supranational Adjudication. *Yale Law Journal, 107,* 273.
Heminway, J. M. (2019). Me, Too and# MeToo: Women in Congress and the Boardroom. *George Washington Law Review, 87*(5), 1079-1094.
Henham, R. (2013). *Sentencing and the Legitimacy of Trial Justice.* Routledge.

Hilbink, L. (2012). The Origins of Positive Judicial Independence. *World Politics, 64(4),* 587-621.

Hirsch, P. M., & Andrews, J. (1984). Administrators' Response to Performance and Value Challenges – Or, Stance, Symbols and Behavior in a World of Changing Frames. In *Leadership and Organizational Culture: New Perspectives on Administrative Theory and Practice*, 170-185.

Hobbes, T. (1998). *Leviathan.* J.C.A. Gaskin (Ed.), Oxford University Press, Oxford.

Hoefnagels, M. (1977). Political Violence and Peace Research. In: *Repression and Repressive Violence*, Amsterdam: Swets & Zeitlinger, pp. 29-39.

Horovitz, S. (2013). How International Courts Shape Domestic Justice: Lessons from Rwanda and Sierra Leone. *Israel Law Review, 46*, 339.

Howard, L. M. (2010). Sources of Change in United States–United Nations Relations. *Global Governance: A Review of Multilateralism and International Organizations, 16(4),* 485-503.

Hurd, I. (1999). Legitimacy and Authority in International Politics. *International Organization, 53*(2), 379-408.

Husketh, E. (Spring 2005). Pole Pole: Hastening Justice at the UNICTR. *Northwestern University Journal of Human Rights, 3*(1).

Hussain, V. (2004). Sustaining Judicial Rescues: The Role of Outreach and Capacity-Building Efforts in War Crimes Tribunals. *Virginia Journal of International Law, 45*, 547.

Hybels, R. C. (August 1995). On Legitimacy, Legitimation, and Organizations: A Critical Review and Integrative Theoretical Model. *Academy of Management Proceedings* (Vol. 1995, No. 1, pp. 241-245). Briarcliff Manor, NY 10510: Academy of Management.

Jones, E. (2009). Output Legitimacy and the Global Financial Crisis: Perceptions Matter. *JCMS: Journal of Common Market Studies, 47*(5), 1085-1105.

Jost, J. T., & Major, B. (Eds.). (2001). *The Psychology of Legitimacy: Emerging Perspectives on Ideology, Justice, and Intergroup Relations.* Cambridge University Press.

Kamatali, J. M. (2005). From the ICTR to ICC: Learning from the ICTR Experience in Bringing Justice to Rwandans. *New England Journal of International and Comparative Law, 12*, 89.

Kelder, J. M., Holá, B., & van Wijk, J. (2014). Rehabilitation and Early Release of Perpetrators of International Crimes: A Case Study of the ICTY and ICTR. *International Criminal Law Review, 14*(6), 1177-1203.

Kerr, R., & Lincoln, J. (2008). *The Special Court for Sierra Leone: Outreach, Legacy and Impact.* Department of War Studies, King's College London: War Crimes Research Group.

Knoke, D. (1985). The Political Economies of Associations. *Research in Political Sociology, 1*(1), 211-242.

Lamb, R. D. (2014). *Rethinking Legitimacy and Illegitimacy: A New Approach to Assessing Support and Opposition Across Disciplines*. Lanham, MD: CSIS and Rowman & Littlefield.

Landman, T. (2014). Social Science, Methods and Human Rights. *The Sage Handbook of Human Rights*, 181-204.

Laws, M., Ntakirutimana, R., & Collins, B. (2019). *'One Rwanda For All Rwandans': (Un)covering the Twa in Post-Genocide Rwanda*. In Grayson, H., & Hitchcott, N. (Eds.). (2019). *Rwanda Since 1994: Stories of Change* (Vol. 10). Liverpool University Press.

Levi, M., Sacks, A., & Tyler, T. (2009). Conceptualizing Legitimacy, Measuring Legitimating Beliefs. *American Behavioral Scientist, 53*(3), 354-375.

Lincoln, J. (2011). *Transitional Justice, Peace and Accountability Outreach and the Role of International Courts after Conflict*. Taylor & Francis.

Lister, M. (2010). The Legitimating Role of Consent in International Law. *Chicago Journal of International Law, 11*, 663.

Locke, J. (2014). *Second Treatise of Government: An Essay Concerning the True Original, Extent and End of Civil Government*. John Wiley & Sons.

MacDonald, Z. (2002). Official Crime Statistics: Their Use and Interpretation. *The Economic Journal, 112*(477), 85-106.

Magnarella, P. J. (2018). *Justice in Africa: Rwanda's Genocide, Its Courts and the UN Criminal Tribunal: Rwanda's Genocide, Its Courts and the UN Criminal Tribunal*. Routledge.

Mamigonian, M. A. (2015). Academic Denial of the Armenian Genocide in American Scholarship: Denialism as Manufactured Controversy. *Genocide Studies International, 9*(1), 61-82.

Manning, P. K. (1992). *Organizational Communication*. Transaction Publishers.

Marschik, A. (2005). The Security Council as World Legislator?: Theory, Practice and Consequences of an Expanding World Power. *New York University School of Law, International Law and Justice Working Papers, 18.*

Matas, D. (1989). Prosecuting Crimes Against Humanity: The Lessons of World War I. *Fordham International Law Journal, 13*,86.

Mazepus, H., Veenendaal, W., McCarthy-Jones, A., & Trak Vásquez, J. M. (2016). A comparative study of legitimation strategies in hybrid regimes. *Policy Studies, 37*(4), 350-369.

Merad, M., & Trump, B. D. (2018). The legitimacy principle within French risk public policy: A reflective contribution to policy analytics. *Science of the Total Environment, 645*, 1309-1322.

Meyer, J. W., & Rowan, B. (1977). Institutionalized Organizations: Formal Structure as Myth and Ceremony. *American Journal of Sociology, 83*, 340-363.

Meyer, J. W., & Scott, W. R. (1983). *Organizational Environments: Ritual and Rationality*. Beverly Hills, CA: Sage.

Meyer, M., Buber, R., & Aghamanoukjan, A. (2013). In Search of Legitimacy: Managerialism and Legitimation in Civil Society Organizations. *Voluntas: International Journal of Voluntary and Nonprofit Organizations, 24*(1), 167-193.

Moghalu, K. (2002). Image and Reality of War Crimes Justice: External Perceptions of the International Criminal Tribunal for Rwanda. *Fletcher Forum of World Affairs 26*(2), 21-46.

Moghalu, K. (2005). *Rwanda's Genocide - The Politics of Global Justice*. Palgrave Macmillan.

Møse, E. (2005). The ICTR: Experiences and Challenges. *New England Journal of International and Comparative Law, 12*, 1.

Murithi, T. (2003). The African Union and the International Criminal Court: An Embattled Relationship? *Institute for Justice and Reconciliation, Policy Brief, 8.*

Nicholson, J. (2017). Strengthening the Effectiveness of International Criminal Law through the Principle of Legality. *International Criminal Law Review, 17*(4), 656-681.

Nielsen, L. B. (2010). The Need for Multi-Method Approaches in Empirical Legal Research. In Cane, P., & Kritzer, H. M. (Eds.). (2010). The Oxford Handbook of Empirical Legal Research. Oxford Handbooks in Law, 951-975.

Nwoye, L. C. (2014). Partners or Rivals in Reconciliation: The ICTR and Rwanda's Gacaca Courts. *San Diego International Law Journal, 16*, 119.

Nyseth Brehm, H., Uggen, C., & Gasanabo, J. D. (2014). Genocide, Justice, and Rwanda's Gacaca Courts. *Journal of Contemporary Criminal Justice, 30*(3), 333-352.

Oomen, B. (2007). Transitional Justice and Its Legitimacy: The Case for a Local Perspective. *Netherlands Quarterly of Human Rights, 25*(1), 141-148.

Oomen, B. (2009). Justice Mechanisms and the Question of Legitimacy. The Example of Rwanda's Multi-layered Justice Mechanisms. In Ambos, K., Large, J., & Wierda, M. (Eds.). (2009). *Building a Future on Peace and Justice* (pp. 175-202). Springer Berlin Heidelberg.

Oosterveld, V., & McManus, J. M. (2002). The Cooperation of States with the International Criminal Court. *Fordham International Law Journal, 25*, 3.

Othman, M. (2002). The 'Protection' of Refugee Witnesses by the International Criminal Tribunal for Rwanda. *International Journal of Refugee Law, 14*(4), 495-508.

Palmer, N. (2012). Transfer or Transformation?: A Review of the Rule 11 *bis* Decisions of the International Criminal Tribunal for Rwanda. *African Journal of International and Comparative Law, 20*(1), 1-21.

Pancani, L., Preti, E., & Riva, P. (2020). The Psychology of Smartphone: The Development of the Smartphone Impact Scale (SIS). *Assessment, 27*(6), 1176-1197.

Paulussen, C. (2016). Arrest and Transfer. In De Brouwer, A. M., & Smeulers, A. (Eds.). (2016). *The Elgar companion to the international criminal tribunal for Rwanda.* Edward Elgar Publishing.

Peskin, V. (2005a). Courting Rwanda: The Promises and Pitfalls of the ICTR Outreach Programme. *Journal of International Criminal Justice, 3*(4), 950-961.

Peskin, V. (2005b). Beyond Victor's Justice? The Challenge of Prosecuting the Winners at the International Criminal Tribunals for the Former Yugoslavia and Rwanda. *Journal of Human Rights, 4(2)*, 213-231.

Peskin, V. (2008). *International Justice in Rwanda and the Balkans: Virtual Trials and the Struggle for State Cooperation.* Cambridge University Press.

Pfeffer, J. (1981). Management as Symbolic Action: The Creation and Maintenance of Organizational Paradigms. *Research in Organizational Behavior, 3*, 1-52.

Pham, P. N., Weinstein, H. M., & Longman, T. (2004). Trauma and PTSD Symptoms in Rwanda Implications for Attitudes Toward Justice and Reconciliation. *Jama, 292(5)*, 602-612.

Plato & Jowett, B. (2009). *The Republic.* Waiheke Island: Floating Press

Powell, W. (1991). Expanding the Scope of Institutional Analysis. *The New Institutionalism in Organizational Analysis*, Chicago, 183-203.

Prost, M. (2017). Hierarchy and the Sources of International Law: A Critique. *Houston Journal of International Law, 39*, 285.

Reyes, A. (2011). Strategies of legitimization in political discourse: From words to actions. *Discourse & Society, 22*(6), 781-807.

Rombouts, H. (2004). *Victim Organisations and the Politics of Reparation: A Case-study on Rwanda.* Intersentia.

Rothe, D. L., Meernik, J. D., & Ingadottir, T. (Eds.). (2013). *The Realities of International Criminal Justice.* Martinus Nijhoff Publishers.

Rousseau, J. J. (1997). *Rousseau: 'The Social Contract' and Other Later Political Writings.* Cambridge University Press.

Ruef, M., & Scott, W. R. (1998). A Multidimensional Model of Organizational Legitimacy: Hospital Survival in Changing Institutional Environments. *Administrative Science Quarterly*, 877-904.

Ruxton, G. F. (2001). The View of the Public Prosecutor of ICTY. In Van Dijk, W. A. M., & Hovens, J. L. (Ed), *Arresting War Criminals.* Wolf Legal Productions.

Salancik, G. R., & Pfeffer, J. (1978). *The External Control of Organizations: A Resource Dependence Perspective.* New York: Harper & Row.

Schabas, W. A. (2005). Genocide Trials and Gacaca Courts. *Journal of International Criminal Justice, 3*(4), 879-895.

Schabas, W. A. (2006). *The UN International Criminal Tribunals: the former Yugoslavia, Rwanda and Sierra Leone.* Cambridge University Press.

Schabas, W. A. (2008a). State Policy as an Element of International Crimes. *The Journal of Criminal Law and Criminology*, 953-982.
Schabas, W. A. (2008b). International Criminal Tribunals: A Review of 2007. Northwestern Journal of *International Human Rights*, *6*, 382.
Scharpf, F. W. (2003). Problem Solving Effectiveness and Democratic Accountability in the EU (No. 03/1). *Max-Planck-Institut für Gesellschaftsforschung (MPIfG) working paper.*
Scheffer, D. J. (1996). International Judicial Intervention. *Foreign Policy, (102),* 34-51.
Scheffer, D. (2013). *All the Missing Souls: A Personal History of the War Crimes Tribunals* (Vol. 11). Princeton University Press.
Schiff, B. N. (2010). Lessons from the ICC for ICC/R2P Convergence. *The Finnish Yearbook of International Law*, *21*(1), 101-105.
Schotsmans, M., & Nsanzuwera, F. X. (2002). *Victims in the Balance: Challenges Ahead for the International Criminal Tribunal for Rwanda*. International Federation for Human Rights.
Schmelzle, C. (2012). Evaluating Governance: Effectiveness and Legitimacy in Areas of Limited Statehood. *SFB-Governance Working Paper*, 26.
Schmidt, V. A. (2013). Democracy and Legitimacy in the European Union Revisited: Input, Output and 'Throughput'. *Political Studies, 61*(1), 2-22.
Seligson, M. A. (2002). The Impact of Corruption on Regime Legitimacy: A Comparative Study of Four Latin American Countries. *The Journal of Politics, 64*(2), 408-433.
Selznick, P. (1957). *Leadership in Administration: A Sociological Interpretation*. Berkeley: University of California Press.
Semeen, H., & Islam, M. A. (2020). Social impact disclosure and symbolic power: evidence from UK fair trade organizations. *Critical Perspectives on Accounting*, 102182.
Serrao-Neumann, S., Di Giulio, G., & Choy, D. L. (2020). When salient science is not enough to advance climate change adaptation: Lessons from Brazil and Australia. *Environmental Science & Policy, 109*, 73-82.
Shany, Y. (2012). Assessing the Effectiveness of International Courts: A Goal-Based Approach. *American Journal of International Law, 106*(2), 225-270.
Shelton, D. (2008). Form, Function, and the Powers of International Courts. *Chicago Journal of International Law, 9*, 537.
Sikkink, K. (2011). *The Justice Cascade: How Human Rights Prosecutions Are Changing World Politics*. WW Norton & Company.
Sluiter, G. (2005). The ICTR and the Protection of Witnesses. *Journal of International Criminal Justice, 3*(4), 962-976.
Smeulers, A., & Grünfeld, F. (2011). *International Crimes and Other Gross Human Rights Violations: A Multi- and Interdisciplinary Textbook*. Brill.
Smit, B. (2002). Atlas.ti for qualitative data analysis. *Perspectives in Education*, *20*(3), 65-75.

Snyder, H. (2019). Literature review as a research methodology: An overview and guidelines. Journal of Business Research, 104, 333-339.

Stephen, C. (2005). *Judgement Day: The Trial of Slobodan Milošević*. London: Atlantic Books.

Sternberger, D. (1968). Legitimacy. *International Encyclopedia of the Social Sciences, 9,* 244.

Straus, S., & Waldorf, L. (Eds.). (2011). *Remaking Rwanda: State Building and Human Rights after Mass Violence.* University of Wisconsin Press.

Suchman, M. C. (1994a). *On the Role of Law Firms in the Structuration of Silicon Valley.* Disputes Processing Research Program, Institute for Legal Studies, University of Wisconsin-Madison Law School.

Suchman, M. C. (1994b). *On Advice of Counsel: Law Firms and Venture Capital Funds as Information Intermediaries in the Structuration of Silicon Valley.* Thesis (Ph.D.) Stanford University.

Suchman, M. C. (1995). Managing Legitimacy: Strategic and Institutional Approaches. *Academy of Management Review, 20*(3), 571-610.

Suddaby, R. (2010). Challenges for Institutional Theory. *Journal of Management Inquiry, 19*(1), 14-20.

Sudetic, C., & Del Ponte, C. (2011). *Madame Prosecutor: Confrontations with Humanity's Worst Criminals and the Culture of Impunity.* New York: Other Press.

Sunshine, J., & Tyler, T. R. (2003). The Role of Procedural Justice and Legitimacy in Shaping Public Support for Policing. *Law and Society Review, 37*(3), 513-548.

Sykes, G. M., & Matza, D. (1957). Techniques of Neutralization: A Theory of Delinquency. *American Sociological Review, 22*(6), 664-670.

Tajfel, H. (Ed.). (2010). *Social Identity and Intergroup Relations.* Cambridge University Press.

Takemura, H. (2007). Big Fish and Small Fish Debate – An Examination of the Prosecutorial Discretion. *International Criminal Law Review, 7*(4), 677-685.

Tankebe, J., Reisig, M. D., & Wang, X. (2016). A Multidimensional Model of Police Legitimacy: A Cross-Cultural Assessment. *Law and Human Behavior, 40*(1), 11-22.

Taraku, S., & Karlsen, G. M. (2002). *Prosecuting Genocide in Rwanda: The Gacaca System and the International Criminal Tribunal for Rwanda.* Oslo: Norwegian Helsinki Committee.

Thirkell-White, B. (2003, March). *Institutional Legitimacy and the International Financial Architecture.* European Consortium for Political Research, Joint Sessions of Workshops, Edinburgh.

Thomson, S. M. (2009). Ethnic Twa and Rwandan National Unity and Reconciliation Policy. *Peace Review, 21*(3), 313-320.

Thomson, S. (2017). The Long Shadow of Genocide in Rwanda. *Current History, 116*(790), 183.

Tippett, E. C. (2018). The Legal Implications of the MeToo Movement. *Minnesota Law Review, 103*(1), 229.

Tost, L. P. (2011). An Integrative Model of Legitimacy Judgments. *Academy of Management Review, 36*(4), 686-710.

Tyler, T. R. (1997). The Psychology of Legitimacy: A Relational Perspective on Voluntary Deference to Authorities. *Personality and Social Psychology Review, 1*(4), 323-345.

Tyler, T. R. (2001). A Psychological Perspective on the Legitimacy of Institutions and Authorities. In Jost, J. T. and Major B. (Eds.). (2001). *The Psychology of Legitimacy: Emerging Perspectives on Ideology, Justice, and Intergroup Relations*. Cambridge: Cambridge University Press

Tyler, T. R. (2004). Enhancing Police Legitimacy. *The ANNALS of the American Academy of Political and Social Science, 593*(1), 84-99.

Tyler, T. R., & Huo, Y. (2002). *Trust in the Law: Encouraging Public Cooperation with the Police and Courts.* Russell Sage Foundation.

Tyler, T. R. (2006). *Why People Obey the Law*. Princeton University Press.

Van Sliedregt, E., & Vasiliev, S. (Eds.). (2014). *Pluralism in International Criminal Law*. Oxford: Oxford University Press.

Vasiliev, S. (2015). Between International Criminal Justice and Injustice: Theorising Legitimacy. In Hayashi, N., & Bailliet, C. M. (Eds.). (2017). *The Legitimacy of International Criminal Tribunals.*Cambridge University Press (2016).

Verpoorten, M. (2005). The Death Toll of the Rwandan Genocide: A Detailed Analysis for Gikongoro Province. Population, 60(4), 331-367.

Von Bogdandy, A., & Venzke, I. (2012). In Whose Name? An Investigation of International Courts' Public Authority and Its Democratic Justification. *European Journal of International Law, 23*(1), 7-41.

Wald, P. M. (2001a). International Criminal Tribunal for the Former Yugoslavia Comes of Age: Some Observations on Day-to-Day Dilemmas of an International Court. *Washington University Journal of Law and Policy, 5*, 87.

Wald, P. M. (2001b). To Establish Incredible Events by Credible Evidence: The Use of Affidavit Testimony in Yugoslavia War Crimes Tribunal Proceedings. *Harvard International Law Journal, 42*, 535.

Waldorf, L. (2006). Mass Justice for Mass atrocity: Rethinking Local Justice as Transitional Justice. *Temple Law Review, 79*, 1.

Weber. M. (1978). *Economy and Society: An Outline of Interpretive Sociology*. Berkeley: University of California Press.

Webley, L. (2010). Qualitative Approaches to Empirical Legal Research. In Cane, P., & Kritzer, H. M. (Eds.). (2010). The Oxford Handbook of Empirical Legal Research. Oxford Handbooks in Law, 926-950.

Weigand, F. (2015). Investigating the Role of Legitimacy in the Political Order of Conflict-torn Spaces. *Security in Transition Working Paper Series*, *4*(SiT/WP/04/15).

Whalan, J. (2017). The Local Legitimacy of Peacekeepers. *Journal of Intervention and Statebuilding*, *11*(3), 306-320.

Wierda, M., Nassar, H., & Maalouf, L. (2007). Early Reflections on Local Perceptions, Legitimacy and Legacy of the Special Tribunal for Lebanon. *Journal of International Criminal Justice*, *5*(5), 1065-1081.

Wüstenhagen, R., & Bilharz, M. (2006). Green energy market development in Germany: effective public policy and emerging customer demand. *Energy policy*, *34*(13), 1681-1696.

Yin, R. K. (2009). Case Study Research: Design and Methods. Sage: London.

Zacklin, R. (2004). The Failings of Ad Hoc International Tribunals. *Journal of International Criminal Justice*, *2*, 541.

Zagaris, B., & Plachta, M. (2020). Genocide, Crimes Against Humanity, and International Tribunals. *International Enforcement Law Reporter*, *36*, 191.

Zaum, D. (Ed.). (2013). *Legitimating International Organizations*. Oxford: Oxford University Press.

Zimmerman, M. A., & Zeitz, G. J. (2002). Beyond Survival: Achieving New Venture Growth by Building. *Academy of Management Review*, *27*(3), 414-431.

Zucker, L. G. (1977). The Role of Institutionalization in Cultural Persistence. *American Sociological Review*, *42*, 726-743.

Legislation

UN Resolutions

United Nations General Assembly, *Resolution 167 (II)*, A/RES/167(II), 20 October 1947.

United Nations General Assembly, *Resolution 50/213C*, A/RES/50/213C, 15 July 1996.

United Nations General Assembly, *Resolution 52/218*, A/RES/52/218, 3 February 1998.

United Nations General Assembly, *Resolution 56/248 A*, A/RES/56/248, 24 December 2001.

United Nations Security Council, *Resolution 827*, S/RES/827, 25 May 1993.

United Nations Security Council, *Resolution 873*, S/RES/872, 5 October 1993.

United Nations Security Council, *Resolution 955*, S/RES/955, 8 November 1994.

United Nations Security Council, *Resolution 977*, S/RES/977, 22 February 1995.

United Nations Security Council, *Resolution 1165*, S/RES/1165, 30 April 1998.

United Nations Security Council, *Resolution 1431*, S/RES/1431, 14 August 2002.

United Nations Security Council, *Resolution 1503*, S/RES/1503, 28 August 2003.
United Nations Security Council, *Resolution 1534*, S/RES/1534, 26 March 2004.
United Nations Security Council, *Resolution 1820*, S/RES/1820, 19 June 2008.

Rwanda

Rwanda: Law N° 47/2001 of 2001 on Prevention, Suppression and Punishment of the Crime of Discrimination and Sectarianism [Rwanda], 18 December 2001.
Rwanda: Law N° 33n bis/2003 of 2003 Repressing the Crime of Genocide, Crimes Against Humanity and War Crimes [Rwanda], 6 September 2003.
Rwanda: Organic Law N° 30/2008 of 25/07/2008 relating to Rwandan Nationality [Rwanda], 25 July 2008.
Rwanda: Law N° 34/2008 of 08/08/2008 on characteristics, description, ceremonial and respect of the national flag [Rwanda], 8 August 2008.

Italy

Italy: Legge 2 agosto 2002, n. 181, di cooperazione con il Tribunale internazionale competente per gravi violazioni del diritto umanitario commesse nel territorio del Ruanda.
(*Law No. 181 of 2 August 2002 on Cooperation with the International Tribunal responsible for Serious Violations of Human Rights Committed in the Territory of Rwanda and Adjacent States*).

Statutory Instruments

London Agreement, *Charter of the International Military Tribunal*, 8 August 1945.
United Nations, *Charter of the United Nations*, 24 October 1945.
Supreme Commander for the Allied Powers, *Charter of the International Military Tribunal for the Far East*, 19 January 1946.
United Nations Security Council, *Statute of the International Criminal Tribunal for the former Yugoslavia* (as amended on 7 July 2009), 25 May 1993. Retrieved from: https://www.icty.org/x/file/Legal%20Library/Statute/statute_sept09_en.pdf.
United Nations Security Council, *Statute of the International Criminal Tribunal for Rwanda* (as amended on 31 December 2010), 8 November 1994. Retrieved from: https://unictr.irmct.org/sites/unictr.org/files/legal-library/100131_Statute_en_fr_0.pdf.
United Nations Security Council, *ICTR Rules of Procedure and Evidence* (as amended on 13 May 2015), 29 June 1995. Retrieved from: https://unictr.irmct.org/sites/unictr.org/files/legal-library/150513-rpe-en-fr.pdf.
United Nations General Assembly, *Rome Statute of the International Criminal Court (last amended 2010)*, 17 July 1998. Retrieved from: https://www.icc-cpi.int/resource-library/documents/rs-eng.pdf.

Case Law - organised in chronological order of decision

District Court of Jerusalem, *Prosecutor v. Adolf Eichman*, Judgement, Case No. 40/61, 11 December 1961.

ICTR, *Prosecutor v. Joseph Kanyabashi*, Decision on the defence motion on jurisdiction, ICTR-96-15-T, 18 June 1997.

ICTR, *Prosecutor v. Jean-Paul Akayesu*, Judgment, ICTR-96-4-T, 2 September 1998.

ICTR, *Prosecutor v. Jean Kambanda*, Judgment and Sentence, ICTR-97-23-S, 4 September 1998.

ICTR, *Prosecutor v. Jean-Bosco Barayagwiza*, Decision on the Extremely Urgent Motion by the Defence for Orders to Review and/or Nullify the Arrest and Provisional Detention of the Suspect, ICTR-97-19-I, 17 November 1998.

ICTR, *Prosecutor v. Jean-Bosco Barayagwiza*, Decision, ICTR-97-19-AR72, 3 November 1999.

ICTR, *Prosecutor v. Jean-Bosco Barayagwiza*, Order, ICTR-97-19-AR72, 25 November 1999.

ICTR, Prosecutor v. Jean-Bosco Barayagwiza, Decision (Prosecutor's request for review or reconsideration), ICTR-97-19-AR72, 31 March 2000.

ICTR, *Prosecutor v. Georges Ruggiu*, Judgment and Sentence, ICTR-97-32-I, 1 June 2000.

ICTR, *Prosecutor v. Athanase Seromba*, Indictment, ICTR-2001-66-I, 5 July December 2001.

ICTR, Prosecutor v. Laurent Semanza, Judgment and Sentence, ICTR-97-20-T, 15 May 2003.

ICTR, Prosecutor v. Jean-Bosco Barayagwiza, Judgment and Sentence, ICTR-97-19-AR72, 3 December 2003.

ICTR, *Prosecutor v. Ferdinand Nahimana, Jean-Bosco Barayagwiza and Hassan Ngeze (Media Case)*, Judgment and Sentence, ICTR-99-52-T, 3 December 2003.

ICTR, *Prosecutor v. Édouard Karemera, Matthieu Ngirumpatse and Joseph Nzirorera*,Decision on Prosecutor's Interlocutory Appeal of Decision on Judicial Notice, ICTR-98-44-AR73(C), 16 June 2006.

ICTR, *Prosecutor v. Athanase Seromba*, Judgment, ICTR-2001-66-I, 13 December 2006.

ICTR, *Prosecutor v. Joseph Nzabirinda*. Sentence. ICTR-2001-77-T, 23 February 2007.

ICTR, *Prosecutor v. GAA*, Judgment and Sentence, ICTR-07-90-R77, 4 December 2007.

ICTR, *Prosecutor v. Siméon Nchamihigo*, Judgment and Sentence, ICTR-01-63, 12 November 2008.

ICTR, *Prosecutor v. Pauline Nyiramasuhuko, Arsène Shalom Ntahobali, Sylvain Nsabimana, Alphonse Nteziryayo, Joseph Kanyabashi and Élie Ndayambaje*, Judgment and Sentence, ICTR-98-42T, 24 June 2011.

ICTR, *Prosecutor v. Theoneste Bagasora and Anatole Nsengiyumva*, Judgment, ICTR-98-41-A, 14 December 2011.

ICTR, *Prosecutor v. Ladislas Ntaganzwa*, Second Amended Indictment, ICTR 96-9-I, 30 March 2012.

ICTR, *Prosecutor v. Augustin Ndindiliyimana, Francois Xavier Nzuwonemeye and Innocent Sagahutu*, Judgment, ICTR-00-56-A, 11 February 2014.

ICC, *Prosecutor v. Omar Hassain Ahmad Al-Bashir*, Decision of the Pre-Trial Chamber II on the Prosecutor's request for a finding of non-compliance against the Republic of the Sudan, ICC-02/05-01/09, 9 March 2015.

United States District Court, *Fuyao Glass America, Inc. v. United States*, 09-CA-201391, 23 June 2017.

ICC, *Prosecutor v. Omar Hassain Ahmad Al-Bashir*, Decision under Article 87(7) of the Rome Statute on the non-compliance by South Africa with the request by the Court for the arrest and surrender of Omar Al-Bashir, ICC-02/05-01/09-302, 6 July 2017.

IR-MCT, *Prosecutor v. Augustin Ngirabatware*, Review Judgment, MICT-12-29-R, 27 September 2019.

Internal Memoranda / Statements / Speeches

Amoussouga, R. K. G. (30 August 2003). *The Challenges and Achievements of the International Criminal Tribunal for Rwanda,* presented by Mr. Roland Kouassi G. Amoussouga, Senior Legal Advisor, Chief External Relations and Strategic Planning Section, Spokesperson of the ICTR at the Annual Conference of the Law Society of Kenya, Whitesands Hotel, Mombasa-Kenya, 27-30 August 2003.

Amoussouga, R. K. G. (16 September 2004). *Press Briefing Notes.* ICTR Press Centre, Arusha.

Annan, K. (23 April 1999). Speech given by the UN Secretary General, Kofi Annan, at the appointment of Judge Asoka de Zoysa Gunawardena to the ICTR.

Byron, D. C. M. (8 October 2010). *Address to the United Nations General Assembly, 15th Annual Report of the International Criminal Tribunal for Rwanda*, Judge Dennis Byron, President. 65th Session, New York, USA, 4 October - 11 November 2010.

Dieng, A. (20 May 2000). Registrar's special address to staff members on their ethical duties and obligations, Arusha, Tanzania.

Dieng, A. (1 March 2002). *Support to Victims of Rwandan Genocide: Legal, Economic and Social Issues* – Opening Statement of the ICTR Registrar at the Brainstorming Session on Victims Support, Kigali, Rwanda.

Dieng, A. (10 May 2002). *Registrar's Statement to ICTR Staff Assembly*, Arusha, Tanzania.

Dieng, A. (6 March 2003). *Statement to the Rwandan Parliament on the progress of the International Criminal Tribunal for Rwanda (the ICTR)* delivered by Mr. Adama Dieng, United Nations Assistant Secretary-General, Registrar, ICTR, Kigali, Rwanda.

Dieng, A. (20 October 2003). ICTR Registrar, Mr. Adama Dieng – *Address to ICA CITRA Annual Conference*, Cape Town, South Africa, 20-25 October 2003.

Dieng, A. (16 January 2004). *Registrar's address to Staff Members*, Simba Hall, Arusha, Tanzania.

Dieng, A. (23 February 2004). *Role and Functions of the Registry of International Criminal Tribunals*. Training Course in International Criminal Law at the European University Institute in Florence, Italy.

Dieng, A. (7 April 2004). *Presentation given during a roundtable meeting with COSEWA* (Construire le Sénégal avec le Président Wadz) in Arusha, Tanzania.

Dieng, A. (10 May 2004). *A few talking points for the Registrar's briefing*, Arusha, Tanzania.

Dieng, A. (11 October 2004). *Address by the Registrar on the occasion of the visit of the Prime Minister of Norway to the International Criminal Tribunal for Rwanda*, Arusha, Tanzania.

Dieng, A. (25 November 2004). *The Challenges of Administration of International Criminal Tribunals with Specific Reference to ICTR*. Presented by Adama Dieng, Registrar at the ICTR at the Prosecutor's Colloquium on the Challenges of International Criminal Justice, Arusha, Tanzania, 25-27 November 2004.

Dieng, A. (8 February 2005). *The Registrar's presentation on the UNICTR's Public Information & Outreach Programme*. Meeting of the Registrars of the International Criminal Tribunals, Arusha, Tanzania, 8-9 February 2005.

Dieng, A. (10 February 2005). *Registrar's address to Staff Members*, Simba Hall, Arusha, Tanzania.

Dieng, A. (20 May 2005). *Registrar's special address to staff members on their ethical duties and obligations*, Simba Hall, Arusha., Tanzania

Dieng, A. (11 July 2007). *The Interpol's Fugitive Investigative Assistance: One of the Most Critical Requirements for the ICTR's Successful Completion Strategy*, 19th African Regional Conference for INTERPOL, Arusha, Tanzania.

Dieng, A. (3 June 2010). *Supplementary agreements, arrangements and other forms of cooperation and assistance, experiences in relation to the Court and other international judicial bodies, a consideration of challenges and how these might be overcome.* International Criminal Court Review Conference, 8th Plenary Stocktaking of International Criminal Justice Cooperation, Kampala, Uganda.

Dieng, A. (20 October 2010). *Welcoming address and opening remarks*, by H. E. M. Adama Dieng, Assistant Secretary-General of the United Nations & Registrar of the International Criminal Tribunal for Rwanda. INTERPOL Second International Training

Course for Investigators of Genocide, War Crimes and Crimes Against Humanity held in room S355, Arusha, Tanzania, 20-29 October 2010.

Gallimore, T. (8 November 2006). *The ICTR Outreach Programme: Integrating Justice and Reconciliation*, Conference on Challenging Impunity, Kigali Novotel, Rwanda. Retrieved from: https://iccforum.com/media/background/outreach/2006-11-08_Gallimore-The_ICTR_Outreach_Program-Integrating_Justice_and_Reconciliation.pdf.

Kama, L. (28 July 1998). *Statement by Judge Laïty Kama, President of the International Criminal Tribunal for Rwanda.* Retrieved from: https://search.archives.un.org/uploads/r/united-nations-archives/e/3/a/e3a14a3f584cf3a7d732933d576164d2d02b248ec61be2eb02d400166421bb97/S-1094-0025-04-00013.pdf.

Kennedy, T. (16 July 2001). *ICTR Newsletter.* Interoffice Memorandum, ICTR/INFO-9-1-128.

Kennedy, T. (16 August 2001). *Note for file, Preparation of Tribunal Bulletin.* Meeting of working group.

Moghalu, K. C. (5 April 2000). The International Criminal Tribunal for Rwanda and the development of an effective international criminal law – legal, political and policy dimensions. *"Replacing the law of force with the force of law – African conflicts and the International Criminal Court"* organised by the Committee for an Effective International Criminal Law in Konstanz, Germany, 5-8 April 2000.

Munlo, L. G. (20 September 2004). *Statement of Mr. Lovemore G. Munlo*, ICTR Deputy Registrar at the Opening Ceremony of the High Level Meeting between Senior Officials of the Government of Rwanda and of the ICTR Registry, Arusha.

Okali, A. U. (1 November 1999). *The Rwandan Tribunal and accountability in Africa*, 26th Ordinary Session of the African Commission on Human and Peoples' Rights, Kigali, Rwanda, 1-15 November, 1999.

Pillay, N. (11 May 1999). *The Future of the International Criminal Tribunals: Exploring the strengths and the weaknesses of the International Criminal Tribunals.* Speech given at The Hague Appeal for Peace Conference, The Hague, The Netherlands, 11-25 May 1999.

Pillay, N. (8 November 1999). *Judge Pillay's address to UN General Assembly as President of ICTR*, UN General Assembly, New York, USA.

News Articles

ICTR News Letter

ICTR Newsletter, January 2005. Retrieved from: https://unictr.irmct.org/sites/unictr.org/files/news/newsletters/jan05.pdf.

ICTR Press Releases

ICTR Press Release (3 October 1997). *The Prosecutor of the International Criminal Tribunals: ICTY and ICTR second workshop on crimes of sexual violence.* Retrieved from: https://unictr.irmct.org/en/news/prosecutor-international-criminal-tribunals-icty-and-ictr-second-workshop-crimes-sexual.

ICTR Press release (1 May 1998). *Ex-Rwandan Prime Minister Jean Kambanda pleads guilty to genocide.* Retrieved from: https://unictr.irmct.org/en/news/ex-rwandan-prime-minister-jean-kambanda-pleads-guilty-genocide.

ICTR Press release (1 May 1998). *Security Council established third Trial Chamber for ICTR.* Retrieved from: https://unictr.irmct.org/en/news/security-council-establishes-third-trial-chamber-ictr.

ICTR Press Release (2 October 1998). *Security Council forwards to General Assembly 18 candidates for judges to ICTR.* Retrieved from: https://unictr.irmct.org/en/news/security-council-forwards-general-assembly-18-candidates-judges-ictr.

ICTR Press Release (20 January 1999). *Trial of Alfred Musema to begin on 25 January 1999.* Retrieved from: https://unictr.irmct.org/en/news/trial-alfred-musema-begin-25-january-1999.

ICTR Press Release (13 October 1999). *Special representative of Rwandan government visits Tribunal.* Retrieved from: https://unictr.irmct.org/en/news/special-representative-rwandan-government-visits-tribunal.

ICTR Press Release (31 March 2000). *Barayagwiza to be tried by ICTR.* Retrieved from: https://unictr.irmct.org/en/news/barayagwiza-be-tried-ictr.

ICTR Press Release (25 September 2000). *ICTR Information Centre opens in Kigali.* Retrieved from: https://unictr.irmct.org/en/news/ictr-information-centre-opens-kigali.

ICTR Press Release (13 December 2000). *Prosecutor outlines future plans.* Retrieved from: https://unictr.irmct.org/en/news/prosecutor-outlines-future-plans.

ICTR Press Release (21 May 2001). *Defence investigator arrested.* Retrieved from: https://unictr.irmct.org/en/news/defence-investigator-arrested.

ICTR Press Release (13 June 2001). *Statement by the Registrar, Mr. Adama Dieng, on some issues relating to the defence of accused persons.* Retrieved from: https://unictr.irmct.org/en/news/statement-registrar-mr-adama-dieng-some-issues-relating-defence-accused-persons.

ICTR Press Release (16 July 2001). *Statement by the Registrar, Mr. Adama Dieng on the non-renewal of the employment contracts of certain defence investigators.* Retrieved from: https://unictr.irmct.org/en/news/statement-registrar-mr-adama-dieng-non-renewal-employment-contracts-certain-defence.

ICTR Press Release (20 September 2001). *Registrars of ICTY and ICTR sign statement on co-operation.* Retrieved from: https://unictr.irmct.org/en/news/registrars-icty-and-ictr-sign-statement-co-operation.

ICTR Press Release (14 December 2001). *Statement of Judge Pillay, President of the Tribunal.* Retrieved from: https://unictr.irmct.org/en/news/statement-judge-pillay-president-tribunal.

ICTR Press Release (21 December 2001). *Nzabirinda arrested in Belgium.* Retrieved from: https://unictr.irmct.org/en/news/nzabirinda-arrested-belgium.

ICTR Press Release (4 April 2003). *ICTR and ICTY Harmonize their Goals.* Retrieved from: https://unictr.irmct.org/en/news/ictr-and-icty-harmonize-their-goals.

ICTR Press Release (9 May 2003). *ICTR Registrar Seeks Support of African Community.* Retrieved from: https://unictr.irmct.org/en/news/ictr-registrar-seeks-support-african-community.

ICTR Press Release (26 May 2003). *ICTR Becomes First International Tribunal to Receive Prestigious Human Rights Award.* Retrieved from: https://unictr.irmct.org/en/news/ictr-becomes-first-international-tribunal-receive-prestigious-human-rights-award.

ICTR Press Release (4 September 2003). *The Security Council Appoints Separate Prosecutors for the two ad hoc UN Tribunals.* Retrieved from: https://unictr.irmct.org/en/news/security-council-appoints-separate-prosecutors-two-ad-hoc-un-tribunals.

ICTR Press Release (15 March 2004). *Joint Statement on Implementation of Inter-Tribunal Co-operation Projects.* Retrieved from: https://unictr.irmct.org/en/news/joint-statement-implementation-inter-tribunal-co-operation-projects.

ICTR Press Release (10 May 2004). *The European Commission to Fund Tribunal Projects.* Retrieved from: https://unictr.irmct.org/en/news/european-commission-fund-tribunal-projects.

ICTR Press Release (27 November 2004). *International Criminal Tribunal Prosecutors Conclude Conference in Arusha.* Retrieved from: https://unictr.irmct.org/en/news/international-criminal-tribunal-prosecutors-conclude-conference-arusha.

ICTR Press Release (17 June 2005). *ICTR President and Prosecutor Meet U.S. Secretary of State.* Retrieved from: https://unictr.irmct.org/en/news/ictr-president-and-prosecutor-meet-us-secretary-state.

ICTR Press Release (29 June 2005). *Second Colloquium of Prosecutors of International Tribunals held in Freetown, Sierra Leone.* Retrieved from: https://unictr.irmct.org/en/news/second-colloquium-prosecutors-international-tribunals-held-freetown-sierra-leone.

ICTR Press Release (31 January 2006). *The Office of the Prosecutor Completes Joint Advocacy Training Programme (25 – 30 January 2006).* Retrieved from: https://unictr.irmct.org/en/news/office-prosecutor-completes-joint-advocacy-training-programme-25-%E2%80%93-30-january-2006.

ICTR Press Release (20 June 2006). *ICTR Appeals Chamber takes Judicial Notice of Genocide in Rwanda.* Retrieved from: https://unictr.irmct.org/en/news/ictr-appeals-chamber-takes-judicial-notice-genocide-rwanda.

ICTR Press Release (21 June 2006). *Irish President Visits Tribunal.* Retrieved from: https://unictr.irmct.org/en/news/irish-president-visits-tribunal.

ICTR Press Release (10 July 2006). *16th Plenary Session of the Tribunal Meets in Arusha.* Retrieved from: https://unictr.irmct.org/en/news/16th-plenary-session-tribunal-meets-arusha.

ICTR Press Release (5 September 2006). *Arrest of Counsel Callixte Gakwaya.* Retrieved from: https://unictr.irmct.org/en/news/arrest-counsel-callixte-gakwaya.

ICTR Press Release (5 September 2006). *Counsel Callixte Gakwaya Released.* Retrieved from: https://unictr.irmct.org/en/news/counsel-callixte-gakwaya-released.

ICTR Press Release (30 November 2006). *Press Statement.* Retrieved from: https://unictr.irmct.org/en/news/press-statement.

ICTR Press Release (23 February 2007). *Tribunal Sentences Nzabirinda to Seven Years Imprisonment.* Retrieved from: https://unictr.irmct.org/en/news/tribunal-sentences-nzabirinda-seven-years-imprisonment.

ICTR Press Release (20 March 2007). *Allegations against Bikindi Co-Counsel not well founded.* Retrieved from: https://unictr.irmct.org/en/news/allegations-against-bikindi-co-counsel-not-well-founded.

ICTR Press Release (13 July 2007). *Press Statement: Interpol Conference Calls for Action on Rwandan War Crimes Fugitives.* Retrieved from: https://unictr.irmct.org/en/news/press-statement-interpol-conference-calls-action-rwandan-war-crimes-fugitives.

ICTR Press Release (28 November 2008). *Roundtable Discussion on International Cooperation.* Retrieved from: https://unictr.irmct.org/en/news/roundtable-discussion-international-cooperation.

ICTR Press Release (23 February 2009). *ICTR Opens Two More Information Centres in Rwanda.* Retrieved from: https://unictr.irmct.org/en/news/ictr-opens-two-more-information-centres-rwanda.

ICTR Press Release (11 November 2009). *International Criminal Justice: Lessons from the Past, Reflections on the Future.* Retrieved from: https://unictr.irmct.org/en/news/international-criminal-justice-lessons-past-reflections-future.

ICTR Press Release (16 November 2009). *Prosecutors of International Criminal Tribunals Call for Full Cooperation.* Retrieved from: https://unictr.irmct.org/en/news/prosecutors-international-criminal-tribunals-call-full-cooperation.

ICTR Press Release (15 November 2012). *Office of the Prosecutor to Host International Workshop on the Prosecution of Conflict-Related Sexual and Gender-Based Violence Crimes.* Retrieved from: https://unictr.irmct.org/en/news/office-prosecutor-host-international-workshop-prosecution-conflict-related-sexual-and-gender.

ICTR Press Release (16 August 2013). *Prosecutor Releases Lessons Learnt Manual for the Tracking and Arrest of Fugitives from International Justice.* Retrieved from: https://

unictr.irmct.org/en/news/prosecutor-releases-lessons-learnt-manual-tracking-and-arrest-fugitives-international-justice.

IR-MCT Press Release

IR-MCT Press Release (16 May 2020). *Mechanism fugitive Félicien Kabuga arrested today.* Retrieved from: https://www.irmct.org/en/news/20-06-09-mechanism-fugitive-felicien-kabuga-arrested-today.

United Nations Press Releases

UN Press Release (26 September 1997). *Secretary-General accepts resignations of Deputy Prosecutor and Registrar of International Tribunal for Rwanda.* Retrieved from: https://www.un.org/press/en/1997/19970226.sgsm6172.html.

UN Press Release (28 August 2003). *Security Council splits prosecutorial duties for Rwanda, Yugoslavia Tribunals, unanimously adopting Resolution 1503 (2003).* Retrieved from: https://www.un.org/press/en/2003/sc7858.doc.htm.

Other News Articles / Blogs

Al Jazeera (19 May 2020). *Rwandan genocide fugitive Felicien Kabuga due before Paris court.* Retrieved from: https://www.aljazeera.com/news/2020/05/rwandan-genocide-fugitive-felicien-kabuga-due-paris-court-200519105137803.html.

All Africa News (31 July 2002). *International Criminal Tribunal Chief Prosecutor to Appoint Deputy Next Month.* Retrieved from: https://allafrica.com/stories/200207310331.html.

All Africa News (18 September 2006). *Rwanda: Gakwaya Fired; Rwanda Demands Details.* Retrieved from: https://allafrica.com/stories/200609190051.html.

BBC (6 April 1994). *Rwanda president's plane 'shot down'.* Retrieved from: http://news.bbc.co.uk/onthisday/hi/dates/stories/april/6/newsid_2472000/2472195.stm.

BBC (18 September 2006). *Rwanda singer on genocide crimes.* Retrieved from: http://news.bbc.co.uk/2/hi/africa/5357062.stm.

BBC (14 December 2015). *Rwanda genocide: International Criminal Tribunal closes.* Retrieved from: https://www.bbc.com/news/world-africa-35070220.

BBC (24 May 2020). *Rwanda genocide: How Félicien Kabuga evaded capture for 26 years.* Retrieved from: https://www.bbc.com/news/world-africa-52758693.

Boston Review (1 December 2003). *Healing Rwanda: Can an international court deliver justice?* Retrieved from: http://bostonreview.net/world/helena-cobban-healing-rwanda.

CTV News (11 February 2013). *Hundreds in Rwanda march in protest over acquittals at genocide tribunal.* Retrieved from: https://www.ctvnews.ca/world/hundreds-in-rwanda-march-in-protest-over-acquittals-at-genocide-tribunal-1.1152276.

Daily News (5 December 2001). *Rwanda claims genocide suspects work at ICTR.*

Foreign Policy Blog (27 May 2011). *My interview with Tim Gallimore, Former Spokesman for the ICTR Prosecutor.* Retrieved from: https://foreignpolicyblogs.com/2011/05/27/my-interview-with-tim-gallimore-former-spokesman-for-the-ictr-prosecutor/.

France24 (2 April 2019). *Seeking Justice: the long hunt for Rwanda's killers.* Retrieved from: https://www.france24.com/en/20190402-seeking-justice-long-hunt-rwandas-killers.

Global Policy Forum (8 May 1998). *UN Chief Leaves Rwanda after Unhappy Visit.* Retrieved from: https://www.globalpolicy.org/component/content/article/190/39200.html.

Global Policy Forum (3 December 2001). *UN Judges Laugh at Rape Victim.* Retrieved from: https://archive.globalpolicy.org/intljustice/tribunals/2001/0512rwa.htm.

Global Policy Forum (29 June 2006). *UN Tribunal Investigating 12 on Its Payroll.* Retrieved from: https://archive.globalpolicy.org/intljustice/tribunals/rwanda/2006/0629payroll.htm.

Global Policy Forum (12 September 2006). *Rwanda: Government could cut links.* Retrieved from: https://archive.globalpolicy.org/intljustice/tribunals/rwanda/2006/0912cutlinks.htm.

InterNews (22 May 2001). *Government welcomes arrest of investigator.* Retrieved from: https://www.thenewhumanitarian.org/report/21514/rwanda-government-welcomes-arrest-investigator.

InterNews (13 May 2002). *Rwanda: Judge Ostrovsky Criticizes Kigali Tribunal.* Retrieved from: https://allafrica.com/stories/200205130370.html.

IOL News (4 December 2001). *UN Court contains genocide suspects.* Retrieved from: https://www.iol.co.za/news/africa/un-court-contains-genocide-suspects-77955.

JusticeInfo (5 November 1999). *ICTR says Rwanda satisfied with judges visit.* Retrieved from: https://www.justiceinfo.net/en/15629-en-en-ictr-says-rwanda-satisfied-with-judges-visit63956395.html.

JusticeInfo (30 November 2001). *ICTR Prosecutor to indict another defence investigator.* Retrieved from: https://www.justiceinfo.net/en/hirondelle-news/16499-en-en-ictr-prosecutor-to-indict-another-defence-investigator72657265.html.

La Repubblica (4 January 2010). *Del Ponte: cacciata dal Ruanda perché volevo fare giustizia.* Retrieved from: http://www.repubblica.it/2003/i/sezioni/esteri/delponte/delponte/delponte.html?refresh_ce.

New York Times (14 April 1994). *Anarchy Rules Rwanda's Capital And Drunken Soldiers Roam City.* Retrieved from: https://www.nytimes.com/1994/04/14/world/anarchy-rules-rwanda-s-capital-and-drunken-soldiers-roam-city.html.

New York Times (29 September 1994). *U.N. Commission Recommends Rwanda 'Genocide' Tribunal.* Section A, Page 13.

New York Times (25 April 1998). *As Crowds Vent Their Rage, Rwanda Publicly Executes 22.* Retrieved from: https://www.nytimes.com/1998/04/25/world/as-crowds-vent-their-rage-rwanda-publicly-executes-22.html.

New York Times (10 May 1998). *Ugly Reality in Rwanda.* Retrieved from: https://www.nytimes.com/1998/05/10/world/ugly-reality-in-rwanda.html.

New York Times (28 July 2003). *Rwanda Is Said to Seek New Prosecutor for War Crimes Court.* Retrieved from: https://www.nytimes.com/2003/07/28/world/rwanda-is-said-to-seek-new-prosecutor-for-war-crimes-court.html.

News24 (3 December 2001). *Judges 'laughed at rape victim.* Retrieved from: https://www.news24.com/News24/Judges-laughed-at-rape-victim-20011202

News of Rwanda (13 February 2013). *Massive Protest Against ICTR Acquittals.* Retrieved from: http://www.newsofrwanda.com/featured1/17083/massive-protest-against-ictr-acquittals/.

Relief Web (24 June 2011). *ICTR record breaking case comes to a close.* Retrieved from: https://reliefweb.int/report/rwanda/ictr-record-breaking-case-comes-close.

Reuters (5 April 2014). *Rwanda's foreign adventures test West's patience.* Retrieved from: https://www.reuters.com/article/us-rwanda-politics-idUSBREA3406L20140405.

Reuters (16 May 2020). *Rwanda genocide suspect Kabuga arrested in France after decades on the run.* Retrieved from: https://www.reuters.com/news/picture/rwanda-genocide-suspect-kabuga-arrested-idUSKBN22S0G5.

Seroussi, J. (4 April 2016). *The devils from the Thousand Hills.* Retrieved from: https://booksandideas.net/The-devils-from-the-Thousand-Hills.html.

The Christian Monitor (11 September 1998). *For Rwandans, Justice Done Only for Others.* Retrieved from: https://www.csmonitor.com/1998/0911/091198.intl.intl.4.html.

The Conversation (1 June 2020). *What Kabuga's Arrest Means for International Criminal Justice – and Rwanda.* Retrieved from: https://theconversation.com/what-kabugas-arrest-means-for-international-criminal-justice-and-rwanda-139393.

The Economist (14 June 2001). *Judging Genocide: Arusha and the Hague.* Retrieved from: https://www.globalpolicy.org/component/content/article/163/28719.html.

The Globe and Mail (26 October 2016). *Kagame government blocked criminal probe, former chief prosecutor says.* Retrieved from: https://www.theglobeandmail.com/news/world/kagame-government-supporters-complicated-un-efforts-to-investigate-crimes/article32524359/.

The Guardian (9 April 1994). *Thousands massacred in Rwanda.* Retrieved from: https://www.theguardian.com/world/1994/apr/09/rwanda.

The Guardian (22 January 2003). *Bloody end as trap for man behind massacres backfires.* Retrieved from: https://www.theguardian.com/world/2003/jan/22/jamesastill.

The New Humanitarian (16 November 1999). *Hundreds protest against Barayagwiza release.* Retrieved from: https://www.thenewhumanitarian.org/fr/node/179881.

The New Humanitarian (17 December 2001). *ICTR denies judges laughed at rape witness.* Retrieved from: https://www.thenewhumanitarian.org/fr/node/198108.

The New Humanitarian (15 March 2002). *ICTR to investigate allegations of witness abuse.* Retrieved from: https://www.thenewhumanitarian.org/report/30753/rwanda-ictr-investigate-allegations-witness-abuse.
The New Humanitarian (2 January 2003). *ICTR investigators to meet new Kenyan government.* Retrieved from: https://www.thenewhumanitarian.org/fr/node/208974.
The New Times (15 May 2012). *Pardoning of Genocide convicts sparks debate.*
The New Times (11 February 2013). *ICTR acquittals shocking but expected.* Retrieved from: https://www.newtimes.co.rw/section/read/62785.
The New Times (11 February 2013). *Rwanda protest against ICTR acquittals.* Retrieved from: http://www.newtimes.co.rw/section/read/62747.
The New Times (12 February 2014). *How the ICTR has let down Rwanda.* Retrieved from: https://www.newtimes.co.rw/section/read/73046.
The New Times (10 February 2015). *Experts on why Rwanda should take custody of ICTR archives.* Retrieved from: https://www.newtimes.co.rw/section/read/185831.
The New Times (14 February 2018). *MICT prosecutor admits to slow progress in hunt for key fugitives.* Retrieved from: https://www.newtimes.co.rw/section/read/230088.
The Telegraph (4 February 2013). *UNs special genocide tribunal for Rwanda a waste of time.* Retrieved from: https://www.telegraph.co.uk/news/worldnews/africaandindianocean/rwanda/9848588/UNs-special-genocide-tribunal-for-Rwanda-a-waste-of-time.html.
The Times (22 December 2002). *Rwandan terror paymaster under protection of Moi aide.* Retrieved from: https://www.thetimes.co.uk/article/rwandan-terror-paymaster-under-protection-of-moi-aide-ktfnrg3ftr9.

REPORTS

ICTR Reports

ICTR (2014). *Best Practices Manual for the Investigation and Prosecution of Sexual Violence Crimes in Post-Conflict Regions: Lessons Learned from the Office of the Prosecutor for the International Criminal Tribunal for Rwanda*, 2014. Retrieved from: https://unictr.irmct.org/sites/unictr.org/files/legal-library/140130_prosecution_of_sexual_violence.pdf.
Kilemi, S. M. (2014). *ICTR Legacy: Administrative Achievements and Challenges*, ICTR Legacy Symposium in Arusha, Tanzania, 6-7 November 2014. Retrieved from: https://unictr.irmct.org/sites/unictr.org/files/publications/compendium-documents/i-legacy-admin-achievements-challenges-kilemi.pdf.

Kilemi, S. M. (2016). *UNICTR Liquidation report: Twenty Plus Years of Challenges, Achievements and Best Practices in Managing an International Criminal Tribunal*, Arusha, Tanzania, July 2016.

ICTR Annual Reports

ICTR, 1st Annual Report, A/51/399-S/1996/778, 24 September 1996. Retrieved from: https://unictr.irmct.org/sites/unictr.org/files/legal-library/960924-annual-report-en.pdf.
ICTR, 2nd Annual Report, A/52/582-S/1997/868, 13 November 1997. Retrieved from: https://unictr.irmct.org/sites/unictr.org/files/legal-library/971113-annual-report-en.pdf.
ICTR, 2nd Annual Report - Corrigendum, A/52/582/Corr.1-S/1997/868/Corr.1, 2 December 1997. Retrieved from: https://unictr.irmct.org/sites/unictr.org/files/legal-library/971202-annual-report-corr-en.pdf.
ICTR, 3rd Annual Report, A/53/429 – S/1998/857, 28 September 1998. Retrieved from: https://unictr.irmct.org/sites/unictr.org/files/legal-library/980923-annual-report-en.pdf.
ICTR, 4th Annual Report, A/54/315-S/1999/943, 7 September 1999. Retrieved from: https://unictr.irmct.org/sites/unictr.org/files/legal-library/990907-annual-report-en.pdf.
ICTR, 5th Annual Report, A/55/435–S/2000/927, 2 October 2000. Retrieved from: https://unictr.irmct.org/sites/unictr.org/files/legal-library/001002-annual-report-en.pdf.
ICTR, 6th Annual Report, A/56/351–S/2001/863, 14 September 2001. Retrieved from: https://unictr.irmct.org/sites/unictr.org/files/legal-library/010914-annual-report-en.pdf.
ICTR, 7th Annual Report, A/57/163-S/2002/733, 2 July 2002. Retrieved from: https://unictr.irmct.org/sites/unictr.org/files/legal-library/020702-annual-report-en.pdf.
ICTR, 8th Annual Report, A/58/140-S/2003/707, 11 July 2003. Retrieved from: https://unictr.irmct.org/sites/unictr.org/files/legal-library/030711-annual-report-en.pdf.
ICTR, 9th Annual Report, A/59/183–S/2004/601, 27 June 2004. Retrieved from: https://unictr.irmct.org/sites/unictr.org/files/legal-library/040727-annual-report-en.pdf.
ICTR, 10th Annual Report, A/60/229–S/2005/534, 15 August 2005. Retrieved from: https://unictr.irmct.org/sites/unictr.org/files/legal-library/050815-annual-report-en.pdf.
ICTR, 11th Annual Report, A/61/265–S/2006/658, 16 August 2006. Retrieved from: https://unictr.irmct.org/sites/unictr.org/files/legal-library/060816-annual-report-en.pdf.
ICTR, 12th Annual Report, A/62/284–S/2007/502, 21 August 2007. Retrieved from: https://unictr.irmct.org/sites/unictr.org/files/legal-library/070821-annual-report-en.pdf.
ICTR, 13th Annual Report, A/63/209–S/2008/514, 4 August 2008. Retrieved from: https://unictr.irmct.org/sites/unictr.org/files/legal-library/080804-annual-report-en.pdf.
ICTR, 14th Annual Report, A/64/206–S/2009/396, 31 July 2009. Retrieved from: https://unictr.irmct.org/sites/unictr.org/files/legal-library/090731-annual-report-en.pdf.
ICTR, 15th Annual Report, A/65/188–S/2010/408, 30 July 2010. Retrieved from: https://unictr.irmct.org/sites/unictr.org/files/legal-library/100730-annual-report-en.pdf.

ICTR, 16th Annual Report, A/66/209–S/2011/472, 29 July 2011. Retrieved from: https://unictr.irmct.org/sites/unictr.org/files/legal-library/110729-annual-report-en.pdf.
ICTR, 17th Annual Report, A/67/253–S/2012/594, 6 August 2012. Retrieved from: https://unictr.irmct.org/sites/unictr.org/files/legal-library/120806-annual-report-en.pdf.
ICTR, 18th Annual Report, A/68/270–S/2013/460, 2 August 2013. Retrieved from: https://unictr.irmct.org/sites/unictr.org/files/legal-library/130802-annual-report-en.pd.f
ICTR, 19th Annual Report, A/69/206–S/2014/546, 1 August 2014. Retrieved from: https://unictr.irmct.org/sites/unictr.org/files/legal-library/140801-annual-report-en.pdf.
ICTR, 20th Annual Report, A/70/218–S/2015/577, 31 July 2015. Retrieved from: https://unictr.irmct.org/sites/unictr.org/files/legal-library/150731-annual-report-en.pdf.

ICTR Completion Strategy Report

ICTR, Completion Strategy Report, S/2003/946, 6 October 2003. Retrieved from: https://unictr.irmct.org/sites/unictr.org/files/legal-library/031006-completion-strategy-en.pdf.

United Nations Reports

United Nations General Assembly (1989). *Current financial crisis and financial emergency of the United Nations*, Forty-fourth Session, 84th Plenary Meeting, A/RES/44/195, 21 December 1989. Retrieved from: https://digitallibrary.un.org/record/82191?ln=en.
United Nations General Assembly (1995). *Fiftieth Session, 52nd Plenary Meeting*, A/50/PV.52, 7 November 1995, New York. Retrieved from: https://digitallibrary.un.org/record/200821?ln=en.
United Nations General Assembly (1997). *Audit and investigation of the International Criminal Tribunal for Rwanda*, Fifty-first Session, A/51/789, 6 February 1997. Retrieved from: https://www.un.org/ga/search/view_doc.asp?symbol=A/51/789&Lang=E.
United Nations General Assembly (1998). *Follow-up on audit and investigation of the ICTR*, Fifty-second Session, A/52/784, 6 February 1998. Retrieved from: https://www.un.org/ga/search/view_doc.asp?symbol=A/52/784&Lang=E.
United Nations General Assembly (2001). *Financing of the International Criminal Tribunal for the Prosecution of Persons Responsible for Genocide and Other Serious Violations of International Humanitarian Law Committed in the Territory of Rwanda and Rwandan Citizens Responsible for Genocide and Other Such Violations Committed in the Territory of Neighbouring States between 1 January and 31 December 1994 (ICTR)*, Fifty-sixth session, A/56/666, 29 November 2001. Retrieved from: https://www.un.org/ga/search/view_doc.asp?symbol=A/56/666.
United Nations General Assembly (2002). *Identical letters dated 4 March 2002 from the Secretary-General addressed to the President of the General Assembly and the President*

of the Security Council, Fifty-sixth Session, A/56/861–S/2002/241, 8 March 2002. Retrieved from: https://undocs.org/pdf?symbol=en/A/56/861.

United Nations General Assembly (2004). *ICTR Financial report and audited financial statements for the biennium ended 31 December 2003 and Report of the Board of Auditors,* Fifty-ninth Session, A/59/5/Add.11. Retrieved from: https://undocs.org/en/A/59/5/ADD.11(SUPP).

United Nations General Assembly (2008). *Financing of the International Criminal Tribunal for Rwanda (ICTR) and the International Tribunal for the Former Yugoslavia (ICTY) for the biennium 2008-2009,* Sixty-third session, A/63/595, 10 December 2008. Retrieved from: https://www.un.org/ga/search/view_doc.asp?symbol=A/63/595.

United Nations Secretariat (1981). *Application of the principle of equitable geographical distribution of the staff of the United Nations Secretariat,* JIU/REP/81/10, Geneva, July 1981. Retrieved from: https://www.unjiu.org/content/application-principle-equitable-geographical-distribution-staff-united-nations-secretariat-4.

United Nations Security Council (1994). *Letter dated 94/09/28 from the Permanent Representative of Rwanda to the United Nations addressed to the President of the Security Council,* S/1994/1115, 29 September 1994. Retrieved from: https://digitallibrary.un.org/record/197773?ln=en.

United Nations Security Council (1994). *Letter dated 1 October 1994 from the Secretary-General addressed to the President of the Security Council,* S/1994/1125, 4 October 1994. Retrieved from: https://www.securitycouncilreport.org/atf/cf/%7B65BFCF9B-6D27-4E9C-8CD3-CF6E4FF96FF9%7D/s_1994_1125.pdf.

United Nations Security Council (1994). *The Situation Concerning Rwanda.* Provisional Report of the 3453rd Meeting, S/PV.3453, 8 November 1994. Retrieved from: https://digitallibrary.un.org/record/167764/files/S_PV.3453-EN.pdf.

United Nations Security Council (1995). *Report of the Secretary-General pursuant to paragraph 5 of Security Council resolution 955,* S/1995/134, 13 February 1995. Retrieved from: https://digitallibrary.un.org/record/198227?ln=en.

United Nations Security Council (1999). *Report of the Expert Group to Conduct a Review of the Effective Operation and Functioning of the International Tribunal for the Former Yugoslavia and the International Criminal Tribunal for Rwanda,* A/54/634, 11 November 1999. Retrieved from: https://digitallibrary.un.org/record/406194?ln=en.

United Nations Security Council (1999). *Report of the Independent Inquiry into the actions of the United Nations during the 1994 genocide in Rwanda,* S/199/1257, 15 December 1999. Retrieved from: https://www.un.org/en/ga/search/view_doc.asp?symbol=S/1999/1257.

United Nations Security Council (2002). *Letter from Rwanda to the UN President of the Security Council,*S/2002/1043, 19 September 2002. Retrieved from: https://reliefweb.int/report/rwanda/letter-rwanda-un-president-security-council-s20021043.

United Nations Security Council (2004). *Rule of law and transitional justice in conflict and post-conflict societies.* Report of the Secretary-General, S/2004/616, 23 August 2004. Retrieved from: https://www.securitycouncilreport.org/atf/cf/%7B65BFCF9B-6D27-4E9C-8CD3-CF6E4FF96FF9%7D/PCS%20S%202004%20616.pdf.

United Nations Security Council (2006). *Report of the Secretary-General pursuant to paragraph 6 of resolution 1644 (2005)*, S/2006/176, 21 March 2006. Retrieved from: https://www.securitycouncilreport.org/atf/cf/%7B65BFCF9B-6D27-4E9C-8CD3-CF6E4FF96FF9%7D/Lebanon%20S2006176.pdf.

United Nations Security Council, (2013). *Construction of a new facility for the International Residual Mechanism for Criminal Tribunals, Arusha branch.* Report of the Secretary-General, A/67/696, 16 January 2013. Retrieved from: https://www.irmct.org/sites/default/files/documents/130116-A.67.696-en.pdf.

United Nations Secretary General (2014). *Commemoration in Kigali – Rwanda*,7 April 2014. Retrieved from: https://www.un.org/en/preventgenocide/rwanda/commemorations-2014.shtml.

United Nations Security Council, (2015). *Letter dated 17 November 2015 from the President of the International Criminal Tribunal for Rwanda addressed to the President of the Security Council*, S/2015/884, 17 November 2015. Retrieved from: https://www.securitycouncilreport.org/atf/cf/%7B65BFCF9B-6D27-4E9C-8CD3-CF6E4FF96FF9%7D/s_2015_884.pdf.

United Nations (2012). *Building Just Societies: Reconciliation in Transitional Justice Settings. Workshop Report*, Accra, Ghana, 5-6 June 2012. Retrieved from: https://www.un.org/peacebuilding/sites/www.un.org.peacebuilding/files/documents/12-58492_feb13.pdf.

Other Sources

Amnesty International (2002). *Annual Report 2002*,27 May 2002. Retrieved from: https://www.amnesty.org/en/documents/pol10/0001/2002/en/.

Human Rights Watch (2003). *Rwanda and the Security Council: Changing the International Tribunal*,Letter to Council Members on the International Criminal Tribunal for Rwanda, 1 August 2003. Retrieved from: https://www.hrw.org/news/2003/08/01/rwanda-and-security-council-changing-international-tribunal.

Human Rights Watch (2008). *Courting History: The Landmark International Criminal Court's First Years*,July 2008. Retrieved from: https://www.hrw.org/report/2008/07/11/courting-history/landmark-international-criminal-courts-first-years.

Human Rights Watch (2014). *Rwanda: Justice After Genocide – 20 Years On*, 28 March 2008. Retrieved from: https://www.hrw.org/news/2014/03/28/rwanda-justice-after-genocide-20-years.

Impunity Watch (2015). *Policy Brief: Enhancing the Societal Impact of International Criminal Tribunals*, February 2015. Retrieved from: https://www.impunitywatch.org/post/enhancing-the-societal-impact-of-international-criminal-tribunals.

Institute of Research and Dialogue for Peace (2003). *Building lasting peace in Rwanda: voices of the People*. Rwanda, IRDP. Retrieved from: https://repositories.lib.utexas.edu/bitstream/handle/2152/4556/3654.pdf?sequence=1.

International Crisis Group (2001). *International Criminal Tribunal For Rwanda: Delayed Justice*,7 June 2001. Retrieved from: https://www.crisisgroup.org/africa/central-africa/rwanda/international-criminal-tribunal-rwanda-delayed-justice.

Jambonews (18 January 2016). *Closing interview with the President of the International Criminal Tribunal for Rwanda (ICTR) – Part I*. Retrieved from: https://www.jambonews.net/en/actualites/20160118-closing-interview-with-the-president-of-the-international-criminal-tribunal-for-rwanda-ictr-part-i/.

Jambonews (4 February 2016). *Closing interview with the President of the International Criminal Tribunal for Rwanda (ICTR) – Part II*. Retrieved from: https://www.jambonews.net/en/actualites/20160204-closing-interview-with-the-president-of-the-international-criminal-tribunal-for-rwanda-ictr-part-ii/.

McKinsey Global Institute (2020). *The Social Contract in the 21st Century. Outcomes so far for workers, consumers and savers in advanced economies*, February 2020. Retrieved from: https://www.mckinsey.com/~/media/mckinsey/industries/public%20and%20social%20sector/our%20insights/the%20social%20contract%20in%20the%2021st%20century/mgi-the-social-contract-in-the-21st-century-full-report-final.pdf.

McLaughlin, D. (2013). *International Criminal Tribunals: a visual overview*. Leitner Center for International Law and Justice. Retrieved from: http://www.leitnercenter.org/files/News/International%20Criminal%20Tribunals.pdf.

Paul Kagame (2013). *Address to the 68th UN General Assembly by President Paul Kagame*. New York, 25 September 2013. Retrieved from: https://www.paulkagame.com/address-to-the-68th-un-general-assembly-by-president-paul-kagame-new-york-25th-september-2013//address-to-the-68th-un-general-assembly-by-president-paul-kagame-new-york-25th-september-2013/.

Penal Reform International (2006). *Eight years on… A record of Gacaca monitoring in Rwanda*. Retrieved from: https://cdn.penalreform.org/wp-content/uploads/2013/05/WEB-english-gacaca-rwanda-5.pdf.

RCN Justice & Démocratie (2015), *The Issues and Challenges faced by Memory Initiatives on Contemporary International Crimes. Lessons learnt from the practices of the actors involved*. Seminars held in Brussels, Belgium, 12 December 2014 & 18-19 June 2015. Retrieved from: https://rcn-ong.be/wp-content/uploads/2020/11/The-issues-and-challenges-faced-by-memory-initiatives-on-contemporary-international-crimes.pdf.

UNICEF (2004). *Rwanda: Ten years after the genocide.* Retrieved from: http://www.unicef.org/infobycountry/rwanda_genocide.html.

Websites

AVEGA	https://avega-agahozo.org/
IBUKA	www.ibuka.rw
ICC, 'Situations under investigation'	https://www.icc-cpi.int/pages/situation.aspx
ICTR, 'About the ICTR'	https://unictr.irmct.org/en/tribunal
ICTR, 'Annual Reports'	https://unictr.irmct.org/en/documents/annual-reports
ICTR, 'Archives'	https://www.irmct.org/en/archives
ICTR, 'Cases'	https://unictr.irmct.org/en/cases
ICTR, 'Chambers'	https://unictr.irmct.org/en/tribunal/chambers
ICTR, 'Completion Strategy Reports'	https://unictr.irmct.org/en/documents/completion-strategy-reports
ICTR, 'Defence and Detention'	https://unictr.irmct.org/en/tribunal/defence
ICTR, 'Financial Reports'	https://www.un.org/ga/acabq/documents/all
ICTR, 'Key Figures'	https://unictr.irmct.org/en/cases/key-figures-cases
ICTR, 'Office of the Prosecutor'	https://unictr.irmct.org/en/tribunal/office-prosecutor
ICTR, 'Registry'	https://unictr.irmct.org/en/tribunal/registry
ICTR, 'Rules of Procedure and Evidence'	https://unictr.irmct.org/en/documents/rules-procedure-and-evidence
ICTR, 'Witnesses'	https://www.irmct.org/en/about/functions/witnesses
International Cities of Peace	http://www.internationalcitiesofpeace.org/cities-listing/
IR-MCT	https://unictr.irmct.org/en/
IR-MCT, 'Searching for the fugitives'	https://www.irmct.org/en/cases/searching-fugitives
IWGA, 'Indigenous peoples in Rwanda'	https://www.iwgia.org/en/rwanda/3502-iw2019-rwanda
Justice4Survivors	https://justice-survivors.com/
McDonald's, 'FAQs'	https://www.mcdonalds.com/gb/en-gb/help/faq/18812-why-is-the-mcdonalds-menu-different-in-different-countries.html
NURC	https://www.nurc.gov.rw/
Original ICTR website, 'Homepage'	https://web.archive.org/web/20070729015544 7/http://www.unictr.org/default.htm
Oxford dictionary, 'legality'	https://www.lexico.com/definition/legality
Oxford dictionary, 'legitimacy'	https://www.lexico.com/en/definition/legitimacy
Oxford dictionary, 'legitimate'	https://www.lexico.com/definition/legitimate

Paul Kagame, Rwandan President	https://www.paulkagame.com/
Rwandan Government, 'About'	https://www.gov.rw/about
Rwandan Government, 'Administrative Structure'	https://www.gov.rw/government/administrative-structure#c4493
The New Times	https://www.newtimes.co.rw/
Tony's Chocolonely, 'Our mission'	https://tonyschocolonely.com/uk/en/our-mission/
Tribunal Voices	http://www.tribunalvoices.org
United Nations, 'About Us'	https://www.un.org/en/about-us/
United Nations, 'UN emblem and flag'	https://www.un.org/en/about-us/un-emblem-and-flag
United Nations Document System	https://documents.un.org/prod/ods.nsf/home.xsp
United Nations Editorial Manual	http://dd.dgacm.org/editorialmanual/
United Nations, 'Rwanda'	http://www.rw.one.un.org/who-we-are/united-nations-rwanda

www.ingramcontent.com/pod-product-compliance
Ingram Content Group UK Ltd.
Pitfield, Milton Keynes, MK11 3LW, UK
UKHW050954290926
15470UKWH00006B/1809

9 789462 362598